Non-Fiction
355.0092 H262m

Harvey, Robert, 1953-
Maverick military leaders : the extraordinary
battles of Washington, Nelson, Patton, Rommel, an

9001000619

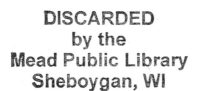

DISCARDED
by the
Mead Public Library
Sheboygan, WI

W9-BPO-175

MAVERICK
MILITARY LEADERS

MAVERICK MILITARY LEADERS

The Extraordinary Battles of Washington, Nelson,
Patton, Rommel, and Others

Robert Harvey

A Herman Graf Book

Skyhorse Publishing

Copyright © 2008 by Robert Harvey.

All Rights Reserved. No part of this book may be reproduced in any manner without the express written consent of the publisher, except in the case of brief excerpts in critical reviews or articles. All inquiries should be addressed to Skyhorse Publishing, 555 Eighth Avenue, Suite 903, New York, NY 10018.

Skyhorse Publishing books may be purchased in bulk at special discounts for sales promotion, corporate gifts, fund-raising, or educational purposes. Special editions can also be created to specifications. For details, contact the Special Sales Department, Skyhorse Publishing, 555 Eighth Avenue, Suite 903, New York, NY 10018 or info@skyhorsepublishing.com.

www.skyhorsepublishing.com

10 9 8 7 6 5 4 3 2 1

Library of Congress Cataloging-in-Publication Data

Harvey, Robert, 1953–
  Maverick military leaders : the extraordinary battles of Washington, Nelson, Patton, Rommel, and others / Robert Harvey.
      p. cm.
  Includes bibliographical references.
  ISBN 978-1-60239-356-1
  1. Military history, Modern. 2. History, Modern. 3. Command of troops--History. 4. Military art and science--History. 5. Generals--Biography. I. Title.
  D214.H37 2009
  355.0092'2--dc22
                              2008039869

Mixed Sources
Product group from well-managed
forests and other controlled sources
www.fsc.org Cert no. SA-COC-1565
© 1996 Forest Stewardship Council
FSC

9001000619

To
Patric Dickinson, this tale of modern knights

Maverick (said to be named from Samuel Maverick, a Texan rancher about 1840 who habitually neglected to brand his calves):

1. (US) In the cattle breeding districts a calf or yearling found without an owner's brand.
2. A masterless person, one who is roaming and casual.

Murray's New English Dictionary, 1908

Some talk of Alexander, and some of Hercules, of Hector and Lysander, and such great names as these, of all the world's great heroes.

The British Grenadiers' marching song

If you can keep your head when all about you
Are losing theirs and blaming it on you,
If you can trust yourself when all men doubt you,
But make allowance for their doubting too;
If you can wait and not be tired by waiting,
Or being lied about, don't deal in lies,
Or being hated, don't give way to hating,
And yet don't look too good, nor talk too wise:

If you can dream – and not make dreams your master;
If you can think – and not make thoughts your aim,
If you can meet with Triumph and Disaster
And treat those two impostors just the same;
If you can bear to hear the truth you've spoken
Twisted by knaves to make a trap for fools,
Or watch the things you gave your life to, broken,
And stoop and build 'em up with worn-out tools

'If', Rudyard Kipling

No more heroes anymore,
No more heroes anymore,
Whatever happened to the heroes?

The Stranglers

Contents

Acknowledgements

I owe an immense debt to the many senior, junior officers and servicemen and women whom I have encountered over three decades as a journalist and politician, who have illuminated me in conversation and by example on the subjects of military leadership, self-sacrifice, motivation and morale. In particular, they have shown that while training, fitness, discipline, hardship and even the ultimate sacrifice are part of the military life; camaraderie, humour, self-fulfilment, professionalism and intelligence also play a huge role.

I owe special thanks to Raleigh Trevelyan, who served with distinction in Italy, for his advice, literary and military; Major Edward Bonnor-Maurice; Colonel Max Morrison, who was in the vanguard of the D-Day landings; Colonel Peter Cannon; Squadron-leader Brab Dowling; the legendary POW escaper Jimmy James (who I met only once, but that was good enough), all of whom helped me to appreciate the qualities of the maverick commander.

I owe a great debt to Colonel Sir John Baynes, whose penetrating insights on morale, as well as his book of the same name, which remains the definitive work on the subject, greatly influenced me in writing this book, and also to Lady Baynes for allowing me to quote from his book.

Still-serving officers whose views have influenced this book would, I am sure, not wish to be named. Former Sergeant-Major Brian Dando in many conversations explained the secrets of training and discipline and the importance of the five Ps: 'Poor preparation produces piss-poor results'.

Sublimely, over many years, I have benefited from the wisdom of several defence correspondents who were journalistic colleagues: Commander Jim Meacham of *The Economist*; Gordon Lee of *The Economist*; John Keegan of the *Daily Telegraph* and Robert Fox of the *Daily Telegraph*.

Finally, the example of my own father, who pretended to be older in order to enlist as a young lieutenant in the Second World War, was captured in fierce fighting in Italy, spent more than a year in a POW camp, and ended the war as a major in charge of the Monuments and Fine Arts section of the British military occupation, has always inspired me – although like so many of his generation he would rarely be drawn into describing his military experiences. My uncle Peter, Lord Harvey of Tasburgh, also had a distinguished war record, as did my maternal uncle, Giuseppe, Marchese Curtopassi, who fought heroically with the Italian partisans against the Germans.

A select bibliography on each of the mavericks is provided at the end of the book. But I wanted to draw particular attention to the most indispensable of them. Sun Tzu's *The Art of War*; written in the closing years of the sixth century BC, remains an astonishing fount of wisdom and good sense two-and-a-half millennia later, its general maxims on warfare still applicable today. By contrast Carl von Clausewitz's *On War*, while a classic, is sometimes inhumane and liable to misinterpretation (as indeed it was, disastrously). Basil Liddell Hart's beautifully written *Strategy* raps Clausewitz over the knuckles, and his *Great Captains Unveiled* provides vigorous pen portraits of great generals. John Baynes' *Morale* remains, as I said, the classic work on this all-important subject. John Keegan's *The Mask of Command* is a major exploration of generalship. General Archibald Wavell's lectures provide the most succinct overview from the horse's mouth, although Montgomery's memoirs also have fine passages on the subject.

I have been stimulated by these and the many other books in the bibliography, for which I am immensely grateful, although the writing, judgements and mistakes are my responsibility entirely.

Finally, I owe enormous thanks to my immensely skilful editors, Leo Hollis and Hannah Boursnell, to the always penetrating and wise counsel of Gillon Aitken, to my indefatigable and accurate assistant, Jenny Thomas and to her historian husband Geoffrey, both of whom have also been extraordinarily courageous, to my mother, and to Jane and Oliver for their love and support.

List of Illustrations and Maps

Illustrations

Portrait of Robert Clive. Oil on canvas, by Nathaniel Dance, c.1773. © *National Portrait Gallery, London, UK / The Bridgeman Art Library* (XCF 268080).

General George Washington at Yorktown, Virginia. Colour lithograph, by James Peale (1749–1831). © *Private Collection, Peter Newark American Pictures / The Bridgeman Art Library* (PNP 257896).

The Death of General Wolfe. Oil on canvas, by Benjamin West (1738–1820), c.1771. © *Private Collection, Phillips, Fine Art Auctioneers, New York, USA / The Bridgeman Art Library* (PNY 153197).

The Death of Nelson, 21 October 1805. Oil on canvas, by Benjamin West. © *Walker Art Gallery, National Museums Liverpool / The Bridgeman Art Library* (WGL 294992).

Admiral Thomas Cochrane. Engraving, by Charles Turner, 1809. © *Private Collection / The Bridgeman Art Library* (XJF 275662).

The Duke of Wellington at the Battle of Waterloo. Engraving, by Matthew Dubourg (*fl.* 1813–20), from *Historic, Military and Naval Anecdotes*, published by Edward Orme, 1815. © *Stapleton Collection, UK / The Bridgeman Art Library* (STC 88721).

Giuseppe Garibaldi. Photograph, by Gustave Le Gray (1820–82), 1860. © *Archives Larousse, Paris, France, Giraudon / The Bridgeman Art Library* (LRS 174407).

General Ulysses Simpson Grant in the field at Cold Harbor, 1864. Photograph, by Matthew Brady (1823–96). © *Private Collection, Peter Newark Military Pictures / The Bridgeman Art Library* (PNP 270120).

Rommel visiting the battlefield at Sollum, published in *Signal*, September 1941. Photograph, by Moosmuller (*fl.* 1941). © *Private Collection, Archives Charmet / The Bridgeman Art Library* (CHT 204093).

Field-Marshal Sir Bernard Montgomery. Photograph. © 2005 *Topfoto* (0873289).

General George Patton with the signal corps, Sicily 1943. Photograph. © 2003 *Topham Picturepoint / Topfoto* (0778846).

General Douglas MacArthur, wading through the water on his return to the Philippines, accompanied by his chief of staff and high ranking officers. Photograph. © 2003 *Topham Picturepoint / Topfoto* (0782384).

Maps

Foreword

This book does not set out to glorify war, nor does it seek to gloss over the considerable defects of many of the military mavericks described in these pages.

Indeed, it seems to me that for the first time in history war may be beginning to be obsolescent, reaching the end of its shelf-life. This may seem a strange statement to make at a time when the world is facing any number of conflicts, from the Caucasus to the Middle East to Africa, and many countries still possess immense numbers of conventional and nuclear weapons. However, the point is that war is increasingly shown to be a not particularly effective way of settling anything. At the most apocalyptic level, nuclear weapons are so devastating that no rational person would ever use them (that is not to say that in a still irrational world they will not be used). It is also increasingly hard to see most modern industrial states actually using the immense conventional forces they still possess in order to settle a dispute between them or to gain territory (again, rationality does not always prevail).

The wars up to the late eighteenth century were primarily dynastic and boundary settling. With the emergence of the nation state, they became primarily colonial. In the last century, with industrialization and mass mobilization, Germany, Japan and Italy sought to acquire empires, and failed. Soon after, the old colonial powers were forced to retreat. Between the major countries of Europe – so long the crucible of war until half a century ago – war is now barely conceivable. For half a century authoritarian Russia desisted from launching a war there, although not against its southern neighbours.

Elsewhere, Latin America's post-colonial boundaries have long been settled; Africa's less so, but on that continent, and even in the volatile Middle East, there are fewer territorial disputes than one might expect. The European colonial powers have long known what the United States is only beginning to learn: however well-intentioned, force does not resolve the most intractable problems. A country can be occupied for a while, but it will eventually oust the occupier.

War is beginning to be the province of a kind of international underclass in the Middle East, India–Pakistan, Afghanistan and parts of Africa – although it may ignite fires which can spread. As countries develop it has become increasingly old-fashioned, costly and distasteful. Wars of aggression, colonial wars and wars for natural resources – Argentina in the Falklands, Iraq in Kuwait – simply no longer deliver: they fail or are beaten back in the short- or long-term. The cost–benefit analysis does not justify war, except in deterring aggression.

Even some of the most powerful military minds have long been pressing for an end to war. Garibaldi, a warrior all his life, argued that 'there should be no more armies and no more fleets, and the immense riches snatched almost always from the needs and poverty of peoples to be squandered in the services of slaughter.' General Douglas MacArthur, broadcasting after the Japanese surrender in 1945, said in a heartfelt plea: 'A new era is upon us. Even the lesson of victory itself brings with it profound concern, both for our future security and the survival of civilization. The destructiveness of the war potential, through progressive advances in scientific discovery, has in fact now reached a point which revises the traditional concepts of war.'

The men in this book were real professionals of war – a selection, necessarily arbitrary, of the greatest geniuses in that art. They were killers by profession and most performed deeds of which few of us would be capable. They were not 'good' or 'bad' men as such: their art was essential to the times in which they lived and when war, or the prospect of it, was almost a feature of everyday life. Some of these men were ruthless, amoral and even abhorrent by the standards of our lives today. Many pursued lives that were careless, to say the least, to those who were closest to them.

However, even in an age when, hopefully, we are getting out of the habit of war, we still remember their extraordinary exploits, not just as history, but as examples of courage and leadership – and, not least, as colourful human beings.

War should never be glorified, but we may glorify the supermen that war provided in the past as so much more real and fulfilling than today's overpaid film and pop heroes. Above all, their courage and self-sacrifice provide examples for us all in the lesser glories of our everyday lives, which are just as valuable but, thankfully, much less risky.

THE GOLDEN AGE OF MILITARY LEADERSHIP

The mavericks were some of the most extraordinary men that ever lived. They were not the best – many were by any standards amoral – but they were capable of feats far beyond ordinary mortals. There were some intriguing similarities between these highly individualistic and very diverse men that only emerged as I wrote the book.

The first is the most common to all: greatness was not thrust upon them. They worked incredibly hard for their achievements, usually encountering the most daunting setbacks along the way that would have discouraged ordinary mortals. However laid back men like Washington, Wellington and MacArthur pretended to be, in reality they were incredibly hard workers. It was not enough to have genius – they had to work very hard to get this genius recognized, and then to stay on top: almost all those in this book fit this category.

To dismiss the concept of supermen (as Tolstoy and many writers have) is to miss the point: the first requirement of such a commander was that, apart from being talented, he had to work beyond the capabilities of ordinary men, and possess the resilience and endurance that lesser mortals lack.

It is easy to point out that some of these men were shambling, unimpressive, lacking in elegance, had bad habits and possessed very human frailties; in the case of the mavericks they got there by determination and talent, not social pedigree, which is why they are so justly remembered today. Superheroes are not just born, but become so only through relentless application and achievement, often requiring a lot of sacrifice and success to become immortal.

The great military leaders have many other characteristics in common, some of them perhaps unsurprising. Many were unruly and hyperactive in youth. A remarkable number were physically unhealthy, and this may have helped to forge the fortitude that led them to be not overly concerned about their own lives.

Some of this was just the vulnerability of men in an era of early medicine, but not entirely. Some may have been psychosomatic, because so many of these men suffered from more than the usual amount of mental afflictions, which surely went hand in hand with their illnesses. Clive was a manic-depressive; Cochrane, described by Lord St Vincent as 'mad', was also vain and impulsive; and Patton was clearly unhinged at moments in his life, and not just in his belief that he had been reincarnated from warriors of old. Clearly, a degree of madness was helpful to the achievement of ultimate warrior status.

There is a further point: some of these illnesses, both physical and mental, may be the product of incredible exertion over a sustained campaigning period, followed by the slough of despondency in which minds fall when the pressure is lifted. Supreme military warriordom of this kind is not based on the steady calculable routine that most of us are used to (indeed we are often unbalanced when this is unexpectedly interrupted), but on immense, almost superhuman mental and physical exertions, sometimes for years, followed by months and years of relative inactivity: the overactive brain crashes. This may be the simplest explanation for the manic-depressive tendencies so common to the mavericks.

Perhaps the most surprising thing about these great men, to a later generation, is that, in an age of intense social immobility, snobbery and class distinction, almost all were self-made men, usually from professional middle-class backgrounds. Only Wellington, from an aristocratic but impoverished Irish family that counted as gentry in England, Cochrane, from a splendid but impecunious

Scottish aristocratic background, and Grant, penniless but descended from America's founding fathers, qualified as aristocracy.

It might be said, in this respect, that war is a great leveller of talent: in peacetime mediocre commanders can prosper. In war, warriors are required and they should be drawn from all sections of society, regardless of class or manners. Today, this may seem obvious; in the stratified society of the late eighteenth, the nineteenth and the early twentieth centuries, it was anything but. To break the glass ceiling of class, a man had to be really talented.

These men were professionals. This is not a distinction that needs to be made too much of: from ancient times, men like Alexander the Great and Caesar were characterized by their devotion to the profession of war and were good at little else; most ancient royal dynasties were founded on proficiency at arms. However, their descendants, who inherited the right to bear arms and raise armies, were often not very good at it. In contrast to these, most of the mavericks were not men who dabbled amateurishly and languidly in war, but who rather devoted themselves wholeheartedly to that activity and ushered in the age of the professional soldier. Only Wellington and Grant downed arms at a relatively early age, in order to lead their countries – not a bad consolation prize!

These men stood at the crossroads between military amateurism and professionalism, and between smallish armies raised from feudal and local origins and massive conscript armies (the French beginning with the *levée en masse*, with the Germans, the British and others following). The British were the first to abandon conscription, the Americans following after the disastrous experience of Vietnam – the dubious advantage (as in Iraq) being that professionals can be ordered into battle, whereas conscripted men will fight only for a cause that they, and the rest of society, believe in; also conscripts in peacetime are usually disgruntled and expensive to train.

Other common characteristics of these superheroes are more obvious: five died violently, and only seven died in their beds. A considerable number were severely wounded in battle: Cochrane once, Garibaldi five times, Rommel twice, while all narrowly escaped death or capture. All, without exception, fell out with their superiors, and no fewer than three suffered imprisonment, exile or both.

A remarkable number moved into positions of enormous political power, or sought this – partly a reflection of their high profiles as a result of military success, partly a consequence of reinvented post-military ambition – Clive (ruler of Bengal), Washington (first President of the United States), Wellington (proconsul of France and Prime Minister of Britain), Grant (President of the United States), Garibaldi (ruler of southern Italy) and Rommel (potential ruler of Germany). Only Nelson and Cochrane were complete political failures, although interested, while Montgomery and Patton showed no interest.

Were these men good or bad? The morality of war creates its own rules when desperate measures are required. While highly principled to those involved, these rules may appear immoral to outsiders. The only, necessarily subjective, measures for the historian are in terms of motivation, as far as that can be judged, and the avoidance of unnecessary ruthlessness.

Did they change the world? They did – and how! Clive created, for good or ill, the British empire in India which was to last for two centuries and was the model for Britain's imperial expansion; Wolfe drove the French out of Canada; Washington was founder of the United States; Nelson and Cochrane ultimately defeated Napoleon by denying him control of the seas; Wellington helped to bring down that empire; Grant won the American Civil War, which ushered into being the most powerful nation the world has ever seen; Garibaldi united Italy; MacArthur ruled Japan – still the second biggest economy in the world – and irrevocably changed the course of its history; Rommel (and Guderian) conquered western Europe and nearly defeated the British in North Africa; Montgomery turned the tide of war there and performed brilliantly, if not flawlessly, in defeating Germany in Europe, bringing a rapid end to the war; and Patton's massive offensive in Europe routed the Germans.

The warriors depicted in this book also reflect the evolution of warfare over these two centuries. Clive used small British forces against massive but ill-equipped armies in a colonial setting; Washington used a mixture of guerrilla and small-scale regular army engagements; Cochrane was the master of surprise and commando tactics; Wellington excelled at defence, the volley and the infantry square, and was an excellent commander of middle-sized armies – and like Washington was a master of the daring rattlesnake strike against the enemy when least expected.

Grant was the first general who used railway-supported armies, and then understood their vulnerability, as well as the effectiveness of frontal attacks – which, however, quickly got bogged down in trench warfare in the nineteenth and early twentieth centuries; Garibaldi was a superb naval captain and guerrilla leader who, remarkably, showed himself also to be a great general of armies in the field; MacArthur was a genius of amphibious tactics, leapfrogging enemy bases and commanding large armies; Rommel, following on from his mentor Guderian, was the greatest mobile tank commander in history; Patton, similarly, was a great trainer of men and a superb tank commander; Montgomery was another great trainer of men and a master of tank in combination with infantry tactics. Truly, these were men who made history.

The spark of leadership is an elusive will-o'-the-wisp that defies definition, like creativity or the origin of life itself. No one has ever been able to describe it with any degree of accuracy or detail. The legendary Prussian military theorist, Carl von Clausewitz, came closest to doing so in a single phrase: *coup d'oeil* – literally the strike of an eye, that moment when the gifted military leader sees his opportunity and turns the tide of battle. Others, like Leo Tolstoy, doubted that there was such a thing as leadership at all, ridiculing the concept of the 'great man' in *War and Peace*, in the person, in particular, of General Kutuzov. Lytton Strachey, in *Eminent Victorians*, famously rebuked General Gordon. The needless slaughter of the First World War further damaged the aura of leadership.

The gifted British military historian John Keegan came close to Tolstoy's view with his phrase 'the mask of command', implying that leadership is no more than the necessary adoption of a façade in order to hide the ordinary and unimpressive mortal.

Keegan suggests that the modern world requires 'post-heroic leadership' – technicians in a nuclear age rather than the dashing man on the white horse.

We may think of a leader as a man with a stentorian voice and self-confidence who acts without hesitation, knows his own mind and whom lesser men will follow. But in reality these are superficial characteristics, not essential to leadership. In regard to men who show such genius as to reach the pinnacles of power in military command, politics or business, attempts to explain their skills are more elusive still, other than to suggest it is done using smoke and mirrors, that these are ordinary mortals who have reached their positions by chance.

Time and again the most improbable figures ascend to the very top: George Washington, impassive and seemingly quite stupid; the Duke of Wellington, with a stiff, carefully cultivated manner and a squeaky shrill voice in action; and, in the twentieth century, Bernard Montgomery, cross and unimpressive, although possessed of a lightning mind.

Are there different styles of leadership for the three dominant powers of our age – military, political and business? It would certainly appear so: obviously a military leader needs courage, a cool eye, an air of command; a political leader needs the power of oratory, an ability to inspire through his words as well as crowd-pleasing charm; a business leader requires the shrewdness to spot an opportunity and to lead a team. Yet these are more interchangeable virtues than they appear, and once again are largely superficial. Moreover, Keegan's thesis might seem vindicated in that politicians have had to tone down their rhetoric, and military and business leaders adapt the bark of command, to a television age where charm and public relations are all important. All three these days have shown a much greater knowledge of the technical aspects of their profession than the deliberately cultivated amateurism of the past.

The real difference between the three remains that a military leader commands by virtue of authority: those lower down the ranks are compelled to obey the orders of those higher up. However,

I will also argue in this book that the really great commanders also wielded the political arts of finding ways of both inspiring and being loved by their men, who can sense the difference between a real leader and a martinet, and perform to the best of their abilities for the former.

Perhaps, indeed, there is more in common than appears. Great military leaders have often shown an almost political ability to charm and inspire their men rather than rely merely on handing down orders; great political leaders have often shown an almost militarist style of command, in place of the usual verbiage and waffle, particularly in times of crisis and conflict; and great business leaders have sometimes shown military-style discipline or political persuasiveness. Perhaps the key to leadership, to genius in any of these three spheres, is the ability to transcend the norms of their professions, to 'think outside the box' – the soldier winning the hearts of his men, rather than their fear. Maybe Clausewitz's *coup d'oeil*, the spark of leadership, the leadership 'gene', is common to all three after all.

In today's society, the hierarchy of the three 'powerful' professions has been reversed from what it was. Business seems predominant to an extent unimaginable half a century ago in an age when it was viewed almost with distaste, as an ungentlemanly activity. Today it attracts the sharpest talents, shapes society through commercialism and advertising, exudes glamour and provides colossal rewards. Politics comes a distant second in most people's eyes, although in reality it is still the most powerful of all human activities. Most people view politicians today with wary cynicism as purveyors of words. The military profession has sunk still lower in the popular esteem. Where once military men were among the most glamorous figures in the land, wearing spectacular uniforms, earning colossal rewards, founding great noble houses and surrounded by women admirers, today few people can recall the name of a single prominent serving soldier – even while wars continue to be fought abroad.

The heroes of modern society are not, in fact, heroes at all, in that they do not risk their lives for their fellow countrymen, or shoulder enormous responsibilities, or generate wealth and employment, or make great discoveries. They are 'celebrities' – pop stars, film stars, fashion models, television personalities, comedians, footballers and other sportsmen – mostly, in fact, powerless entertainers and commercial creations.

In one sense this is thoroughly healthy: a society that does not glorify war surely has its priorities right. Yet the very underpinnings of the peaceful society in which a harmless celebrity culture can thrive are the victories and sacrifices made against threats to our familiar way of life, be they uncontrollable aggressors like Napoleonic France, racist Nazis or totalitarian communists. At a time when external threats were much more visible, military dash and courage were rightly prized.

These men – almost exclusively, although there was no shortage of valiant women, for example in special operations in France and in frontline nursing – were the rock and film superstars of their age. The profession of arms not being one of the highest callings intellectually, many were as stupid as their modern counterparts, narcissistic beefcakes prancing and preening in colourful clothes and on horseback. But as with any calling, those at the top of their professions had to have something besides looks to have got there and, unlike their modern counterparts, most of whom are prima donnas rather than team players, these men had to lead thousands of others into that most dangerous of all places, battle, risking death or disability.

Such men, of course, were no more angels than their modern counterparts, perhaps much less so. Many led disgraceful private lives and were deeply inconsiderate to their loved ones. Yet that is to miss the point: they were not selected for their saintly qualities. They were chosen for their genius at generalship, as supreme professionals capable of getting the job done, and although it was a bloody one, they believed the consequences of failure would have been far worse for their country. Nor should those in a leisured age be too ready to criticize those who fight wars in an age of conflict.

This book is about 12 of these men, drawn from what I have described as the 'Golden Age of Military Leadership', the nearly

200 years from 1757, the date of the Battle of Plassey, to 1945, the defeat of Germany and Japan. Through the study of these extraordinary men the reader may arrive at an intuitive understanding of what makes a warrior and in the process, I hope, enjoy the retelling of their astounding exploits.

How can the 'golden age' label be justified? War, after all, is an activity as old as humanity itself and there were countless great heroes whose exploits redound from antiquity right up to the eighteenth century. Like all historical categorizing, the period chosen is somewhat arbitrary. It marks the period following that when warfare was essentially a matter for small armies between kings or princes, and before it became a much larger, more professional affair increasingly commanded by men chosen at least in part for their ability. Moreover, with the political authority in the shape of the monarch or his princes no longer present, individual commanders – many if not most chosen from outside the ranks of the aristocracy – wielded enormous independent authority in an age when orders took weeks to cross land and sea: they were genuinely autonomous battlefield commanders, masters of their own armies.

The 'golden age' really began with a revolution in military thinking among French and British staff officers, both on land and at sea, against the conventional and rigid military tactics initiated by Frederick the Great of Prussia (1712–86). However, it is often forgotten that Frederick's own tactics were themselves revolutionary, a far more effective and organized way of winning battles than the haphazard, smaller assemblages of rival forces that had characterized warfare all the way back to the Middle Ages. Frederick was the first general to harness the power of the new breech-loading rifle, in place of the arrow, crossbow and, later, the clumsy musket. This new rifle could be reloaded much more rapidly and had a significantly longer range, delivering effective and disciplined volleys and producing a wall of fire that was almost impossible to resist. By the mid-eighteenth century, however, officers were chafing once more at the inflexibility of the Prussian tactics.

Unlike Frederick, Napoleon Bonaparte relied on a combination of tactics which, although used individually in the past, had rarely been used in unison. On many occasions he pushed his cavalry forward in an attempt to defeat their counterparts in the enemy lines and force the infantry into squares, which while effective defensively had much less firepower than a general line. Napoleon then sought to break up the squares, with horses supporting the infantry to sow confusion.

Napoleon also broke with another age-old tradition and insisted on unity of command. His generals were guided by him alone and the French were thus spared the confusion of competing commanders and armies that so plagued eighteenth-century battles. In addition, he kept his men deployed along a wide front, at a distance from the enemy, which encouraged opposing forces to do the same. He would then choose a point of attack and bring his forces together with speed to overwhelm the enemy's weakest point of breakthrough.

The speed with which Napoleon moved his troops displayed all the brilliance of a natural guerrilla commander. In part this derived from the high morale of the troops and the spoils promised to them. They were not grudging peasants who had to be coerced every inch of the way, but men who believed they would win and enrich themselves if they obeyed the commands of their superiors. Time and again victories were won by men marching through the night and appearing suddenly out of the blue, surprising and demoralizing the enemy.

Napoleon's other favourite tactic was the flanking movement: he rarely attacked from the front except when forced to. When he did, he always ensured that another force would materialize on a flank or to the rear to surprise the enemy (the '*mouvement sur les derrières*' – which excited many a ribald comment). The trick here was to bring his army up in corps, each with its own cavalry and artillery, dispatching one (usually weak) force to engage the enemy in frenetic battle, and then sending a separate flanking force to strike from the side or rear. Sometimes the flanking force would be quite small, or sometimes it would be the main force, but it had to arrive precisely in time to rescue the frontal or so-called 'pinning' force and engage the enemy on two sides.

This required accurate timing: the enemy ideally would have committed their own reserves to battle in an effort to overwhelm the frontal force before the flanking attack appeared. A century-and-a-half later, Patton pursued exactly this tactic to great effect. Another favourite strategy was to drive a wedge through the 'hinge', the weakest point between enemy armies (often a hill, wood or river), and then take on the separate forces one at a time.

Napoleon, despite his tactical mastery, realized the limits of a purely mechanical approach to war: 'Tactics, evolution and the sciences of the engineer and the artillery officer may be learned from treatises, much in the same way as geometry, but the knowledge of the higher branches of the art of war is only to be gained by experience and by studying the history of man and battles of great leaders. Can one learn in a grammar to compose a book of the *Iliad*, or one of Corneille's tragedies?'

—⁂—

The other great revolution in the mid-eighteenth century lay in what military men call morale – the management of men, or what is today termed, rather more clinically, 'human resources'. In the past soldiers were essentially either coerced or enlisted men from the lowest ranks of the peasantry or the urban classes, under the control of officers drawn from the gentry or aristocracy, who viewed them with contempt ('the scum of the earth' Wellington called them).

In this, the French Revolution was the prime instigator of change. The first and most dramatic development was the introduction of the '*levée en masse*', or mass conscription. This transformed warfare through numbers alone, providing France with huge manpower reserves. Alongside this came a revolution in '*esprit de corps*', or morale. The immediate post-revolutionary conscription drive was set up by General Dumouriez. The primary motivation for 'joining up' in Jacobin times was, initially, fear: those who refused to join, were unenthusiastic or deserted, were executed summarily. But with remarkable speed Napoleon set about turning the army into an elite military caste.

He introduced powerful incentives, carrots rather than sticks, and permitted his men the freedom to feed off the land – an added advantage being that they were then unencumbered by baggage trains – and saw to it that they were paid on time, usually through plunder. He also inspired them with injunctions to honour and glory, the ultimate 'carrot' being the award of the Légion d'honneur. To be a soldier in Napoleon's army was not to be a wretched, coerced minion destined to be cannon fodder, but a (reasonably) well fed and clothed member of an almost invariably victorious army in the service of France and revolutionary idealism. They felt they were fighting for their country, not their feudal lords.

As with the French, British army reformers tried to professionalize the officer corps, brought in a meritocracy and improved the attitude of the fighting men through a more enlightened approach. The British army, on the eve of its first great continental commitment since the Duke of Marlborough's campaigns in the mid-seventeenth century, had very little reputation to speak of at all. Discipline was enforced in inhumane ways (except under rare, more enlightened officers), as befitted an army officered by the upper classes and manned by the very lowest. So savage were the beatings given out as punishment that Americans protested at the treatment inflicted by the British on their own men in the American War of Independence.

At the time, the tactics were Prussian – with the emphasis on drill, smart appearance, clean uniforms and powdered hair; they marched in column and fought in line. This had rendered the army highly vulnerable to the tactics of the American irregulars, particularly when they had been supported by disciplined French soldiers who had absorbed the lessons of American-style fighting in employing irregular skirmishers and light divisions to fight alongside the main forces.

Yet the British possessed one apparent advantage in the war against France: as a volunteer army, unlike their French counterparts and the many subject nationalities conscripted by the Austrians, they seemed to show much greater bravery and eagerness to fight.

Nonetheless, they were plagued by a lack of imagination in their commanders: mediocre generals like John Burgoyne and Henry Clinton were outclassed by the merely competent William Howe and Charles Cornwallis. With the outbreak of the wars in 1793, an even worse commander had been appointed: George III's favourite son, Frederick, the Duke of York. Fat and florid, he was no leader of men in battle, as his dismal performance in Flanders during the first campaign of the war amply demonstrated (although in London he later proved a surprisingly good administrator). Occasional British commanders had shown modest flair – Sir Ralph Abercromby in the West Indies; Sir David Baird, a dour and competent lieutenant-general who had served with distinction in India; and Sir John Stuart, who boldly supported the Calabrian insurgency. But these were not Nelsons or Cochranes, nor even Howes or St Vincents.

Britain was desperately short of military heroes in the first few years of the war. But then it appeared to find a real hero at last, a man of the hour. Of Nelson and Napoleon's generation, he had been born in November 1761, of humbler origins even than the former, the son of a doctor from Glasgow. John Moore seemed to be Britain's answer to Napoleon.

Moore quickly realized that British army tactics were in radical need of revision to meet the challenges posed by the new French strategies. Securing the support of the Duke of York, he started training British units to become light infantry and reconnaissance forces. An experimental Rifle Corps was set up at Horsham, recruiting men from 15 regiments. His reforms were designed firstly to motivate the soldiers and improve their morale; secondly, to introduce greater mobility – a speciality of his which was the basis of his decision to take soldiers off the parade ground and train them in the field, bivouacking them outside towns and villages; and thirdly to improve tactics. Moore abandoned the rigid discipline enforced through the hanging and flogging of his predecessors. Instead he believed in the 'thinking, fighting man'.

Moore put these ideas into practice with a thoroughly modern approach: officers, who in the past had been discouraged from fraternizing with their men, were encouraged to get to know them, observing their strengths and weaknesses. Soldiers who had previously been discouraged from independent action or thought, for fear of encouraging indiscipline or even insubordination against their officers (and who were often judged as too stupid to make a worthwhile contribution anyway), were taught to use their initiative and encouraged in Napoleonic-style regimental pride. Moore's objective was 'that each individual soldier knows what he has to do. Discipline is carried on without severity, the officers are attached to the men and the men to the officers.' Another officer wrote admiringly of the 52nd Regiment, Moore's showpiece, that 'officers were formed for command and soldiers acquired such discipline as to become an example to the army and proud of their profession'.

Despising parade-ground exercises, Moore instructed his light infantry in the new art of marching – an easy rhythm for general marching without the discomfort of the old Prussian-style stiff marching. He also taught his soldiers to have their wits about them at all times, to be aware of all that went on around them, to reconnoitre and to observe. This was a radical change for soldiers accustomed to marching, wheeling about and manoeuvring with parade grounds stiffness and firing as a separate manoeuvre.

Soldiers were instructed to shoot to kill, and to fire independently as well as in a volley, which was easier with rifles that had a 300-yard range (500 for sharpshooters). They were also taught to reload and fire quickly – five rounds per minute. The British tactic of repeated, disciplined volleys was in fact a refinement of Prussian tactics, and could be effective. However, the tactic of withholding fire until the last moment, which of course required discipline and courage, was the most effective new introduction of all.

Modern research, for example by Brent Nosworthy, suggests that victory was often achieved by a single volley at closer range followed by a bayonet charge. As Nosworthy writes:

> The overall psychological and physical dynamics underlying the British infantry tactic were pre-eminently simple: wait until the distance separating the two forces has been reduced to where, when the fire was finally delivered, it could not help but be

effective, if not overpowering. Then, while the enemy is still recoiling from the shock caused by the devastating volley, rush in with lowered bayonets. The enemy, staggering from their casualties and totally overawed by a ferocious charge delivered in a moment of vulnerability, almost inevitably turns and flees.

The coolness of the troops under fire was carefully inculcated under psychological pressure, with officers exhorting their men to be 'steady, lads, steady', in contrast to the equally deliberate French technique of advancing to drums and shouts, to give the men courage. Moore's revolution in British tactics and morale can hardly be overstated. The British army had grown in strength from around 100,000 regulars in 1803 to double that in 1807, although Castlereagh failed in his attempt to introduce conscription into a nation averse to martial influence. Moreover, a huge quantity of recruits were attracted by the desire to fight for king and country against the seemingly barbarous Napoleon: the army was no longer merely a refuge for 'undesirables'.

———·∿∿·———

The three immense changes in warfare – greater tactical flexibility, the formation of semi-autonomous divisions under the overall control of a commander and the massive improvement in morale – coupled with the great expansion of the armies in Europe to counter the French threat, presented an entirely new strategic challenge that was to be associated with one man, Carl von Clausewitz. Clausewitz's military doctrines or, some argue, a distortion thereof, were to dominate the continent for over half a century until they were ground into the mud of Flanders during the First World War.

The basic Clausewitz theory was a purist, 'Kantian', one – that ideal warfare existed in a vacuum of all other pressures, and that a war should end in a complete victory by one side over another – an 'absolute war' which would be conducted with the 'outmost violence'.

In reality, Clausewitz deliberately set up this target in order to knock it down, arguing that 'war is not an isolated act', that it 'does not consist of a single isolated blow' and that in real life, it was 'never absolute'. He argued passionately that war was essentially the fulfilment of a political objective, and famously, 'the continuation of policy by other means'. This was interpreted to mean that killing people was merely part of the political process, while he in fact meant the opposite – as absolute victory was never attainable, war was limited by political objectives. Clausewitz went on to argue that war was 'of all the branches of human activity, the most like a gambling game', that 'maxims, rules and even systems for the conduct of war' cannot be established, that morale was the key ingredient. Nevertheless the damage was done.

However much Clausewitz sought to qualify the ideal of total war, he also came up with a further series of controversial maxims: 'The best strategy is clearly to be very strong, concentrating one's forces at the decisive point'. 'Superiority of numbers is the most important factor in deciding victory, surprise the second'. More sensibly, Clausewitz viewed retreat as merely a tactical extension of attack, something to be used to an army's advantage.

Many of these ideas displayed moderation and insight, but Clausewitz gave no importance at all to diplomacy or the use of sea power, which had been enormously effective in destroying Napoleon, whose strategy was the source of his analysis. Clausewitz went on to elaborate his most controversial dictum:

> ...the effect of a victory will naturally depend on its greatness, and that of the mass of the conquered troops. Therefore the blow which, if successful, will produce the greatest effect, must be made against that part of the country where the greatest number of the enemy's forces are collected together; and the greater the mass of our own forces which we use for this blow, so much the surer shall we be of this success. This natural sequence of ideas leads us to an illustration by which we shall see this truth more clearly; it is the nature and effect of the centre of gravity in mechanics.

> As a centre of gravity is always situated where the greatest mass of matter is collected, and as a shock against the centre of gravity of a body always produces the greatest effect, and further, as the most effective blow is struck with the centre of gravity of the power used, so it is also in war.

In fact Clausewitz modified and qualified this position too. But that was not how the German general staff, and in particular Field-Marshal Von Moltke saw it: for him Clausewitz's thinking was, baldly, that the victor was the one who had the bigger forces and used them without scruple or mercy to drive towards the very centre of enemy forces and destroy them. German victory in the Franco-Prussian wars appeared to prove this very point. The Germans carried on the strategy into the First World War, and the British general staff also adopted it, at a time when the introduction of the machine-gun and other fixed defences made it mass suicide, with the terrible results observed on the Western front.

Basil Liddell Hart, the great British interwar strategist, was horrified by the waste in that war:

> By the reiteration of such phrases Clausewitz blurred the outlines of his philosophy, already indistinct, and made it into a mere marching refrain – a Prussian Marseillaise which inflamed the blood and intoxicated the mind. In transfusion it became a doctrine fit to form corporals, not generals... for by making battle appear the only 'real warlike activity', his gospel deprived strategy of its laurels, and reduced the art of war to the mechanics of mass-slaughter. Moreover, it incited generals to seek battle at the first opportunity, instead of creating an advantageous opportunity.
>
> Clausewitz contributed to the subsequent decay of generalship when in an oft-quoted passage he wrote: 'Philanthropists may easily imagine that there is a skilful method of disarming and overcoming the enemy without great bloodshed, and that this is the proper tendency of the Art of War... That is an error which must be extirpated...' Clausewitz's phrase would henceforth be used by countless

blunderers to excuse, and even to justify, their futile squandering of life in bull-headed assaults.

The most dangerous of all Clausewitz's frequently misunderstood maxims was that of concentration of force and direct attack. Liddell Hart in particular believed passionately in the indirect approach – encircling the enemy, severing their lines of communication (but leaving a way of escape so they did not have to fight to the finish), stacking the odds in advance of battle so that the enemy had no choice but to surrender, above all undermining their morale through surprise and fear.

Liddell Hart's championing of the indirect approach interestingly, and surely not coincidentally for so great a student of military history, mirrored that of the great Chinese strategist and general Sun Tzu (who also inspired Mao Zedong) as far back as the sixth century BC.

———❧———

This then was the great strategic debate that dominated most of the past two centuries, against which the exploits of these maverick military commanders were played out. The mavericks flourished when the battlefield was mobile and they had independence of command. Frederick the Great's fixed formations of infantry, cavalry and artillery were followed by the military revolution of the late-eighteenth century which permitted much greater mobility and flexibility, before becoming frozen again in the Clausewitzean doctrines of total warfare and direct frontal assault, which culminated in the slaughter of the First World War.

In the Second World War, thanks to air power and tank warfare, tactics became as mobile as in the Napoleonic wars, before being frozen again in the Maginot mentality of the Cold War which, in part due to the lethal deterrent of nuclear weapons, narrowly avoided a total, annihilating war – Clausewitz taken to appalling extremes.

Now, as the immediate fear of a nuclear exchange has, for the most part, lifted, and as troops find themselves in smaller-scale conventional operations like those in Iraq and Afghanistan, warfare seems to be becoming more mobile again. So-called asymmetrical warfare – terrorist and guerrilla attacks against a (usually significantly larger) conventional armed force – is also a new challenge.

In the Second World War, while one of the two main Clausewitzean doctrines was pursued to its logical conclusion – total defeat and unconditional surrender (as opposed to the armistice with Germany that in the First World War arguably rendered another war inevitable) – the other, the doctrine of direct attack on the main concentration of enemy force (which had yielded such disastrous results in the First World War) was not. In large part this is thanks to the foresight of men like Liddell Hart.

This leads us to a more radical conclusion: there are no hard and fast rules of military strategy. An approach that may be right at a particular moment, may also be entirely wrong at another. On this all the great strategists concur, even though it appears to refute their own elaborately conceived military strategies. Napoleon said: 'The art of war does not require complicated manoeuvres; the simplest are the best, and common sense is fundamental.' The lesson may be that in different circumstances, entirely different strategies and tactics apply. It is possible that neither Clausewitz or Liddel Hart is right. Sometimes it is right to attack '*sur les derrières*', sometimes to flank, sometimes to retreat, sometimes to advance, sometimes to concentrate forces, sometimes to disperse, sometimes to divide the enemy and even sometimes to launch a full frontal attack.

—◦◦◦—

Another factor common to many of the commanders in this book is the way they strengthened morale through their actions and their solicitude to their men. Not only was *esprit de corps* the underpinning of the motivation and success of one's own side, but throwing the morale of the enemy off-balance was a key to victory in battle – hence the impact of unconventional and unpredictable surprise tactics. Catching the enemy unawares could lead, almost instantaneously, to catastrophic retreat.

Sir John Baynes, in his definitive book, *Morale* (1967), has a fine passage on the subject:

> The truth is that a brilliant plan of battle in the tactical sense can be a complete failure if morale is bad, while a poor plan can be made to work well if morale is good... war is a desperately muddled, confusing, and chaotic business...
>
> It is my contention that high morale can spring from two sources, which I would call 'nobility of spirit' and 'bloody-mindedness'... Nobility of spirit, found in the person with a background of love and affection, gives rise to the characteristics usually quoted in connection with good morale. They include love of a cause, love of one's country, loyalty, *esprit de corps*, and unselfishness...

Baynes's book is probably the only full-length study of this all-important subject. However, Field-Marshal Bernard Montgomery brilliantly captured just this point in an eloquent passage of his autobiography:

> The raw material with which the general has to deal is men. The same is true in civil life. Managers of large industrial concerns have not always seemed to me to have understood this point; they think their raw material is iron ore, or cotton, or rubber – not men but commodities. In conversation with them I have disagreed and insisted that their basic raw material is men. Many generals have also not fully grasped this vital matter, nor understood its full implications, and that is one reason why some have failed.
>
> An army must be as hard as steel in battle and can be made so; but, like steel, it reaches its finest quality only after much preparation and only provided the ingredients are properly constituted and handled. Unlike steel, an army is a most sensitive instrument and can easily become damaged; its basic ingredient is men and, to handle an army well, it is essential to understand human nature. Bottled up in men are great emotional forces which have got to be given an outlet in a way which is positive and constructive, and which warms the heart and excites the imagination. If the approach to the human factor is

cold and impersonal, then you achieve nothing. But if you can gain the confidence and trust of your men, and they feel their best interests are safe in your hands, then you have in your possession a priceless asset and the greatest achievements become possible.

The morale of the soldier is the greatest single factor in war and the best way to achieve a high morale in war-time is by success in battle. The good general is the one who wins his battles with the fewest possible casualties; but morale will remain high even after considerable casualties, provided the battle has been won and the men know it was not wastefully conducted, and that every care has been taken of the wounded, and the killed have been collected and reverently buried...

The remarkable thing about each of the commanders in this book is that they appreciated the importance of their men and morale, and in turn they were trusted by their men, who would follow them to the ends of the earth or, more importantly, to the ends of their lives if necessary – perhaps the single most important ingredient of military command. In this respect John Keegan may be wrong that the age of heroic leadership is past: heroism was not just required to impress public opinion back home, but to instil confidence in men to go into battle and risk their lives. With fewer, if any, senior commanders exposing themselves on the frontline, that role may have passed to more junior officers: but without their courage and example, many men would not be prepared to lay their own lives on the line.

—⁓—

To Baynes' analysis of morale, there needs to be added another more modern-day development. Patriotism has sharply changed over the years: the soldiers and sailors that built the British empire were principally motivated by greed and the prospect of spoils, as well as by coercion in the lower ranks. In a society where self-advancement was hard to obtain at home, abstract patriotism probably didn't rank very highly.

Yet by the late-eighteenth century, the time of the Napoleonic Wars, Baynes' analysis carried more weight. Although soldiers were often reluctantly recruited to escape lives of extreme poverty, and many sailors were press-ganged, there was a feeling that Britain was under threat from a hostile and alien ideology led by an ogre, Napoleon Bonaparte, who threatened the British way of life, their families and their wellbeing. As the nineteenth century progressed, it was noticeable that the British did better in wars justified by some measure of idealism rather than naked self-interest. The Crimean War was a disaster, whereas – whether consciously or not – Britain saw itself on a civilizing mission in lands like India and much of Sub-Saharan Africa. The wars in Sudan and the Boer War were further disasters with muddled objectives. The First World War, with public opinion whipped up against the 'Huns', was also seen as a moral war – at least until troops started blaming their incompetent commanders. The Second World War was perhaps the ultimate moral war against the perceptible evil of Hitler and Nazi mass murder and aggression. As the two centuries progressed, the degree to which morale – so key to winning the war – could be buttressed by the perception that Britain was fighting in a good cause, not for purely patriotic or chauvinistic reasons, had increased perceptibly.

The United States, of course, has often used a moral argument to justify its military motivation – first the War of Independence against its British colonial oppressor, the Civil War to end slavery, the frontier wars to 'civilize' their lands, the First World War to establish self-determination for the European peoples, the war against the barbarous Japanese and murderous Hitler, and finally the crusade against communism in Asia, now metamorphosed into a crusade to establish democracy in the Middle East.

If anything, the desire to fight for moral reasons has increased since then, as the most ordinary person and army private is subjected to television, newspapers and the internet as never before: it is always a huge mistake to underestimate the degree of understanding and passion felt about political issues by even some of the most modest in society. Baynes concludes:

One can, perhaps, say that morale is an unchanging quality, and that
the ways of sustaining it are in principle unchanging as well, but that
where the change comes in is in the methods of applying these principles. As men get more used to comfort, more sophisticated and
more intelligent it becomes essential to take more trouble over their
morale. The problem is not to discover what keeps the soldier in
good heart, but how to apply lessons learnt throughout history to the
pattern of modern life in its increasing complexity.

Today superior technology and firepower is perhaps considered
the defining reason why a war is won or lost. But in the period
considered in this book, it was the morale and good leadership of
men, always inextricably intertwined, that played the key role.
Curiously enough the demand for these qualities may be returning
as the great military machine and the threat of awe-inspiring
means of mass destruction posed by nuclear weaponry become
increasingly substituted by much smaller scale fighting with guerrillas and even terrorists. Maybe the idea of old-fashioned leadership of men is not quite dead yet: the heroes of this book may yet
have much to teach us.

—〰—

To turn briefly to the issue of generalship and command itself,
as noted earlier, many have tried to define this quality without
succeeding. But their attempts are instructive. Sun Tzu wrote:

> All warfare is based on deception. A skilled general must be master
> of the complementary arts of simulation and dissimulation; while
> creating shapes to confuse and delude the enemy he conceals his true
> dispositions and ultimate intent. When capable he feigns incapacity;
> when near he makes it appear that he is far away; when far away, that
> he is near. Moving as intangibly as a ghost in the starlight, he is
> obscure, inaudible. His primary target is the mind of the oppos-
> ing commander; the victorious situation, a product of his creative
> imagination...

The expert approaches his objective indirectly. By selection of a devious and distant route he may march a thousand *li* without opposition and take his enemy unaware. Such a commander prizes above all freedom of action. He abhors a static situation and therefore attacks cities only when there is no alternative. Sieges, wasteful both of lives and time, entail abdication of the initiative.

The wise general cannot be manipulated. He may withdraw, but when he does, moves so swiftly that he cannot be overtaken. His retirements are designed to entice the enemy, to unbalance him, and to create a situation favourable for a decisive counter-stroke. They are, paradoxically, offensive. He conducts a war of movement; he marches with divine swiftness; his blows fall like thunderbolts 'from the nine-layered heavens'. He creates conditions certain to produce a quick decision; for him victory is the object of war, not lengthy operations however brilliantly conducted. He knows that prolonged campaigns drain the treasury and exhaust the troops; prices rise, the people are hungry: 'No country has ever benefited from a protracted war'.

The expert commander strikes only when the situation assures victory. To create such a situation is the ultimate responsibility of generalship. Before he gives battle the superior general causes the enemy to disperse. When the enemy disperses and attempts to defend everywhere he is weak everywhere, and at the selected points many will be able to strike his few.

Socrates, writing a little later, was practical:

The general... must be observant, untiring, shrewd; kindly and cruel; simple and crafty; a watchman and a robber; lavish and miserly; generous and stingy; rash and conservative. All these and many other qualities, natural and acquired, he must have. He should also, as a matter of course, know his tactics; for a disorderly mob is no more an army than a heap of building materials is a house.

The Duke of Wellington claimed that officer leadership was essential, observing:

...how odd it was that the Spaniards, such fine and brave men as individuals, should make such indifferent troops. That happens from want of confidence in their officers. And how should they have any? Their officers had seen no service and knew nothing... Romana was a good-natured, excellent man, most easy to live with – and very clever too – knew all about the literature and poetry of his country more than any Spaniard I ever knew, but he knew nothing of troops at all. I never in my whole life saw a man who had acted at all with troops understand so little about them. I liked him very much – he died in my arms – at least I was in the room at the time – but as to his generalship!

General Archibald Wavell, in a famous essay, saw moral toughness as the first quality of a general:

Now the mind of the general in war is buried, not merely for 48 hours but for days and weeks, in the mud and sand of unreliable information and uncertain factors, and may at any time receive, from an unsuspected move of the enemy, an unforeseen accident, or a treacherous turn in the weather, a bump equivalent to a drop of at least a hundred feet on to something hard. Delicate mechanism is of little use in war; and this applies to the mind of the commander as well as to his body; to the spirit of an army as well as to the weapons and instruments with which it is equipped. All material of war, including the general, must have a certain solidity, a high margin over the normal breaking strain. It is often said that British war material is unnecessarily solid; and the same possibly is apt to be true of their generals. But we are certainly right to leave a good margin.

It is sometimes argued whether war is an art or science... I know of no branch of art or science, however, in which rivals are at liberty to throw stones at the artist or scientist, to steal his tools and to destroy his materials, while he is working, always against time, on his picture or statue or experiment. Under such conditions how many of the great masterpieces of art or discoveries of science would have been produced? No, the civil comparison to war must be that of a game, a very rough and dirty game, for which a robust body and mind are essential. The general is dealing with men's lives, and must have a certain mental robustness to stand the strain of this responsibility. How great that strain is you may judge by the sudden deaths of many of the commanders of the late War. When you read military history take note of the failures due to lack of this quality of robustness.

...He must have 'character', which simply means that he knows what he wants and has the courage and determination to get it. He should have a genuine interest in, and a real knowledge of, humanity, the raw material of his trade; and, most vital of all, he must have what we call the fighting spirit, the will to win. You all know and recognise it in sport, the man who plays his best when things are going badly, who has the power to come back at you when apparently beaten, and who refuses to acknowledge defeat. There is one other moral quality I would stress as the mark of the really great commander as distinguished from the ordinary general. He must have a spirit of adventure, a touch of the gambler in him. As Napoleon said: 'If the art of war consisted merely in not taking risks glory would be at the mercy of very mediocre talent'. Napoleon always asked if a general was 'lucky'. What he really meant was, 'Was he bold?' A bold general may be lucky, but no general can be lucky unless he is bold. The general who allows himself to be bound and hampered by regulations is unlikely to win a battle...

A general who speaks to men individually may sometimes receive a disconcerting answer. A story is told of Haig, who usually inspected men in a complete and stony silence, that one of his staff told him that it would make a better impression if he spoke to one or two men. Accordingly he said to a man, 'Where did you start this War?' 'I didn't start this War, sir; I think the Kaiser did,' was the reply. Allenby once, on a visit to the trenches, found a man sitting on the fire-step delousing his shirt. 'Well, picking them out, I see,' he remarked. 'No, sir, no,' replies the man looking up, 'just taking them as they come'.

The British soldier himself is one of the world's greatest humorists. The Germans held an investigation after the First World War into the causes of morale, and attributed much of the British soldier's staying power to his sense of humour. They therefore decided to encourage this in their own soldiers, including in their manuals instructions on how to cultivate it. They gave as an illustration in the manual one of popular British cartoonist Bruce Bairnsfather's pictures of 'Old Bill' sitting in a building with an enormous shell-hole in the wall. A new chum asks: 'What made that hole?' 'Mice,' replies Bill. In the German manual a solemn footnote of explanation is added: 'It was not mice, it was a shell'.

———

War is not a matter of diagrams, principles or rules. The higher commander who goes to Field Service Regulations for tactical guidance inspires about as much confidence as the doctor who turns to a medical dictionary for his diagnosis. And no method of education, no system of promotion, no amount of commonsense ability is of value unless the leader has in him the root of the matter – the fighting spirit... 'No battle was ever lost until the leader thought it so'. And this is the first and true function of the leader, never to think the battle or the cause lost. The ancient Romans put up a statue to the general who saved them in one of Rome's darkest hours, with this inscription: 'Because he did not despair of the Republic'.

This has changed since the Second World War. With the acceleration in instant modern communications, command and control has been taken to absurd limits, with staff headquarters thousands of miles away micro-managing operations, with even politicians and their media 'spinners' getting in on the act. The invasion of Iraq, for example, was heavily supervised by US Central Command in Tampa, Florida, overseen by Defence Secretary Donald Rumsfeld, a civilian heavily criticized by his generals. In Britain, decisions are increasingly taken by the political hierarchy to present the best possible public relations veneer back home.

Whatever the benefits or disadvantages of this approach, it greatly reduces the autonomy of even mid-level commanders in the field except in the very thick of battle, where one suspects *coup d'oeil* will still make the difference between victory and defeat. But precisely because these men are middle-ranking officers, their readiness to improvise, let alone defy orders, is likely to be less.

Real 'warrior' moments are increasingly few: one exception was General Sir Michael Jackson's tough stand against Russia in Serbia – when he briefly freed himself from his political leash. Other 'names', against all odds, have been Colonel 'H' Jones in the Falklands and General Sir Michael Rose. Apart from intense control and political scrutiny, the drabness of modern uniforms and the specialization of much modern soldiery, with its laptops and targeting systems, have cut the ground from under the old-fashioned warrior-hero. Again, these developments are probably inevitable in a technological age, but they make the emergence of Boys' Own commanders even less likely in the future 'post-heroic age'.

The main qualities exhibited in varying degrees by most, but not all, of these lost mavericks can be summarized as follows:

1. Outstanding and exemplary courage under fire.
2. The ability to think coolly and rationally on the battlefield.
3. Remarkable determination in making their way to the top on merit.
4. Extraordinary stamina.
5. Resolution in the face of terrible setbacks.
6. A strategic grasp geared to seizing opportunities, often after long periods of frustrating caution, and staging strikes of great boldness.
7. An ability to improvise and seize unexpected tactical advantage on the battlefield and manoeuvre skilfully.
8. Verve and charismatic leadership often executed through consummate diplomacy, flamboyance and eccentricity – perhaps the earliest form of public relations.
9. A penchant for fighting against superior odds that could catch a complacent enemy unawares.
10. A fatherly devotion to their own men, seeing to their needs during the long periods of inaction and refusing to risk their lives unnecessarily.
11. An intense interest in raising morale.

12. Skill in selecting subordinates.
13. The command and control system on the battlefield that ensured orders reached the right people at the right time (which so often went wrong prior to modern telecommunications), as well as the necessary discipline and ruthlessness to forge a modern, efficient fighting machine.
14. High intelligence, often concealed under a veneer of military bluffness, and communications skills.
15. A record of insubordination and questioning authority in their own rise to the top – something they would not tolerate in others.
16. An instinct to question, revise or ignore traditional tactics.

Chapter 1

CLIVE OF INDIA: BRITISH WARRIOR-EMPEROR

Robert Clive was Britain's first professional soldier-hero – which was strange because he was not trained as a soldier at all. From a middling gentry family, he emerged as a rebuke to the aristocratic, amateurish British officer class to deliver a dazzling array of battlefield successes in India, executed with an almost unerring eye and extraordinary boldness, using small manoeuvrable forces staging surprise flanking attacks of a kind that had rarely been tried before. As a result he conquered a third of the continent and founded the British empire in India.

Clive was born into a respectable gentry family on 29 September 1725, at Styche, near Moreton Saye in Shropshire. Something of a young tearaway who climbed the local church steeple, he appeared to have few prospects in Britain. At the age of 17, he was sent off to make his fortune at the East India Company headquarters in the prosperous British settlement of Madras where, it is said, he was so homesick and bored that he attempted to commit suicide, but his pistol twice failed to go off.

When the French East India Company, under the formidable governor of Pondicherry, Joseph-François Dupleix, suddenly attacked and occupied Madras in 1746, the 21-year-old Clive and three companions escaped, disguised as Indians, and made their way to Fort St David, 50 miles to the south. Clive took part in defending the fort against French attack, and in a failed attack on the French stronghold of Pondicherry. Madras was finally restored to the British under the Treaty of Aix-La-Chapelle.

Clive's first real command came in 1749 when a tough professional soldier, Major Stringer Lawrence, put him in charge of 30 British troops and 700 Indians in an assault on Fort Devikottai; the fearlessness of his attack caused the hostile local Indian ruler to abandon the fort.

The French, meanwhile, sought to gain control of most of southern India by besieging the Indian ruler of Trichinopoly, Mohammed Ali. Some 800 French and 20,000 Indians besieged 60 English and 2,000 Indian troops inside the colourful citadel. Clive was sent as an aide to an incompetent Swiss mercenary, Captain Rudolf de Guingens, commanding a relief force. Contemptuous of de Guingens and impatient for action, Clive persuaded his superiors in Madras to despatch him to seize the fortress at Arcot, citadel of France's Indian allies, while most of their army was at Trichinopoly.

Clive's small army, which dwindled to 120 British troops and 2,000 Indians, marched through monsoon thunderstorms to seize the fortress, which was abandoned on his approach. With his tiny force occupying the sprawling fortress, Clive held out against the assault of an Indian army of some 15,000 men for 53 days.

On 13 November 1751, Clive's exhausted, parched and half-starved men, only two-thirds of them fighting fit, were subjected to a full-scale attack by their Shia adversaries. It was the last day of Muharram, the great Shia Muslim festival commemorating the martyrdom of the grandsons of the Prophet, Hassan and Hussein. The latter had been butchered after all around him had been slain. His head was carried to the enemy leader, who struck at it with a stick, and, it was said, his lips were then seen pressed to the lips of the Prophet. If a Shia Muslim died on this holy day, he would go straight to heaven. Shia is the most zealous branch of Islam; their leader, Raza Sahib, had no trouble working his men into a religious frenzy.

Clive and his soldiers could hear the wailing ululations and shrieking outside, along with the drum-banging and trumpet-blowing of an army drunk on liquor and high on drugs as they worked themselves into a fever of vengeance. Even for Clive, the terrifying sounds outside the fort that still late autumn evening must have been chilling. The fort had withstood two ham-fisted attacks, a series of bombardments and relentless musket fire. But could just a few hundred battle-fit soldiers stand up to a whole religious-crazed army of more than 15,000?

Just before dawn a large number of the enemy were seen running forward, carrying ladders. Behind them, elephants with huge protective iron plates on their foreheads charged forward to batter down the gates. Further behind, a torrent of enemy soldiers with muskets and spears surged as far as the eye could see.

Clive, entirely cool in a crisis and apparently fearless, promptly gave orders for his men to shoot at the unprotected flanks of the elephants. They stopped and reared up under the intense pain; and then turned and stampeded into the soldiers following them. The gates remained secure. However, simultaneous attacks were being mounted in two major breaches caused by the French guns, and the besiegers were spurred on by their religious frenzy 'with a mad kind of intrepidity'. Clive had organized his tiny force to fire and then hand back their muskets to loaders, who would promptly pass on another gun, so as to make use of both his active and inactive soldiers. This concentrated fire caused the attackers to waver. Meanwhile, grenades were being hurled from the ramparts at the second line of enemy troops.

At the northwest breach, the leader of the assailing forces, Abdul Kodah Khan, led his troops forward across the moat and to the first trench, waving his flag – before being struck by a bullet and knocked into the water below. Beside the other breach, the moat was still deep, and the attackers had launched a raft with some 70 men on it. This came under intense fire from two small English guns. Clive himself grabbed one of them and raked the vessel with the most accurate shots, causing the men on board to panic and capsize the raft. The moat was soon full of struggling figures under fire.

The French, meanwhile, were nowhere to be seen. The French commander, Goupil, had disapproved of Raza Sahib's decision to storm the fort, and had kept aloof. By now, wave after wave of brave if undisciplined attacks had been driven off, and Raza Sahib decided to withdraw. His men tried to return to retrieve the bodies of the dead, a custom traditionally allowed by the enemy in India. But the British fired as they advanced, driving them back, either mistaking this for a new assault or as part of a deliberate tactic by Clive to terrify the enemy.

It was just before dawn, and the fierce fight, which had seemed interminable, had only lasted an hour. Robert Orme, Clive's first biographer, described how the British were 'left to gaze at each other in the first garish brilliance of the suddenly uplifted sun'.

The scene must have been eerie. The screams, battle chants and trumpets, the yells and groans of conflict, had been replaced by the moans of the dying. Around 300 of the enemy lay strewn outside the wall; just four British soldiers had been killed and two Indians wounded. It had been a testament to the incredible difficulty of storming a well-defended fort, as well as to Clive's leadership.

Even so, the young captain, while triumphant, could hardly afford to rest. The enemy was almost certainly regrouping for another attack; they had a manpower reserve of some 15,000 fighters. The next attack could not be long in coming. Clive's exhausted men could hardly keep up the resistance indefinitely.

Two hours later, a relentless barrage of musket and cannon fire began. This was presumably the softening up needed to deter his men from manning the ramparts again. Clive embarked on his rounds once more, cheering up and cajoling his men while checking on the defences. After more than four hours the relentless bombardment, which had set all of them on edge, ceased, and a small party arrived under a white flag requesting permission to carry off the bodies of the dead, which were already decomposing under the intense midday sun. The request was granted.

Two hours later the pounding began again. The garrison rested as best it could. The bombardment continued for a full 12 hours; Clive imagined the enemy were seeking to exhaust the garrison mentally in preparation for the next assault. When it ceased at 2 a.m., the jangled nerves of Clive and his men were tensed for the attack. All night they watched and waited for the next pre-dawn assault.

When the sun rose a second time, there was no sign of the enemy, although their guns and baggage were strewn before the fort. They had left the city, and the bombardment had been a cover to allow them to retire in good order, in case the formidable enemy within the fort sallied out to attack them.

Two more hard-fought battles ensued, a set-piece one at Arni and an enemy ambush at Kaveripak, which Clive won narrowly before he returned to Trichinopoly, which was still under siege. Along with Major Stringer Lawrence, he carried the battle to the French who were encamped on a narrow tongue of land behind the immense pagoda complex at Srirangam to the north, protected by the Cauvery and Coleroon rivers. Clive relentlessly bombarded the French and Indian forces while Lawrence closed the trap from the landward side, forcing surrender. Clive's whirlwind of activity in his first tour of India ended with the decisive capture of two French forts, Covelong and Chingleput. He returned in glory to Madras, where he married the redoubtable Margaret Maskelyne, and received a hero's welcome in England as the man who had saved Britain's southern settlements in India at the age of just 27.

In London he quickly squandered his new wealth, much of it on an expensive but unsuccessful attempt to enter the House of Commons, and in 1755 was compelled to return to India to seek his fortune again. On the journey back he took part in the successful storming of the pirate stronghold at Gheria, near Bombay, before taking up his new post as commander of Fort St David on 22 June 1756 – coincidentally just two days after the Black Hole of Calcutta incident, the (much exaggerated) atrocity conducted by Siraj-ud-Daula, the Nawab of Bengal, following the seizure of the main British settlement in Bengal, Fort William, which the governor, Roger Drake, had shamefully abandoned to its fate.

As soon as the news from Calcutta reached Madras, the British started to organize an expedition to regain the settlement with Clive as one of three commanders. On 16 October one of the mightiest expeditionary forces assembled in the eighteenth century set sail. The people of Madras turned out in their hundreds to wave goodbye to this formidable and magnificent spectacle. There were four major ships of the line: the *Kent*, Admiral Charles Watson's flagship, with 64 guns; the *Cumberland*, under Admiral Pocock, with 70 guns; the *Tyger*, with 60 guns; and the *Salisbury*, with 50. In addition, there was a smaller ship, the *Bridgwater*, with 20 guns, and a fireship named, without imagination, the *Blaze*. They were escorting three company warships (also equipped with some guns), the *Protector*, *Walpole* and *Marlborough*, and three ketches. There were more than 500 British company soldiers, 150 marines, 100 artillerymen, nearly 1,000 Indian troops and 160 support troops. Including the crews, over 2,500 sailed with six weeks' worth of provisions.

George Pigot, governor of Madras, had tried to tie Clive's hands with the admonition that 'the sword shall go hand in hand with the pen'. He now sent Siraj-ud-Daula a threatening letter which also held out the hope of avoiding hostilities:

> The great commander of the King of England's ships has not slept in peace since this news and is come down with many ships, and I have sent a great *sardar* who will govern after me, by name Colonel Clive, with troops and land forces... You are wise: consider whether it is better to engage in a war that will never end or to do what is just and right in the sight of God.

However, Clive was not to be inhibited by Pigot, who would soon be several hundred miles away in Madras. Clive had been bewitched by Calcutta on his only visit there, as by the river Hugli that led away into a kingdom of vast wealth and extent. Siraj-ud-Daula had furnished him with the pretext for going after it. As the prows of the ships steered proudly northwest, and the cheers from the quayside grew more distant, Clive, who had been so scarred by the humiliation of the British surrender at Fort St George years earlier, felt pride surge in his breast. He had been picked to command the restoration of British rule to another scene of national shame and humiliation. He knew that he was at another turning point in his life.

His previous exploits, while remembered, had propelled him only to the status of a minor British hero, and his personal ambitions in Britain had been frustrated and his fortune diminished. His immense abilities and energies, though, were in their prime and leavened by experience. He understood that a defeat would never be acceptable to a restless tyrant like Siraj-ud-Daula. Nothing less than the removal of the Nawab of Bengal from his throne would secure British rule in Calcutta again. But if the Nawab were to be removed, why should the British make terms with another oriental despot? They would be mad to relinquish any authority they acquired. A new law was to apply to Clive's gains in Bengal: the law of accelerating ambitions. To secure a gain it is always necessary to annex more land, and then secure that, and so on.

After a bombardment, the looted and largely destroyed Fort William was retaken. In revenge for the attack on Calcutta, Clive marched upriver and took the town of Hugli, which was also abandoned by the Bengalis. But this provoked Siraj-ud-Daula to march south back to Calcutta. Clive now faced his most formidable foe.

Siraj-ud-Daula differed sharply from any of the conventional dissolute princes of India, described in the classic *Raghuvamsha* by the Sanskrit poet Kalidasa as being manipulated by a senior minister who 'accustoms him to the pleasures of a life of luxury and gives him every possible opportunity to indulge in them... he accustoms [the young ruler] to believe that the ruler's share in royal authority consists merely in sitting on the throne, shaking hands, being addressed as Sire, and sitting with women in the seclusion of the harem'. Siraj-ud-Daula was dissipated, but he was also ambitious, hyperactive, and showed considerable cunning, if not statecraft. Apart from his pathological contempt for his own nobility, three other traits stand out: an insatiable sexual appetite, a penchant for frivolous cruelty and a loathing of the British.

Siraj-ud-Daula's cruelty was legendary. He would rip open the stomachs of pregnant women to satisfy his curiosity as to how the child lay in the womb. According to his ally, Jean Law, head of the French settlement at Kosimbazar, 'he was often seen, in the season when the river overflows, causing ferry boats to be upset or sunk, in order to have the cruel pleasure of seeing the confusion of a hundred people at a time, men, women and children, of whom many, not being able to swim, were sure to perish'. To the British trader William Watts, Siraj-ud-Daula was 'that imbecile murderer who breaks birds' wings and cuts off men's privities'. But he was also bold, decisive and a ruthless and skilful military commander.

Clive bravely decided on a pre-emptive attack on the Nawab's camp at Dum Dum, outside Calcutta, in February 1757. But for once things went wrong: when a fog lifted he was left exposed to a far superior enemy force and he had to cut his way hurriedly through the Bengali camp to escape, inflicting some 1,500 casualties in the fighting. Siraj-ud-Daula nevertheless retreated further up the river Hugli after this display of British determination, and forged an alliance with the nearby French settlement at Chandernagore. Clive promptly replied by bombarding and taking the French enclave.

Clive now set his sights on total victory over the Nawab and embarked on a policy of duplicity for which he would later be much criticized. Yet it is hard to see what else he could have done, in view of the overwhelming force arrayed against him. William Watts was sent to seek a secret agreement with Siraj-ud-Daula's chief general, Mir Jafar, to betray his master and attach his forces to the British side in any battle. This also involved double-crossing an untrustworthy go-between, the merchant Omichand, with a false treaty promising him huge rewards for his help. But by the time Watts secretly left the Bengali capital of Murshidabad, there was no certainty that the Indian general would come to the aid of the British.

Clive, with a small army of 3,000 men, marched up the river Hugli to confront Siraj-ud-Daula and historically ordered his men to cross a tributary as the rising waters, swollen by monsoon rains, cut off their line of retreat. On the wrong side of the river, his men faced massacre if they lost. He took up a position at the Nawab's beautiful hunting lodge at Plassey. To the south there was an immense mango grove, to the west the river.

When dawn broke, Clive was on the roof of the lodge, telescope in hand. What he saw must have shaken him. He had heard reports that the Nawab's army was only 8,000 strong, because his treasury had failed to pay the rest of his men. Others believed the number to be much greater; but the evidence suggests Clive was reasonably confident the numbers were on the low side. Instead, in the clear light of the morning, while the sun cast its early cold light and the monsoon clouds began to gather, there lay before him a rolling sea of enemy troops – the standing army of Rai Durlabh reinforced by the whole might of Murshidabad, including Mir Jafar – which was fanning out towards and around the British position.

One of Clive's aides wrote: 'What with the number of elephants, all covered with scarlet cloth and embroidery; their horse, with their drawn swords glittering in the sun; their heavy cannon drawn by vast trains of oxen; and their standards flying, they made a most pompous and formidable appearance.' Pennants were flying, bands with trumpets and cymbals were playing. Elephants with exotically tailored, clanking, suffocating armour bore the major commanders.

A large and well-trained cavalry was among them, their swords at the ready. A large number of cannon was in their midst, heavily outnumbering the English; they were on mobile wooden platforms, each pulled by some 50 oxen; behind, elephants pushed them forward. The odds were the worst that Clive had ever faced. The forces against him were relatively well disciplined. He had less than a tenth of their cannon and no cavalry; he had no native supporting armies, unlike at Trichinopoly.

His position, although a good defensive one, was hardly a fort. Against his 3,000 men was an army of at least 50,000: 35,000 disciplined infantry, admittedly often mutinous, but just sweetened by large sums of back pay, along with 15,000 of the best cavalry available – Pathans, fine fighters and riders from the northwest border. In addition, the Nawab had more than 50 cannon; the most advanced of these had sophisticated screw devices to raise and lower their barrels and, more threatening still, they were maintained and fired by 50 Frenchmen under the control of M. de St Frais, who was bent on avenging the defeat at Chandernagore.

There had been no reply, in the night or early morning, from Mir Jafar. As the forces before Clive began to outflank the British to the south, he wondered whether he would soon be entirely surrounded and cut off with his back to the river. He had never been in such dire straits; he feared that he had lost his gamble. He remarked grimly, 'We must make the best fight we can during the day and at night sling our muskets over our shoulders and march back to Calcutta.'

Clive watched as St Frais and his Frenchmen entrenched themselves with their guns behind earthworks near a mound only 200 yards from the British, deliberately provoking them. Between the Frenchmen and the river two more guns were set up to give cover to 5,000 cavalry and 7,000 infantry. This force was commanded by Mir Madan, a loyal favourite of the Nawab.

In response, Clive ordered his men well beyond the shelter of the grove, to a position directly in front of the enemy line. He placed three of his small guns on either side, and hundreds of his soldiers in between. Sepoys guarded his flanks. A little further back he placed his two remaining six-pound guns and howitzers protected by brick kilns. Not until Gordon's stand at Khartoum more than a hundred years later can a more hopeless position have been defended by the British, and so few have faced such overwhelming odds to so little apparent purpose. They faced a wipeout; it looked like the last stand of a defeated army. To the south the Nawab's huge armies continued relentlessly to encircle him.

—⁓—

At 8 a.m. the first cannonade from the French guns began, and the British replied. The British fire ripped through Mir Madan's men, but the French had killed 10 British soldiers and 20 Indians within half an hour. Clive's boldness in venturing beyond the mango grove had been an absurd mistake in the face of the overwhelming firepower directed by the accurate French.

He was quick-witted enough to realize the consequences and gave his men the order to pull the guns back to the grove; the cannon were moved behind a mud bank, where they could fire through holes while being protected. Only the howitzers remained in a forward position. One, by an incredibly lucky shot, seriously wounded Mir Madan.

Not knowing this, the position appeared quite desperate to Clive. The enemy cavalry were moving forward to attack and he decided to pull back his remaining guns. The enemy cannon were blasting huge holes in the Nawab's beloved mango trees, but inflicting few casualties as the British continued to shelter behind the mud bank. The two sides continued exchanging relentless fire in this way for three hours.

Clive summoned his commanders to suggest that they concentrate on holding out until midnight and then resort to his old tactic of a surprise night attack as a last desperate measure. Clive believed he could hold his position to the front, provided the forces moving to encircle him did not attack from the flank or the rear. Significantly – although he did not know it – these forces were commanded by the three main conspirators: Mir Jafar, Yar Latuf Khan and Rai Durlabh. The possible rebels were waiting and circling like vultures to see which side would prevail. While they would not attack until the battle moved decisively to one side or another, as soon as it did they would join the victors. All the intense plotting and negotiating of the past month had at least entombed a large part of the Nawab's army into a kind of neutrality – but no more than that.

The cannonade continued on both sides. In the shelter of the mango grove, Clive's hope was that a direct frontal attack could be repulsed. Then, suddenly, the monsoon clouds, which had been building up for hours, broke; the rain, although lasting only half an hour, was torrential, soaking all, including Clive, to the skin. The British hastily pulled tarpaulins over the ammunition as soon as the downpour started; the Bengali ammunition was drenched. Throughout the downpour the British guns continued to fire, while the enemy ones fell silent. The sound of thunder mixed with that of cannon. As one of Clive's officers wrote, 'We had some apprehension that the enemy would take advantage of this opportunity and make push with their horse, but our guns continuing to play very briskly prevented any such motion. The enemy's guns during the rain, which lasted half an hour, did not fire a shot.'

Unknown to Clive, Mir Madan, the Nawab's best commander, was taken to camp behind the lines, where he died of his wounds. Another loyal commander, Bahadur Ali Khan, was also killed in the British cannonade. This left only his favourite, the foppish Mohan Lal, who fought with remarkable bravery at the head of the troops attacking the English line.

—⁓—

Siraj-ud-Daula was now beginning to panic: Mir Jafar and the other senior commanders had so far taken no part in the fighting, although their flanking move had continued and they were now in a position to attack from the side, and very nearly from the back, cutting Clive off. The Nawab sent repeatedly for Mir Jafar, who came at last on horseback with a huge and magnificent escort, in case there was an attempt to assassinate him. Mir Jafar advised the Nawab to call off the attack.

When Clive, depressed and soaked to the skin, saw to his astonishment that the enemy frontline was beginning to pull back, he assumed this was a temporary lull in the fighting and went to change his clothes; as he was pulling them off, he was informed that some of his forward troops under Major Kilpatrick were going after the retreating enemy – and preparing to attack the French gunners' strategic position on a piece of high ground.

This was madness. Clive had no men to spare for a chase that could overextend his forces and lead them into a trap. He was beside himself with rage and went off in pursuit; he needed every man to defend the British position. He caught up with Kilpatrick just as the troops reached the now abandoned French position. The French had retreated, with their guns, to a nearby redoubt. Furious, he ordered Kilpatrick put under arrest, but the latter apologized and was ordered back to the mango grove to take charge there, while Clive took command of the forward troops.

He resolved that having already advanced, the British could not retreat, and ordered Major Eyre Coote to bring up reinforcements. Although Mohan Lal's men poured musket fire into the exposed British position, it held with some difficulty. Then the Bengalis turned and advanced again, and were met with withering British fire. But the British were in trouble, under the fire of French guns, and potentially faced by a third of Mir Jafar's forces.

The Bengali cavalry now prepared to charge the British on open ground. Clive asked desperately for more reinforcements, only to be told that another cavalry attack was being prepared against the mango grove itself. Clive countermanded the first order. The few British cannon blazed away at the oxen dragging the Indian cannon and forced them back. Although Bengali infantrymen attacked bravely and in waves, they were not reinforced. Under intense British fire, their elephants were rearing up and getting out of control.

When Mohan Lal's forces began to pull away, Clive ordered his soldiers forward to take the foremost Bengali positions. Simultaneously, one of the enemy ammunition dumps blew up: Eyre Coote captured the little hill in front of Plassey House, while St Frais's men fled the redoubt from which their guns had kept the British pinned down for so long.

Siraj-ud-Daula, hearing that the British were attacking, had jumped aboard a camel and fled back with 2,000 horsemen towards the capital. The Bengalis, after fighting so furiously, were faced with the flight of the Nawab, the death of two senior commanders and the near-desertion of three others. The huge army now also fled, their panic becoming a rout. As the British moved forward, hardly believing their luck, they found the stores and baggage of the encampment abandoned. Around 500 of the enemy had been killed compared to just 20 dead and 50 wounded on the British side.

The consequences both for the British in India and Clive person-ally were momentous. The East India Company and Britain had acquired, at a stroke, effective control of the largest and wealthiest part of the subcontinent. Taken together with their superiority in the south, they now held nearly a third of India's land area. Only the central belt, divided between the Marathas and the French, the north, controlled by the Nawab of Oudh, and the wild northwest eluded them. Clive had effectively doubled the British area of occupation. The Company was now indisputably the major power in India. The foundations had been laid for British rule that was to endure for two centuries.

Clive himself was in a position of unparalleled power for any British national in history, before or since. He had a kingdom of 40 million people at his feet, more than six times the subjects of the British monarch. There was no effective control over his personal rule from the civilian authorities in Madras or Calcutta. His rivals – Charles Watson and Eyre Coote – although acquitting themselves well in the campaign, had shrunk to insignificance.

The gamble he had taken in crossing the river Hugli tributary had been his, and his alone, supported only by Coote and disavowed by Watson and the Calcutta councillors. Just as he would have had to face the consequences if he had failed and his force was surrounded and defeated, now he took the credit, feeling fully vindicated. He had reached his finest hour, his crowning moment of glory. Francis Drake and Walter Raleigh had achieved extraordinary feats, but had never ruled over an empire. Clive's was larger than that of either Cortés or Pizarro.

He was the new Nawab of Bengal – king, emperor and effective dictator rolled into one. In Lord Thomas Babington Macaulay's words, 'great provinces [were] dependent on his pleasure, an opulent city afraid of being given up to plunder; wealthy bankers bidding against each other for his smile; vaults piled with gold and jewels thrown open to him alone.' He also now faced ultimate temptation, the possession of absolute power over a country much more populous than Britain, unchecked by the rule of constitutional law.

Yet it would be wrong to say that Clive ruled as a conqueror through force of arms alone. The Emperor of Delhi, the nominal source of authority, had refused to recognize Siraj-ud-Daula as Nawab of Bengal, preferring his cousin, Shaukut Jang. The Nawab's other senior courtiers had turned against him, also making use of the argument that he lacked imperial recognition. Clive from the first ruled through Mir Jafar as the legitimate Nawab; and Clive was not to assume legal responsibility for governing Bengal until he was granted the *diwani* (management of the revenue) in perpetuity by the Emperor in 1765. Clive was always scrupulous to observe the legal proprieties, whatever the realities of power might be, and in deposing the Nawab he had a strong case for arguing he was acting with legal sanction in the interests of the Bengalis themselves.

Clive entered Murshidabad in triumph. After lengthy haggling, it was agreed that the Nawab should pay half of what he now owed the British immediately, two-thirds in bullion and one-third in jewels, plate and gold, and the rest in equal instalments over the next three years. Clive visited the treasury himself to satisfy his curiosity. From this was to derive his most famous remark before an inquiry of the House of Commons: 'When I recollect entering the Nawab's treasury at Murshidabad, with heaps of gold and silver to the right and left, and these crowned with jewels, by God, at this moment do I stand astonished at my own moderation.' He was led into the large chamber, where fabulous wealth glittered all around him: King Solomon's mines could not have been more resplendent. In addition to his 2 lakhs under the treaty, Clive was given a personal gift by the new Nawab of 16 lakhs: altogether he took some £230,000 (a colossal fortune worthy of an English duke). It was true he could have taken more, and that he turned down the gifts of the Hindu nobility, but by any standards his victory had made him fabulously wealthy.

Within a couple of days, the first half-payment to the British was loaded on to 75 boats, each carrying a lakh (around £15,000). This procession, bearing around £1m altogether, perhaps the largest shipment of booty in history, set off in a large and colourful regatta of music, drums and flags, and was joined at Hugli by an impressive British naval escort. To those that watched, it must have seemed that the very wealth of Bengal was being taken downriver.

Mir Jafar, the new Nawab, had Siraj-ud-Daula killed. He was heavily dependent on the British. Clive, the real power in the land, consolidated the British hold on India, sending armies under Francis Forde and Stringer Lawrence to fend off a determined French attempt to take the Carnatic. Sir Eyre Coote routed the French at the Battle of Wandewash in 1760 and a year later took Pondicherry and razed it to the ground.

A further revolt threatened in northern India under the leadership of the heir to the Moghul emperor, the Shahzada, who was to become Shah Alam II. Clive himself marched forward and defeated the enemy, also indulging in uncharacteristic cruelty in destroying 300 villages in Pulwansing. After the triumph he extracted from Mir Jafar a *jagir*, an annual payment of £27,000 a year, a staggering sum for those days, to be paid out of the annual rent the East India Company was supposed to pay the Nawab for the lands around Calcutta. Clive's many enemies in Britain complained of his becoming the recipient of the Company's rents. Mir Jafar conspired against the British with the Dutch at their settlement of Kasimbasar. The Dutch attacked the British downstream from Calcutta but in a short, bloody and decisive action were routed on the Plains of Badaw, with the Dutch losing 320 men for 10 British dead.

In February 1760, the absolute ruler of much of India set sail for Britain where he again attempted to become a significant force in British politics. But this brilliant commander in the field and outwitter of the Indians proved no match for the scheming Prime Minister, the Duke of Newcastle, and he also incurred the enmity of the chairman of the East India Company, Laurence Sullivan, and others jealous of his success. Meanwhile, conditions in India deteriorated steadily, with widespread allegations of corruption and the formation of military alliances among Indian princes against the British.

—⁓—

In June 1764, the seemingly indispensable Clive returned to India to restore order. On arrival he set out to Murshidabad in a budgerow, a luxury houseboat, where he formally reduced the

Nawab's status to that of puppet monarch. His next appointment was with the Emperor, Shah Alam II, who languidly declined to come forward to meet him, sending him ludicrously inconsequential letters instead. If the Mogul could not go to Clive, Clive must go to the Mogul, and he set off to Allahabad on 9 August to meet the largely powerless figure with the greatest family prestige on the subcontinent, a man who approved every princely appointment yet commanded barely any real forces or territory – except those the British were about to give him.

As the Shahzada he had been one of Clive's most persistent and troublesome foes; he was far from being the usual decadent holder of his throne. He had proved himself strong-willed, a good and tenacious fighter, not excessively given to cruelty, and something of a tactician and a statesman, carving out for himself a role from the very poor hand he had been dealt as the son of a puppet, however distinguished.

Clive found him to be a very dark young man with a 'grim deportment bordering upon sadness'. The Emperor repeated his old ambition for the British to restore him to the throne at Delhi, which Clive politely declined. In exchange for the *diwani* – his seal of approval for British tax collection for Bengal, Bihar and Orissa – he accepted the two provinces of Oudh that were offered him and an income from Bengal of 26 lakhs. The following day, in a slightly ludicrous ceremony in Clive's tent, the lugubrious young man was placed on a throne consisting of a draped armchair on a dining room table, and awarded the *diwani* to Clive, his subject, beneath him. Thus occurred the formal beginning of the British Raj in India.

Clive now plunged into a whirlwind of administrative reform to establish the foundations of colonial government in India, including an anti-corruption drive – an ironic rebuttal of accusations of his own past profiteering – and to provide secure boundaries for British India. He set up a Society of Trade to regulate commerce, he proposed establishing a class of salaried civil servants (an idea only adopted under his successor, Warren Hastings), a crackdown on extortion, a new postal system and a land survey of Bengal.

He faced down intense local opposition, followed by a strike by Company civil servants and finally, most dangerously, a full-scale mutiny by his own British officers centred around the city of Monghyr. He rushed up there and, with only a single escort, walked into the garrison, ordering the rebels to lay down their weapons. When they did so he said, 'Now I am satisfied you are British soldiers and not, as I was erroneously informed, assassins.' The following year he left India for the last time, at the remarkably young age of 42.

Clive indulged his own vast wealth to buy and improve a succession of large estates. He improved his old family home at Styche in Shropshire, added to his lovely house at Walcot, bought the beautiful seat of Oakly and completely refurbished the magnificent estate of Claremont in Surrey, the home and creation of Sir John Vanbrugh, with gardens laid out by William Kent and then, under Clive, by Capability Brown. He also bought the magnificent 45 Berkeley Square in London and the Earl of Chatham's house in Bath. He was estimated to be worth some £55,000 at the time – a colossal fortune for those days.

However, his enemies were gathering again. In India, the warrior Hyder Ali launched a furious rebellion against the British and news also arrived of the 1769–70 famine in Bengal, in which millions perished, with blame unfairly falling on British maladministration. Clive had to defend himself manfully against his detractors, first on a House of Commons committee, then in a vote of censure on the floor, which he carried by 155 to 95 votes in 1774. Clive was now in a position to be considered for the post of commander of British forces in the seemingly inevitable war with the American colonies.

On 22 November 1774, Clive was found in the lavatory of his Berkeley Square home with his throat cut. His body was hurried up for burial that same night at the tiny church of Moreton Saye. The secrecy surrounding his burial, as well as the fact that he was buried in an unmarked grave, suggested that Clive, often prone to depression and illness, had committed suicide: it was a shocking act for a man who had survived so many battles.

It also seems possible that he was murdered, or more likely sought in an emergency to cut his own throat to remove an obstruction, which was not uncommon in those days, a theory which is sup-ported by at least one prominent surgeon today. So perished, in tragic circumstances, one of the greatest British commanders of all time, characterized by gambling against huge odds, decisiveness, speed, manic energy and always going straight for his opponent – as well as the only non-royal Englishman who can properly be described as having founded and run an empire. The nation which had so often been grudging about his achievements belatedly granted him real recognition by giving his eldest son, Ned, the title of Earl of Powys.

How does Clive rate by the 16 standards of the true warrior, as set out in the Introduction? He was extraordinarily courageous in bat-tle, with cool judgment and an instinctive eye for an opportunity on the battlefields, and he was a superb tactician – witness his march on Arcot and its defence, his subsequent victories, his suc-cess at the siege of Trichinopoly, saving his army from disaster at Calcutta and the whole extraordinary progress up the Hugli, culmi-nating in the triumph at Plassey against vastly superior odds. He had to fight his way from being a humble clerk to ruler of Bengal and one of the richest men in Britain. He had enormous determina-tion and resilience from setbacks – as the Battle of Calcutta showed. His career was one of spectacular ups and downs – fighting against the East India Company, then censure by the House of Commons.

He also showed a remarkable grasp of what today would be called public relations, behaving more like a Moghul emperor on occasion than a British general, awing his followers and enemies alike with his court and lavish entertainments – which nearly proved his ruin, stirring up colossal resentment back home. Clive took care of his men, leading them into battle himself and not running unnecessary risks. He was skilful in his choice of subordinates, selecting power-ful figures in their own right, and not yes-men, even though this led to his quarrels with commanders like Eyre Coote, Hector Munro and Francis Forde. Clive's armies were small and manoeuvrable so that issues of command and control rarely arose – although an incident of autonomy by a junior officer nearly lost him the Battle of Plassey.

His intelligence and quickness of mind were remarkable, as was the subtlety of his diplomacy and deception in the negotiations with Mir Jafar and Omichand. His oratory could on occasion rise to a very high order: 'I stand astonished at my own moderation.' Clive was a brilliant political leader and administrator of an empire of 40m people. He was also a hugely successful and shrewd businessman in his own interest. His downside was a restless quality manifest in many of the mavericks, bouts of manic-depression and, rarely, displays of cruelty as in the failure to protect Siraj-ud-Daula from being murdered and the laying waste of Pondicherry and Pulwansing. He had a highly dubious sense of morality in amassing his fortune – which was not, however, uncommon at the time. Occasionally, he behaved like an oriental despot, above the law. He was a surprisingly loyal subaltern to Stringer Lawrence, but his own man when given independent command. His treatment of Watson and Coote, nominally his superiors, on the expedition to retake Bengal verged on the mutinous, as did his contempt for his bosses in the East India Company. He ticks virtually every box of maverick military genius. He was one of the greatest warriors Britain has ever produced and the actual ruler of a domain far larger than that hitherto ruled even by any British monarch.

Chapter 2

WOLFE OF QUEBEC: THE FIRST AMPHIBIAN AND COMMANDO

Of all the maverick military leaders, James Wolfe is perhaps the most one-dimensional, partly a consequence of his early death on 13 September 1759 at the age of just 32, and partly as a result of the inevitable jealousy surrounding this Icarus-like figure who ascended to the heavens and fell to earth, dying in a blaze of glory. Wolfe's career, unlike those of most of the mavericks, rested on a single achievement, the taking of Quebec – a little unfairly, because he performed with courage and flair in a number of other engagements during his short adult life.

Wolfe also – sadly such things count – was not as dashing or striking-looking as Wellington with his haughty manner, or Cochrane the red-headed giant. He was the epitome of the British chinless wonder, with a snooty pointed nose, receding chin and a goofy expression, oddly enough resembling William Pitt the Younger, the son of his own patron. He was immensely able, ambitious and precocious, a death-or-glory man because – as we shall see – he welcomed oblivion on the battlefield.

He had the maverick qualities in abundance: above all, he changed the world. The British capture of Quebec was one of the turning points in history, banishing the French from control of the North American continent in favour of the British and their allies and inadvertently, by so doing, opening the way for the

American colonies to declare their independence from Britain – which they would not have dared to do if they were still seriously threatened by France. Not least, it brought into being one of the world's most pleasant and civilized countries, Canada.

Wolfe was the son of a middle-ranking soldier, Edward Wolfe, who had served under the Duke of Marlborough and against James Francis Stuart, the Old Pretender, in the rebellion of 1715, and was descended from a prominent Anglo-Irish family dating back to the fifteenth century. Wolfe's father settled at Westerham, outside London, and the boy was brought up near Greenwich. When his father took part in the ill-fated Cartagena expedition in 1740, James, aged just 13, became imbued with the military spirit; it was planned that he should go with his father as a young volunteer, but he fell ill.

By the age of 15, however, he had a commission in the marines, serving in Flanders. His first experience of action was at Dettingen, in June 1743, when the teenager showed his extraordinary toughness. He was promoted to lieutenant and then captain, which was unusual for a young man with few connections, rising solely on merit. He performed bravely at Fontnoy and was promoted to major by the Duke of Cumberland, who had noticed his abilities.

Wolfe was then sent to Newcastle to serve under General Hawley – known as Hangman Hawley for his brutal suppression of the rebellion of Bonnie Prince Charlie – and served in the army that was repulsed by the Jacobites at Falkirk. When Cumberland arrived to lead the army, Hawley and his young major joined the campaign which ended in the decisive and brutal battle of Culloden. Wolfe took part in hunting down the rebels, although it is not known how assiduously the young man carried out his superior's more savage orders.

Wolfe returned to Holland in 1747 and was wounded at the battle of Laffeldt. By 1749, the young man, aged 21, had taken part in five major battles in three campaigns, and was a full major. But peace intervened, to his frustration, and he was sent to Scotland where, again at an astonishingly young age, he became effectively commander of his regiment. He displayed a keen concern for his men, but utter boredom at his fate:

> I shall be sick of my office: the very bloom of life nipped in this northern climate... barren battalion conversation rather blunts the faculties than improves my youth and vigour bestowed idly in Scotland; my temper daily charged with discontent; and from a man become martinet or monster... the men here are civil, designing and treacherous, with their immediate interests always in view; they pursue trade with the warmth and necessary mercantile spirit, arising from the baseness of their other qualifications. The women, coarse, cold, and cunning, for ever enquiring after man's circumstances. They make that the standard of their good breeding.

Wolfe was almost constantly unwell, and his attempts to marry a Miss Lawson, maid of honour to the Princess of Wales, were firmly rebuffed, possibly because his social origins were not impressive enough, possibly because of his looks. He went from Glasgow to Perth, an even grimmer, bleak, windswept posting, and then secured a more interesting appointment in Paris. However, he wrote, 'I find it impossible to pursue the business I came upon and to comply with the customs and manners of the inhabitants at the same time. No constitution, however robust, could go through all.' At court there were 'men that only desire to shine, and that had rather say a smart thing than do a great one... A Frenchman that can make his mistress laugh... is at the top of his ambition... The natives in general are not handsome either in face or figure; but then they improve what they have.'

Back in Glasgow his waspish side re-emerged with a vengeance: he wrote of dinners and suppers of 'the most execrable food upon earth, and wine that approaches to poison. The men drink till they are excessively drunk. The ladies are cold to everything but a bagpipe. I wrong them: there is not one that does not melt away at the sound of an estate; there's the weak side of this soft sex.' He was described at this time as a 'tall thin officer astride a bay horse, his face lit by a smile, and conversing pleasantly with the officer who rode by his side'. Appointed lieutenant-colonel, he acerbically continued to kick his heels until he was ordered to become quarter-master general in Ireland.

William Pitt the Elder, now in power, ordered an attack on the French naval stronghold of Rochefort on the Atlantic coast, and Wolfe was sent to take part, at last being called back to action after nearly nine frustrating years of peacetime duties. Wolfe's frustrations emerged in a letter he wrote at the time:

> Few men are acquainted with the degree of their own courage till danger prove them, and are seldom justly informed how far the love of honour and the dread of shame are superior to the love of life... Constancy of temper, patience, and all the virtues necessary to make us suffer with a good grace are likewise parts of our character, and... frequently called in to carry us through unusual difficulties. What moderation and humility must he be possessed of that bears the good fortune of a successful war with tolerable modesty and humility, and he is very excellent in his nature who triumphs without insolence. A battle gained is, I believe, the highest joy mankind is capable of receiving to him who commands; and his merit must be equal to his success if it works no change to his disadvantage. Lastly, a defeat is a trial of human resolution, and to labour under the mortification of being surpassed, and to live to see the fatal consequences that may follow to one's country, is a situation next to damnable.

Wolfe was not just a grumbler and martinet thirsting for battle. He was a keen-minded tactical innovator, a convinced believer in the perfection of firepower and the volley:

> firing balls at objects teaches the soldier to level incomparably, makes the recruits steady, and removes the foolish apprehension that seizes young soldiers when they first load their arms with bullets. We fire, first singly, then by files 1, 2, 3, or more, then by ranks, and lastly by platoons; and the soldiers see the effects of their shot, especially at a mark or upon water. We shoot obliquely, and in different situations

of ground, from heights, downwards, and contrarywise... We are lazy in time of peace, and, of course, want vigilance and activity in war. Our military education is by far the worst in Europe. We are the most egregious blunderers in war that ever took the hatchet in hand... I'm tired of proposing anything to the officers that command our regiments; they are in general so lazy and so bigoted to old habits.

On arrival off the island of Aix he reconnoitred ashore and urged an amphibious frontal attack, which his dilatory superiors refused. He angrily set out his own principles of amphibious operations, a largely virgin field for military tacticians.

Pitt, impressed by the intelligent, aggressive young man, appointed him brigadier to Colonel Jeffrey Amherst on the other side of the Atlantic for the exploration of Louisburg, the great fortress in modern-day Nova Scotia which controlled the approaches up the St Lawrence River to Canada. Amherst, nominally serving under a pompous commander, General James Abercromby, who made a huge hash of operations further south, was a 40-year-old of little more experience than Wolfe. Pitt, the 'Great Commoner', was determined to bring forward men of talent, regardless of social origin.

The British expeditionary force consisted of no fewer than 50,000 men – a huge number for those days. Against these the French had an army of 10,000 and a militia of some 16,000. The French had been deserted by their Native American allies, and a famine in 1757–8 made life even more uncomfortable in Canada. The French commander, the Marquis de Montcalm, was extremely able, but despaired of his chances of success.

On 8 June 1758, Amherst decided to make his first landing on Cape Breton Island, covering the approaches to the St Lawrence. He arranged for two diversionary landings near the fortress of Louisburg itself, while sending Wolfe to command the main force by Freshwater Cove in Gabarus Bay. This was Amherst's own idea, in contrast to Wolfe's plan to land at three points close to the fort and then converge, while the fleet staged a diversionary attack on the well-defended positions at Gabarus Bay. Wolfe's boats came under fire and had to row back, at last finding a sheltered spot nearby and taking the main French gun battery. Another force landed further west, threatening to cut the French off in a pincer movement: they fled. Wolfe's force had suffered 100 casualties and only succeeded, he commented angrily, 'by the greatest good fortune imaginable'.

Wolfe resolved to seize the battery on Goat Island, which protected the harbour at Louisburg. He occupied Lighthouse Point opposite and erected a battery which by the end of June had destroyed the Goat Island battery. However, Admiral Edward Boscawen, the naval commander, hesitated and the French sent ships to block the harbour entrance. It was necessary to engage in an old-fashioned landward siege of zigzagging trenches, bringing forward cannon to blow a breach in the wall. By 6 July, cannon were breaking the walls and mortar bombs and incendiaries were deluging the city. Soon the King's Bastion, the main external defence, was on fire.

On 25 July, in dense fog, Boscawen sent boats to cut out the two remaining French battleships, setting the *Prudent* on fire and taking the *Bienfaisant*, the French flagship. Over the next 12 hours, from both sea and land, 1,000 British shot bombarded the Louisburg fort: some 400 Frenchmen were killed and 1,300 wounded. The greatest French fortress in the New World surrendered the next day. Wolfe openly criticized Amherst for not moving instantly on Quebec. He expressed disgust for American colonial soldiers, as the 'dirtiest, most contemptible, cowardly dogs that you can conceive'. However, he understood the importance of the New World, and showed foresight: 'This will, some time hence, be a vast empire, the seat of power and learning. Nature has refused them nothing, and there will grow a people out of our little spot, England, that will fill this vast space, and divide this great portion of the globe with the Spaniards, who are possessed of the other half.'

Wolfe set about attacking French villages on the Gulf of St Lawrence, but his always fragile health broke and he returned temporarily to Britain to take the waters at Bath, where he fell in love with Katherine Lowther, who was also smitten.

Pitt, highly impressed by Wolfe, appointed him to command an expedition to Quebec in 1759. He chose as his lieutenants Robert Monckton, Lord George Townshend and James Murray. King George II appointed him major general with the remark, when it was suggested that Wolfe was mad, 'Mad is he? Then all I can hope is that he'll bite some of my other generals.' Wolfe was given an army of around 9,000 based at Louisburg against the French army of 16,000 under Montcalm.

The French had just been reinforced by three frigates and 20 storeships that slipped past the British and up the St Lawrence once the ice had broken. Quebec was a strongly defended position perched on a rocky hill overlooking the St Lawrence, defended from the south by the cliffs which rose up to the plateau known as the Heights of Abraham, and from the south and north by the Montmorency and St Charles rivers. It was thus virtually impregnable.

The British sent 60 warships up the treacherous St Lawrence, navigated at their head, with immense skill, by Captain James Cook of later fame. They landed at Ile d'Orléans, four miles below Quebec, on 27 June 1759. The French promptly deployed seven fireships against the British, but brave seamen rowed out and towed them away from the fleet. Wolfe seized Point Levis, directly opposite Quebec, and began to bombard the city, to little effect. He ordered two brigades across to the north side of the river, east of Quebec, just below the Montmorency, in an effort to lure Montcalm out of his garrison, which again failed.

Undaunted, Wolfe sent a frigate and other ships upriver past Quebec, which the British continued to bombard from the Point Levis side; Montcalm at last responded by sending 600 men to guard the cliffs. Wolfe considered landing there, but judged the risk of sending a body of men across the water, who could be cut off and picked off at will, too great. He turned his attention to the east, below Quebec, where, reinforced by two brigades from across the shallower reaches of the Montmorency, he planned to land on a strip between the river and the heights, below the spectacular 250-foot falls. This new attempt to lure Montcalm out of his fastness and into an open fight was abandoned when Wolfe observed that the French were well-defended on his proposed landing ground.

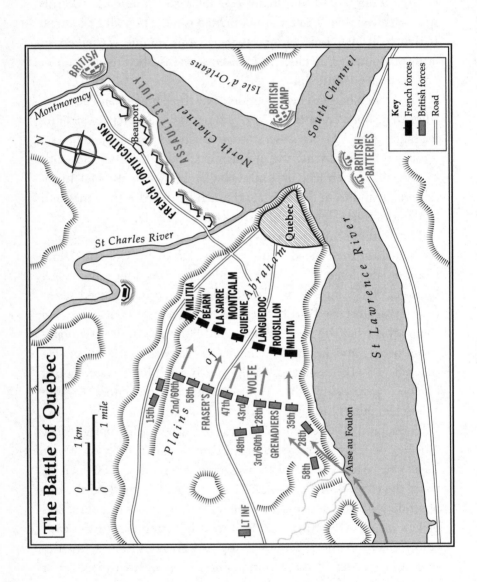

The Battle of Quebec

Key
French forces
British forces
Road

BRITISH

Montmorency

Beauport

ASSAULT 31 JULY

FRENCH FORTIFICATIONS

Isle d'Orléans

North Channel

South Channel

BRITISH CAMP

BRITISH BATTERIES

St Charles River

Quebec

Plains of Abraham

St Lawrence River

MILITIA
BEARN
LA SARRE
MONTCALM
GUIENNE
LANGUEDOC
ROUSILLON
MILITIA

15th
2nd/60th
FRASER'S 58th
47th
WOLFE
43rd
48th
3rd/60th 28th
GRENADIERS
35th
28th

LT INF

58th

Anse au Foulon

N

0   1 km
0   1 mile

Later in the day he decided to land between his forward troops and the French positions; his men were mauled before reinforcements could be brought to bear, while a rainstorm engulfed them, making the slopes they were climbing slippery and damaging their powder. More than 200 were killed and around 450 wounded. It had been a major disaster. Montcalm exulted, 'There is no more anxiety about Quebec.'

It had been a devastating setback for the precocious 32-year-old commander. He had fought with verve and skill at Louisburg, his greatest achievement so far, but his acid criticism of Amherst and others had earned him many enemies, not least from those jealous of his rapid promotion and youth: his three subordinate commanders joined in the backbiting. His campaign so far had been a fiasco and he was running out of ideas as to how to dislodge the French.

He then initiated a brutal 'starvation' campaign against the surrounding countryside, intended to deny supplies to the French: at least 1,400 farms were destroyed and atrocities were committed – rapes, killings and scalpings, including a priest and 30 families at Sante Anne on 23 August. Wolfe himself ordered women and children to be treated humanely and strictly forbade 'the inhuman practice of scalping except where the enemy are Indians or Canadians dressed like Indians'. But he must bear the responsibility for initiating this savage campaign, possibly a throwback to his experiences at Culloden, and also a manic reaction to his setback on the banks of the Montmorency. Criticized by his lieutenants, it was the darkest moment of the career of this arrogant young commander. His frustration was evident in a letter to his mother:

> My antagonist has wisely shut himself up in inaccessible entrenchments, so that I can't get at him without spilling a torrent of blood, and that perhaps to little purpose. The Marquis de Montcalm is at the head of a great number of bad soldiers, and I am at the head of a small number of good ones, that wish for nothing so much as to fight him – but the wary old fellow avoids an action doubtful of the behaviour of his army.

Wolfe sought to cut off the supply run downstream from Montreal to the west, sending several ships and 1,200 troops there to harass French boats and settlements. Meanwhile, he had fallen desperately ill of fever and kidney stones, increasing the sense of urgency in his mind that, nearing death, he must achieve a great victory. He decided to evacuate the Montmorency companies as a futile avenue of attack, moving his troops to concentrate on the south bank and putting more aboard ships. The French at Montreal, upstream, countered by sending 500 more men. Wolfe was in an increasingly desperate frame of mind, with his reputation at stake – by the end of September 1759, the British fleet would have to withdraw to avoid being stuck in the winter ice and it lacked sufficient provisions for the winter. If he must, he wanted to die gloriously.

He consulted his three brigadiers, Monckton, Townshend and Murray, at a council of war and their view was that the British force should abandon Quebec and move up river to cut off Montcalm's line of supply from Montreal. All three men, from noble backgrounds, looked down upon Wolfe, a professional and low-born officer in an age of aristocratic military officers, and one whose sharp tongue and quick mind they distrusted.

Wolfe at this stage appears to have made contact on 6 September with a former British soldier called Captain Robert Stobo, who had been a prisoner in Quebec but had escaped down the St Lawrence. Stobo knew of a footpath at L'Anse au Foulon – Fuller's Cove – a precipitous ascent of the cliffs to the Plains of Abraham about two miles north of Quebec. It was now clear to Wolfe's grumbling subordinates that he was preparing for an attack, and they recommended that he should launch one at Cap Rouge, much higher up the river, or at Pointe aux Trembles. He sent some 20 warships and transports with 3,100 men upstream to a position opposite Cap Rouge. Montcalm observed the movement of a large force but believed it to be a feint: he was still convinced the British would attack from the east, at Beauport. Just in case, he reinforced his defences to the west under Louis-Antoine de Bougainville, in the wooded and difficult country beyond the Plains of Abraham.

On 10 September, as the two sides eyed each other warily in anticipation of battle, a heavy storm occurred which rendered the path up the cliff slippery and impassable. The same day, Wolfe ordered a further 1,000 of his men upstream, virtually abandoning the Ile d'Orléans. On the evening of 12 September, at around 8 p.m., Wolfe made elaborate preparations for his likely death: he summoned a friend, John Jervis, a stern and waspish personality like himself, who later became Earl of St Vincent and Horatio Nelson's mentor, and handed over his papers, his will and a miniature of Miss Lowther. He also recited the words of Thomas Gray's 'Elegy Written in a Country Churchyard': 'The paths of glory lead but to the grave', and remarked, 'I would sooner have written that poem than take Quebec.'

Wolfe and Jervis were interrupted by a perplexed message from his army subordinates, aware that an attack was to take place but still none the wiser where it was to happen. Wolfe informed them that he intended to be in the first boat and that the objective 'is the Foulon Distant upon 2 or 2½ miles from Quebec where you remember an encampment of 12 or 13 tents and an abbatis below it'. He issued his famous order: 'The officers and men will remember what their country expects of them... resolute in the execution of their duty.'

When two lanterns were hoisted on the flagship, HMS *Sutherland*, the troops were to be carried down on the tide to the landing place. Wolfe's extraordinary secrecy towards his own commanders can be explained partly by the mutual antipathy between them, partly because he feared they would object to the plan as sheer madness, although they were duty bound to execute his orders, and also by his almost obsessive desire for secrecy to protect his plan from becoming known. In a masterstroke, Wolfe ordered Admiral Charles Saunders – he seemed to trust sailors better than soldiers – down to Beauport before sunset, where his men began to drop buoys as if to indicate a passage for landing boats. The sailors rowed noisily about and then opened fire from a distance at the French on the river bank. Montcalm himself had arrived to supervise the defence at the camp and kept watch through the night.

At 2 a.m. the lanterns were raised and Wolfe's flotilla drifted down with the tide: challenged by a sentry, a British officer replied in excellent French. The moon was a quarter one and the night was calm and dark. With only half an hour to dawn – rather too close for comfort – the boats landed. A specially selected group of men under General William Howe disembarked and silently climbed up the sheer 175-foot precipice along the path, where they surprised the French soldiers at the top, exchanging musket fire: it was the first and most famous commando raid. The French captain was able to despatch just a single runner to warn Quebec.

Wolfe himself followed up at around 4 a.m., while other troops were still disembarking below. A French battery upriver opened fire to little effect and was quickly silenced by Howe's men. A further 1,200 men under Colonel Burton had landed from the south at day-break, in a fine rain. Some seven British battalions and two six-gun cannon were brought laboriously up the path, while there were now 20 ships down below.

Wolfe had been a pioneering advocate of the disciplined volley, writing papers on the subject. The British advanced, 4,500 of them, strung out in the first 'thin red line' of troops. However, they came under fire from Canadian and Indian irregulars to the right and left, and Wolfe ordered them to lie down. The British were in an extremely dangerous position: they could not retreat under fire by the path they had ascended in secrecy, while Bougainville's force of 2,000 was positioned behind them and could have caught them in a pincer with the French force in front. The British could have easily defeated the former alone, who were some eight miles and three hours' marching away, but not if caught between two fires.

Like Clive of India at Plassey, Wolfe's retreat was cut off and he had no alternative but to press on, as he must have realized when he devised the whole plan. Wolfe's objective was to draw the French out on to the open plain, where he believed the British would inevitably win. What if the French would not come out? The western wall of Quebec was weak and with the element of surprise Wolfe might just have stormed it. He could not bring with him the entrenching equipment to mount a classic, slow siege – which anyway would have given time for the French to reinforce: he had gambled everything on surprise and a quick victory.

Montcalm, summoned from his bed after an exhausting night supervising his troops for the attack on Beauport that never came, had by now hurried disbelievingly to the scene, leaving 1,500 men behind in case that was, after all, to be the main thrust of the British attack. He ordered four brigades out in front of the walls of the city. Montcalm was visibly thunderstruck, and at 9 a.m. decided he had no choice but to attack the British on open ground, believing 'the enemy is entrenching, he already has two pieces of cannon. If we give him time to establish himself, we shall never be able to attack him with the sort of troops we have.'

If Wolfe's troops were stretched out as a line of soldiers across a 1,000-yard front, there was good reason, for he had to avoid his flanks being forced into that narrow plain. Unfortunately for the French, their regular troops were mixed in with militia who, at 500 yards from the British, broke into a headlong disorganized run: they would only have one chance to loose off a ragged volley before engaging with bayonets; they mistook the lack of British response for vulnerability. The British, most of whom were veterans, walked coolly forward in double ranks.

At around 150 yards the French dropped on one knee and fired. Wolfe, young, tall and commanding in a resplendent uniform, was shot in the wrist, but barely seemed to notice. The British muskets stayed silent. The French continued to advance in increasingly uncoordinated groups. Wolfe's instruction had been that 'a cool, well-levelled fire is much more destructive and formidable than the quickest fire in confusion'. The left and right of the British opened fire when the French were within 60 yards, with the 43rd and 47th regiments in the centre joining in when they were within 40 yards, delivering, according to a captain present:

> As heavy [a] discharge, as I ever saw performed at a private field of exercise, insomuch that better troops than we encountered could not possibly withstand it: and, indeed, well might the French officers

say, that they never opposed such a shock as they received from the centre of our line, for that they believed every ball took place and in such regularity and discipline they had not experienced before... our troops in general, and particularly the central corps, having levelled and fired – *comme une coup de canon*. [H]ereupon they gave way and fled with precipitation, so that, by the time the cloud of smoke was vanished, our men were again loaded, and, profiting by the advantage we had over them, pursued them almost to the gates of the town... redoubling our fire with great eagerness, making many officers and men prisoners.

Wolfe, leading the grenadiers on the right, headed the British charge; he was shot in the groin and the lungs, and was carried off by two officers and two men. He gave orders to the last: 'Go one of you, with all speed to Colonel Burton and tell him to march Webb's regiment down to the St Charles River and cut off the retreat of the fugitives to the beach.' His final words were, 'Now God be praised, I die happy.'

Montcalm had also been shot in the lungs. Murray was caught in a fierce skirmish so Townshend was sent for as commander: he reordered the British and tried to turn to face Bougainville, now approaching from the west: the Frenchmen withdrew at once. Townshend ordered his men not to attack the city, and set them digging trenches, burying the 58 killed and tending to the 600 wounded – about the same as the French. Montcalm's wound was mortal and he died early the next morning. The Marquis de Vaudreuil, the French-Canadian commander at Beauport, decided to save what was left of his army and ordered its evacuation.

Some 2,200 militia and soldiers, and a few sailors, were left to defend Quebec, along with 4,000 civilians and only three days' provisions. As the British brought up siege equipment, the French shelled them. Finally, as British cannon prepared to open fire, the French sought terms and surrendered.

Wolfe inevitably appears as a somewhat limited figure, and perhaps even as a personally unpleasant and brutally arrogant young man. After a precocious military career in Flanders and Scotland, his main achievements of the solid success at Louisburg and the astonishing seizure of Quebec were elevated by his martyrdom at just 32 years old. He is certainly not to be compared with some of the other commanders in this book who conducted several campaigns and fought many battles.

But what a battle for which to be remembered! It was the epitome of romantic heroism and an audacious gamble that could so easily have gone wrong. It was executed at dead of night up a steep cliff path, surprising and routing the enemy in a perfect execution of maverick tactics that were all the more remarkable for his having been a somewhat conventional soldier until then.

The historic consequences of Wolfe's achievements were momentous, spelling the beginning of the end of French ambitions in North America. Ultimately, they paved the way for the American Revolution and even helped to trigger the disillusion with French aristocratic military tactics that was one of the prime causes of the French Revolution.

Wolfe was not just a lucky commander: he was one of the brightest minds in Britain's eighteenth-century army, as his sharp and incisive writings revealed. He was one of the foremost exponents of the power of the withheld volley to destroy the enemy's cohesion with precision; a clever practitioner of feints and diversionary attacks; an unconventional tactician prepared to disperse his forces – for which he is often criticized – if he could eventually regroup them while confusing the enemy; and, above all, the pioneer of the amphibious assault, coordinating ship movements and mass military landings at night. His was the first and one of the greatest commando raid in British military history.

Wolfe's brave stand in front of his troops on the Plains of Abraham showed reckless courage under fire, even if his illness may have given him a death wish. His ability to choose his moment and to pounce, after a policy of caution, was evident at Quebec. His eccentric and charismatic leadership, his sense of discipline, order and communications skills, his intelligence, his persistent questioning of his superiors and the originality of his tactics all qualify him as a maverick.

He was never a political figure, although he impressed Pitt the Elder; he was as prickly with subordinates as with superiors, and his career was not a rollercoaster – rather, just an uninterrupted if brief rise – but it would certainly have slumped dramatically if he had failed at Quebec. Instead, he established himself by one bold strike but paid the ultimate price in a heroic death. He qualified eminently as one of the last warriors, both in life and in the dramatic manner of his death. Who knows what he might have gone on to achieve had he lived?

Chapter 3

WASHINGTON: THE FIRST AMERICAN

George Washington was not a man of dash or verve like Clive. Indeed, they seem barely to inhabit the same planet, although they were contemporaries. Washington was dour, austere, grey, a pillar of sobriety, seemingly dull-witted, economic in speech and style of dress, and in some ways the epitome of the conservative, dutiful military figure. He rarely directly engaged the enemy and was cautious and patient through winters of extreme privation. He has been compared to the dutiful Roman Emperor Cincinnatus, refusing the leadership of his country to retire frugally to his home farm until forced by destiny to assume the presidency.

Yet, under the surface, there are similarities with the conqueror of northern India. Like Clive, Washington was often hot-tempered and intolerant. Like Clive he had to govern on a leash – Clive answering to his masters in the East India Company, while Washington was responsible to Congress – and both frequently grumbled about their distant masters. Like Clive, Washington was a master of military intrigue who repeatedly undermined, and then destroyed, potential rivals.

Washington's reserved exterior made him seem less of a risk-taker than he really was: his seizure of Boston was a master stroke; his retreat from New York a well-executed military retreat; his crossing of the Delaware River an action of great daring. His preservation of the core of his army in the face of appalling winter conditions was a fine display of leadership and endurance. His southern strategy was correct and executed brilliantly by his best general, Nathanael Greene. His sudden pincer movement to trap the British at Yorktown was one of the greatest and most decisive *coup d'oeil*'s in history, yielding instant triumph. Improbable as it might seem, this well-dressed, prosperous Virginia gentleman was in essence a guerrilla leader, leading a ragged army to harass the British enemy and avoid direct engagement until it was essentially exhausted.

—⁓—

Washington was born in 1732 to a newly wealthy family of planters which attempted to blazon its social status with a curious mixture of pedigrees, claiming a minor gentry background in Britain as well as descent from one of the executed leaders of Wat Tyler's 1381 rebellion, the Peasants' Revolt. He was a fourth-generation American – one of the oldest – whose father died when he was 11. He spent the rest of his childhood growing up in the shadow of his terrifying mother. Astonishingly, he managed to teach himself the practical skills of life: at the age of 13 he was already interested in accountancy and legal work. He was physically tall, six-foot-two (1.88m), well-built, slightly stiff and awkward in manner, and extremely strong. He was shy, reserved and tongue-tied to an almost paralytic extreme.

Washington's mentor was his half-brother Lawrence, a distinguished soldier, who encouraged the teenage George in manly pursuits, including living out in the open in the western wilderness, and who left him his large estate on his death, when the young man was only 19. Washington was less of a dullard than appeared. He was a man of immense ambition and hoped to prosper in the British army. Although on the losing side, he came away with a formidable reputation from the Seven Years War and felt deeply slighted by his failure to gain a commission. In 1759 he married a wealthy heiress, Martha Dandridge, who already had two children, and settled down to nearly 16 years as a farmer within the Virginia squirearchy, leading a life of stolid and agreeable dullness, exchanging visits with his friends, attending balls, hunting with hounds and owning slaves, whom he treated humanely.

Although deeply frustrated and profoundly anti-British as a result of the slights against him, Washington was astonishingly self-controlled. Abigail Adams wrote: 'He has a dignity which forbids familiarity married with an easy, appealing mind which creates love and reverence.' He was extremely modest, rushing from the room when made commander-in-chief of American forces. John Marshall, one of his closest friends who became chief justice of the United States, wrote that his innate and unassuming modesty was 'Happily blended with a high... sense of personal dignity, and with a just consciousness of the respect which is due to station.'

Washington was not a superman or a saint. He was a highly successful, slightly frustrated man who beneath his modest exterior harboured an iron will. As is so rarely the case, the iron will was married to a brilliant military and political mind – he was imaginative, risk-taking and unbound by convention, yet he was wedded to the need for discipline that his idiosyncratic troops so singularly failed to regard as necessary.

He was in many ways a cold, unattractive, detached, controlled man who could be something of a martinet. He told his officers: 'Be easy and condescending [i.e. natural] in your deportment to your [junior] officers, but not too familiar, lest you subject yourself to a want of that respect which is necessary to support a proper command.' However, his skills were wide-ranging. His ascent to the front rank of global heroes was aided by his ability to pluck victory from defeat on innumerable occasions and to shape the nature of the regime that followed independence. He was also to show the ruthlessness, ability to improvise and strike, resilience in adversity, and capacity to rein in his own ambition at crucial moments that mark true greatness. He could never be accused of being dictatorial and his command was all the more effective for that.

Despite the dull exterior, this rich man on the margins of the Virginia aristocracy was to display leadership, strength, political skill and dignity of such an order that ultimately the whole American Revolution came to revolve around him. Many of the reputations of the 'founding fathers' have been grotesquely inflated; Washington's, if anything, was understated through his own deliberate choice, and his very failings only serve to strengthen the reputation. He was an astonishing man, not just a founding father, but, after Samuel Adams, *the* founding father.

—⁓—

Washington's military career began, crucially, as a subordinate in the British Army. The 'Great War for the Empire' commenced with a skirmish in which Washington, a 22-year-old major of the militia, was sent in to drive out the French who had encroached on Virginian land at Fort Duquesne in June 1754. Washington surprised and killed a score of Frenchmen, along with their commander, at a site called Great Meadows. The French surrounded Washington in his crude log stockade, Fort Necessity, and forced him to surrender. As the colonies appeared under imminent threat of a French–Indian invasion, the British rushed a large number of troops there to buttress the ill-coordinated efforts of the locals.

On their arrival, the British troops were appalled by what they perceived as the greed of the colonists: they were made to pay for access to water from privately owned wells, charged exorbitant prices and billeted in very expensive lodgings. 'I never saw such a set of people, obstinate and perverse in the last degree,' complained one British general.

Major-General Edward Braddock, the self-important British commander, set out in 1755 to conquer the disputed territory of northwestern Virginia. Sixty years old, bluff and overconfident, Braddock was infuriated as he made his preparations for the expedition. Above all, the British could not obtain horses or dogs. It was a local Pennsylvania politician, Benjamin Franklin, who obtained some for them, but his assessment of Braddock was shrewd and less than flattering: 'Braddock might probably have made a good figure in some European war. But he had too much self-confidence; too high an opinion of the validity of regular troops; too mean a one of both Americans and Indians.'

Braddock wanted to take Fort Duquesne and then march on to Niagara, in spite of Washington's misgivings. Franklin tried to warn him that in such country he would be exposed to ambush. Braddock replied patronizingly: 'These savages may, indeed, be a formidable enemy to your raw American militia, but upon the King's regular and disciplined troops, sir, it is impossible they should make any impression.'

At length, the expedition departed for the wild country of north-western Virginia, advancing at a painfully slow pace, until it crossed the Monongahela River, 10 miles from Fort Duquesne. On 9 July 1755, Braddock's force marched forward in disciplined ranks across a clearing surrounded on both sides by thickly wooded ravines and was ambushed by the French and Indians from the cover of the trees. Unable to see the enemy, the ranks broke into a headlong retreat. Braddock fought furiously and had four horses shot from under him, before being shot himself in the lungs. Some 750 of his men were killed and wounded, about two-thirds of the total, against enemy losses of just 51. Braddock's dying words were: 'We shall know better how to deal with them the next time.'

Not for the last time, the British had grossly underestimated the toughness of local fighters and the very different kind of terrain from Europe. Washington rallied what was left of the force, complaining bitterly that the 'dastardly behaviour of the British soldiers exposed all those who were inclined to do their duty to almost certain death'. The British retreated to Fort Cumberland.

—·∾∾·—

Washington disappeared to his estate in Virginia, where he led the agreeable life of a wealthy, slave-owning landowner until he suddenly emerged as commander of the forces of the newly emergent independent colonies who were trying to throw off the shackles of British rule. The choice of Washington was dictated by the need to secure the support of the southern plantation states and to deny the job to the wealthy John Hancock, the Massachusetts merchant who had played a key role in the first round of the struggle against the British, but who lacked any military qualifications.

At the Second Continental Congress in Philadelphia, May 1775, John Adams rose to nominate George Washington: 'A gentleman whose skill and experience as an officer, whose independence, great talents and excellent universal character would command the approbation of all America and unite the cordial exertions of all the colonies better than any other person in the union.'

It proved to be the key decision of the Congress, and perhaps of the whole American Revolution until 1787. Washington, certainly the most distinguished soldier in that assembly, was pointedly dressed in military uniform, but his acceptance speech was a model of restraint:

> Though I am truly sensible of the high honour done me in this appointment, yet I feel great distress, from a consciousness that my abilities and military experience may not be equal to the extensive and important trust. However, as the Congress desire it, I will enter upon the momentous duty, and exert every power I possess in the service, and for the support of the glorious cause. I beg they will accept my most cordial thanks for this distinguished testimony of their approbation.
>
> But, lest some unlucky event should happen, unfavourable to my reputation, I beg it may be remembered by every gentleman in this room, that I, this day, declare with the utmost sincerity, I do not think myself equal to the command I am honoured with.

The general chosen to command the unified American army was, by an extraordinary stroke of fate for the Americans, a man of quite astonishing ability. This was anything but apparent at the time. Washington had been a compromise choice, slotted in for a straightforward political motive: to secure the support of the southern states and their aristocracy, of which he was a rather new but impressive representative, behind the northern conspiracy that had triggered hostilities with Britain in Massachusetts.

Knowing the importance of securing Boston as soon as possible, Washington travelled north with apprehension. However, he was eager to take up his command and arrived in Cambridge on 2 July with his two chief subordinates, Charles Lee and Philip Schuyler from New York. The professional soldier from Virginia was appalled by the militia who had started the American Revolution and now lay outside Boston besieging the British.

He found that men would wander in and out of camp at will, abandon their sentry duty when they felt like it, take pot-shots at the British and even sometimes fraternize with the enemy. Their camps were filthy, with latrines filled to overflowing. Needing to elevate the army to a level of professionalism, he set about issuing detailed orders including demands that 'stale and unwholesome' food be thrown away, clean bedding should be given to the men, new latrines should be dug and the rubbish around the camps should be removed.

The soldiers were expected to conform to new standards of discipline: officers were cashiered and men fined and lashed. He ordered the powder the army was so sorely lacking and built up new fortifications against the British. Meanwhile, Washington had women sympathizers up and down the colonies make no fewer than 14,000 coats. One major problem was the terms of enlistment, under which most of the men's service expired on 31 December. Washington introduced the concept of year-long enlistment, and tried to regroup the army into 26 infantry regiments of eight companies (some 700 men) each, a rifle regiment and an artillery regiment.

Enthusiastic as the Massachusetts men had been during the fervour of high summer, getting them to obey the new discipline through the rigours of a New England winter was another matter altogether. Only 12,500 men had joined the new 'continental army', and Washington was forced to depend on 7,000 of the ill-disciplined militia he hated. This was hardly evidence of popular enthusiasm for the rebel cause.

Washington himself got off to a poor start in the field, despatching an expedition to take Quebec which was easily beaten off by the British. His next move, however, was a triumph of intrigue and daring. In November 1775, Washington despatched a large, tall, fat, gregarious colonel of artillery, Henry Knox, to Ticonderoga to retrieve the British cannon captured there. In an astonishing piece of military professionalism and endurance, Knox succeeded beyond Washington's wildest expectations. He arranged the removal of 44 guns, 14 mortars and a howitzer from the fort on flat-bottomed boats across Lake George. This colossal armoury was then transported 300 miles across the mountains on sleds, crossing the Hudson River no fewer than four times along the journey. By late January 1776, at the height of the New England winter, Knox had reached Framingham and by February his guns were ready for action outside Boston.

Washington was overjoyed. He had by now had time to organize his army, although not to bring it up to full strength, and was pressing furiously for action. He urged an attack across the ice from Cambridge to Boston. His fellow commanders rejected this, but accepted a lesser plan to mount the artillery on Dorchester Heights to the south of the town, from which they could pound Boston to bits at their leisure. Astonishingly, the British had made no move to occupy the Heights.

On 2 March 1776 the Americans launched a bombardment of Boston which was replied to heavily but ineffectively by the British. Under the cover of darkness, 2,000 men quietly ascended Dorchester Heights with the cannon and huge bundles of equipment. Because of the hardness of the ground, it was impossible for the Americans to dig in, so they hit upon the ingenious solution of erecting barricades of earth which was brought up on 300 ox carts.

Meanwhile, Washington prepared forces for an attack across the ice should the British attack Dorchester Heights. The British general, William Howe, awoke the following morning to find the American guns in place. His naval commander, Admiral Molyneaux Shuldham, who had succeeded the irascible, incompetent Admiral Sir Thomas Graves, told him that the navy would have to move out of reach of the American heavy guns immediately. General Howe had no choice but to attack or to watch as Boston was blown to bits.

However, that night a violent storm made it necessary for Howe to postpone his attack and the British fleet to put out to sea. He decided to evacuate the garrison rather than risk a repeat of the 1775 Battle of Breeds Hill, which the British had won but only at the cost of 800 men. It was a decision that should have been executed much earlier. Boston was a city under siege in hostile territory protected only by water: the men in it had no chance of breaking out without reinforcements and much more vigorous leadership.

After negotiations under a flag of truce, Washington agreed not to attack provided the British left Boston intact. On 17 March, the British sailed away to Staten Island, where they would be free to regroup and pursue a much more vigorous and aggressive strategy with the help of reinforcements from Halifax and Nova Scotia. The first phase of the war was over. Without losing a single man, Washington had won the first real American victory. It proved a powerful shot in the arm to a cause dispirited by the recent humiliation in Quebec.

Several weeks after landing at Staten Island, Howe's forces arrived on Long Island. After his triumph at Boston, Washington had withdrawn the bulk of his army for the defence of New York, where the British attack was rightly expected to come. It was the Americans' turn to be overconfident, and Washington now put on a staggering display of military ineptitude, revealing his army to be amateur in tactics and strategy. Believing their own propaganda, Washington and the Americans concluded that the ambush at Concord and Lexington which marked the beginning of the war in Massachusetts, the Battle of Breeds Hill and the British evacuation of Boston had brought the British to their knees – when they were actually only very limited victories.

In New York, matters were altogether different from Massachusetts. The state was a hotbed of loyalist, pro-British, 'Tory' sentiment, but the rebels, arguing that all Americans hated the British, were deeply unwilling to acknowledge this. Moreover, the positions in New York were reversed from those in Boston. Washington, holding the city, would be subjected to the same difficulties that the British had been in Boston: his army would be cut off by a numerically superior enemy in countryside that was largely hostile. Washington's best tactic would have been to stay out of the city altogether, to give him freedom of manoeuvre, or even to move his forces south to New Jersey. However, abandoning New York would have been a devastating admission of weakness and of the falseness of Congress's claim to represent the majority of Americans.

Washington, believing his own forces to be stronger, and the British much weaker, than they were, decided to make his stand there. In an effort to avoid being overtaken by the same fate as befell the British in Boston, he stationed his forces across the river in Brooklyn: for if the British gained control of this area, New York would be at the mercy of their cannon.

In doing this, Washington displayed serious tactical flaws which were nearly to cost America the war at its outset. Placing his forces across the East River meant that they could be surrounded and cut off by the British army and navy. He wrongly believed his position to be strong. On his right he was protected by the salt marshes at Gowanus Creek. Just in front of Brooklyn village, he placed his vanguard under General Israel Putnam. This position was protected by the Hills of Guan which stretched out in a much longer line to the south. They were heavily wooded and believed to be impassable except in four places – Gowanus on the sea, the Flatbush Pass a mile to the east, the Bedford Pass a mile further on and the Jamaica Pass three miles beyond that. General Jack Sullivan was placed in charge of the troops holding the Guan Heights.

To the Americans, accustomed to fighting in such terrain, and who had already inflicted major casualties on British troops storming their positions from above at Breeds Hill, it must have seemed an almost impregnable position, and one which would force the British to string their men out in a long line instead of concentrating their forces at a single strongpoint. Unfortunately Sullivan, possibly believing the British could not stretch their forces that far, or ignorant of the topography, sent only five men to defend the Jamaica Pass, to the Americans' far left.

Washington sent a stirring invocation to his men to do their best, coupled with a warning against desertion:

Remember officers and soldiers, that you are freemen, fighting for the blessings of liberty – that slavery will be your portion, and that of your posterity, if you do not acquit yourselves like men: Remember how your courage and spirit have been despised, and traduced by your cruel invaders... Be cool, but determined; do not fire at a distance, but wait for orders from your officers. No such scoundrel [deserters] will be found in this army; but on the contrary, every one for himself resolving to conquer, or die, and trusting to the smiles of heaven upon so just a cause, will behave with bravery and resolution: Those who are distinguished for their gallantry, and good conduct, may depend upon being honourably noticed, and suitably rewarded.

Washington's words were stirring, but General Howe was now to show his greater experience and skill as a commander. Carefully scouting the rebel lines, he arranged for feint attacks to be made on the three eastern passes in the early morning of 27 August 1776. Howe despatched his army, with himself in charge of the main force, Sir Henry Clinton in the vanguard and Lord Charles Cornwallis in the rear, to the virtually unguarded Jamaica Pass. They arrived there at 3 a.m., seized the five defenders and moved along the old Jamaica Road as silently as they could at dead of night – behind the American frontline in the hills.

These perfectly executed moves caught the American forces in a trap, and only the right flank succeeded in escaping to the Gowanus marshes. By noon around 1,000 Americans had been killed, wounded or captured in the bogs at the expense of only a handful of casualties among the British – a vastly more complete victory than the American 'triumphs' at Concord and Lexington and Breeds Hill. British officers were eager to chase the Americans into their entrenched positions around the village of Brooklyn, and might have succeeded in routing the demoralized Americans altogether. However, Howe's caution and concern to keep casualties as low as possible among his own men mistakenly prevailed. There were still some 7,500 Americans facing the 15,000 British.

In desperation, Washington had 2,000 troops ferried across from New York, to reinforce the Americans in Brooklyn. He was tightening the noose around his own neck, for the British now began to construct trenches and breastworks, as well as a battery, 600 yards away from the American line in preparation for a siege. All that was needed was the British fleet, under the command of Admiral Richard Howe, the general's brother, to sail up the East River and cut the rebels off.

Providence intervened on the American side. On 28 August, a violent northeasterly storm soaked both sides, damping their ammunition and rendering the Americans vulnerable to a bayonet charge, which many British officers urged their commander to mount. More significantly, the weather prevented the British fleet sailing up the East River. General Howe now misjudged badly. Possibly assuming that he would get his chance once his brother closed the trap, or that the Americans would be equally immobilized by the storm, or that they would surrender, or even conceivably that if he showed mercy peace negotiations were possible, he bided his time. As Israel Putnam put it: 'General Howe is either our friend or no general. He had our whole army in his power... and yet offered us to escape without the least interruption... Had he instantly followed up his victory, the consequence to the cause of liberty must have been dreadful.'

Washington had now been convinced by his officers that his position was untenable and that he must evacuate. During the night of 30 August the storm subsided and a dank and impenetrable mist settled on both positions. The choppy river settled to glass-like smoothness. For the first time in a career so far more marked by the suggestion of ability than any real proof of it, Washington displayed his genius as a commander. The entire American force of 9,500 men, together with all their provisions, ammunition and most of their guns, were evacuated over the river to New York. The British only discovered that the bird had flown the following morning.

Howe promptly decided that instead of attacking New York City, which would antagonize the inhabitants and lead to house-to-house fighting and destruction, he would organize his men in a flanking movement further up the East River and bottle up Washington's forces in the city, where once again they would be caught in a trap. This was sensible, as destroying the pro-British city would have needlessly antagonized its inhabitants, but the British would have to act with alacrity in cutting off the American forces.

In spite of their miraculous escape, there was no disguising the demoralization and sense of defeat on the American side. Hundreds of members of the militia deserted outright, while Washington and his officers sought frantically to organize musters, court martials and whippings to stop them. In an army lacking British-style discipline, this was next to impossible.

To the British, it must have seemed that the end of the war was very near. Washington's army had escaped total annihilation by a fluke, and it could now be cut off in New York, which the American commander was doggedly and stupidly determined to defend – until ordered by Congress not to do so. Generals Putnam and Greene also both urged a withdrawal from the city, the latter arguing that it should be burnt down, as it was a Tory stronghold – an indication of the ruthlessness with which the rebels were prepared to punish even their own people.

On 13 September, British ships sailed up the East River and blasted away at American defensive earthworks at Kip's Bay. The militia then promptly abandoned their positions, while the British landed hundreds of men unopposed. Washington, hearing of the landing, took to his horse at the head of two New England brigades while, with eminent good sense, Putnam furiously led a headlong retreat from the New York trap up the west side of Manhattan Island, carrying as many provisions and ammunition as possible, but leaving the guns behind.

On reaching his fleeing men, for the first time in his career Washington lost his ice-cool composure and started whipping officers and men with his riding cane, dashing his hat on the ground and raging, 'Are these the men with whom I am to defend America?' The American commander-in-chief feared that he faced another debacle to match that on Long Island. After his triumphalism in Boston, this would be humiliation indeed.

Astonishingly, in spite of his perfectly executed landing, Howe once again held back from springing the trap. He sent his troops north and south up the main road, but failed to cross over to the western, Hudson River side of Manhattan Island and cut off Putnam's line of retreat. By evening, the American forces were relatively safe at Harlem Heights to the north of the city.

A skirmish the following day gave a bloody nose to the British advance guard below the Heights, but one of America's best soldiers, Colonel Thomas Knowlton, was killed. Having almost caught their prey, the British veered off into another attack on a defended uphill position, and the fleeing American army was momentarily safe once again. Meanwhile, the British had taken New York easily.

It is easy to understand why, by this time, the British were contemptuous about the fighting abilities of their enemy. All the same, Howe, who feared that he had too few troops to risk sacrificing them in a significant engagement, remained remarkably cautious. Rather than storming the Heights, his forces remained entrenched for the best part of a month while preparing the next movement – a pincer this time, leaving a garrison in New York and sending a force up the Hudson and another up the East River. The strategy was once again impeccable, but leisurely executed. Some 400 men were landed at Throgg Point, at the bottom of Long Island Sound, on 14 October.

This prompted Washington four days later to march north to White Plains, evacuating Harlem Heights altogether. He was proving an adept runner. The ever-cautious Howe waited several days before disembarking more troops further north at Pell's Point and Myer's Point and marching to attack the far left of the American position at Chatterton's Hill, which the British took with difficulty at the cost of 229 men to 140 Americans.

Washington was forced to retreat again to a better position at North Castle Heights, only to see the British suddenly withdraw southwest towards an American fort, Fort Washington, he had inexplicably left unprotected. It was a skilful tactical movement that left Washington floundering. He decided to leave 10,000 men behind and cross the Hudson with 5,000 to threaten the British should they choose to attack the two forts on either side of the river, Forts Washington and Lee. These garrisons, which contained 3,000 men and 2,000 respectively, were supposed to blockade the

British fleet from moving upriver, but were otherwise quite useless; and they were sitting ducks for the British.

What followed was glorified by Washington as a 'war of posts', or a 'defensive' war. It was, in fact, nothing less than a British chase and an American retreat as the British forces marched quickly and skilfully in pursuit of the bedraggled and confused American forces. Washington had made another major blunder in leaving these useless garrisons behind his lines and he could do nothing now to save them. On 16 November 1776, in a classic attack on three sides, the British surrounded and routed the American lines around Fort Washington. Three hundred British died compared to only 54 Americans, but the garrison of 2,900 men and all their stores were captured. It was the biggest victory so far in the war.

Four days later, the ablest British commander, Lord Cornwallis, crossed the Hudson to a position just below the other redundant American garrison, Fort Lee, and General Nathanael Greene, the commander there, evacuated his 2,000 men in great haste. He joined up with Washington's men in a desperate attempt to escape yet another British trap. Moving with furious urgency, Washington and Greene reached Newark, New Jersey, on 22 November. There they sought to rally their men to make a stand but 2,000 soldiers, with their terms of enlistment at an end, decided to abandon what seemed a lost cause. Washington had now had his fill of bitterness, defeat and retreat.

He was reduced to a force of just 3,000 men. These escaped in the nick of time as Cornwallis arrived in hot pursuit, and even on occasion in sight, on 28 November. Washington reached New Brunswick the following day, and would have been caught but for an order from General Howe to Cornwallis not to engage.

Washington's next place of refuge was Princeton. The British, now rejoined by Cornwallis, resumed their march under Howe and almost surrounded them there, but the depleted American forces escaped and at last reached the Delaware River, which they crossed, destroying every boat for 70 miles in the process. Howe lingered on the north bank for a week before deciding to pursue no further and return to winter quarters.

It had been one of the great chases in military history, covering some 170 miles in two months. At its end, Washington had narrowly escaped with the rump of the American army. The flame of resistance was still flickering, but barely more than that. His whole campaign from New York to Delaware had been a string of disasters, defeats, miscalculations and retreats. He had been wrong to risk his army in the defence of New York; wrong to send the bulk of it across to Long Island and to reinforce it there; wrong in his half-baked defence of Brooklyn; wrong to seek to hold New York after this disaster; wrong to flee north to White Plains instead of seeking to concentrate his forces in New Jersey; and wrong to leave a large garrison at Fort Washington to be picked off in his wake.

The idea of a united American effort to overthrow the British oppressors was in tatters. New York, New Jersey and Rhode Island had wholly failed to follow New England's lead and emerge as hotbeds of armed resistance to the British. All were now virtually under British control. The American army had lost around 5,000 men in casualties and prisoners to around 1,000 British soldiers. In total, it had been slashed by war, disease and destruction from around 20,000 men to just 3,000 under Washington's command, with a further 5,000 left behind under the control of General Charles Lee at North Castle and Peekshill.

—∾∾—

Despite the losses, Washington's superb political skills were never more in evidence: even at the very darkest moment of his command, he turned defeat into long-term advantage, both for America's cause and his own authority. He also displayed another characteristic of great politicians and (sometimes) great soldiers: with his back to the wall, this normally most cautious and cool-headed of leaders decided to gamble everything on a single, bold throw of the dice.

Even though he seemingly held no cards, had neither authorization nor a sensible strategic objective, and had been hounded across the length of two states, barely escaping with his life, Washington had two overriding reasons for a bold stroke: to secure a desperately needed propaganda success with which to rally the Americans, and to stage a single victory that would enable Congress to justify retaining him in his command. He was facing imminent dismissal as a disastrous leader, and he knew it; self-interest as much as idealism continued to guide this intensely ambitious and proud man. Risking the remnants of the army, which now faced annihilation if defeated, in a last-ditch bid to save America's and his own reputation, was a colossal gamble indeed.

He was aided by good intelligence, which revealed the British state of complacency and lack of preparation, as well as their depleted numbers now that General Howe had gone back to winter quarters in New York. To Washington, this was too good an opportunity to miss, even for his ragged forces. He was now about to stage one of the greatest guerrilla strikes and propaganda victories in history – even though it was, despite American claims, to prove little more than a couple of outsize skirmishes in purely military terms.

Howe had made two colossal misjudgements after the successful autumn campaign, both born of the British belief that victory was now inevitable and that a mopping up of the remnants of American forces was all that would be required the following spring. Firstly, he decided to leave the desperate, cornered Americans across the Delaware River alone, and retired with the bulk of his army; and, secondly, he left the front line defended by some 2,000 troops from the German state of Hesse, strung out in a long line from Trenton to Burlington under the overall command of General Carl von Donup, with the Trenton troops under Colonel Johann Rall.

The German hussars were undoubtedly brave and tough, but were not great ambassadors for the British cause. Although instructed to pay for any provisions they needed, they showed little inclination to behave with such gentility and succeeded in antagonizing many of the local people. Consequently, with the main British force withdrawn, the rebels were free to move about the countryside, stirring people up and ambushing and harassing British patrols, which were safe only in the towns.

Fond of drinking and gambling, the Hessian officers could be counted on to be engaged upon both on Christmas night, 1776.

Washington, well-informed by his scouts about the Hessian troop positions, planned his attack with precision. He was to command the central thrust crossing the Delaware with some 2,400 men some nine miles north of Trenton. Further downstream, directly opposite the town, a force of 700 would land as a diversion while a smaller force would attack Donup at Mount Holly, a feint designed to tie up his troops and prevent Trenton being reinforced.

The conditions were grim as night fell. Huge blocks of ice flowed down the freezing river and a snow blizzard descended as the American troops embarked on flat-bottomed craft usually used to convey iron ore downriver. The biggest problem was ferrying the horses and 18 cannon which were under command of the huge and efficient Henry Knox. The half-frozen troops, many wearing only cloths rather than shoes around their feet, left trails of blood in the snow. They only completed the river crossing by 3 a.m. on 26 December.

Washington divided his main force into two columns, one to attack from the river side to the west, the other from the northeast, in an effort to surround the town. One of the southern contingents was sent to secure the bridge on Assunpink Creek to the south of Trenton, to complete the loop. Marching forward in the dark, Washington's troops arrived at around 8 a.m. to find Trenton barely guarded, with the garrison snug in bed after the night's carousing: it seemed inconceivable that the ragged and God-fearing Americans would mount an attack at Christmas, especially after such a terrible night.

Moving quickly in the muffled silence of the snow, the Americans set up field guns in the streets. Awoken from their slumbers, the Hessians fired from their windows and tumbled downstairs to take up defensive positions. They were mown down by musket and artillery fire. Colonel Rall bravely tried to make a stand on the east side of town, but he was mortally wounded by a bullet.

Within an hour the battle was over, with only three Americans dead and six wounded compared with 22 Hessians dead, 98 wounded and 1,000 taken prisoner. The Hessians had been caught napping. It had been a beautifully executed and heroic (under the arctic conditions) night ambush. Some 500 Hessians escaped to the south across the Assunpink. In addition the Americans had captured six cannon and 1,000 muskets. It was a remarkable triumph for careful planning and boldness.

—◆◆◆—

Washington himself took little part in the next great offensive operation, despatching his rival generals Horatio Gates and Benedict Arnold to the north, where they brilliantly lured General John Burgoyne's British troops into a trap at Saratoga. Washington then again showed his ruthless streak by tearing up the surrender terms, which allowed for the repatriation of the British army, negotiated by Gates: this was an unprecedented breach of faith, and also undercut Gates, his rival.

Meanwhile, Washington had lost the rebel capital, Philadelphia, thanks to a daring British military coup and his own poor leadership. General William Howe's plan for an attack on Philadelphia had four objectives: to lure Washington's army into open battle and defeat it; to control as much of the countryside as possible, so as to encourage loyalists to come out on the British side; to gain control of the major eastern cities; and to strike a devastating psychological blow at the enemy by seizing their capital. The seizure of Philadelphia would serve all four ends.

It was a brilliant concept, with only two drawbacks: by embarking his troops, Howe would for a time make it impossible to reinforce New York or march to Burgoyne's aid if necessary; and the Delaware River was effectively blocked by the Americans. Further, in refusing to march back across New Jersey, the British would give the impression that they had abandoned the many loyalists in the state. However, Howe seems to have feared an ambush from the west.

While he spent the next three months preparing for his expedition, Howe staged several sorties and feints both to lure Washington into battle and to deceive him as to his true intentions. He marched his forces beyond the Raritan River, which prompted Washington to move southwards from Morristown to the heights of

Middlebrook. Then Howe withdrew and, when Washington fol-lowed, turned on him, nearly crushing the Americans in open bat-tle. He sent forces up the Hudson Valley and then into Long Island Sound, while the Americans watched bemused as to his objectives.

Washington, knowing that the British were massing for an attack from Canada, was certain that Howe's ultimate destination was Albany, where he would link up with Burgoyne. It was with incredulity that the American commander learnt on 23 July 1777 that Howe had embarked 36 battalions and a cavalry regiment, totalling 18,000 men, on board 260 boats.

Washington never believed that Howe would sail up the Delaware to capture Philadelphia. On 31 July he learnt that the British fleet had been sighted off the Delaware. He then learnt that the ships, even more remarkably, had sailed on, deterred by the strength of the American defences on the river.

It was not until 15 August that the British reappeared, this time in Chesapeake Bay, after a stormy and extremely hot 47 days at sea which killed most of Howe's horses. He landed his troops on one side of the Elk River. To the last, the British commander had kept the Americans guessing, with Washington believing that Howe was headed much further south.

At the beginning of August, Washington moved his army of 16,000 towards Philadelphia, the American capital, establishing quarters at Wilmington. The British meanwhile marched forward, ecstatic after their gruelling sea journey, and plundered the well-stocked countryside – although Howe imposed severe penalties for those caught. Washington sent detachments to harry the British, while his main force occupied Brandywine Creek, a watercourse bounded by wooded slopes, in an effort to block the British from advancing on Philadelphia.

So far Howe had shown both audacity and skill, avoiding the trap on the Delaware River and catching the Americans by surprise with his move up the Chesapeake. He was now to engage in another display of tactical ability in what was by far the most dazzling British campaign of the war. As in the Battle of Brooklyn, Howe's response to Washington's attempt to block him was to stage a frontal feint attack on the main American force, which was stationed at Chad's Ford across the Brandywine. At 10 a.m. on 10 September his artillery, under the German general Wilhelm von Knyphausen, opened fire across the Brandywine as a prelude to the expected assault.

However, Howe had already despatched his main force six hours earlier on a long march across Jefferson Ford to the north, beyond the furthest American positions. Washington had learnt of this move an hour earlier, but failed to take it seriously enough, so the British succeeded in occupying the strategic heights of Osborne's Hill and advanced on the Americans from the rear: the rebels had been caught napping.

The main American forces along the river rapidly and desperately wheeled around to avoid being taken from behind and to engage the British force. Washington hastily asked General Nathanael Greene, whose troops had been standing by to support the American forces awaiting General Knyphausen's attack across the Brandywine, to bring his troops up to plug a gap in the new American frontline created by the rapid manoeuvre. This Greene did at a run, his troops covering four miles in 45 minutes. The British coolly descended the hill in perfect formation to the strains of the 'The British Grenadiers' marching song and plunged into a vicious battle.

The sound of battle gave Knyphausen his cue to attack across Chad's Ford. The German bravely led his men across the river under withering fire and the Brandywine soon being 'much stained with blood'. Knyphausen seized the artillery and took on the American infantry. Caught between two pincers, the Americans yielded and then panicked, but after some four miles encountered another American force which slowed them into an orderly retreat.

The American army had survived to fight another day, but they had lost the decisive battle for the defence of the capital. Some 200 Americans had been killed, 500 wounded and 400 captured, compared to around 100 British killed and 450 wounded. Howe had faultlessly and seemingly effortlessly outmanoeuvred Washington.

Howe was not slow to follow up his advantage: the following day he set off towards Reading, travelling along the Schuylkill River, while Washington's forces sought to keep up with him on the other side. Then, dramatically, he turned back and crossed a ford behind the Americans, despatching a force under Lord Cornwallis to seize Philadelphia while his main army camped at Germantown, five miles to the north. Congress had already fled the capital, and Cornwallis entered Philadelphia to the strains of 'God Save the King'. The date was 26 September 1777, just over 14 months after the signing of the Declaration of Independence in the same city.

To many Americans, it seemed that the war was all but over. In propaganda terms, the British victory had been overwhelming. The Americans had been defeated in every pitched battle they had dared to fight and had been completely outmanoeuvred by Howe on this occasion. With Philadelphia lost as well as New York, the American cause seemed hopeless indeed.

Washington decided, against the odds, to try and stage another desperate counterattack, akin to his masterful strike across the Delaware the previous winter, to restore the morale of his side. He was given faith by the fact that Howe kept his army dispersed. The bulk of the British forces were near Philadelphia at Germantown – some 9,000 men – while 3,000 were guarding the supply line from Elktown. Some 4,000 men were stationed in Philadelphia itself and some 2,000 had been sent along the Delaware.

Washington, with an army barely larger than that of the British at Germantown, decided to attack. Once again he was on the ropes, and he invoked his men to do great deeds: 'Let it never be said that in a day of action you turned your backs on the foe; let the evening no longer triumph.'

On the night of 3 October 1777, he staged a forced march from his camp 20 miles to the west, deploying the army in separate columns down the four roads into the scattered village of Germantown. It was a curious tactic, for it dispersed the American advantage in numbers. Starting at 5 a.m. in a heavy fog, the Americans had the advantage of stealth.

Howe was taken by surprise. He had had only an hour's sleep after spending the night up gambling – one of his favourite pastimes. He jumped on a horse, shouting 'Form! Form!' at his men, but was made to fall back. The Americans were in savage mood, and gave no quarter. A number of British soldiers took refuge in Chew House, an old, large stone building, and futile attempts to dislodge them delayed Washington's army for hours.

Nathanael Greene, advancing down Limekiln Road to the east, sent one of its units into the fray, which mistakenly attacked one of the main American columns under General Anthony Wayne. This confusion, and the delay at Chew House, persuaded Howe, with astonishing speed and improvisation, to regroup and launch a counterattack, to devastating effect. The Americans were forced to retreat some 20 miles, their offensive in a shambles.

Unsurprisingly, the British were in no state to pursue. The Americans were later to make much of this, characteristically trying to portray a major defeat as a victory, but the truth was that Washington's surprise attack had ended in disaster: the British had been caught unawares, but had reacted with speed and skill. The attackers should have had the advantage, but Washington's tactic of dispersing his army along four roads had been a blunder, his troops had been badly led in firing upon one another and they had wasted time attacking Chew House. Some 650 Americans had been killed or wounded, compared to 500 British; around 450 Americans were captured. The British had snatched victory from a seemingly certain defeat. It was one of their most impressive performances to date.

Washington now showed his capacity for stoic endurance. The loss of Philadelphia had been a major strategic setback for the American cause. Worse, he had retreated to a valley near White Marsh, some 12 miles south of the capital, only to be ambushed by the British there at the beginning of December 1777. After a standoff between the two forces, Washington felt compelled to retreat a further 12 miles to a safer refuge at the village of Valley Forge. The site had been chosen because the Schuylkill River and Valley Creek provided natural defences on two sides and it featured several thickly wooded hills which could be easily defended. It was also well placed for watching British troop movements. To Washington it seemed not unlike his choice of Morristown the previous year.

However, the area suffered from three severe disadvantages over Morristown: there were virtually no buildings there; the people of the area were themselves suffering extreme privation and could provide scant supplies; and the winter of that year was far fiercer than that of the previous year. The army this time was also much larger: some 11,000 men, of whom around 8,000 were fit for duty. They had barely a change of clothing, few shoes and no soap. The absence of food and provisions was reflected in the lack of enthusiasm of most people in the middle colonies towards the American cause. The states, too, preferred to hang on to their supplies, however much Congress might try to cajole them.

The army set about building log cabins, 14 by 16 feet, to contain 12 men at a time. The soldiers slept on the floors, and subsisted off firecake, a type of bread made of flour and water. At the end of December, and then again in early January and mid-February 1778, the troops virtually ran out of food. Some 500 horses died of starvation.

From its confined quarters in Yorktown, Congress was officially in charge of provisioning but proved woefully inept. Produce bought in New Jersey went rotten because it could not be transferred and Philadelphian farmers preferred to sell their crops to the British, who could pay in hard cash, while others shipped flour to New England. Washington quarrelled bitterly with his congressional critics. Meanwhile, the American commander had countered an attempt, dubbed the Conway Cabal after its commander, James Conway, to supplant him by Horatio Gates.

The War of Independence had become entrenched, and 1779 and early 1780 offered few decisive moments. American spirits were even lower than at any other time during the war. The army was reduced to a wretched rump and the news filtering back from the south was uniformly bad. The French had recognized the independence of the colonies in 1778 and now openly supported the American effort, but their intervention had so far proved, from the American point of view, completely ineffectual. A new system of raising provisions, so much vaunted in milder weather under

Greene the year before, had failed, and Washington himself could not escape his share of the blame.

In May 1780, when news of the catastrophic loss of Charleston reached Washington, his spirits plunged further. Then, in June, the British, under the Hessian general Wilhelm von Knyphausen, even dared to stage an offensive aimed at the American base of Morristown, but were blocked at Springfield. To the north, Washington was in as dire straits as ever. He had just survived another wretched winter in which he had descended from the uplands to intimidate General Henry Clinton, who had replaced Howe as the British commander-in-chief in 1778, but he did not dare to attack him frontally. Then, in January 1781, there were two serious mutinies by the enlisted men who were now entering their fourth winter in camp, long after they had expected to return to their families. They had originally been enlisted for a period of three years or until the end of the war (whichever was the longer). The first mutiny was bought off with concessions from Congress which Washington opposed for fear they would lead to another. He was right. The second was suppressed with his customary ruthlessness in times of necessity: two of the ringleaders were shot.

Washington himself was bitter and realistic about the Americans' plight at the beginning of 1781. The French, increasingly sceptical about the Americans' chances, proposed a peace leaving each side in control of the territory it occupied, and there was a real prospect that this would end the conflict. With Washington's army having dwindled to around 3,500 men huddled in West Point, and with the 4,000-strong French standing idle and stranded at Newport, Rhode Island, for more than a year, American prospects seemed dismal indeed. The 11,000-strong British garrison in New York seemed impregnable.

In the north, elsewhere in the colonies, the rebels could point to no great upsurge in support for independence, no massive inflow of new recruits and no real control of the countryside. Most Americans were weary and unenthusiastic, if not hostile to both sides, who sat glowering in their strongholds across a desert of popular indifference. The revolutionary cause had always been – as most revolutions are – a minority one imposed on an indifferent or hostile people. The cause was never less popular than in the spring of 1781, when most histories suggest it was gathering irresistible momentum in advance of the devastating defeat of Yorktown.

From a strategic point of view, the prospects for Washington were scarcely more encouraging and he showed only marginally more initiative than the wretched Clinton. His chief fear seems to have been that Cornwallis would return to the south to threaten Greene. In order to pre-empt this, he toyed with the idea of attacking New York, while holding out no great hopes of doing so successfully, but he hoped that the timorous Clinton would order Cornwallis north to New York, where their combined troops would be pinned down. Washington was tired and dispirited even as he prepared for the siege of New York. His appeal to Congress for support was less than stirring:

> We must not despair. The game is yet in our own hands; to play it well is all we have to do, and I trust the experience of error will enable us to act better in future. A cloud may yet pass over us, individuals may be ruined, and the country at large, or particular states, undergo temporary distress, but certain I am that it is in our power to bring the war to a happy conclusion.

Victory for both sides seemed as elusive as ever. The contest seemed likely to be determined by whichever side grew weary of the stalemate first. It was by no means certain that the British would be the first to back down. Although both the British Parliament and public opinion were deeply weary of the extensive and endless conflict, the number of troops committed to America was not enormous and Britain had the resources to continue.

The Americans were almost out of money, their regular army was at an all-time low by the summer of 1781 and their leadership under Washington seemed uninspiring. If Clinton could not expect to wipe out Washington's small army, which had the ability to retreat in depth, nor could the American commander seriously hope to prise the British out of New York. But he felt he had no alternative but to prepare for a long, grim siege.

———∿∿∿———

Something entirely unexpected happened that dramatically turned the deadlock upside down, scattering the pieces on the chessboard. Suddenly, briefly, the British lost control of the sea. Washington, patient, plodding, tough-minded, ruthless, cold and seemingly bereft of initiative, was provided with an opportunity which galvanized him into one of his rare displays of dynamic action. And, as at Saratoga, the British were dogged by an extraordinary succession of mistakes and bad luck that were to deliver them into their enemy's hands.

As late as 13 August 1781, the British still probably held the initiative in this tired war. By the following day the Americans did: the news had arrived that François Joseph Paul, Comte de Grasse, had sailed from Santo Domingo at the head of 28 warships, accompanied by smaller vessels, with 3,300 French regular troops.

In May, de Grasse had set out from France for the West Indies to try and challenge Britain's domination of the region, where Admiral Lord George Rodney had been making a great nuisance of himself. De Grasse now travelled northwards, but his destination was not New York, where the new American–French land offensive was being planned by Washington at that very moment, but the much closer Chesapeake Bay, where Cornwallis' smaller army was much more exposed. The choice may have been dictated by expediency: de Grasse had promised the Spanish that he would return to help them in the West Indies by November. Almost certainly, he could pounce successfully provided, first, that Cornwallis did not move out of the Yorktown Peninsula beforehand, second, that American and French troops could get there overland in time to close the trap, and, third, that the French continued to enjoy control of the sea.

None of these things was by any means certain, or even highly likely. Cornwallis, apparently safe in the Yorktown Peninsula,

which was surrounded on three sides by sea and a heavily defended
'neck', had orders to construct a naval base for the British and,
refusing to send his troops north to bolster Clinton in New York,
was waiting for the opportunity to take them south again. It seems
not to have occurred to him that the British might lose their naval
superiority, although there were strong rumours by mid-July 1781
that de Grasse might sail north. With a large fleet in the Caribbean
under Rodney, and a smaller one under Admiral Sir Thomas
Graves at New York, the British felt ready to meet any challenge.

Nor had the British apparently given much thought to the possibility of a joint American–French expedition to Virginia. The
British had intercepted a letter from Washington to Gilbert du
Motier, Marquis de Lafayette, the Frenchman responsible for the
defence of Virginia, saying that New York would be the target of
their proposed offensive as indeed, at that stage, it was. After a year
of enforced idleness, the French army under the Comte de
Rochambeau had crossed over from Newport to Providence in good
order, with a force of 4,000 men, and travelled 220 miles to
Philipsburg in Westchester County to meet up with the Americans
at the beginning of July.

Washington's proposed assault of New York was on schedule and
the two armies began to manoeuvre in preparation for a long
siege. Clinton, meanwhile, remained completely inert. The joint
American–French army was now in a position to threaten the fortifications at Kingsbridge across from Manhattan Island, as well as
those on Long Island. A month later, on 14 August, the news
arrived that de Grasse's fleet was on the way, as well as a message
from Lafayette stating with uncharacteristic understatement that
'should a French fleet now come to Hampton Roads, the British
army would be ours, I think'. With remarkable speed, Washington
and Rochambeau decided to put all their plans into reverse and
seize the opportunity being offered by marching their army across
the 450 miles to Chesapeake Bay.

Washington alerted Lafayette: 'By the time this reaches you, the
Count de Grasse will either be in the Chesapeake or maybe looked
for every moment... you will immediately take such a position as

will best enable you to prevent [the] sudden retreat [of the enemy] through North Carolina, which I presume they will attempt the instant they perceive so formidable an armament.' However, Lafayette's army had already proved it was no match for Cornwallis' force and would not have been able to prevent a British breakout from the Yorktown Peninsula. Just four days later, on 19 August, the joint army set out, consisting of 4,000 Frenchmen and 2,500 Americans, leaving just 3,500 defending the upper reaches of the Hudson around West Point.

The march itself is justly described as an epic. One of the longest in the entire war, it was an act of astonishing boldness. It is comparable to Washington's crossing of the Delaware in 1776, but on a much larger scale. Washington had left his small force at West Point virtually unprotected from Clinton's army of 11,000, and he himself was also vulnerable to attack from his rear. He calculated, correctly, that Clinton would do nothing.

More serious was the risk that Cornwallis would slip away and the whole enterprise would prove to be futile, further dispiriting the flagging American cause. To prevent this, Washington engaged in a subtle show of deceit, wheeling around after crossing the Hudson to a position opposite Staten Island and Sandy Hook, giving the impression he was preparing to attack New York from the south. Roads were improved and a bakery was even set up to make French bread. Boats were commandeered to reinforce this feint. It was only when Washington crossed the Raritan at Brunswick on 30 August that even his own officers realized he was heading south. The news reached Clinton two days later.

The following day Washington reached the Delaware River and Trenton, and he and Rochambeau spurred forward to enter Philadelphia, followed by the American troops on 2 September and the French on 3 September. They were received rapturously in the American capital. The French were bemused by the speed of the march, though. Rochambeau's chaplain complained of being woken at 2 a.m. to march until the sun rose and grew too hot, when they would rest exhausted while the baggage train caught them up, bringing provisions. One burning day, 400 men collapsed from the heat.

The news that de Grasse had left the West Indies was correctly interpreted by Admiral Rodney. He promptly despatched a ship to warn Admiral Graves in New York; this, however, was intercepted. Meanwhile, Rodney, who had fallen ill, sent his second-in-command, Rear-Admiral Sir Samuel Hood, with 14 ships after de Grasse, who had a three-day lead. Hood's seamanship was such, however, that he overtook de Grasse inadvertently and reached the Chesapeake before him. Finding no one there, not even a despatch ship from Admiral Graves, Hood concluded that de Grasse had gone on ahead with New York as his destination.

It was a fatal miscalculation. Hood abandoned the bay, leaving Cornwallis' army without naval protection, but for the best of reasons: he feared that New York was under severe threat. Reaching Sandy Hook on 28 August, he met up with Admiral Graves three days later. The latter had been off on a reconnaissance mission to Boston and, not finding de Grasse, the two men realized what must have happened. The incompetent Graves, as the senior officer, now took command of the combined fleet of 19 warships, which promptly sailed for the Chesapeake. Graves bore the disturbing news that another French fleet, consisting of eight warships, four frigates and transports of siege equipment and guns, had sailed from Newport under Admiral Comte de Barras.

Although his intelligence was fragmentary, by this time Cornwallis knew that Washington was closing in on him in a pincer movement on land but chose not to make a break for safety. He was still confident of Britain's ability to rule the waves, unaware of the approach or size of de Grasse's fleet. Moreover, he had grown tired of running and the prospect of a victory on land must have seemed remote. It was safer to stay where he was and hope for evacuation by sea.

Clinton had been completely out-manoeuvred by Washington. With his dithering, he had already missed the best opportunity to come to Cornwallis' aid. He had made no preparation for an expedition out of New York and was not prepared to improvise at the last moment. The result was that the biggest British army in America – some 11,000 men – was completely out of the picture as events unfolded, while Cornwallis had by now very little choice but to stay where he was.

When news that de Grasse's fleet had actually arrived at Chesapeake Bay reached Washington, one French observer reported: 'I have never seen a man so thoroughly and openly delighted.' Back in Philadelphia the news was announced at a banquet for French officers, which erupted into cheering. Outside, there was a carnival atmosphere in the streets. With the fleet's protection, the French and American armies could be safely embarked across the bay and the French now had the advantage of being inside the immense natural harbour.

But they had not yet won control of the sea. This happened in a battle on 5 September. De Grasse, who had just landed 3,000 troops under the Marquis de Saint-Simon on James Island, had positioned some of his fleet in the James River to prevent the British slipping away to the south, as well as other ships at the entrance to the York River to the north. Meanwhile, troop transports had been sent to pick up Washington's allied land armies, which had marched to Baltimore and were now waiting at Head of Elk to be ferried across to the neck of the Yorktown Peninsula. The French commander sighted the British fleet at 8 a.m. and realized that it threatened to block the transportation of troops across the bay. De Grasse's first instinct was not to be trapped by the British and he ordered his 24 warships out of the bay as the British fleet of 19 warships closed in from the northeast.

As the French spread out, the British commander, Graves, adopted entirely conventional tactics, bringing his flagship, the *London*, to windward of the French fleet which was sailing about three miles away on a parallel course. As his flagship was about halfway down the British line, to the rear of the French fleet, the seven British ships behind him were shadowing no one, but Graves gave no order that they should close up. The results were that the seven were left out of the ensuing battle altogether.

He ordered his flagship and the ships ahead to close with the French, who were struggling to order their lines in their haste to escape the bay, and they opened fire at 5 p.m. The battle raged for two hours until just after sunset, when Graves belatedly ordered the redundant ships to his rear to close. It was too late: the French had peeled away from the engagement.

In spite of the initial disadvantage of five ships, increased to 12 through Graves' ineptitude, the British ended the battle with honours about even with the French. One French ship, the *Diademe*, had lost 120 men and had received more than 100 holes in her hull, virtually knocking her out of action. A British ship, the *Terrible*, was also so badly damaged that she had to be set on fire. Some 90 British seamen were killed and 25 wounded. The French losses were greater. This commendable performance in battle could not disguise the fact that Graves' incompetence had thrown away what ought to have been a British victory. Backed by a favourable wind, he had had every opportunity of routing a confused French line. Hood, who commanded the ships that had never been ordered into battle, had been beside himself with fury.

The two fleets now manoeuvred within sight of each other in the open sea. Graves, a stickler for the rule book and a commander of caution bordering on cowardice, refused to engage again on the grounds that his ships had suffered enough damage. De Grasse was similarly afraid of a fight, and had come to realize that leaving Chesapeake Bay had been a mistake. It was impossible to be completely trapped in a stretch of water so large. He would have been much better protected there and his ships would have been able to concentrate their attack on British ships entering the bay. True, the British might have tried to stage a blockade, but he was going to be there for a while anyway and the opportunity would surely have occurred to slip out to sea after a storm, for example, even if the British did not grow tired and need to resupply.

Hood, impatient of Graves' refusal to engage, urged that the British fleet move into the bay and thus ensure the survival of Cornwallis' army. They would have been able to slip away to north or south across the York or James rivers and also could have possibly intercepted the enemy troops being ferried across to the Yorktown Peninsula. However, Graves was even more obsessed with not getting his ships trapped than de Grasse, and preferred to stay in the open sea. This was sheer madness. Had Graves had the courage to move into the bay, de Grasse would almost certainly have stayed outside and the disaster at Yorktown would have been averted. Unlike Saratoga, there was no inevitability about Yorktown until the very last moment.

While the two main fleets shadow-boxed, de Barras's smaller French fleet, with its eight warships, military engineers and siege equipment, slipped into the bay behind them. When the wind turned favourable again, de Grasse was able to correct his initial error and also sail back into the bay. It was one of those rare Anglo-French naval confrontations in which the French showed more cunning, seamanship and courage than the British.

Graves arrived two days later and found a combined French fleet of 36 warships inside the bay at anchor. He chose not to engage, gave up the struggle altogether and returned to New York. He left Cornwallis to his doom. Cornwallis was now trapped, and he knew it, but he was determined to make a fight of it nevertheless. He hoped that Graves might soon return, or that Clinton in New York would bestir himself to come to his relief by land – both forlorn expectations in view of the character of the two men involved. However, Clinton had made it clear in a letter on 24 September that a relief force would arrive by sea on 5 October. Graves' withdrawal, he intimated, had been no more than a tactical one to allow some 7,000 troops to be embarked, while his fleet was reinforced to 25 warships, two 50-gun vessels and eight frigates.

Clinton and Graves knew that risks had to be taken if Britain was not to lose an entire army to Washington's forces, but both were men of such caution that they refused to engage unless the odds were heavily stacked their way. Cornwallis committed three mistakes of his own. Firstly, he made no attempt to break out of the trap on the landward side: in early September, as the American and the French armies were being ferried across Chesapeake Bay, he could probably have broken through Lafayette's army, even though it had been reinforced by Saint-Simon's 3,000 troops. Secondly, he failed to take advantage of the few British ships he had on the York River to ferry his men across to the British enclave in Gloucester that was held by Banastre Tarleton and his cavalry; to do so, of course, would have brought his own army out into the open, and Washington could have easily diverted his forces landing on the Yorktown Peninsula to catch him. Thirdly, and worst of all, he abandoned his outer defences across broken and difficult ground nearly a mile to the west of Yorktown, which would have taken several days for Washington to break through.

Cornwallis' inaction only made sense in the certainty that relief was close at hand. As Cornwallis put it to Clinton: 'Under all these circumstances, I thought it would have been wanton and inhuman to the last degree to sacrifice the lives of this small body of gallant soldiers, who had ever behaved with so much fidelity and courage, by exposing them to an assault which, from the numbers and precautions of the enemy, could not fail to succeed.'

In fact, he had every reason to feel confident, even in this dangerous situation. The British navy was still almost the equivalent of the French in size, having been only slightly damaged in the battle of Chesapeake Bay, and any competent commander should have been able to force his way into the bay, with its wide neck. Furthermore, as New York was now spared the danger of Washington's threatened attack, Clinton would surely fulfil his promise to come to Cornwallis' rescue with the large majority of his troops. Clinton even saw amongst the unfolding events an opportunity to trap the Americans and the French, who had at last been brought into the open, into a classic engagement which the British could hope to win.

As long as reinforcements seemed likely, Cornwallis regarded it as his duty to stay at Yorktown, conserving his army behind a defensive position rather than risking it out in the open against a currently far superior enemy force. He made a gross error of judgment in permitting himself no means of escape should reinforcements fail to arrive. It would not be the first time Clinton failed to arrive in time and relations between him and Graves were notoriously poor, hampering the effort to relieve Yorktown. In the event the relief expedition did not set out until the second week of October – a week later than Clinton had promised it would arrive.

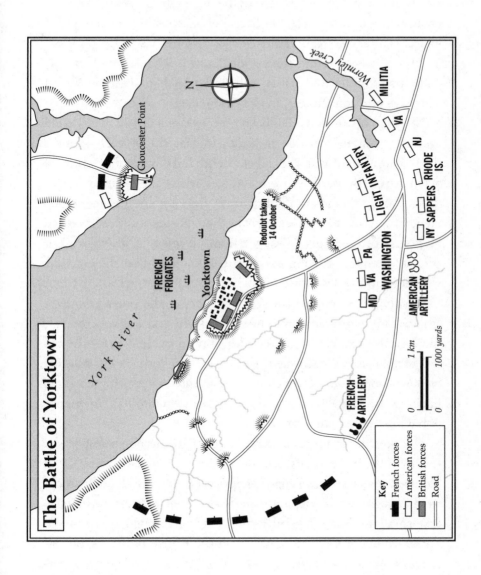

The Battle of Yorktown

Key
French forces
American forces
British forces
Road

Washington's combined American and French forces, who were in position to begin the siege on 28 September, were surprised at Cornwallis' rapid abandonment of the outer perimeter and his comparatively restrained defence thereafter. Cornwallis, in spite of his image as a reckless general, knew the deficiencies in his position. Yorktown was no more that a small town defended by a hastily built, half-constructed earth wall and trench and a handful of defensive positions. It was, in fact, wide open.

The siege of Yorktown has been portrayed as a classic of its period against a heavily fortified position. In fact the British defences there barely deserved the label. Behind its inadequate line of defence were sheltering some 8,800 men whose supplies were dwindling. Facing them was Washington's army totalling some 18,000 men, with at least 90 guns, many of them heavy, and the advanced French siege equipment brought from Newport. Both sides went through the motions, almost as a ritual, knowing that the outcome was inevitable unless relief came.

Washington occupied the four redoubts of the outer perimeter which had been abandoned by the British, and constructed two more of his own. He was obsessed by a need to close in for the kill before relief could reach the British from New York. 'A vigorous use of the means in our power cannot but ensure success,' he remarked impatiently. The Americans revelled in the unfamiliar experience of having their enemy at bay.

The French set up their main batteries to the northwest of the town, while the artillery was drawn up to the southwest. On 6 October, under cover of night, 4,300 American and French troops were brought up to the southwestern corner to start work on a first parallel – a 1,000-yard trench cutting through the south of Yorktown about 400 yards away from the British positions, out-of-range of all but the biggest cannon. The British guns had been blazing away at campfires set up as a decoy to one side. Washington himself ceremonially broke the first ground in the construction of the trench with a pickaxe.

The following morning, the earthwork and the trench were in place. By noon on 9 October the guns and emplacements were ready along the trench. Washington permitted a French gun, in recognition of the work done by the force of 600 French artillery-men present, to fire the first shot. With several 24-pounders in place against the smaller British guns, the contest was unequal from the first. All of Yorktown was well within range.

So accurate was the French and American fire that the British were forced to close down their guns by day and use them only at night, when their embrasures could not be seen. Most of the small British flotilla in the York River was destroyed in this first artillery assault. The following night, some 1,000 shells landed on Yorktown. But Cornwallis had not yet given up all hope. On the night of 11 October, American and French positions came under intense British fire. The spectacle of red-hot shot being lobbed through the night between the two sides was almost surreal. Considerable courage was displayed by the French and the Americans as they completed a second parallel just 300 yards from British lines. They were now able to blast away straight into the British positions. By this time Cornwallis had been driven out of the governor's house, which had been half-destroyed, and into a kind of cave by the riverside at the bottom of the garden.

Cornwallis now knew that it was almost over. Clinton's relief force was more than a week overdue. On the night of 14 October, the French were surprised at the British failure to counterattack. Cornwallis, as though merely going through the motions, obliged them the following night, sending 350 men under Abercromby to spike the American and French guns facing them. They gained control of the second parallel, killing and wounding 17 men and driving off the rest. However, they had only the time and means to jam bayonets into the touchholes of six guns instead of pouring liquid metal into them to disable them permanently before retreat-ing. When the Americans and the French returned, the spikes were removed without much difficulty.

The uneven bombardment resumed. With the British positions being pummelled to devastating effect by the superior French guns, now at point-blank range, the half-built British defences proved of little use. Cornwallis tried one last throw. On the night of 16 October, in a final, desperate bid to stage a breakout, he began to ferry his troops, in whatever boats he could muster, across the York River to Gloucester. Surprisingly, de Grasse had not yet closed off this escape, being wary of moving too far upriver. It was more astonishing perhaps that Cornwallis had not tried this before, but he had been slow to realize the impossibility of his position and the fact that help would not arrive in time. That night, after he had ferried 1,000 men across to Tarleton's enclave, a storm blew up, and he realized that it was hopeless; there would be too few troops to successfully break through the enemy lines outside Gloucester. When the storm abated, the troops there were rowed back to avoid unnecessary carnage.

At 1 a.m. on 17 October, a lone drummer appeared on the British defences and the cannonading stopped. Washington suspended the firing for two hours as Cornwallis sent his terms. Like Burgoyne, who had surrendered at Saratoga on the very same day five long years before, the British commander sought a negotiated surrender which would allow his men to be spared. Washington, who had objected to the first agreement (which had been subsequently reneged upon by Congress), refused and was in a strong position to dictate terms.

On 18 October representatives on both sides met to discuss the terms. Washington made them deliberately humiliating: the British were to come out with their colours folded up, they were to give up their arms and they were all to be treated as prisoners of war. Their drums were to play a British march, for fear they would try to mock an American tune, as had happened at Saratoga. They were given until 11 a.m. the next day to agree to these terms, or the murderous barrage would be resumed.

At 2 p.m. on 19 October the British filed out to the tune of 'The World Turned Upside Down'. Cornwallis snubbed Washington, though, claiming to be ill. Instead, he sent his second-in-command, Brigadier Charles O'Hara, who even more pointedly presented his sword to General Rochambeau at Washington's side, a gesture signifying that the British had been defeated by the French, not by the

Americans. Rochambeau pointed to the American commander. In a cold and controlled fury, Washington passed Cornwallis' subordinate on to Benjamin Lincoln, the American general defeated at the siege of Charleston, who ordered the British down a gauntlet of French troops on the left and American soldiers on the right to a field where, according to some witnesses, the British threw down their arms contemptuously.

The bitterness over, O'Hara was entertained cordially at dinner by Washington. Then, at last, Cornwallis appeared at a banquet in a field tent and addressed Washington with a double-edged compliment: 'When the illustrious part which your Excellency has borne in the long and arduous contest becomes a matter of history, fame will gather your brightest laurels from the banks of the Delaware rather than those of the Chesapeake.'

The aristocratic French officers present were generous to the defeated foe, fulfilling the best traditions of gentlemanly eighteenth-century warfare. Rochambeau loaned Cornwallis £10,000 while the Vicomte de Noailles lent him a popular book on tactics. None of these men could have known that Revolution would soon visit Europe, where the French aristocratic order would be swept away by a whirlwind of hatred far more severe, uncontrolled and violent than that which had spread across the 13 colonies.

Yorktown was the decisive victory in the American War of Independence. It was certainly the turning point. Yet Cornwallis' bitterness was not entirely ill-founded: it had been little more than a minor battle in terms of the casualties involved, with 156 killed and 326 wounded on the British side, and 75 killed and 200 wounded on the French and American side. However, more than 8,000 troops had surrendered – double the number at Saratoga. For the British army, it had been a humiliation almost without parallel. Famously, the British Prime Minister Lord North took the news 'like a bullet in his breast', exclaiming 'It is all over.' George III showed greater aplomb and sense of proportion: 'I have no doubt when men are a little recovered of the shock felt by the bad news, and feel that if we recede no one can tell to what a degree the consequence of this country will be diminished, that they will find the necessity of carrying on the war, though the mode of it may require alterations.'

Yorktown was the greatest strategic coup of the war. For the Americans and the French to have moved with such precision to take advantage of the enemy's strategic situation remains one of the greatest feats in military history. Cornwallis might well scoff at the battle itself; the real achievement had been Washington's rapid march of the allied forces across more than 450 miles of territory to trap him. The march on Yorktown was the culminating feat in a remarkable career, and established the greatness of George Washington in the field. Knowing the territory as well as he did, he was very much the leader of the joint expedition, as the French admiringly acknowledged.

The achievement showed him in his most attractive light: as in crossing the Delaware River, he was a man capable of great feats of boldness and daring, when he judged them to be appropriate. One of the greatest tests of military command, as of statesmanship, is to resist the clamour of all those about you to do something, but to move as swiftly as a panther when the opportunity presents itself. Washington had displayed caution bordering on inertia, year after year, and then he had suddenly sprung into action at the decisive moment to deliver a fatal blow to his enemy.

This was leadership of the very highest order, displaying self-control, patience, extraordinary good sense and – so rare in a man of this type – the ability to strike with lethal speed at exactly the right time. The campaign that led to Yorktown undoubtedly defined Washington's greatness as a general, even though the battle itself was militarily a limited one. To trap an enemy is arguably an even greater achievement than to defeat it in open battle, with great quantities of blood spilt, and this is what Washington achieved at Yorktown.

The British never recovered from the battle. They evacuated New York City, their final major stronghold, in November 1783 and Washington took possession of the city. He resigned his commission as commander-in-chief soon afterwards. In 1789, he was unanimously elected as the first president of the United States of America.

—∿—

Washington was outstanding in his courage under fire, his ability to think coolly and rationally on the battlefield and his seizing of opportunities such as the taking of Boston, crossing the Delaware and setting the trap at Yorktown. He also showed a fatherly devotion to his own men at Valley Forge and other grim winter quarters. He was skilful in selecting talented subordinates, although ruthless and jealous towards potential rivals. He proved to be good at command and masterful in his relations with Congress. Like Clive of India, he was an able political operator and, as president, a skilled administrator. In youth he had shown insubordination by rebelling against the British. He was a gifted guerrilla tactician although perhaps not so good in set-piece battles. Although something of a gilded youth, he had determination in spades and an ability to roll with the punches: his career was one with almost constant setbacks which he manfully overcame. He was, however, a ruthless disciplinarian who showed little penchant for fighting against superior odds and almost entirely lacked the qualities of charismatic leadership. However, he certainly passes muster as a maverick, a military genius and one of the last warriors – as well as one of America's greatest political leaders.

Chapter 4

NELSON: SAILOR SUPERSTAR

Horatio Nelson, possibly the most extraordinary fighter that Britain has ever produced, was born in provincial obscurity. He was born on 29 September 1758, the son of a well-to-do parson, Edmund Nelson, whose wife had aristocratic connections. She was related to Sir Robert Walpole, the British First Minister who was the dominant but corrupt statesman throughout the reigns of George I and George II. His son, Horace Walpole, fop, dilettante and creator of Strawberry Hill's Gothic architectural style, was Nelson's godfather, a powerful connection indeed.

When aged just 12, the boy Horatio, by common consent a forceful personality even in childhood, asked his uncle, Captain Maurice Suckling, whether he could serve on his ship which was due to see service against Spain in the dispute over the remote Falklands Islands in the South Atlantic. He was appointed midshipman, but the international crisis eased and he was posted under Suckling aboard a guard-ship in the Medway, the 74-gun *Triumph*.

As a middling son in a gentry family, Horatio would be expected to make his own way in life and the navy presented an attractive career for a resourceful boy. In academic studies at the respectable Royal Grammar School in Norwich, Horatio had shown little aptitude for academic work except in his written English, which was to show later in his despatches. As a midshipman aboard a formidably large two-deck ship of the line, he pursued a simple, spartan and unexceptional life of mundane duties while acquiring the skills of seamanship from the bottom; he also served aboard a merchant ship to acquire sailing experience.

In 1773, at the age of 14, he was granted his first adventure. The *Carcass* was due to sail to seek the fabled Northwest Passage across the top of America to the East Indies. The young midshipman begged his uncle Captain Suckling to be allowed to go on the expedition. The ship's captain, Skeffington Lutwidge, was a friend of Suckling; Horatio got his way. The journey took four months and brought Nelson within 10 degrees of the North Pole. Another midshipman vividly described the 24-foot ice wall which threatened to destroy the ship and the walrus to which they harnessed it to try and tow it to safety. The Northwest Passage went undiscovered, but it was an exciting expedition for the boy, who was given command of a cutter with 12 men and boasted of his navigational abilities. Later writers embroidered the journey with a supposed encounter between Horatio and a bear which he was supposed to have fought off with the butt of a musket.

On his return he was promoted to a frigate, the *Seahorse*, bound for the East Indies. He went on the fabled route across the Atlantic but was blown back by the trade winds to the Cape of Good Hope. He later formed a favourable impression of Trincomalee in Ceylon, visited the magnificent British settlements at Calcutta and Bombay and even sailed up the Persian Gulf to the fetid port of Basra.

The first significant event in his life occurred when he contracted malaria, which was to recur all his life, and was despatched on the six-month journey home, ailing and seemingly condemned to obscurity in his profession. He even voiced thoughts of committing suicide by throwing himself overboard (malaria is a notoriously depressive illness). He had already acquired the frail and delicate appearance that made others want to mother him but seemed so implausible in a hero. In his fevered state he experienced a curious conversion, believing that he would become 'a hero and confiding in Providence that I will brave every danger'. Intriguingly, Robert Clive of India had experienced such a call of destiny following his own failure as a young clerk to commit suicide with a pistol.

Horatio may have felt that, having escaped death, he was unafraid to brave it in future.

On his arrival back in Britain at the age of 17 in the summer of 1776, as the American colonies raised the banner of independence, he found his fortunes had changed dramatically for the better. Captain Suckling had been appointed to the key post of Controller of the Navy. His young protégé was promptly appointed acting lieutenant aboard the 64-gun *Worcester*, under Captain Mark Robinson, which sailed to Cadiz.

The keen young man evidently made a good impression and the following year he took his lieutenant's examination before three captains – the chairman of which, in a not uncommon display of nepotism in the supposedly egalitarian navy, was none other than Captain Suckling. He passed with flying colours and, unlike so many of his more frustrated peers, was immediately appointed second lieutenant aboard the 32-gun frigate *Lowestoffe*, under Captain William Locker.

By the age of 19, the young man had twice travelled halfway around the world to its coldest northern reaches and its most tropical equatorial climates, experienced a dozen of the world's ports and now, under the close patronage of a very senior naval figure, seemed embarked on a solid if unexceptional career.

Locker, as was his custom towards his younger officers, commissioned the first known portrait of the young Horatio. He emerges as slim and fresh-faced, with a delicate, almost feminine complexion and an expression of great sensitivity. His keen, alert eyes and his dominant nose are offset by the gentle lips and chin: at that tender age Horatio exuded a curious mixture of determination, intelligence and grace. He looked more like a foppish, art-loving young nobleman than a naval warrior.

Horatio tended to get on with his superiors and he and Locker hit it off right from the start. The young lieutenant admired Locker for his dictum 'Lay a Frenchman close and you will beat him' (which was reminiscent of his own advice to the young Thomas Cochrane years later: 'always go at 'em'). He was fearless from the start, his courage belying his slight frame. He was appointed to the Jamaica station, notorious for its tropical diseases, where he boarded a French privateer in a gale in his first real naval action; afterwards he admitted to his enjoyment of danger. Admiral Sir Peter Parker, the fleet commander in the West Indies, was an old friend of Horatio's uncle and took him aboard his flagship as third lieutenant, soon promoted to first. Sadly, Suckling died, but Parker took over as Horatio's mentor.

The war between Britain and France and its rebellious American allies was now under way. Horatio soon showed his mettle, taking part in the capture of three prizes of which he was entitled to a 32nd share, securing his first modest financial capital. In 1779 he was made master and commander of his first ship, the *Badger*, a small two-masted brigantine. With this he rescued the crew of a sloop which had been accidentally set on fire. Under Parker's patronage Horatio continued his effortless rise, being appointed to the coveted position of post-captain of the *Hinchinbrook* in June 1779. Still only 20, he was one of the youngest ever to reach this rank – a faster rise than either Samuel Hood or John Jervis, Lord St Vincent.

He was largely untested except as a promising seaman: he had never been in a significant engagement but, by being respectful, loyal, disciplined and a fine sailor, he clearly had an uncanny ability to impress his superiors. As promotion to admiral was merely a matter of seniority among post-captains, Nelson was now clearly in the fast stream to the top. He was the same age as his near-contemporary William Pitt when the latter first became a member of parliament. Another contemporary, Napoleon Bonaparte, was then aged just 10 and, when he reached the same age, was still no more than an obscure lieutenant dabbling in the even obscurer politics of his native island, Corsica.

Due to illness and to his bitter disappointment, Nelson was unable to take up his new command, the *Janus*, a 44-gun frigate. He was shipped back to Britain once more and sent to convalesce at Bath, where he spent months recovering. It was a terrible setback for a man with an apparently golden staircase to the top. He had still not seen any significant action. He reflected that his 'dream of glory' would yet be fulfilled: 'It is the climate that has destroyed my health and cowed my spirit.'

In the autumn of 1791, while still not yet in full health, he was given a new command: the 32-gun *Albermarle*, a French prize of unprepossessing appearance. Still less promising was his mission: dull escort duty for convoys of merchant ships in the Baltic and the North Sea. His ship was accidentally rammed by a merchant ship in a gale and was only just saved. It was now despatched on convoy duty to Quebec. There, at last, he ran into the enemy: he was pursued by five French ships of the line and a frigate for 10 hours before, in a superb display of seamanship, he eluded them in fog and crossed the shoals of St George's Bay where the larger ships could not follow.

In Quebec, too, he first experienced his other great pleasure. He fell in love with the daughter of the provost marshal of the garrison, the 16-year-old Mary Simpson. When he was ordered to New York – perhaps because her father disapproved – he displayed his romantic streak by threatening to disobey the command in order to stay with her. In New York, his old talent for ingratiating himself with his superiors did not desert him and Admiral Hood, another old friend of Suckling, took an immediate shine to him, although he turned down the 24-year-old's extraordinarily ambitious request to command a ship of the line.

Hood later gave him command of the small 28-gun frigate *Boreas*, which was just back from the West Indies. Arriving in Barbados in the summer of 1784, just after the conclusion of the final peace with France, Nelson fell into the parochial bitchiness that is typical of expatriate military duty at peace. For once, he took an instant dislike to his superior, Admiral Sir Richard Hughes; flirted openly with the Governor of Antigua's pretty young wife, Mary Moutray; and admirably led a one-man crusade against local merchants who were illegally trading with the now independent American colonies. In the latter, at least, he showed integrity and courage.

Having offended almost everyone he could in this peaceful small-town backwater, he met Fanny Nisbet, the daughter of a prominent local judge, who was a young widow with a five-year-old son. One of Fanny's friends vividly described the young Horatio Nelson in a letter to her:

> It was impossible, during this visit, for any of us to make out his real character; there was such a reserve and sternness in his behaviour, with occasional sallies, though very transient, of a superior mind. Being placed by him, I endeavoured to rouse his attention by showing him all the civilities in my power; but I drew out of him little more than yes and no. If you, Fanny, had been there, we think you would have made something of him; for you have been in the habit of attending to these odd sort of people.

By the summer of 1785, Nelson was plainly infatuated by Fanny, declaring that to live in a cottage with her would be like living in a palace with anyone else, and writing passionate letters to her. She was a petite, dark-haired, nervous young woman, graceful and good-looking, but whose shyness and reticence were to gain her, unfairly, a reputation for coldness. At the time, she was housekeeper to her mother's brother, John Herbert, the wealthy president of the island council, descended from the distinguished Herberts of Powys and Pembroke.

He begged Herbert for her hand, but the rich old man counselled delay. Nelson was a highly promising, if rather odd, young man, yet in poor health and someone who had upset the local establishment. It was unsurprising that Herbert thought this impecunious captain something of a comedown for his beloved niece who belonged to the most prominent family on the island and would one day inherit his fortune.

Nelson found himself with the task of escorting Prince William, who had been appointed captain of the frigate *Pegasus* at the age of 21. William was soon at odds with his ship's officers and regarded Nelson as his best friend as he careered around the Leeward Islands in search of amusement. As Nelson complained:

> How vain are human hopes. I was in hopes to have been quiet all this week. Today we dine with Sir Thomas [Shirley], tomorrow the prince

has a party, on Wednesday he gives a dinner in St John's to the regiment, in the evening is a mulatto ball, on Thursday a cock fight, dine
at Col Crosbie's brother's and a ball, and on Friday somewhere but I
forget, on Saturday at Mr Byam's the president [of Antigua]... Some
are born for attendance on great men, I rather think that is not my
particular province.

The Prince acted as best man at Nelson's wedding when it finally
took place on 11 March 1787 at Herbert's extensive house,
Montpelier. It was celebrated with an enormous banquet and ball
attended by 200 people.

When William angrily upbraided a highly experienced first lieutenant over a trifle, Nelson took the Prince's side. The Prince travelled to Jamaica, where the fleet captain gently rebuked him for his
reprimand of the first lieutenant and refused to hold a court martial
which would have been embarrassing to the fleet – something the
ingratiating Nelson should have done in the first place. The offend-
ing first lieutenant was promoted to Hood's flagship, a calculated
snub to the Prince.

Nelson, who was suffering from one of his periodic bouts of ill-
health, had at the time turned into something of a disciplinarian,
flogging three of his men with two-dozen lashes for using mutinous
language – a very severe punishment. He then sentenced another
man to death for desertion, but the sentence was not carried out.
On his return to Britain he had another 14 crewmen flogged. By
the time he had paid off the men on his ship, the *Boreas*, he had
ordered the flogging of 61 of its 142 crew – a huge proportion for
the time.

In Britain, Nelson continued to fawn on Prince William, which
won him no favours with the Admiralty. Together with his brothers, the Prince of Wales and the Duke of York, William was seen to
be opposing William Pitt's government more or less openly, much
to the irritation of his father, the King.

Nelson constantly badgered his superiors for a ship but obtained
none: this was peacetime and few were available. Moreover, he was
regarded for the first time with disfavour as an undiplomatic young

man who had offended just about every vested interest in the West Indies, associated too closely with Prince William and had risen above his station. He had seen little action, been promoted largely through connection, and, apart from a few minor skirmishes and a few acts of seamanship, he was anything but a hero. There were many others with far better claims. No doubt his disciplinarian streak did not go unnoticed: it was regarded with approval by some, disapproval by others. Both Lord Richard Howe and Lord Samuel Hood of the Admiralty were pestered with demands for a ship for Nelson, which annoyed them. Angrily Nelson contemplated entering the service of the Tsar of Russia as a mercenary.

Meanwhile, he introduced his wife to his father, Edward, who got on famously with the modest, charming and beautiful young bride. Seven-year-old Josiah, her son, went to school in Norfolk. Nelson was to spend another three years in Norfolk, bombarding the Admiralty with demands for a ship – even a cockleboat, he remarked caustically.

After his own dazzling start, Nelson had to wait until the beginning of 1793, when he was aged 34, for another chance to prove himself. He was given command of the *Agamemnon*, a fine 64-gun ship, the smallest of the line, as war with France inexorably approached. Meanwhile, Nelson had succeeded to modest wealth, having inherited £4,000 from an uncle. Josiah, his stepson, was appointed a midshipman aboard the *Agamemnon*. He left Fanny in order to captain his new ship to Cadiz and then sailed to the French port of Toulon.

The people of Toulon had rebelled against the French revolutionary government and Hood, Nelson's commander, offered them his protection. Nelson was despatched to seek troops from the court of Naples, which was allied to Britain. There, he first made the acquaintance of the boorish King Ferdinand IV, his formidable queen, Maria Carolina, and the British ambassador, Sir William Hamilton. The young British captain was received in state and dined with the King, who lent him the 4,000 soldiers he sought. He and young Josiah stayed six days in the fabulous but decadent court at the dazzlingly splendid place at Caserta.

Nelson was entranced to meet Hamilton's wife, Emma, a celebrated beauty who, as Nelson wrote to his wife innocently, had been 'wonderfully kind and good to Josiah. She is a young woman of amiable manners who does honour to the station to which she is raised.' This may be a reference to her humble origins as a blacksmith's daughter who had mothered an illegitimate child at 16 and had been mistress to several men of importance, including the painter George Romney, who painted her fresh sensuousness frequently. It was rare in those days for marriage to a member of the lower orders not to attract social opprobrium; possibly she had succeeded because of her beauty and charm, and the ease with which she fitted into upper-class society. She danced beautifully, spoke Italian and French and became Queen Maria Carolina's best friend. The middle-aged captain was enchanted.

Returning to Toulon, Nelson was despatched to establish a British naval base on the island of Corsica where, to his dismay, he learned that Toulon had been regained by the French thanks to the enterprise of a daring young French artillery officer, Napoleon Bonaparte, although the name would barely have registered with the British officer. Nelson ordered his sailors to disembark in Corsica and set up guns outside the port of Bastia, which was bombarded and blockaded by sea. Towards the end of May 1794 the town surrendered.

Nelson now repeated the feat at Calvi, but was twice wounded by enemy fire; his right eye was blinded by splinters in the second attack. Some consider his fearlessness reflected a morbid death wish; in fact, Nelson and many other officers considered that exposing oneself to the same dangers as the men was an essential part of leadership; if there was any unusual psychological element it is that Nelson, unlike most men, felt entirely calm under fire and possibly even relished the heat of battle, as so many natural warriors have in the past.

Calvi surrendered in August 1794. The army commander, Colonel John Moore, an extremely able officer, later asserted that both ports could have been taken by simple blockade – this was possibly an excuse for his own caution. Nelson and Hood claimed the credit. The former, by his ceaseless activity and reckless bravery, had taken the chance to demonstrate what a leader of men he could be under fire and had somewhat redeemed the setback suffered with the loss of Toulon.

In March 1795, near Genoa, he experienced fleet action, pursuing the French two-decker *Ça Ira* along with 15 lesser warships. The *Agamemnon*, the fastest ship in the 14-strong British fleet under the Mediterranean command of Admiral William Hotham, caught up with the *Ça Ira*, which was already being fired upon by a small British frigate, the *Inconstant*, and skilfully manoeuvred to stay out of range before coming up to deliver a full broadside, thus disabling the French ship.

Nelson continued to fire upon her until other French ships came to the rescue, while the rest of the British fleet in the meantime hurried up to reinforce him. Soon both the *Ça Ira* and another French ship struck their colours. Some 350 men were killed or wounded aboard the French ships, compared to just 13 aboard Nelson's own.

—*◦∿◦*—

By the beginning of 1797, Britain's predicament was truly appalling. Napoleon was on his final mopping-up operation in Italy and about to inflict the blow that would knock Austria out of the war. That would leave Britain with just one ally on the entire European continent – small, loyal Portugal. Meanwhile, the British had been all but expelled from the Mediterranean with the fall of Corsica: only the troops that had been taken from the island to Elba remained, along with the outposts of Malta, Minorca and Gibraltar.

The fate of the British was now to rest decisively in the hands of two very different men. The first was a small man with an elfin, sardonic, bitter expression, a cunning squashed rodent face at once harsh, determined and slightly humorous. Sir John Jervis, who was to become the 1st Earl of St Vincent and was known as 'Black Jack', was one of the most feared and detested commanders in the navy, known for his unbending love of discipline as for his tongue-lashing of subordinates. He seemed to possess a cruel, even sadistic streak: he once ordered all his fleet's chaplains aboard his flagship in a gale – merely to summon these wretched and scared men to a routine meeting. He would make junior officers bow low before him – 'lower, sir, lower' – for his own amusement. He resorted frequently to the lash and the death sentence. The second man was Horatio Nelson, who had been given the dangerous duty of evacuating the British troops on Elba with just two frigates, the *Minerve* and the *Blanche*.

As Nelson set off on 19 December 1796, he ran into Spanish frigates at nearly midnight. He called, 'This is an English frigate,' and told the captain of one of the Spanish boats to surrender. A voice shouted back with a Scottish accent, 'This is a Spanish frigate, and you may begin as soon as you please.' The captain was a descendant of the Stuart dynasty. A furious gun-battle ensued. Nelson three times offered a ceasefire in exchange for surrender and received the answer 'Not while I can fire a gun.' After some 90 minutes the two Spanish ships struck their colours, but being in Spanish waters, another Spanish frigate had heard the noise of the cannon and was upon Nelson. He had to cast off his prize and engage the third boat, but at dawn he saw two huge Spanish battleships approaching. Heavily outgunned, he had no choice but to run before them for a whole day.

On eventually reaching Elba, he performed his task of taking off the island garrison and then returned to Gibraltar on 9 January 1797, where he learned that the Spanish fleet had slipped the British blockade and was heading out into the Atlantic. He set off to join the main fleet on 11 January, but was soon pursued by two Spanish ships of the line.

At that moment one of the *Minerve's* sailors fell overboard, and a boat commanded by Lieutenant Thomas Masterman Hardy was lowered to go to the rescue. The boat was quickly swept away by the tide and Nelson had to decide whether to abandon his men or go to their rescue and risk coming within range of the huge ships chasing him. He decided to pick up his men. The Spanish ships, seeing to their amazement the British ship backtracking, were confused, wondering whether a trap was being sprung with some as yet unseen British ships lurking over the horizon: why else would a tiny ship sail directly towards two huge ones? They held back while the *Minerve*, having picked up the little boat, returned to its former course.

Then the chase was on again. When night fell, Nelson ordered all the lights to be hidden and changed course suddenly: he thus threw off his pursuers. He was congratulating himself on the coup as the ship rolled in a gentle swell beneath the stars. It then became apparent that the stars were rather too low: they were ships' lights. It was too late to engage in any manoeuvre that might draw attention to his ship in the dark: he was in the middle of the missing 30-ship Spanish fleet. He was astonished to observe it sailing south and imagined it was heading for the West Indies, so he tagged along during the night to sense its direction, taking the colossal risk of detection and annihilation or capture. Abruptly, the fleet changed course west after Nelson had watched a barrage of signal lights being exchanged in the gloom. Still pretending to be part of the fleet, the *Minerve* skilfully drifted away, with its lights hidden, to report the Spanish fleet's direction to Jervis.

Nelson returned at last to the British fleet. It was stationed on the barren southwestern extremity of Portugal off Cape St Vincent (São Vicente), which was dominated by an old fort at the very tip of continental western Europe. In the winter roll of the Atlantic, with thousands of miles of ocean extending to the west, it is a particularly bleak place.

Nelson reported directly to the acerbic older man and then raised his flag aboard the *Captain*. That night the signal guns of the Spanish fleet were sounding eerily off to the southwest. In the morning, a thick mist blocked the view of both fleets. It was a tense moment, one that would be crucial to the war. If Britain lost, the way would be open for the enemy to command the Channel and ultimately to the invasion of Britain.

The mist suddenly lifted to reveal one of the most awesome and picturesque fleets ever assembled, a floating township of thousands of men. There were no fewer than 27 Spanish battleships; including the biggest ever made, the four-decker, 212-gun *Santissima Trinidad*, six three-deckers with 112 guns each, two 80-gun vessels and 17 74-gun ships. In terms of firepower, it was perhaps the greatest armada ever hitherto assembled. With a low swell that morning, the sight of this colossal fleet of baroque castles gently bobbing in the western Atlantic left the British sailors speechless with awe. Nelson described the ships as 'the finest in the world [but] the Spaniards, thank God, cannot build men'. There was a deathly calm about the whole scene, while Jervis' fleet continued to observe strict silence.

On paper, the strength of the Spanish fleet was overwhelming: it had a total of 2,292 guns compared to the 1,332 guns of the 15-strong British fleet. Yet compared to the extremely tight formation of the latter – Nelson remarked, in a rare tribute, 'of all the fleets I ever saw I never beheld one in point of officers and men equal to Sir John Jervis's' – the Spanish lines were straggly and ill-ordered. Perhaps they had never expected the British to be so near.

Jervis soon spotted a weakness in the Spanish defence: the six ships at the rear were several hundred yards away from the main fleet. If he could cut through the gap, the six would be at his mercy. He signalled from his flagship, the *Victory*, and the two perfectly ordered British lines – each ship at an equal distance from the other – quickly formed a single line.

With Thomas Troubridge in the *Culloden* leading, they made at full canvas for the gap; the *Victory* was in seventh place and Nelson's *Captain* was in 13th, nearly at the rear, a position held by Cuthbert Collingwood in the *Excellent*. The six isolated Spanish ships sought desperately to tack against the wind and rejoin their main fleet, which was also trying to close the gap. At about the time the *Culloden* reached the gap, the Spanish vice-admiral's ship, the 113-gun *Principe de Asturias*, veered round into a position where it faced the seventh ship – Jervis' own *Victory* – in the British line which was severing the Spanish fleet in two. A tremendous broadside from the British ship raked the Spanish one, which with-drew hastily to leeward.

Just ahead, three ships from the main Spanish fleet had slipped past the point of the British spearhead. Nine Spanish ships were now isolated from the main fleet. They were to leeward of the British and were reluctant to do battle with a far superior force: they were effectively out of the fight, and now sailed off in head-long flight. The odds between the main fleets were now much more even: 18 Spanish ships to 15 British ones.

As the Spanish fleet turned with the wind to try and escape past the tail of the British line, Troubridge tacked skilfully from his southwesterly course to a northerly one. Nelson, in one of the two rearmost ships, spotted the Spanish manoeuvre, which would per-mit the whole fleet to escape past the back of the British line before Troubridge could lead it back up. Nelson threw the rule book to the winds and broke the British line, steering the *Captain* in a reverse course around the ships immediately behind and crossing the front of Collingwood's *Excellent* to try and intercept the fleeing Spanish fleet. He was set on engaging the biggest ships leading the entire Spanish fleet in an attempt to delay them while the British fleet could come up to attack. The *Excellent* followed his example by breaking the line.

The flag captain of Jervis' *Victory*, seeing this blatant flouting of orders, was outraged and insisted that a signal be sent to recall them, but Jervis, usually the most punctilious and disciplinarian of men, had realized what they were doing and refused. The little *Captain* found itself facing the main body of the entire Spanish fleet. It was headed by the four-decked *Santissima Trinidad* itself, flanked by two 112-gun ships, the *San Josef* and the *Salvador del Mundo*, each larger than Jervis' own flagship, with three 80-gun ships immediately following them: the *Captain* seemed destined to become matchwood before these behemoths as they bore down on it.

Undaunted, Nelson made straight for the *Santissima Trinidad*, all guns blazing. For nearly an hour the little ship endured the simulta-neous fire of six much bigger ships, but many of the shots went wide and hit other Spanish ships. Soon the *Captain* was reduced to a floating hulk, but Collingwood furiously engaged one of its tormentors and compelled it to surrender before moving upon the next, the *San Nicholas*, and from a distance of just 10 feet gave her 'the most awful and tremendous fire', as Nelson wrote.

The Spanish fleet began to veer away, perhaps out of astonishment at the boldness of the attack by just two small ships. At that moment Troubridge's *Culloden*, leading the British line on its new northwest course, reached the scene of the fighting and the battle swept past Nelson's disabled *Captain*. Even in this condition he renewed the attack on the nearest ship, the 80-gun *San Nicholas*, which had been dismasted. The British sailors swarmed up the remaining masts and spars of the *Captain* in order to drop aboard the *San Nicholas'* deck, which towered above the smaller British ship; others grabbed the Spanish ship's cable. Nelson himself broke through a window on the lower deck. The leader of the British boarders on the upper deck furiously cut down the Spaniards facing him and then enterprisingly hauled down the Spanish colours as officers began to surrender to him.

Down below, the Spanish guns were still firing at a nearby British ship, the *Prince George*, while another Spanish giant, the *San Josef* on the other side of the *San Nicholas*, was crammed with marines firing their muskets at the British boarders. Nelson ordered his men to stand by the hatchways with their muskets to prevent the still-fighting Spaniards below from pouring on to the deck, and then summoned a boarding party to attack the *San Josef*, which was passing just six feet away and was in turn being raked by the muskets of the British marines.

Nelson climbed up the ropes of the *San Josef* and was astonished to encounter a Spanish officer announcing surrender – their admiral had been hit and was dying. The British captain made the officers hand over their swords. As Collingwood later wrote: 'On the deck of the Spanish first-rate San Josef he received the swords of the officers of the two ships, while a Johnny, one of the sailors, bundled them up with the same composure he would have made a faggot, and twenty-two of their line still within gunshot!'

Nelson had captured a 112-gun enemy three-decker by raiding across the deck of an 80-gun Spanish three-decker from his own much smaller two-decker: the feat became known as 'Nelson's patent bridge for boarding first-rates'. Meanwhile, the missing leeward flotilla of Spanish ships had veered round to attempt to rejoin the main Spanish fleet. Jervis formed a line to prevent the junction and protect the four Spanish ships he had taken as prizes, as well as the disabled *Captain*. By this stage, the Spanish fleet had had enough. Headed by the limping *Santissima Trinidad*, it made for Cadiz.

Nelson now had to face a foe every bit as dangerous as the Spanish: the wrath of the disciplinarian Jervis for so blatantly flouting the fleet's orders. As he climbed wearily and apprehensively aboard the *Victory*, with part of his hat blown away by shot, he was astonished to find the usually bitter, sarcastic and unemotional Jervis rush forward to embrace him. The disapproving flag captain reminded the admiral that Nelson had disobeyed orders. 'He certainly did,' exclaimed Jervis. 'And if you ever commit such a break of orders I will forgive you also.'

Jervis thus established his immortality as a man who recognized boldness and genius when he saw it, even though the rules were flouted. Later, it was said that Nelson alone had saved the day and that Jervis had been largely out of the battle. This was untrue – the latter had headed straight for the fight and had initiated the first engagement with a Spanish ship; he had also shown speed in veering his ships around when the Spaniards nearly outmanoeuvred him to return to the battle. Above all, he had displayed the boldness to engage a far superior fleet, while traditionally admirals would decline battle unless the odds were much more even. Nelson was later to turn this into an art form, but Jervis had shown the way. Finally, for all his severity, Jervis' obsession with order had ensured a perfect formation and clockwork manoeuvring by his fleet. He was rewarded with the title Earl of St Vincent.

When, soon after the Battle of Cape St Vincent, it was learnt that Spanish treasure ships with some £6m in bullion were to dock at

Tenerife, Nelson, now a rear-admiral, promptly suggested that the island should be seized. This was no easy task. On 21 July 1797 he set out with a force of around 1,000 sailors and marines and launched a surprise attack at night, commanded by his friend Thomas Troubridge, on the capital, Santa Cruz. However, a gale arose when they were still a mile from shore and as dawn broke they were compelled to return. On the following day they succeeded in landing and climbed a hill opposite the citadel, but again retired without achievement.

On 24 July, Nelson himself led the attack – which as a rear-admiral and flag officer broke with precedent and placed his life in danger. It is easy to see why he was so impatient after previous failures. He later wrote: 'Had I been with the first party, I have reason to believe complete success would have crowned our endeavours... My pride suffered; and although I felt the second attack a forlorn hope, yet the honour of our country called for the attack, and that I should command it. I never expected to return, and am thankful.'

The now-alerted enemy had some 8,000 troops on the island, instead of the few hundred the British believed, and were in command of a heavily fortified citadel: the enterprise was doomed from the start. Some of the boats containing Nelson and his 600 men missed the pier in the night darkness and were smashed into splinters by the surge. A cutter, the *Fox*, was destroyed by Spanish fire from some 40 cannon and nearly 100 men were lost. The remainder of the men scrambled ashore and were raked with fire from the citadel, although they succeeded in capturing a convent.

Nelson and Captain Thomas Fremantle commanded two of the boats that succeeded in finding the pier – only to discover that it lay directly beneath the citadel from whence came a withering burst of fire. Grapeshot shattered Nelson's right arm as he stepped ashore. Josiah, his stepson, improvised a tourniquet and Nelson was rowed out to the *Theseus* where his arm was amputated.

Meanwhile, the remainder of the force was still without means of evacuation. Troubridge, Nelson's second-in-command, attempted to bluff his way, declaring that, unless boats were found to lift his men off safely, the town would be bombarded from the sea and attacked by the British force ashore. When this was met by no response, Lord Samuel Hood cannonaded the town until the island's governor offered to help them evacuate and to provide supplies to the ships.

Nelson bore his terrible wound and the failure of the expedition bravely, although he feared it would be the end of his career: no one, he believed, would have any use for a left-handed admiral.

Nelson was allowed to return home after more than four years at sea and was reunited with his wife and father at Bath. He had changed hugely: with his missing arm, white hair, frail frame and blind eye, he was almost unrecognizable. The face was no longer pampered and immature. While his good eye continued to blaze forth with determination and stern impatience, his cheekbones were more prominent and his nose had become the rudder of a thinner, hungrier visage. His mouth was now pursed and tight-lipped and the slight curl of arrogance, even cruelty, of the later portraits had made its appearance, which made him all the more attractive to women.

If his daring success at Cape St Vincent had made him a name familiar across England, the disaster at Tenerife, which should have destroyed his career for its recklessness and inadequate preparation, cemented his reputation as a great national hero. The perception of the dashing, fearless seaman who had led his men into battle under murderous fire and was now armless, his sleeve pinned to his uniform, with a patch slung, pirate-like, over one eye (he never in fact wore one) had come to stay. In a country desperately in need of popular heroes – the army had furnished none yet – it was an incredibly romantic image.

Despite his disabilities, Nelson was given a ship, the *Vanguard*, as soon as he was fit enough for service. In March 1798, with Edward Berry as his flag captain, he set sail to rejoin Lord St Vincent, who assigned him command of a Mediterranean squadron to discover why the French were assembling a huge fleet in great secrecy at

Toulouse. On the way the *Vanguard* nearly foundered in a storm. Nelson's new maturity, after the loss of his arm, was enshrined in a letter to Fanny: 'Figure to yourself a vain man on Sunday evening at sunset walking in his cabin with a squadron about him who looked up to their chief to lead them to glory... Figure to yourself this proud conceited man, when the sun rose on Monday morning his ship dismasted, his fleet dispersed and himself in such distress that the meanest frigate out of France would have been a very unwelcome guest.'

More seriously, however, the three fast frigates accompanying Nelson, which were his most effective means of scouting out the French fleet, had disappeared in the storm. They were crucial to his reconnaissance of the Mediterranean to find the French fleet. 'Were I to die at this moment, want of frigates would have been stamped on my heart,' he remarked. He had been given orders to do virtually as he pleased in order to destroy the French Mediterranean fleet, but all he had left were three battleships now that he had lost the frigates.

British intelligence was lamentably defective as to the destination of the huge fleet being prepared at Toulon. To confuse the British, the French had dubbed the fleet the 'Left Wing of the Army of England'. A French newspaper had deliberately hinted that the force was being prepared for an attack on Britain or Ireland, and it seemed likely that the idea was to link up with the Brest fleet beforehand. *The Times* considered Portugal or Ireland the most likely targets. Pitt himself opined on 31 May 1798 that the destination was Ireland.

However, the suspicion was beginning to dawn on the acutely intelligent Nelson that the French were destined for Egypt. In June, learning that the French had given him the slip from Toulon, he travelled down to Naples, where the ever-welcoming Sir William Hamilton had intelligence that the French had gone to Malta. Nelson wrote, with his usual naval insight, 'I shall believe that they are going on their scheme of possessing Alexandria, and getting troops to India – a plan concerted with Tippoo Sahib, by no means so difficult as might at first view be imagined... Be they bound for the Antipodes, Your Lordship may rely that I will not lose a moment in bringing them to action, and endeavour to destroy their transports.'

So the *pas de deux* began between two evenly matched fighters, Nelson and Napoleon. Both were men who lusted after glory to the point of insanity and were fearless, impetuous, decisive and ruthlessly convinced of their mission. It was to be the only duel between the two men that ever occurred in person. They knew each other by reputation, which in neither case was as inflated as it was later to become.

Having at last divined the French intention, Nelson turned to attack. Believing the French fleet to be no more than six days' sailing time ahead, he crowded on the canvas. On 20 June 1798, he pushed through the Strait of Messina between Italy and Sicily; the French armada was about 160 miles away. Napoleon, to his consternation, learnt of the presence of a new, reinforced British fleet moving towards the eastern Mediterranean and set off towards Crete to baffle his pursuers.

On nearly parallel eastward courses, the two fleets, one immense, the other compact, came within a few tantalizing miles of each other on the night of 22 June, which was shrouded in dense fog. The smaller British fleet, under as much sail as it could raise, simply cruised past the cumbersome, slow-moving French armada with its vulnerable troop transports, which would almost certainly have been annihilated had they been discovered. It proved to be an incredible stroke of luck for the French.

At Alexandria, Nelson was dismayed to find that the French fleet was not there and gave the order to sail west, back to Sicily. He did not realize that he had merely arrived too early. On the very same evening that the British sailed away, the French finally arrived off the port. Napoleon, well aware of the danger to his expedition every day his army stayed aboard ship with a hostile British fleet cruising around the area, ordered its disembarkation with characteristic speed and impetuousness on 1 July.

At first it seemed that Horatio Nelson had been made to look a fool: his career appeared about to plunge again as it became apparent that the French fleet had completely eluded him. After the disappointing, frenzied chase, Nelson now lapsed inexplicably into inertia while having his ships revictualled at Siracusa. It was surely his duty to resume the chase as quickly as possible – to find out whether the French fleet had indeed gone west or remained in the eastern Mediterranean rather than dawdle for three weeks at anchor. His newly acquired golden touch seemed to have faded. Nelson did not leave Siracusa until 23 July 1798 to resume his fruitless search, travelling eastwards again, directly towards the Peloponnese. Five days later, he at last heard reliable news that the French fleet was at Alexandria and sailed south.

At 2.45 p.m. on 1 August, a lookout from the masthead of the *Zealous* shouted that he had spotted a huge line of topmasts against the sky. Its captain signalled the news to Nelson in his flagship, the *Vanguard*. Instantly, he threw off his depression. He summoned his officers to dinner and declared that the following morning he would either be in the House of Lords or Westminster Abbey.

With a favourable following wind, he ordered his captains to proceed under full sail to attack the French fleet. He later recalled:

> When I saw them [the French ships] I could not help popping my head every now and then out of the window (although I had a damned toothache) and once, as I was observing their position, I heard two seamen quartered at a gun near me, talking, and one said to the other, 'Damn them, look at them. There they are, Jack, if we don't beat them, they will beat us'. I knew what stuff I had under me so I went into the attack with a few ships only, perfectly sure that the others would follow me, although it was nearly dark and they might have had every cause for not doing it, yet they all in the course of two hours found a hole to poke in at.

Only at around 4 p.m., as the British fleet approached under full sail, did the astonished French admiral, François-Paul Brueys d'Aigailliers, realize Nelson's intention to attack at once. Brueys summoned his three senior admirals to discuss whether to meet the British at sea or at anchor. The arguments for staying at anchor prevailed: the French crews were inexperienced and could not be expected to sail and fight at the same time; the ships had only provisions for a day and could not escape into the Mediterranean; and three of the French battleships were anyway in poor condition.

The two foremost British ships, the *Zealous* under Lord Samuel Hood and the *Goliath* under Thomas Foley, were in a race to be the first to engage. The *Goliath* ran up its staysails and suddenly pushed forward, taking the lead. Foley had a captured, although inaccurate, French chart and did not pause to make soundings as he aimed for the narrow gap between Aboukir Island and the foremost French ship, the *Guerrier*.

The mortars on the island opened up, but their range fell short. At 6.30 p.m., the sun was just beginning to set spectacularly fast off the Egyptian coast, the giant red ball visibly disappearing beneath the horizon, when Foley gave the order to fire as he arched around the *Guerrier* and an overwhelming broadside rocked the French ship. Foley put out his anchor to stop the *Goliath*'s momentum, but it failed to 'bite' into the sea floor and the *Goliath* shot past to stop opposite the *Conquerant*, the second ship in the French line.

The French admiral in charge of the vanguard, still on his way back from his meeting with Brueys, waved frantically at his captains to open fire – which they were reluctant to do without orders. By the time they did, the second British ship, the *Zealous*, was in place to rake the unfortunate *Guerrier* with another broadside. The French response was lamentable: they had not even managed to run out most of their guns.

The *Orion* followed the other two British ships on their outside, dangerously close to the shoals, and slipped in to engage the French. A French frigate had the temerity to open fire on it, and was destroyed with a single broadside from the *Orion*, which had also raked the *Guerrier* for a third time, bringing down its remaining mast and leaving it a wreck. The *Orion* engaged two ships simultaneously.

The *Theseus* came next. It once again poured shot into the *Guerrier* and then navigated the small channel between the British and French ships between broadsides, exchanging fire with the latter before curving around the *Orion* to engage another French ship; this was flawless seamanship of the highest order. The French guns' elevation was aimed at the other British ships, so the *Theseus* took advantage to run under the arch of the shot. Another British ship followed on the inside.

Nelson, in his flagship the *Vanguard*, was next and led the way down the outside of the French line to engage its third ship, the *Spartiate*, which was already under attack from the *Theseus*, between two fires. Pounded by a combined total of 148 guns, the ship quickly surrendered. The *Bellerophon*, behind the *Vanguard*, found itself in the already fallen darkness engaging the huge French flagship, *L'Orient*, which had 120 guns. The British ships could be distinguished in the darkness by the four horizontal lights on the mizzen peak.

Two of the *Bellerophon's* masts fell under the intense fire from *L'Orient*, which set her on fire three times and killed a third of the crew before she drifted off, crippled, to port. Immediately, three more British ships took up the fight against the deadly three-decker. The brave but devastated *Guerrier* had by now struck her colours, as had two other French ships, the *Conquerant* and the *Spartiate*, attacked by Nelson.

Nelson had once again been seriously wounded, an inch of skin falling from his brow over his good eye, with blood pouring down his face. 'I am killed,' he said. 'Remember me to my wife.' He was carried below for treatment. The French admiral, Brueys, was also injured. No sooner had he dismasted the *Bellerophon* than he was nearly cut in two by a cannonball at 7.30 p.m. He refused to go to the infirmary so that he might die on the bridge.

Meanwhile, disaster had struck a British ship, the *Culloden*, commanded by Sir Thomas Troubridge, regarded as second only to Nelson in the British fleet. He had sailed too close to Aboukir Island and ran aground. With two British ships out of action compared to three French, the battle was far from won.

Then, under fire from three much smaller ships, it became apparent that the giant *L'Orient* was ablaze. Some historians allege, based on a second-hand story from the poet Samuel Taylor Coleridge, that phosphorous firecrackers had been thrown on to the deck by the British, but this would have been very difficult to achieve with the three-decker French ship towering over the British ships. Also, it was the French rather than the British that carried phosphorous firecrackers. The French believed that oil cans left behind by painters started the fire.

At about 10 p.m., after fighting the fire for well over an hour, Honoré Ganteaume, who had succeeded Admiral Brueys, gave the order to abandon ship. A nine-year-old boy who refused to leave his injured father, Captain Casabianca, was immortalized in verse as the 'boy stood on the burning deck whence all but he had fled'. The colossal ship blew up a few minutes later, at about 10.15 p.m., with a blast that was felt some 25 miles away, lighting up Alexandria and Rosetta, and sending blazing timbers and bodies far into the air.

After the awesome explosion, there was a 10-minute silence, as all the gunners on both sides, subdued by the spectacle, stopped firing. Out of 1,000 men aboard *L'Orient*, only 70 were saved, including a lieutenant who, when picked up by a British ship, was naked except for his hat which he had saved, he explained, to prove he was an officer. With *L'Orient* sank some £600,000 in gold coins, ingots and diamonds – the treasure looted from the Knights of Malta, which was supposed to finance Napoleon's expedition.

The French ship *Franklin* was the first to recommence firing after the deathly lull, although two-thirds of that ship's company had been killed or wounded. She surrendered at 11.30 p.m. Another French ship, *Le Peuple Souverain*, was a wreck by 11 p.m. and *L'Artemise* drifted ashore and was set on fire by her crew; it blew up in the morning. By then the flagship was no more, six of the French ships had struck their colours, three ships had gone ashore and the *Tonnant* was a floating wreck, although it was the last to have surrendered with 120 men killed and 150 wounded. Only two French ships remained and they made good their escape.

The most unexplained part of the whole battle was the failure of the commander of the rear, Admiral Pierre-Charles de Villeneuve, to order his ships to come to the aid of those in the vanguard. Napoleon was later scathing: 'It was only at 2pm the following afternoon that Admiral Villeneuve seemed to take notice of the fact that there had been a battle going on for the past 18 hours... it was in Villeneuve's power to turn the battle into a French victory even as late as daybreak.' This is clearly unfair, but Villeneuve gave no satisfactory explanation. He and Nelson were destined to meet again.

It was a famous victory for the exhausted British. The French had lost 11 of their 13 battleships and some 4,000 men to two British ships and some 900 men. More than 3,000 French prisoners had been taken, most of whom were later set loose ashore as the British could not care for them. The French fleet had been virtually annihilated. At a stroke the British were masters of the Mediterranean, although a considerable French fleet still remained in the Atlantic. Napoleon's army in Egypt was stranded. True, the troop transports remained at Alexandria, but without the protection of the French fleet they could be picked off at will by the British.

Nelson, in the aftermath of the battle, despatched Sir James Saumarez with six French prizes to Gibraltar. He himself left with three ships for Naples, leaving behind three battleships and three frigates to blockade the coast of Egypt. All communications between Napoleon's army and France had been severed. The French generals Jean-Baptiste Kléber and Jacques-François Menou were fearful that Nelson would attempt an attack on Alexandria itself, but he declined as he believed the French defences there to be stronger than they actually were.

—⁓—

When Nelson arrived in Naples after the Battle of the Nile, Queen Maria Carolina exclaimed, 'Oh brave Nelson! Oh God bless you and protect our brave deliverer.' The simple-minded King Ferdinand called him his 'deliverer and preserver'. Suddenly, it seemed for the first time that French domination of Europe was not inevitable after all and that those few places such as Naples which still held out could survive. Nelson was made a baron – Lord Nelson of the Nile. Pitt had wanted to confer a viscountcy, but the

King was reluctant to confer even a peerage, perhaps disapproving of his support of Prince William. There was a small outcry that he had not been granted a greater title. Pitt ordained that a colossal pension of £200,000 a year be set up for Nelson and his two male heirs (£20m at today's values). Fanny Nelson was received by the Queen. However, Josiah Nisbet, the stepson to whom Nelson was devoted, was not promoted. Nelson appealed to St Vincent:

> That part of your letter relative to Nisbet has distressed me more than almost anything in this world, as probably his mother's life and my happiness is wrapt up in this youth, if he drinks it is a vice not only lately learnt but which he could not have been taught by me, as to his company I can say nothing about it except that till you had the goodness to promote him he never was in any company but mine. As a seaman he is I can assure you the best of his standing of any I have ever seen, I wish I had half as good I could then sleep which I have not done since I left you, and as I owe my life to him I cannot but be interested for his having a good frigate, which I hope you will manage to give him.

Nelson suffered nausea and splitting headaches from his new wound, and he was also plagued again by malaria. He increasingly felt himself to be a child of destiny, writing that 'Almighty God has made me the happy instrument in destroying the enemy's fleet.' He wrote later, almost mystically: 'I prayed that, if our cause was just, I might be the happy instrument of His punishment against unbe-lievers of the supreme and only true God – that if it was unjust I might be killed. The Almighty took the battle into his own hand, and with his power marked the victory as the most astonishing that ever was gained at sea: all glory be to God! Amen! Amen!'

His mood was understandable. After his career had once more teetered because of his failure to find the French fleet, its destruc-tion had conferred greatness beyond any expectation. He felt at last that he enjoyed a niche in British hearts that could not be removed. He had served God, the King and his country to the very summit of duty and glory. Moreover, he felt himself increasingly under divine protection, for he always sensed he was close to the next world. He had nearly died in the Indies of disease and in Nicaragua of illness; in Cape St Vincent he had risked his life in open combat; in Corsica he had just survived; he had nearly been killed in Tenerife; now again he had escaped death by the narrowest of margins. Yet, as so often with this strange, attractive, romantic, severe, duty-driven genius of a naval commander, pride came before a fall: hubris was followed by nemesis.

Arriving in Naples to have his crippled flagship refitted, he was greeted by the kind of welcome only the Neapolitans can give. When the *Vanguard* arrived on 22 September 1798, it was surrounded by a small flotilla of boats and the sound of music. Nelson was wholly seduced. He wrote to Lord George Spencer, First Lord of the Admiralty: 'You will not, my lord, I trust, think that one spark of vanity induces me to mention the most distinguished reception that ever, I believe, fell to the lot of a human being... If God knows my heart, it is amongst the most humble of the creation, full of thankfulness and gratitude.'

Nelson was lodged in the splendid palazzo of Sir William and Lady Hamilton, who bathed his wounds in ass's milk. On his 40th birthday, some 1,700 people were invited to a ball, 80 of them supping with the Hamiltons. The Sultan of the Ottoman Empire sent him an aigrette, a superbly embossed if bizarre clockwork jewel.

Nelson moored at Palermo, where his old morbid streak returned with a vengeance, as it often did after a period of immense exertion. This fault was now mixed with a greater arrogance and ruthlessness. In the summer of 1799, following Naples' brief period as the French-backed Parthenopaean Republic, he assisted the retaking of the city on behalf of the local monarchy. At King Ferdinand's request, it seems that he reneged on a peace treaty and had his fleet fire upon the ships of the republican forces who were preparing to leave Naples. He then allowed the execution of many prisoners, including respected local dignitaries. Nelson accepted a dukedom offered by King Ferdinand in thanks. The severity of his actions against the republican movement has long provided fuel to his detractors, and was perhaps the biggest stain on his reputation.

Then, three times he ignored the direct orders of the new commander of the Mediterranean fleet, Admiral Lord Keith, to send ships to protect Minorca. In the end he sent four under-armed sloops. He wrote sarcastically to Lord Spencer, alluding to Keith's failure to catch the combined French and Spanish fleet – something for which Keith was in fact widely blamed throughout the Mediterranean fleet. The Admiralty wrote back congratulating him on rescuing Naples but chiding him for disobeying Keith. However, the rear-admiral was by now virtually out of London's control, for their lordships could not easily act against the British hero they had built up in the public's mind. To Keith's alarm, Nelson was appointed commander-in-chief of the Mediterranean fleet.

Nelson neglected his duties to set off on a five-week pleasure cruise aboard his flagship with the Hamiltons, visiting Siracusa's Roman ruins and then Malta. During one of his 'nights of pleasure' on the trip, Emma conceived a child by Nelson. Hamilton discreetly turned a blind eye.

In 1800, Nelson was recalled to Britain and took the opportunity to conduct a European tour with Lady Hamilton on the way. They journeyed by land to Trieste in four carriages with three luggage wagons, and on to Vienna. Nelson, now emaciated and prematurely old, made an odd contrast with the by now vast Lady Hamilton. They were feted like royalty. Nelson and the Hamiltons then travelled overland across Europe before travelling up the Elbe to catch a ship to Yarmouth. Nelson spent some £3,500 on the journey – some £350,000 at today's prices. At Yarmouth the crowds detached the horses from his carriage and pulled it themselves.

He stayed with Fanny on his first night home, where she underwent the ordeal of entertaining the Hamiltons to dinner. He was mobbed in the Strand and was given a ceremonial sword by a grateful City of London. But the newspapers were full of ribaldry: the caricaturist George Cruikshank depicted the *ménage à trois* smoking pipes, with Lady Hamilton commenting, 'The old man's pipe was always out, but yours burns with full vigour.' Nelson replied, 'Yes, I'll give you smoke, I'll pour a whole broadside into you.' The unhappy Fanny had to endure fraternizing in public with Nelson and his mistress. At the theatre on Drury Lane she uttered a cry and fainted from the strain of appearing with them.

—⁓—

In 1800, Britain was wary that Russia, Sweden and Denmark were siding with the French in the protracted conflict and that Tsar Paul I had gone so far as to organize a 'League of Armed Neutrality' to protect the region's trade with France using force. Nelson, who had just been appointed a vice admiral, and a formidable fleet were placed under the orders of a senior admiral, Sir Hyde Parker, in March 1801. When the fleet arrived off Copenhagen – which Nelson regarded as a secondary target, Russia being the real cause of the trouble – Parker attempted to negotiate with the Danish government, but was rebuffed. The scene was set for a battle unlike any other of Nelson's major engagements – it was not to be a fight in the open between fleets, but a brutal war of attrition between the British fleet and the shore defences of a city.

Parker had placed Nelson in command of 10 ships of the line, two 50-gunners, seven frigates and nine small craft. The senior admiral remained in command of eight more ships of the line some three miles away. Nelson was presented with his trickiest challenge yet – to attack down a narrow channel between a huge shoal – the Middle Ground – and the smaller shoals along the coast of Copenhagen. The latter was guarded by a gauntlet of 18 men-of-war, although many of them were in poor condition and were no more than grounded gun batteries. In addition, to the north of the channel, there were two forts.

On the morning of 1 April 1801, the wind was favourable for Nelson to sail up the dangerous channel between the Middle Ground and the coastal shoal. The local pilots refused to help for fear of causing the fleet to be grounded. Captain Murray in the *Edgar* led the way. The plan was meticulous: the fleet would pass the first four ships firing broadsides; then the *Edgar* was to anchor beside the fifth ship, the two ships behind her overtaking to engage the next two ships, and then the following ships to pass on ahead to engage the other ships, one by one, as they moved further forward. Thus, each ship would rake the first four Danish ships with repeated broadsides, but without stopping, and then engage the rest.

Disaster struck almost immediately: the *Agamemnon* went aground on the southern tip of Middle Ground, while the *Bellona* and the *Russell* also went ashore a little way further up. Nelson himself was in the next ship, the *Elephant*, and saw that he was only likely to find the elusive deep-water channel if he passed to the west of the stranded ships. As his ships sailed down the Danish line, now just 700 feet away, the two sides exchanged murderous broadsides.

The exchange lasted four terrible hours, with dreadful carnage being inflicted on both sides. On the *Edgar*, 142 crew members were killed; on the *Monarch*, 218 lost their lives. Nelson, deprived of three of his main ships, sent the frigates led by Captain Edward Riou to exchange fire with the powerful 90-gun batteries on Three Crown Island at the northern tip of the channel.

Admiral Parker was watching helplessly more than a mile away to the northeast of the Middle Ground, entirely uncertain how the fighting was going as smoke enveloped the ferocious battle. Captain RW Otway, his flag captain, went in a boat to discover what was happening, and while he was away Parker ran signal 39 from the mast of his flagship, the *London*: this meant 'discontinue the action'. The frigates, exchanging a terrible pounding with the short batteries, obeyed, although Riou, already wounded, was deeply upset, and exclaimed, 'What will Nelson think of us?' He was then almost cut in two by fire from the Danish shore battery.

So arose one of the most celebrated incidents in Nelson's career: According to Colonel William Stewart, who was beside him, Nelson saw the signal and made no comment but continued pacing the deck. His signal-lieutenant asked whether he should raise the same signal over the *Elephant*, so as to pass the message down the fleet. 'No, acknowledge it,' said Nelson. Then he asked, 'Is my signal – number 16 [for close action] flying?' 'Yes my lord.' 'Mind you keep it so.' Nelson turned to his flag captain, Thomas Foley, and remarked, 'You know Foley, I only have one eye. I have a right to be blind sometimes.' He raised his telescope to his blind eye and said, 'I really do not see the signal. Damn the signal. Keep mine for close action flying.'

This version was first given in 1809 in Clarke and McArthur's extensive *The Life of Admiral Lord Nelson*. Southey's classic *The Life of Nelson*, written in 1813, repeated the same story, as well as that of the ship's surgeon – that Nelson ordered his own signal for close battle to be nailed to the mast – which must have been hearsay, for surely the surgeon would have been down below tending the wounded. Colonel Stewart himself wrote three versions of the story, and the 'blind eye' gesture only emerged in the last. The tale may be a later piece of embroidery, but it obscures the more important aspects of the battle. Nelson undoubtedly did the right thing in disregarding an order from an admiral far from the scene of the battle. To continue the action was the only thing that he safely could do, for to withdraw would have exposed all his ships to withering and destructive broadsides as they ran the gauntlet to get out of the channel.

Nelson was facing one of the trickiest situations of his career: unlike at Cape St Vincent, he could not confront the enemy fleet in open seas; unlike the Nile, he could not send his ships inshore to attack the Danes on both flanks. Trapped between shoals, he was committed to a straightforward exchange of fire against an enemy with far superior firepower. There was no room for imagination or dramatic manoeuvring: it was more like a classic land battle than a naval one.

His position began to look critical. His flagship, the *Elephant*, and the *Defiance* at the northern end of the line were under intense fire and seemed likely to be destroyed, while the *Monarch*, which was also in the vanguard under the guns of the fort, had sustained huge casualties. It looked as if Nelson was facing his first defeat in a major fleet action. Then the *Dannebrog*, the Danish flagship, spectacularly caught fire and, with its cables cut, drifted down the Danish line sowing alarm. At 3.30 p.m. it blew up. Other floating batteries had also cut their cables and some had sunk; but still Nelson could not lead his ships to safety under the intense fire of the Three Crown Island shore batteries.

Coolly, with his ship continuing firing, he resorted to a brutal threat. He addressed a letter to the Danes: 'Lord Nelson has directions to spare Denmark when no longer resisting but if the firing is continued on the part of Denmark Lord Nelson will be obliged to set on fire the floating batteries he has taken, without having the power of saving the brave Danes who have defended them.' He insisted on sealing the letter with wax, and did so with great care while Stewart asked him why he was taking so long. Nelson replied that he did not want the Danes to believe he was acting in a hurry. This missive was received by the Danish Prince Regent, Frederick.

The young prince was less concerned by the fate of the men aboard the now helpless hulks than the possibility that the British, in this desperate situation, might bombard his capital – something which Nelson, for all his reputation for ruthlessness acquired in Naples, refused to do. The Danes, who had no real quarrel with the British and were already regretting their alliance with Russia, acquiesced, to Nelson's intense relief.

He was able to extricate his ships from the channel of death. Even then two ships collided, including his own *Elephant*, three of them running aground: they would have been helpless if the Danish batteries had still been firing. The following day he was able to refloat his three beached ships at the southern end of the mudbank. He had salvaged all of his ships with the loss of around 350 men killed and 600 wounded: the Danes had lost some 1,800 men and 3,500 were taken prisoner in the captured ships. It was a victory on points, and the least decisive of Nelson's greatest battles.

Nelson was to be criticized for his actions but they worked and involved the minimum loss of life after a bloody battle: somewhat bogusly, he said he was acting out of 'humanity'. He was accused of ruthlessness in threatening to burn helpless ships with so many men aboard: but such threats are commonplace in battle and in the event were not carried out.

After the battle Nelson said apprehensively to Foley, 'Well I have fought contrary to orders and I shall perhaps be hanged. Never mind. Let them.' When the new prime minister, Henry Addington, later commented that he had been brave to disregard his superior's order, Nelson said it was the duty of an officer to take responsibility in such a situation, but then disingenuously added: 'In the midst of it all, I depended on you. I knew that, happen what might, if I did my duty you would stand by me.' The delighted doctor-politician declared it was the greatest compliment he had ever received in his life.

———

After his success at Copenhagen, Nelson's career plunged down the big dipper in its now familiar fashion. He was to gain a command of his own – but one he did not want. On his return to Britain in July 1801 he resumed his affair with Emma Hamilton, but was promptly appointed to command the Channel Fleet in case of French invasion.

Nelson was deeply sceptical that any such possibility existed, justifiably so, although there were 2,000 French soldiers still at Boulogne, supposedly getting ready. Unable to stay passive for long, on 4 August, Nelson despatched a flotilla of gunboats and bomb vessels, as well as a ship of the line, to bombard Boulogne. Thousands of spectators lined the cliffs of Dover and Deal to watch the action with telescopes. The attack did minimum damage, but served to warn the French to be on their guard.

The impatient Nelson then summoned some of his youngest captains to plan for a frontal attack: five squadrons would be involved. The aim was to attack the ships moored across the harbour at night, with boarding parties supported by mortar ships, when the French ships could not be expected to fire back for fear of hitting their own. It was a 'cutting-out' expedition on a grand scale.

However, his adversary was France's greatest naval commander, Admiral Louis-René de Latouche-Tréville, and he was prepared: netting had been strung down from the upper rigging to the ships' sides to repel attack and the ships were attached to one another by chains with strong cables securely anchored to the seabed. The French commander observed the British making preparations during the day of 15 August. That same night, boatloads of British

sailors were dropped off the coast wearing white armbands for identification at night and carrying cutlasses, pikes, tomahawks, pistols,
muskets and knives. It was to be a daring inshore raid – except that
the French were fully alert to them. The netting and chains did
their job, and the British sailors were easy pickings.

By about 4 a.m. the boats returned, having utterly failed in their
task, while Nelson stood watching from a frigate off the French
coast. At midday on 16 August, the British sailed back to Deal,
with 44 men killed and 128 wounded and not a single prize; only
10 Frenchmen had been killed and 34 wounded. The raid had been
a complete, if relatively minor, fiasco. The French sang joyfully:
'Off Boulogne, Nelson poured hell-fire! But on that day, many
a drunk/Instead of wine, drank salt water/off Boulogne!' Nelson's
reputation plummeted once again.

———

In January 1805, Napoleon, who had been amassing his forces, at
last got his break. Admiral Edouard Missiessy, with four ships of the
line and 3,500 troops, escaped from Rochefort in a snowstorm,
evading the blockading fleet which was sheltering in Quiberon Bay.
The British believed that he then headed towards the West Indies.
A week later Admiral Villeneuve escaped with nine ships of the
line from Toulon while Nelson was loading supplies in Maddalena
Bay in Sardinia. Nelson immediately sailed to Cagliari and to
Palermo to defend these ports: he proceeded all the way to
Alexandria and found nothing.

Napoleon unveiled his grand design for landing in Ireland and
stirring up a rebellion there, attacking the West Indies and staging
an invasion of Britain from across the Channel. He ordered
Admiral Ganteaume to sea on 26 March 1805 to carry out the first
stage. The French admiral's 21 ships found their way to Ireland
blocked by 15 British ships. He asked for permission to engage.
Napoleon refused, so he remained bottled up.

However, Villeneuve, spurred by the wrath of Napoleon, slipped
out of Toulon once again at dead of night on 30 March. There now

began the greatest naval chase in history. Villeneuve's objective was to fulfil his assigned role in Napoleon's latest plan, which at least had the merit of simplicity. Villeneuve's fleet was to rendezvous with Ganteaume at Martinique, along with the troops in the West Indies. The aim was to lure the British fleets after them; the joint French fleet would then return across the Atlantic, pick up more French ships and at last defeat what remained of the British fleet in the Channel so that the French invasion force could cross. It seemed a madcap scheme, but it almost worked.

Meanwhile, Nelson cruised anxiously back to Sicily, unsure of the enemy's intentions. There was considerable shock in Britain that Villeneuve had escaped. The French 'can get out when they choose', declared a fashionable lady. Nelson was blamed. The British admiral, having gone in entirely the wrong direction, now had to battle against unfavourable winds across to the western Mediterranean. At one point he advanced just 15 miles in two days and his progress was continually slow, averaging 90 miles a day, owing to a laggard in his fleet, the *Superb*.

Napoleon was delighted by news of Villeneuve's escape. Never convinced by Nelson's reputation, he had watched the British commander repulsed off Boulogne in 1801 and now outwitted by Villeneuve. The latter set off for the West Indies.

The new First Lord of the Admiralty, Sir Charles Middleton, now Lord Barham, a genius who as controller of the navy had revived the senior service after the American war, had ordered Sir Alexander Cochrane to reinforce the five British warships in the West Indies with his own. He further ordered a flying squadron of seven more warships under Cuthbert Collingwood to reinforce Cochrane.

Meanwhile, William Pitt, who had returned as prime minister in 1804, assembled a 'secret expedition' of several thousand soldiers under Sir Eyre Coote, a British Indian veteran, and Sir James Cruz to sail for the Mediterranean where they were to liaise with a Russian force from Corfu to liberate Naples. Pitt feared that Villeneuve had sailed to intercept it and Nelson, who was supposed to be protecting the Mediterranean, had disappeared. Barham now ordered Collingwood to go to the rescue of the secret expedition, stripping the western approaches of the Channel of ships so as to bring his force up to 18 warships.

To the astonishment of both Barham and Napoleon, Missiessy suddenly turned up with his four battleships off Rochefort. The reports had been false: he had not fled to the West Indies. Meanwhile Nelson, who had at last reached Gibraltar, learnt of the secret expedition which had then arrived at the mouth of the Tagus in Portugal and had occupied the forts there in anticipation of the arrival of Villeneuve's fleet. The expedition's commanders in turn learnt that Nelson was nearby and they sailed in delight to meet him. There, escorted by two battleships, they made their way eastwards towards Gibraltar. Pitt's secret expedition was safe.

After this wholly unnecessary diversion, Nelson decided to leave for the West Indies in pursuit of Villeneuve. Leaving 20 of his 23 cruisers behind in the Mediterranean, he now had 10 ships of the line and three frigates to pursue a fleet twice as large. Soon after he departed, Collingwood arrived to escort the secret expedition; he despatched two more battleships across the Atlantic to reinforce Nelson.

News arrived that Villeneuve had reached Martinique on 16 May 1805. Barham immediately feared that when Nelson arrived in the West Indies, Villeneuve would sail straight back to Europe where the Straits of Dover had been stripped of most of their defences. Lord Cornwallis, who was blockading Brest, was ordered to send 10 of his battleships to reinforce Collingwood's small Channel flotilla. The remainder of the scrappy Channel fleets – Cornwallis' 12 ships, five which were still off Rochefort and several more in British ports – were to join together if Villeneuve suddenly materialized in British waters.

Nelson's fleet crossed the 3,200 miles from Gibraltar to Barbados in just three weeks – an average of 135 miles a day, an extraordinary feat as his slowest ship, the *Superb*, was barely seaworthy. Nelson could not be certain of finding Villeneuve and was ready to sail back immediately if he did not. On 4 June, the British fleet reached Barbados where they learned that the French had indeed arrived, and had left. Nelson was exultant, believing he had caught his man. He made the signal, 'Prepare for battle'.

On the advice of General Brereton, the British commander at St Lucia, he sailed for Trinidad in pursuit, where he found no sign of the Franco-Spanish fleet. Nelson was furious: 'But for General Brereton's d——d information Nelson would have been, living or dead, the greatest man in his profession England ever saw. Now, alas! I am nothing... If either General Brereton would not have wrote or his look-out man had been blind, nothing would have prevented my fighting [Villeneuve] on June 6.'

Nelson immediately made for Grenada to the north. There he learnt that Villeneuve had been sighted at Martinique on 5 June – the two fleets had passed within a hundred miles of each other. The unsuspecting Villeneuve, who had lost 3,000 of his men through sickness, had orders to remain in the West Indies until joined by Ganteaume and to capture as many British islands as possible. He had sailed to Guadeloupe to pick up troops, and to his shock had learned that Nelson had been anchored off Barbados just days before. In spite of his overwhelming naval superiority, that was enough for Villeneuve: he set sail immediately back across the Atlantic to Ferrol.

Nelson had succeeded in his first objective without a fight: the West Indies had been saved for Britain. When Nelson reached Antigua, he discovered that he was four days behind Villeneuve, but he had no idea where the French fleet had gone. He had a difficult decision to make: had Villeneuve set off to attack Jamaica, or had he sailed for Europe? He was relieved at last to hear from a young captain that Villeneuve's 32-ship fleet had been sighted making for the northeast. On 13 June, Nelson set sail for Gibraltar.

Villeneuve arched back across the Atlantic to the north: he had the choice of liaising with the Rochefort or Ferrol squadrons and assembling a mighty fleet of more than 40 ships of the line in the Channel to crush the few British ships still there. Nelson sent the *Curieux*, his fastest ship, on ahead to warn Barham of Villeneuve's return, and this overtook the French fleet to arrive at Plymouth on 7 July.

Hearing the news, Barham acted with speed and ordered 10 ships from the Channel fleet and five from the Rochefort blockade to stand in Villeneuve's path. The unimaginative Sir Robin Calder was put in charge. On 22 July, after a delay of three days, Calder's squadron was cruising off Ferrol in thick fog as Villeneuve's 20 ships of the line came near, neither fleet seeing the other. At noon the fog lifted and Calder was daunted by the size of the enemy fleet. After five hours of hesitation he ordered his ships to engage as fog descended again. The fighting was inconclusive and confused, lasting several hours before two of Villeneuve's fleet surrendered.

The following day dawned with the two fleets having drifted 17 miles apart, again separated by fog. Neither of these cautious commanders chose to attack. It was a deeply unimpressive dress rehearsal for a much larger battle. Nelson would have shown no such hesitation. On 20 July, Villeneuve reached the safety of Ferrol, which Calder had been seeking to blockade. Calder withdrew with his tail between his legs to join Cornwallis' blockading squadron at Brest.

Nelson had already left his ships at Brest and sailed back to Britain for a long-deserved leave – his first for more than two years. He was bitterly disappointed and neurotically ill again, and sought solace with Lady Hamilton. The great chase across the Atlantic had failed. The French fleet had escaped. He had travelled nearly 7,000 miles in vain. This histrionic, highly strung seeker after glory was plunged into despair.

Nelson should not have been so disappointed: the West Indies were safe while his speedy crossing of the Atlantic, which surprised Napoleon, and Barham's decision to intercept Villeneuve's fleet had frustrated Napoleon's latest attempt at an invasion.

—◦◦◦—

On 2 September 1805, the peace of Nelson's domestic household in the country was disrupted by an official arrival: a messenger bearing the news that Villeneuve had moved to Cadiz. What could it mean – another invasion attempt? Nelson hurried to see Pitt. Neither man could know that Napoleon had already abandoned the whole enterprise.

Pitt's orders this time were for Nelson to assume the Mediterranean and Atlantic commands and destroy the French fleet. He immediately drew up his battle plan and, as usual, departed from convention with a decision to attack in two lines. He then had a fraught farewell with Emma Hamilton and ordered a coffin already made out of the broken timbers of the French flagship *L'Orient* to be prepared for him. He hugged his little daughter Horatia five times before leaving on the night of 13 September. He must certainly have anticipated his death.

He embarked before a large crowd. Many were in tears, many kneeling and blessing him. His flagship was the *Victory* again. Arriving to join the fleet blockading Cadiz, he showed compassion towards Admiral Calder, who had been relieved, giving him the dignity of a 90-gun ship of the line, which he could ill-afford to spare in the coming battle, to take him home.

Nelson received a rapturous welcome from the fleet. He summoned his captains aboard and set out his plan of action in great detail. The captains crowded into the low-ceilinged, wood-panelled cabin of the *Victory* were famous names in themselves: Nelson's second-in-command was Collingwood, a bluff, uncomplicated man and an unimaginative fighter, but an excellent sailor; there was Nelson's flag captain, Thomas Hardy, and Israel Pellew, as well as Thomas Fremantle, Edward Codrington, George Duff, Thomas Louis and others, all towered over by the giant Captain Benjamin Hallowell, a striking contrast to the slight, delicate figure before them, towards whom they felt almost protective.

Now there was nothing to do but settle down to the tedious business of blockade, waiting for the French to make their move. If they had any sense, they would make none for months, although the huge 35-strong combined Franco-Spanish fleet was running short of supplies. The timorous Villeneuve and his admirals were determined to stay in safety in Cadiz.

The adventurous Sir Sidney Smith suggested they be forced out by a rocket attack or a kind of primitive torpedo developed by the indefatigable American military inventor, Robert Fulton, who had defected from assisting the French. Nelson understandably remained unconvinced. For once in his life Nelson seemed calmly resigned to waiting, watching his sailors perform a play for the amusement of the officers and crew, ordering all his ships to be painted yellow with black stripes, like giant wasps, for easy identification in battle, and insisting on having better provisions served to his men.

With characteristic skill he kept his fleet well out of sight of Cadiz, some 50 miles to the west, communicating through a small line of signalling ships with a small frigate squadron watching the port. With a westerly wind blowing he knew he would be able to close in quickly on Cadiz. If an easterly blew, he could take refuge on the African side of the Straits of Gibraltar, which would allow him to remain within striking distance of Cadiz.

Villeneuve received a letter from the Emperor Napoleon: he proposed to replace him if his 'excessive pusillanimity' kept him at Cadiz. The Emperor 'counts the loss of his vessels for nothing if he loses them with honour', he declared, with his usual unconcern for the lives of his own men. This accusation of cowardice was too much for any man of honour to bear. On 19 October, Villeneuve decided to take advantage of a light wind from the northeast to carry the fleet south and escape through the Straits of Gibraltar.

However, the French, after being bottled up in harbour for so long, made their exits clumsily – only 12 ships emerged by nightfall. Villeneuve had ordered a third of his fleet to remain behind, to form a reserve French fleet to come to the aid of the main French fleet if attacked. This further complicated the departure and only on 20 October did the remainder emerge to form five straggling columns nine miles long.

The fleet consisted of 18 French and 15 Spanish ships, mostly of 74 guns, although four possessed more than 100 guns. The great and sinister red-and-black Spanish *Santissima Trinidad*, the towering four-deck veteran of the Battle of Cape St Vincent, towered above them all with its 150 guns. The colossal *Santa Anna* was entirely draped in funereal black. To those crowding along the shore of the

Spanish mainland to watch, it was a mighty armada of magnificent ships rolling in the high sea like a stately procession of ducks, colourful in plumage, stately in bearing, but ragged in line.

On receiving the news from his signal frigates that the French had broken out, Nelson wrote to Emma: 'My dearest, beloved Emma, dear friend of my bosom, the signal has been made that the enemy's combined fleet are coming out of port. We have very little wind, so that I have no hopes of seeing them before tomorrow. May the God of Battles crown my endeavours with success...'

He sailed slowly towards the shore to cut off the French. The wind changed direction twice, and he altered his course accordingly. When Villeneuve saw the British fleet in an orderly line on the horizon on the morning of Monday, 21 October, he realized to his horror that it consisted of 27 ships, not 18 as he had expected. He considered making a bolt for the Straits and escaping to Toulon, but then decided to go north and make a run back to Cadiz. He abandoned his tactical dispositions and ordered his captains to form a single uneven line. He issued his last instruction: 'There is nothing to alarm us in the sight of an English fleet. Their 64-gun ships have not 500 men on board; they are not more brave than we are; they are harassed by a two years' cruise; they have fewer motives to fight well.'

The day dawned pleasantly, with a soft breeze. To the west, Nelson was at ease, touring the gun decks of his ship where he was cheered by his 1,000 men. He knew he could catch up with the French and put his plans into action at leisure. The prospect of action always seemed to induce an unnatural calm in this twitchy hypochondriac. He had decided to lead the first column himself, with Collingwood leading the second.

He sat down to write a prayer of moving simplicity:

> May the great God, whom I worship, grant to my country and for the benefit of Europe in general a great and glorious victory, and may no misconduct in anyone tarnish it, and may humanity after victory be the predominant feature in the British Fleet. For myself individually, I commit my life to Him who made me and may his blessing light

upon my endeavours for serving my country faithfully. To Him I resign myself and the just cause which is entrusted me to defend. Amen, amen, amen.

He then issued his famous signal: 'England expects that every man will do his duty.' This visibly irritated Collingwood, who believed signals should be reserved for practical instructions.

The battle commenced to the west of Cape Trafalgar. The Franco-Spanish fleet was sailing in between the British fleet, about 20 miles out to sea, and the shore of the Cape. At the last moment, perhaps out of impatience, Nelson seems to have decided to attack at right angles straight into the French fleet, rather than closing at a more oblique angle, perhaps to present a smaller front to the fire of French ships as his column approached. Captain Blackwell, who had been ordered aboard the *Victory* to be at his side, urged Nelson to shift his flag to the *Euryalus*, where he could direct the battle from safety. Nelson brusquely refused, and rejected another suggestion that the *Temeraire* under Captain Eliab Harvey should lead the attack.

The two fleets were now in a slow motion drama impelled by the slightest of breezes, the French and the Spanish extending in a great crescent about four miles long, the British in their two columns, which had in fact broken up into bunches with every ship trying to be first into the action, heading for the centre and rear like two slow-moving spears.

As picturesque as these elegant sailing craft, with their sleek wooden hulls and their billowing sails, might appear, they were colossal engines of war, packed with explosives, approaching each other with the purpose of inflicting as much damage and killing as many people as possible. It seemed improbable to the spectators on shore that the beauty and peace of this slow-moving scene, the stately procession of magnificent, gaudy and multicoloured ships with their bosomy sails billowing almost as far as the eye could see, would soon engage in horrific and destructive conflict.

The fleets were not evenly matched; the French had some 400 more guns than the British and double the number of men.

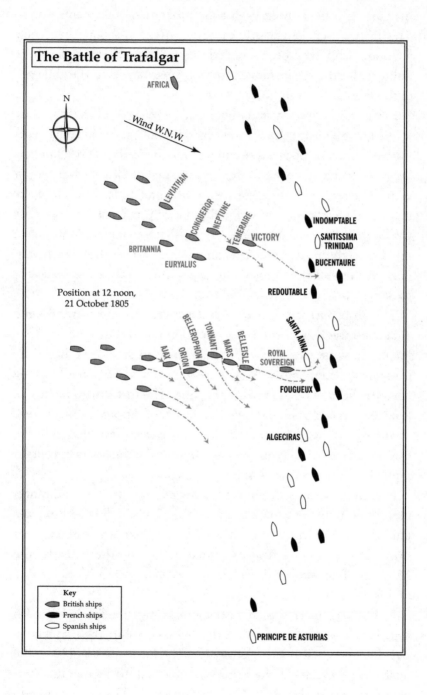

The Battle of Trafalgar

N

Wind W.N.W.

AFRICA

LEVIATHAN

CONQUEROR

NEPTUNE

TEMERAIRE

VICTORY

INDOMPTABLE

SANTISSIMA TRINIDAD

BUCENTAURE

BRITANNIA

EURYALUS

REDOUTABLE

Position at 12 noon,
21 October 1805

BELLEROPHON

TONNANT

AJAX

ORION

MARS

BELLEISLE

SANTA ANNA

ROYAL SOVEREIGN

FOUGUEUX

ALGECIRAS

PRINCIPE DE ASTURIAS

Key
British ships
French ships
Spanish ships

However, Nelson had compensated for this by his tactics, and his guns also fired twice as fast as the French and Spanish ones. The British were also vastly more experienced sailors than their enemies, who had been cooped up in port. Slowly, elegantly, unhurriedly, the spears moved towards their targets in the great arc of the Franco-Spanish fleet.

It was Collingwood and the *Royal Sovereign*'s glory that they arrived first beneath the sinister black hull of the *Santa Anna*. This was the moment of greatest danger. The huge ship and its neighbours were able to concentrate their fire on the British ship, which could not return it as its guns were not broadside. The *Fougueux* behind the *Santa Anna* attempted to block the *Royal Sovereign*, but Collingwood steered straight for it, as though to ram it. At just after midday, as the *Royal Sovereign* came within range, the French ship opened fire and the British ship pressed forward as the *Fougueux* took evasive action to avoid collision.

The *Royal Sovereign* broke the line between the stern of the *Santa Anna* and the bow of the *Fougueux*. Collingwood raked both ships broadside as he passed. 'What would Nelson give to be here!' he exclaimed triumphantly. 'How I envy him,' said Nelson, observing from the head of his slower-moving line. The first British broadside disabled some 14 guns and killed some 300 of the *Santa Anna*'s crew. Swinging her helm round, the *Royal Sovereign* came alongside the towering Spanish ship on the lee (shore) side; the Spanish captain replied with his own broadsides.

Five ships were soon firing at the *Royal Sovereign*. For 15 minutes more 'that noble fellow Collingwood', as Nelson dubbed him, was entirely alone in the action: it was extraordinary that his ship was not destroyed. Then he was joined at last by the *Belleisle*, the *Mars*, the *Tonnant*, the *Bellerophon*, the *Orion* and the *Ajax* coming up his column.

Nelson's column was at last approaching the Franco-Spanish line. He had intended to attack the enemy flagship, the *Bucentaure*, but there was nothing to identify it, so he made for his old foe, the *Santissima Trinidad*. As the *Victory* approached the French fired single shots to test whether she was within range. The seventh blew a hole in the *Victory*'s topsail. The British held their breath for two minutes more: then a pandemonium of fire broke out from the enemy fleet as she approached.

For nearly 40 minutes more she ploughed on, unable to return fire under this gauntlet of shot. At 500 yards' distance the mizzen topmast came down. The ship's wheel was disabled and its sails were shredded. A single shot killed eight marines in the poop and another struck a launch, showering splinters on Nelson and Hardy, who were standing on the quarterdeck. Another cannonball ripped John Scott, Nelson's secretary, who was standing beside them, in two. 'This is too warm work, Hardy, to last long,' declared Nelson without emotion. Some 50 officers and men were killed in those first volleys.

As they approached the French line they spotted Villeneuve's flag flying aboard the *Bucentaure*, but the *Victory* could not veer towards it without exposing her side to fire from the *Redoutable* and the French *Neptune* (there was a British ship of the same name in the battle). 'Take your choice,' Nelson instructed Hardy. The *Victory* steered past the stern of the French flagship and at last opened fire with a 50-gun broadside directly into the *Bucentaure*'s bow at point-blank range. Some 20 guns were disabled and 400 men killed.

The *Victory* turned alongside the *Redoutable*, which closed her lower-deck gun ports to avoid being boarded. The two ships became entangled. Meanwhile the French *Neptune* , the *Bucentaure*, the *Redoutable* and the *Santissima Trinidad* were pouring fire into the *Victory*, but she was soon supported by the *Temeraire*, the next in line, then the British *Neptune*, the *Leviathan*, the *Conqueror*, the *Africa* and the *Agamemnon*. Meanwhile, the vanguard of the Franco-Spanish fleet had sailed ahead, leaving two clusters of ships fighting about half a mile apart from each other, where Nelson's and Collingwood's squadrons had penetrated the French line.

The *Victory* raked the *Redoutable* with broadsides, but its Captain Jean Jacques Lucas was a formidable fighter. Although his ship was crippled, the sharpshooters he had placed in the tops were still firing lethally down on to the deck of the *Victory*. A French mariner called Robert Guillemard, who was one of Lucas' best marksmen, described the fateful moment of the battle:

> The two decks were covered with dead bodies, which they had not time to throw overboard. I perceived Captain Lucas motionless at his post, and several wounded officers still giving orders. On the poop of the English vessel was an officer covered with orders, and with only one arm. From what I had heard of Nelson, I had no doubt that it was he. He was surrounded by several officers, to whom he seemed to be giving orders. I saw him quite exposed and close to me. I could even have taken aim at the men I saw, but I fired at hazard among the groups I saw of sailors and officers. All at once I saw great confusion on board the Victory; the men crowded round the officer whom I had taken for Nelson. He had just fallen, and was taken below, covered with a cloak.

If this is accurate, and Guillemard indeed fired the fatal shot, he was not aiming specifically at Nelson but at a group of British officers, even though he had recognized the Admiral. Hardy made a much bigger and more impressive target in his captain's uniform. The sharpshooter was aiming at a distance of 50 yards in the heat of battle from a swaying ship on to the deck of another. Even an excellent marksman could not have been sure of his target, so it is understandable that he just chose to fire at the group.

Nelson has been much faulted for exposing himself to danger and wearing his decorations in battle: certainly admirals like Sir Hyde Parker at Copenhagen and Lord James Gambier later at Aix were careful to be a long way from the scene of battle. Yet his uniform was dusty and the decorations were stars sewn into it, not his usual glittering ones. The Frenchman claimed he recognized him from his single arm as well, something Nelson could not cover up. It is hard to believe that Nelson had a death wish, as some have alleged, or that he actually sought death in the field of battle. He was a man who loved glory and the acclaim of his countrymen: in decimating the enemy fleet as he intended, he would already have acquired a place of glory and in the affection of Britons to the end of his days, which he wanted to share with his beloved Emma and their daughter Horatia.

Much more likely, for a man accustomed to leading his men by exposing himself to their risks by showing cool detachment in the face of great odds which allowed him to direct the course of the battle, he believed he could cheat death as he had so many times before. He knew the risks, but it was his style of leadership to seek to defy them: his place was at the head of his men, in uniform and decorations, so that he could be recognized by them and show that he did not fear the enemy, or possible death, and nor should they.

It was meaningless to talk of his staying out of battle and directing operations from afar. As had been shown in Admiral Peter Parker's case, no admiral could direct operations where he could neither comprehend the course of the action nor expect to be obeyed by the captains in the thick of it. Once battle was joined it had to be carried through to the end in ship-to-ship engagements until one side or the other broke it off: this was not a land battle that could be directed from a hill with orders to various units to advance, retreat or redeploy.

Only if Nelson was seen as a venerable national treasure to be preserved should he have stayed aloof, and he had no intention of being seen as such. He had stayed back from such minor actions as the attack at night on Boulogne, but this, he knew full well, was the decisive engagement between two colossal fleets that might determine the outcome of the war and change the course of history. The withering criticism that would have been rained upon him had he stayed distant from so historic an engagement, or taken shelter in his cabin, can only be imagined.

Nelson was no coward: the very basis of his extraordinary career and the esteem in which he was held by his fellow countrymen were that he exposed himself fearlessly to risk. Other naval commanders had done just the same – Lord Richard Howe at the glorious First of June, John Jervis at St Vincent, Lord Duncan at Camperdown. History has not been kind to those who stayed at a safe distance. Young Captain Blackwell was later to lament in self-guilt 'what a horrid scourge is war... I wish to God he [Nelson] had yielded to my entreaties to come on board my ship. We should all have preserved a friend, and the country the greatest admiral that ever was, but he would not listen to it.' But Nelson was wholly innocent: he had no other choice but to lead his men and expose himself to risk.

The bullet passed through his left shoulder, was deflected into his chest, ruptured an artery and shattered his spine. It could hardly have been more damaging. 'They have done for me at last, Hardy,' he said as he fell slowly. 'My backbone is shot through.' He covered his face with a handkerchief so as not to be recognized and dishearten his men. A marine and two sailors carried him down to the cockpit. His crew had little chance to observe what had happened. The fighting was as fierce as ever.

—◦◦◦—

With the deadly fire of the French marksmen having all but cleared the top deck of the *Victory* and the *Redoutable* itself wrecked and on the point of surrendering, the latter's sailors tried desperately to board the British flagship without success. The French crew had fought with unbelievable tenacity and ferocity: of its complement of 643 men, 522 were killed or wounded, an extraordinarily high casualty rate, particularly for a smaller ship attacking a larger. Nearby the *Tenerife* had also attacked the *Redoutable*, and came under fire from the *Fougueux* and the French *Neptune*.

However, the French flagship, the *Bucentaure*, proved less formidable: badly damaged by the fire from the *Victory* and under attack from the *Conqueror*, its last mast fell and Villeneuve surrendered. A British marine officer, three marines and two sailors came aboard and found 'a very tranquil, English-looking Frenchman, wearing a long-tailed uniform coat and green corduroy pantaloons'. The marine took Villeneuve and his two companions aboard his little launch, and tried to return to the *Conqueror*. He could not find it in the bedlam of fighting around him, so he escorted his eminent prisoner aboard the nearest English ship, the *Mars*.

The *Conqueror* had taken on another giant ship, the *Santissima Trinidad* itself, which was also under fire from several others. The behemoth's mainmast came crashing down, like a huge skyscraper at sea. According to a British officer:

> This tremendous fabric gave a deep roll, with a swell to leeward, then back to windward, and on her return every mast went by the board, leaving her an unmanageable hulk on the water. Her immense topsails had every reef out, her royals were sheeted home but lowered, and the falling of this majestic mass of spars, sails, and rigging plunging into the water at the muzzles of our guns was one of the most magnificent sights I ever beheld.

The giant Spanish ship threw a Union Jack over its side in surrender, but the *Conqueror* was already off in search of new prey. The *Africa* took possession of it, despatching a lieutenant who found a solitary Spanish survivor on the main deck. At that moment several ships of the Spanish vanguard, which had at last tacked about, seemed to be coming to the rescue, so the Spaniard replied that the ship was still fighting, and the lieutenant hastily retreated to his boat unmolested. In the end the *Santissima Trinidad* was not rescued but was captured by another British ship, the *Prince*.

In Collingwood's battle cluster, his flagship was pounding away at the other giant Spanish ship, the *Santa Anna*, and beat it into submission. After an hour-and-a-half, though, the *Royal Sovereign* was in almost as bad a state, with just its foremast left standing, and had to be taken in tow. Around Collingwood, the battle raged: the British *Belleisle* took on three ships one after the other, including the *Fougueux*. The *Belleisle* was soon dismasted. The *Mars* came to her rescue, drawing off one of the attackers, but another French ship joined in. Undaunted, the *Belleisle* continued to pour shot into the nearest Frenchman, which struck.

Along with the *Mars*, the *Leviathan* and the *Polyphemus* arrived at the scene of the battle, followed by the *Swiftsure*. The *Mars* went on to engage four ships simultaneously, a Frenchman on each side with a Spaniard behind reinforced by a Frenchman. The last's broadside killed her captain, George Duff. Codrington's *Orion* closed silently into battle, under orders not to fire until it was alongside a French ship before bringing down all three of its masts in a devastating broadside, forcing it to strike its colours. The *Orion* proceeded to attack *L'Intrepide*, which it also quickly forced to surrender. The *Tonnant* was engaged with the *Algeciras*, which attempted to board it; a single Frenchman succeeded in getting aboard and was captured. The *Tonnant* went on to capture two prizes.

Perhaps the most desperate fight by a British ship was that of the *Bellerophon*, which found itself under fire from a ship on either side, and three from behind, after breaking the enemy line. The ship was entirely dismasted and as her sails fell they caught fire. The captain and some 115 men were killed, but the wreck still fought on and forced the *Monarco* to surrender. The *Bellerophon* then pounded the *Aigle* into submission. As all her launches were out of action, an officer dived overboard, swam to the *Aigle* and climbed up her rudder chains to claim the prize. The *Bellerophon* – dubbed the 'Billy Ruffian' by her non-classically minded men – was later to play an even more fateful part in the Napoleonic saga.

Aboard the *Victory*, the long, immortal, heroic, pathetic and tragic tableau of Nelson's death was unfolding. When the ship's surgeon, William Beatty, reached his side, Nelson told him, 'I am mortally wounded. You can do nothing for me, Beatty. I have but a short time to live.' Beatty prodded the wound with his finger and realized his admiral was right. He was running a high temperature and desperately thirsty. 'Drink, drink, fire, fire,' he kept repeating and was given lemonade, water and wine. He asked repeatedly for Hardy. The captain came after an hour during a lull in the fighting. 'Well Hardy, how goes the day with us?' Nelson asked. Hardy replied that 12 or 14 ships had surrendered. When Nelson said, 'I hope none of our ships have struck, Hardy?' the captain replied, 'No, My Lord, there is no fear of that.'

'I am a dead man, Hardy,' said the admiral. Hardy returned to his duties and Nelson turned back to the doctor: 'All pain and motion behind my breast is gone and you know I am gone.' Beatty concurred. 'God be praised. I have done my duty,' breathed Nelson. Meanwhile the counterattack by the returning French vanguard had been blunted by the *Victory* and other ships; three more prizes were taken. Hardy returned to inform Nelson that it was now certain that 14 or 15 prizes had been taken. 'That is well. But I had bargained for 20,' was the grudging reply.

Nelson gave his last order. The growing swell, in spite of the fine weather, had alerted the great man that seriously bad weather was on the way: catastrophe threatened the partially disabled British ships and the wholly disabled prizes which could be driven by the wind on to a lee shore. With all his energy Nelson suddenly called out, 'Anchor, Hardy, anchor!' Hardy remarked that Collingwood was now in charge. 'Not while I live, I hope Hardy. No, do you anchor Hardy?' After a while he said, 'Don't throw me overboard. You know what to do.' Nelson's seamanship and prescience had remained to the last. The fleet, having comprehensively defeated its enemies, was now facing a more dangerous one still: catastrophe from the weather, a threat Collingwood, in the thick of battle, seemed to be neglecting.

With the poignancy of a child facing an unknown threshold about to be crossed, Nelson called out for human comfort: 'Kiss me Hardy.' The burly captain kissed his cheek. 'Now I am satisfied. Thank God I have done my duty.' Hardy leaned over to kiss him again on the forehead. 'Who is that?' 'It is Hardy.' 'God bless you Hardy.'

After Hardy had left again for the quarter deck, Nelson told the ship's chaplain, who was rubbing his chest to ease his pain, 'Remember that I leave Lady Hamilton and my daughter Horatia as a legacy to my country.' He added a moment later, 'I have not been a great sinner, doctor.' He wept, repeating 'Thank God I have done my duty.' His last words were 'God and my country'. He died at about 4 p.m., 21 October 1805.

The battle raged on a little longer before Pierre Dumanoir le Pelley, commander of the French vanguard, called off his four ships. Fifteen minutes later the Spanish Admiral Federico Carlos Gravina ordered his remaining – crippled – 10 ships back to Cadiz. After about another half hour, the fighting ended. The 'grim and awful scene', as Codrington was later to describe it, was over. The fact that it had taken place at sea in those huge floating wooden stately homes that were the great ships of the time could not conceal the fearsome toll of the battle. More than 7,000 men had been killed or badly wounded, the casualty levels of a major land battle. The decks were covered in blood, with bodies and limbs lying everywhere. The swelling sea itself was reddened and packed with floating corpses as the hulks of great and crippled vessels milled about without direction.

Alongside the sheer horror of the scene, awareness of a colossal British victory began to dawn on the men. Seventeen French and Spanish ships had been taken in all, and one had blown up spectacularly in battle. The remaining 15 had escaped. The British had not lost a single ship, although several were badly disabled. The British had some 450 killed and 1,400 wounded, compared to 3,400 French dead and 1,200 wounded, and 1,000 Spanish killed and 1,400 wounded. Some 4,000 prisoners had been taken.

Of the remaining French and Spanish ships, 11 escaped to Cadiz while Dumanoir le Pelley's four vessels were attacked off Cape Ortegal a fortnight later by a British squadron under Captain Richard Strachan, and were captured without a fight. Of the 11, five attempted a breakout two days after Trafalgar, recapturing two of the British prizes, but three were lost in the gale. The remainder were virtual prisoners in port, and the French ships were eventually seized by the Spanish. The colossal fleet of 33 warships was effectively annihilated. Although not quite as complete as the Battle of the Nile, it had been an overwhelming victory.

The significance of the Battle of Trafalgar went even further, although no one realized it at the time, for the French consoled themselves with the thought that their shipyards could always rebuild the fleet. However, the battle made a major contribution to the Spanish decision to turn against the French. Napoleon was to attempt a major naval engagement only once more – and that a cautious one. The plans for invading England were now shelved for good. He would never consider the project seriously again: Britain was safe. Trafalgar was the equivalent of the Battle of Britain in the 1940s – a lifting of the shadows of invasion and enemy occupation.

The travails of those exhausted, exultant seamen were not over yet. As the dying Nelson had realized, with his last fevered ounce of seamanship, a fate almost as dangerous as an enemy fleet would soon be upon them: as though in heavenly rage at the passing of Nelson, or at the appalling suffering inflicted by man that day, a truly devastating gale struck the British fleet. Collingwood had decided to ignore Nelson's orders to anchor, partly because some of the anchors aboard the British ships had been lost in the fighting, and partly to move as far as possible from the dangerous lee shore of Spain, with its treacherous shoals at Trafalgar.

Whether he was right or not, Collingwood sailed straight into the teeth of the gale on that fateful night of 21 October 1805. Colossal waves battered the ships, many of them already crippled with gaping holes and hundreds of wounded and agonized men aboard, and they rolled about helplessly. The *Redoutable*, the French hero of the fight, sank behind the ship towing her. The French flagship *Bucentaure* had to be cut adrift and was seen crashing on to the shoals three miles away with the loss of the remainder of its crew. The whole fleet was being driven back towards the rocks. During the gale, as the ships struggled to maintain position and feared that they would all perish ashore, the wind veered abruptly, allowing them to gain a few miles distance. However, as dawn struck the storm continued and almost all the other French prizes went aground, sank, or had to be destroyed. The British limped home with none of their ships lost but only four prizes.

In the hold of the *Victory*, the body of Nelson had been preserved in a huge cask filled with brandy, and then turned upside down.

Nelson was perhaps the Zeus, the first among equals, of all the mavericks. This extraordinarily puerile person seemed to belong on the stage more than real life. Watching the progress of this slip of a man as he gradually shed an arm, then an eye, then finally his life in brave exposure to enemy fire held not just his own men, but the whole nation, agog. His passionate and reckless affair with Emma Hamilton seemed drawn from the pages of a romantic novel, eclipsing the much quieter personal lives of Clive and Washington, as did his brief sojourn with the decadent and murderous court of Naples.

Yet these were the accompaniments to a spirit of naval genius that delivered four astonishing victories, each in entirely different circumstances and requiring different tactics – Cape St Vincent, the Nile, Copenhagen and Trafalgar. The first was a vainglorious display of sheer boldness by a single ship against overwhelming odds. The second was his most brilliantly complete and technically skilled victory, attacking at dusk without delay, giving the enemy no time to think and turning the rule book on its head while engaging in dangerous and unconventional tactics by navigating between the enemy ships and the land. The third was a battle of attrition and insubordination towards his commander, which completely wrong-footed the enemy. The fourth was a brilliant major operation, the product of long hours of brooding in his cabin, which again threw convention to the winds by attacking a fleet line of battle in two columns, dividing the enemy and inflicting a decisive defeat.

Nelson had a grim determination to succeed on merit from relatively modest origins, and sailed back up to the crest after each trough in his career, of which there were many. He never hesitated to fight against overwhelming odds, calculating that surprise and superior manoeuvrability gave him the advantage, was regarded with awe and devotion by his men (even though when young he was a strict disciplinarian) and was brilliant at picking his subordinates, although he quarrelled with some of them, notably Troubridge. Nelson was superb at informing and coordinating his senior commanders to follow his plans, was a superb tactical innovator and his intelligence and mastery at sea as a commander of ships has never been equalled. At Cape St Vincent and Copenhagen, he directly disobeyed his superiors in the heat of battle – even though his early career shows a remarkable degree of ingratiation in the attempt to rise to a position of command.

Unlike most of the other mavericks, he was politically inept and naive, although he showed some business skills in amassing a fortune. He was a man of colossal faults – extraordinary vanity, petulance and on occasion callousness, as in Naples. Nothing, though, can eclipse his brilliance as an admiral or the results he achieved. He was the master commander par excellence, one of the very greatest of the last warriors, the giant military genius at the top of the pantheon in the golden age of leadership. His was heroic leadership incarnate.

Chapter 5

COCHRANE, THE SEA WOLF: THE NAVAL MARAUDER

Eccentricity, verging on madness, seems to have been the rule for many military mavericks. Thomas Cochrane may have been the most deranged of all, enjoying a career of dizzying rises and falls, carrying out an astonishing succession of feats at sea, and even occasionally on land.

In a country deprived of great statesmen following the deaths of William Pitt the Younger and Charles Fox and the departure of William Grenville, and of heroes after Horatio Nelson's fall on the deck of the *Victory*, an extraordinary Don Quixote of the seas emerged with as much bravery and glamour as Nelson, yet who was more wayward, unconventional and determined to snub his superiors.

Although far too individualistic and not senior enough to be a fleet commander, Cochrane was if anything an even better seaman than Nelson and shared with him a fearlessness that very nearly made him an equal. Unlike the bourgeois Nelson, this young man was born the elder son of a line of impoverished aristocrats. While his predecessor was sickly and frail, the newcomer was tall, sandy-haired and dashing.

Born in 1775, Thomas, Lord Cochrane, was the eldest son of the Earl of Dundonald, an eccentric Scottish inventor and lord of Culross Abbey House on the Firth of Forth. As a shy, gangling and awkward 17-year-old, he enlisted aboard ship as a midshipman under the command of his uncle, Sir Alexander Cochrane, a distinguished sailor. He served without seeing action in the North Sea and the Atlantic before transferring to the Mediterranean under Admiral Lord Keith. There, he encountered Nelson, who gave him the never-forgotten advice: 'Never mind manoeuvres; always go at 'em.' Nelson gave Cochrane his first command, putting him in charge of a disabled French prize which he conveyed safely, in the teeth of a gale, from Italy to Minorca.

Then, in 1800, Cochrane was given his first ship: the little 158-ton *Speedy*, a brigantine equipped with just 14 tiny four-pound guns and manned by just six officers and 84 men. His cabin was no more than four feet high, and the gawking six-foot-two (1.88m) youth had to shave by poking his head through the skylight. It seemed an unpromising start. Cochrane knew he was either still being tested by his superiors, or that they had decided to dispose of him quietly as being too independent-minded. After many years as an officer aboard a flagship, he had every reason to suspect the latter. They little realized that the small craft, and its captain, would soon become famous. For the moment, Cochrane at least had the satisfaction of no longer being bound by the stuffy protocol of a flagship or of having to kowtow to men he regarded as incompetent, inferior seamen, lacking in courage.

In the summer of 1800, in the brilliant sun off Cagliari in Sardinia, the *Speedy* emerged on its first mission to convoy 14 merchant boats; the 24-year-old commander proudly gazed over his ship's company, which included an energetic and able second-in-command, Lieutenant William Parker, and his own brother Archibald, still a midshipman. After several hours sailing across the glittering blue sea, one of his lookouts noticed a boat moving in like a shark to pick off one of the dispersed convoy's stragglers. Cochrane promptly ordered the *Speedy* to turn around and caught up with the little French privateer, the six-gun *Intrepid*. After firing a warning shot, the crew of the *Speedy* boarded the prize and hauled her in. It had been a battle of the pygmies, secured without bloodshed, but Cochrane's first day's fighting had yielded a catch – the first in his career – 'my first piece of luck'.

The long journey to Leghorn (Livorno) on the coast of Italy proceeded. Four days later, five 'sharks' moved in on two more stragglers in the convoy and boarded them. Once again, Cochrane immediately turned the *Speedy* about and caught up with the two stricken vessels. The five gunboats made off, but were forced to abandon their prizes. Arriving a week later in Leghorn, Cochrane delivered one prize and 50 French prisoners to Admiral Keith – not bad for a first outing.

Cochrane's tactic was simple: always go on the offensive. The following month he captured three prizes, and then three more in July. To the young commander, zigzagging across those dreamy blue seas at the height of summer, capturing craft with a warning shot and a boarding party, the whole dance seemed unreal and idyllic. He was a man in control of his ship, utterly confident of his seafaring skills, and he faced little resistance from the small French privateers. He was fishing minnows, although to the captured merchant ships they must have seemed like predators until they were rescued. The impression of the firefly skimming across the waters was captured in the young commander's log:

> June 16 – Captured a tartan off Elba. Sent her to Leghorn, in the charge of an officer and four men.
>
> 22 – Off Bastia. Chased a French privateer with a prize in tow. The Frenchman abandoned the prize, a Sardinian vessel laden with oil and wool, and we took possession. Made all sail in chase of the privateer; but on our commencing to fire she ran under the fort of Caprea, where we did not think proper to pursue her. Took prize in tow and on the following day left her at Leghorn, where we found Lord Nelson, and several ships at anchor.
>
> 25 – Quitted Leghorn, and on the 26th were again off Bastia, in chase of a ship which ran for that place, and anchored under a fort three miles to the southward. Made at and brought her away. Proved to be the Spanish letter of marque Assuncion, of ten guns and thirty-three men, bound from Tunis to Barcelona. On taking possession, five gun-boats left Bastia in chase of us; took the prize in tow, and kept up a running fight with the gun-boats till after midnight, when they left us.

29 – Cast off the prize in chase of a French privateer off Sardinia. On commencing our fire she set all sail and ran off. Returned and took the prize in tow; and the 4th of July anchored with her in Port Mahon.

July 9 – Off Cape Sebastian. Gave chase to two Spanish ships standing along shore. They anchored under the protection of the forts. Saw another vessel lying just within range of the forts; – out boats and cut her out, the forts firing on the boats without inflicting damage.

For the commander of the *Speedy*, life must never have seemed so intoxicating. Not only could he show off his naval skills: the delightful, if occasionally oppressively hot or squally, Mediterranean offered a wide range of exotic ports and landscapes, from the bustle and volubility, fine wines and even better food of a port like Leghorn to the reserved and sleepy atmosphere of British-dominated Minorca, Corfu or Malta, to the mutual incomprehension and suspicion experienced by the British in the narrow-alleyed ports of North Africa. Sun-baked, whitewashed dwellings, huddled in the picturesque amphitheatres of northern Mediterranean ports or labyrinthine south Mediterranean casbahs, were now Cochrane's playground. It was a heady brew.

Lord Keith ordered Cochrane to the west to attack enemy ships off the coast of Spain. This was more serious, for the *Speedy*, if it got into trouble, would have no support within striking distance from the British fleet at Port Mahon in Minorca, and there were more likely to be large enemy warships about. However, the young commander jumped at the chance as it gave him a perfect opportunity to improvise and fight close with the enemy.

Left to his own devices, he adopted an unusual tactic which gave the first real sign that he was not some ordinary if brave young lieutenant, but a commander of real intelligence and ability. He kept well away from the Spanish coast by day and then moved in by night to attack vulnerable and unsuspecting ships. This required total command of his crew and their full respect, as well as immensely skilful seamanship, for the dangers of running aground were multiplied at night.

Cochrane and the *Speedy* struck again and again, picking off prizes without resistance. As he did so, his reputation grew not only among the British public, but among the enemy. The mighty Spanish fleet was increasingly irritated at this gadfly operating off its coast and was irked enough to deploy real warships to go in chase of it. It was time to swat the insect. But audacity was not the 24-year-old commander's only virtue. Now, for the first time, he was to deploy another exceptional skill: deception.

As Cochrane buzzed about harassing Spanish merchant ships, he fought no real engagements, but instead showed superb sailing skills, mostly at night, to seize his prizes. But the risks were always present, as he well knew. He had his men repaint the *Speedy* in the colours of a Danish ship, the *Clomer*, which he had observed in the area. He recruited a Dane and dressed him up as an officer; he was preparing the ground for the inevitable Spanish counterattack.

In the blustery, cold winter of 1800, on 21 December, he was intrigued to see that a group of gunboats twice made out of Barcelona to attack him and then turned tail, challenging him to give chase. This he did. Soon a huge ship appeared. As he approached, broadside, the ship's portholes suddenly opened to reveal that it was bristling with cannon. The trap was deliberate: the Spaniards had caught the fly. However, they had reckoned without his indifference to intimidation and brazen resourcefulness. He immediately ran up a Danish flag as he watched this large Spanish frigate lowering a boatload of men to board him. Cochrane ordered his Danish crewman to parley with them, saying that they were a Danish ship coming from Algeria.

Undeterred, the Spanish boat continued towards them – and then Cochrane raised the yellow flag of quarantine. The Dane explained that the plague was rampant in Algeria – which was true – and that there were cases aboard. The Spanish party was aghast. If this was true, any Spaniard climbing aboard was liable to die. The boat rowed back to the mother ship, preferring to give the Dane the benefit of the doubt. Cochrane had bluffed his way through by a whisker. The young lieutenant wrote afterwards:

By some of my officers blame was cast on me for not attacking the frigate after she had been put off her guard by our false colours, as her hands – being then employed at their ordinary avocations in the rigging and elsewhere – presented a prominent mark for our shot. There is no doubt but that we might have poured in a murderous fire before the crew could have recovered from their confusion, and perhaps have taken her, but feeling averse to so cruel a destruction of human life, I chose to refrain from an attack, which might not, even with that advantage in our favour, have been successful.

Cochrane saw in the New Year of 1801 on the friendly territory of Malta. He dressed up, as a jape, in the clothes of an ordinary seaman for a fancy dress ball, but his entry was blocked by a group of status-conscious French royalist officers. Cochrane may have been drunk, unusually for him, and he lashed out at one of them. Although it was quickly clear that Cochrane was the audacious young British lieutenant who was making a name for himself off the coast of Spain, the Frenchman demanded satisfaction.

The two of them went through the absurdities of a duel, with Cochrane wounding the Frenchman in the leg and being himself hit in the ribs. But the experience shook him: 'It was a lesson to me in future, never to do anything in frolic which might give even unintentional offence.' It was a narrow early escape for the still immature young man, but it should have shown him the dangers of taking life too lightly, and of losing his temper – the latter a problem which unfortunately was to dog him for the rest of his career.

A couple of months later he pursued a French brigantine into Tunis harbour, violating its neutrality and plundering its cargo of ammunition but setting its crew free by ordering that the ship's boat be lowered into the water and left unguarded. Taking his prize back to Port Mahon in mid March 1801, he suddenly realized that the *Speedy* was being shadowed by a large Spanish frigate. Knowing he was no match for her, he flew before the wind at such speed that a sail fell from the mast. As he raced on regardless through the night, he thought he had lost the frigate, but in the grey of the morning he saw that the pursuer was still on his heels, although out of range.

He pressed on through the next day, while the frigate, with its superior sail-power, steadily closed on him. By nightfall it was almost within range and Cochrane's crew was exhausted. In a last attempt to escape, Cochrane instructed the ship's carpenter to secure a lantern to the top of a barrel and lower it from the stern, changing direction the moment the barrel was bobbing in his wake. The Spanish frigate bore down on the barrel, all eyes on the single light glowing in the dark, and found that the *Speedy* had disappeared.

—*◊◊◊*—

It was inevitable, however, that, sooner or later, the daring young man would be caught. On 5 May 1801 the reckoning came. Almost insolently close to Barcelona, the centre of Spanish naval power in the Mediterranean, Cochrane set off in pursuit of a group of small Spanish gunboats, capturing one and then returning for another among the fishing ships clustered near the harbour the following morning.

From behind those ships there suddenly emerged one of the most powerful Spanish frigates: the gunboats had been deliberately sent out as a decoy to lure Cochrane in. It was the *Gamo*, four times the size of the *Speedy*, carrying 319 men with 32 guns – 22 12-pounders, eight 8-pounders and two 24-pound carronades (the nastiest of all guns, capable of firing a huge amount of grapeshot). The *Speedy*, by contrast, had just 54 men, which was only half of its full complement because so many men had been sent off to crew prizes. Its pathetic firepower of 14 four-pounders could inflict only minimal damage at 50 yards, and none at all at 100 yards.

Cochrane had three possible courses of action. Firstly, he could surrender. Secondly, he could make a break for it and run, but the *Gamo*, by far the bigger and faster ship, would overtake him and was already nearly within range: it seemed inevitable that, if he ran, he would be caught. Or, thirdly, he could commit apparent suicide and engage this monster. In what was to become one of the classics of naval engagement between a small ship and a bigger one, he chose the latter course – perhaps because he realized there was no other hope.

He sailed straight towards the *Gamo* and placed the *Speedy* within range of its guns, although his own puny ones were still out of range. The crew of the *Gamo*, astonished, fired a warning shot. Cochrane ran up the American flag to gain time. The Spanish captain, Francisco de Torres, already amazed by the *Speedy's* decision to approach him, was thrown momentarily into confusion: perhaps, after all, this was not the nuisance that had been preying Spanish coastal shipping for so long, but a neutral ship. The decision was made not to open fire, partly because the Spaniards knew that the little ship could not escape.

At this time, the guns on all ships could not be aimed at a specific target: they were locked into position and the skill was to open fire when the movement of the sea placed a vessel at the best possible advantage to do damage to its opponent. The *Speedy*, which was windward of the *Gamo*, made the perfect target, and was within range. Cochrane's objective was to get around to the other side, where the *Gamo's* hull was low and the guns would be aiming into the sea. The Spaniard's hesitation permitted him to do just that, and he felt emboldened to run up the British flag. The result was an immediate broadside from the Spaniard which, as he expected, fell short of the *Speedy* and into the sea.

The next British manoeuvre was more startling still: the *Speedy* moved straight towards the side of the *Gamo* as the other ship rolled back with the sea and reloaded its guns frantically. Its aim was to get so close that the next Spanish broadside would fire harmlessly overhead. This involved a combination of seamanship, the movement of the sea itself and split-second timing: a few seconds too late and the *Speedy* would have faced a devastating broadside. Cochrane succeeded, and the spars of the *Speedy* actually locked with those of the *Gamo*, they were so close, while another large Spanish broadside belched deafeningly forth to pass way over the smaller ship's decks, which were 10 feet below those of the *Gamo*.

What now? The fly seemed merely to have closed with the spider and was still easy prey. But Cochrane had made his preparations: like a boxer grappling with a larger opponent at close quarters, preventing him landing a punch, he had ordered his cannon to be 'treble-shotted' and 'elevated' – aiming upwards as far as possible. With the swell tilting his ship sideways so that it aimed up into the *Gamo* (technically, he was to leeward), he was able to fire straight up into the other ship's gun deck.

He was incredibly lucky: the captain, de Torres, was killed by this first devastating broadside from below, which did remarkable damage for such small guns because it was at point blank range. The little ship was still too close for the *Gamo*'s broadsides to harm it. As Cochrane put it later: 'From the height of the frigate out of the water the whole of her shot must necessarily go over our heads, while our guns, being elevated, would blow up her main deck.'

The two ships now engaged in a bizarre *pas de deux*. Cochrane spotted Spanish marines assembling and preparing to board the little ship; he veered away just far enough to prevent this, but not so far as to bring the ship into a position where the Spanish guns could bring their guns to bear. Then he returned to inflict a further upwards broadside. This happened three times during the course of an hour, the precision of sailing involved being extraordinary because one slip could bring about a collision, or result in boarding, or permit the Spaniards to fire a devastating volley.

Of course, Cochrane's smaller ship had the advantage of much greater manoeuvrability. However, he was locked in: if he bolted, he would be picked off easily. Once again, attack seemed the only option available to him, even against a ship with six times as many men. He told his crew that the Spaniards would give them no quarter if they won and ordered several to blacken their faces in preparation for boarding. The *Speedy* moved forward to the *Gamo*'s bows and, cutlasses in mouth as though in some old pirate story, some 20 of its men, including the young Archibald Cochrane, climbed up on to the Spanish ship. Cochrane described the scene:

> The fellows thus disguised were directed to board by the head, and the effect produced was precisely that calculated on. The greater portion of the Spaniard's crew was prepared to repel boarders in that direction, but stood for a few moments as it were transfixed to the deck by the apparition of so many diabolical-looking figures

emerging from the white smoke of the bow guns; whilst our other men [including Cochrane himself and Lieutenant William Parker], who boarded by the waist, rushed on them from behind, before they could recover from their surprise at the unexpected phenomenon.

In difficult or doubtful attacks by sea – and the odds of 50 men to 320 comes within this description – no device can be too minute, even if apparently absurd, provided it have the effect of diverting the enemy's attention whilst you are concentrating your own. In this, and other successes against odds, I have no hesitation in saying that success in no slight degree depended on out-of-the-way devices, which the enemy not suspecting, were in some measure thrown off their guard.

In the confusion, the Spanish did not know how heavily they outnumbered the British attackers. Cochrane yelled at Dr Guthrie, who had been left in charge of the *Speedy*, to send in the next wave of attackers – although he knew that there was actually no one else left on board. The startled Guthrie yelled back that he would. The Spanish officers heard and believed that another boarding party was on its way. They thought that they had been lured into a trap and that the *Speedy* was crammed with attackers.

Cochrane yelled at one of his men to lower the Spanish colours, which, with remarkable coolness and skill, he did. The leaderless Spaniards, confused and demoralized, took this to be an order to surrender. The battle was over. Fifteen Spaniards, including the captain, had been killed and 41 wounded; just three British seamen had been killed and 18 wounded, one of them the valiant Parker, slashed in his leg and wounded by a musket shot.

Cochrane could not yet pause. Before the 300 or so remaining Spaniards could realize that fewer than a sixth of their number had taken them prisoner, the fighting captain ordered them into the hold and had the two most powerful guns on the ship, the carronades, trained down upon them and manned by British sailors with burning fuses. Cochrane appointed Archibald to command the giant prize, which the little *Speedy* proudly led into Minorca.

Cochrane's astonishing feat did not capture the imagination of the old men in the Admiralty. The start of the feud between the dashing young commander and his superiors can be dated from this moment – and it was the latter that initiated the hostilities. It is far from clear what underlay the Admiralty's vindictiveness. The best guess is simply that, in a service deeply reliant on hierarchy, deference and subordination, Cochrane had refused to play to the rules. He was regarded as insubordinate and was to be punished accordingly.

When he had been appointed to the command of the insignificant little *Speedy*, his superiors had never envisaged such a triumph as this; their attempt to tame him or relegate him to obscurity had backfired. He had performed spectacularly as an individual commander operating on his own; this grated on men accustomed to coordinated team action. He had been continually contemptuous of such men as Lieutenant Philip Beaver, his immediate superior, and he had too full an opinion of himself. The crusty John Jervis, Earl of St Vincent, now elevated to First Sea Lord, was not impressed by Cochrane's reputation for insubordination, and possibly even less so by the popular interest his spectacular action had aroused. The old man had almost certainly heard of Cochrane's criticism for the escape of the French fleet in the Mediterranean in 1799.

The young hero, who, although critical of his superiors, bore no particular grudge against them and was in the full flush of success, suddenly found himself steamrollered by the naval establishment. It was as though, far from having achieved one of the most spectacular single-ship victories in British naval history, he had committed a major transgression. Even after a much lesser triumph, it was customary for an officer to be made post-captain (the modern equivalent of captain). Cochrane was denied this accolade for capturing a ship four times bigger than his own.

It was normal, too, for a warship of such enormity as the *Gamo* to be absorbed into the British navy, with a large part of the prize money being paid to those who had captured her. Instead, it was announced by the Admiralty, without explanation, that the *Gamo* would be sold off as a merchantman to the ruler of Algiers, so that there would be virtually no prize money. Most offensively of all, the Admiralty resolutely blocked Cochrane's attempts to secure promotion for his able and courageous second-in-command, William Parker, who had been badly wounded in the fighting. Cochrane has been much faulted for his prickliness and insubordination even by sympathetic biographers, but these actions, which fired in the still extraordinarily young lieutenant resentments that until then had only been smouldering, were unprovoked assaults upon him by the Admiralty.

Disappointed in promotion, Cochrane was allowed to resume his raiding career in the *Speedy*, soon capturing a six-gun Spanish privateer which he put under the command of his brother Archibald. He then embarked on a successful but dangerous raid in conjunction with a bigger ship, the *Kangaroo*, on the Spanish convoy at the port of Oropesa.

It was at this time, as he continued to capture prizes relentlessly, that Cochrane began to develop a paranoid hatred of the Admiralty's system for awarding prize money. His obsession with prize money, although driven by a strong mercenary trait in his character, was far from unjustified. It was fashionable in those times for those born wealthy to deride those motivated by money; but Cochrane, although of impeccable aristocratic pedigree from one of the most distinguished titled families in Scotland, had no money; he can hardly be faulted, like those without either wealth or title, for seeking to acquire some. The system of prize money, and the possibility that large sums might be obtained thereby even by ordinary seamen, provided the navy with one of its greatest romantic attractions and motivations, as it had since Sir Francis Drake's day.

Cochrane's success was startling: by July 1801, after just a year in command of the *Speedy*, he had captured more than 50 prizes equipped with 122 guns and taken 534 prisoners. This meant that his own ordinary seamen were better rewarded than the officers in some other ships – another reason why the crew was so loyal to Cochrane. However, in a great many cases the prize money obtained was surprisingly derisory and Cochrane felt he had been cheated.

Cochrane's evident concern for his men was a particularly attractive feature of life on the *Speedy*. It was observed from the first how
extraordinarily easy it seemed to be for the young lieutenant to get
the best out of them. This was no easy task in some ships, where
sullen and resentful men would barely do the bidding of their commanders and took recourse in slowness and inefficiency rather than
outright insubordination.

Cochrane secured this respect in part because he was as good a
seaman as any on board, in part because of his approachability and
unfailing courtesy, and above all because of his dazzling success. It
was exciting to serve under such a commander and the men would
follow him willingly into danger because he had the kind of magic
that led them to believe they would emerge unscathed. Cochrane
was unfailingly solicitous about the lives of his men; he lost remarkably few because he calculated the odds so carefully in undertaking
such apparently suicidal actions as the attack on the *Gamo*. At
Oropesa, for instance, all 10 British casualties were aboard his sister
ship; moreover, Cochrane did not have command of the operation.
Although he ran his ship efficiently, discipline was not excessive
and he never had a man flogged – although he did not express
opposition to flogging in principle. It was just that he had no need
to resort to this deterrent. He was a natural-born captain.

The legendary career of the plucky little *Speedy* was brought to an
end, fittingly, in one of its most glorious actions. To Cochrane's
fury, in the summer of 1801 he was assigned to act as convoy to the
mail packet that ran between the British naval base of Port Mahon
in Minorca and Gibraltar. This in itself was a glaring example of
minor corruption: because the packet ship was barely seaworthy,
the mail was transferred to the *Speedy* as soon as the two ships were
out of port, and then back aboard the packet as they approached
Gibraltar, to give the impression the packet had carried the mail all
the way – which meant that the contractor who had provided this
unseaworthy boat could pocket the ample fee paid.

Impatient and frustrated, Cochrane cruised along the coast, keeping an eye out for possible prizes. He soon spotted some small merchant ships near Alicante, and got close. The Spaniard ships ran aground, but Cochrane could not disembark to capture them where they lay beached without risking the flimsy packet boat in his charge, so he fired his cannon at them to set them on fire. One happened to be carrying oil, which blazed fiercely through the night, to Cochrane's satisfaction.

However, the flames attracted the attention of three French battleships also heading for the Straits of Gibraltar. Cochrane's lookouts spotted the magnificent top-sails on the horizon the following morning. As Toulon, from which these warships had emerged, was supposed to be under British blockade, and the Spanish fleet was bottled up in Cadiz, Cochrane concluded that they must be Spanish treasure ships, presenting him with a wonderful opportunity. This was a fatal mistake. As he sailed towards them, wasting valuable escape time, it gradually became apparent that they were the pride of the French fleet – the *Indomitable*, the *Dessaix* and the *Formidable* – and they were fast closing on the *Speedy*, which was trapped between them and the shore.

Faced with such odds, any other commander would have surrendered at once; with the French ships' awesome sail-power, there was no chance of escape. Once they came within range, a single broadside by any one of them would be enough to sink the *Speedy*; as there were three of them they could close in on him and block his routes of escape up or down the coast. However, Cochrane was determined to make a break for it, believing, as with the *Gamo*, that he could surprise his enemies with such a bold move. He put on all possible sail, dumped his little guns overboard – they would be of no use to him in any action against the overwhelming firepower of the French ships – as well as all other surplus weight, and began to tack as the ships approached so as to ensure that he was never broadside to them.

The French guns in bow and stern managed to damage his rigging, but his bobbing and weaving prevented them from concentrating their fire. He suddenly made a break for it between the

Dessaix and the *Formidable*. The astonished French, who had expected the *Speedy* to flee from them at their approach, managed to let off a single broadside as the little ship sped past, but it missed. The *Speedy* made it out into the open sea. Captain Christie-Pallière of the *Dessaix* turned and went after it.

For a moment it seemed Cochrane had succeeded, but as repeated shots from the Frenchman's bows ripped into the *Speedy*'s canvas, the little ship began to slow and the *Dessaix* caught up after an hour, at last overhauling it. Cochrane later reported:

> At this short distance she let fly at us a complete broadside of round and grape, the object evidently being to sink us at a blow, in retaliation for thus attempting to slip past, though almost without hope of escape. Fortunately for us, in yawing to bring her broadside to bear, the rapidity with which she answered her helm carried her a little too far, and her round shot plunged in the water under our bows, or the discharge must have sunk us; the scattered grape, however, took effect in the rigging, cutting up a great part of it, riddling the sails, and doing material damage to the masts and yards, though not a man was hurt. To have delayed for another broadside would have been to expose all on board to certain destruction, and as further effort to escape was impotent, the Speedy's colours were hauled down.

Cochrane was rowed aboard the *Dessaix* and offered his sword to Christie-Pallière. 'I will not accept the sword of an officer who has for so many hours struggled against impossibility,' the Frenchman told him chivalrously, in exultation at having at last brought to an end the career of the legendary terror of the Spanish coast and its commander. Cochrane was treated with full courtesy on the remainder of the trip to anchorage at Algeciras near Gibraltar.

When they reached Algeciras, Cochrane was informed of the approach of a squadron of six British warships of 74 guns each under the command of Admiral Sir James Saumarez. Christie-Pallière asked him whether they would attack. Cochrane replied: 'An attack will certainly be made, and before night both the French and British ships will be at Gibraltar, where it will give me great

pleasure to make you and your officers a return for the kindness I
have experienced on board the Dessaix.'

The French commander ordered his ships to move closer to the
protection of the Spanish batteries but, in their haste, the three
ships ran aground. As the two men had breakfast the following day
a cannonball smashed into the cabin, spraying them with glass from
a shattered wine bin nearby. They ran on deck to witness several
marines being cut down by intense British fire. Cochrane, not wishing to be killed by his own side, discreetly withdrew to a safe place.
He recounted what happened next:

> The Hannibal, having with the others forged past the enemy, gal-
> lantly filled and tacked with a view to get between the French ships
> and the shore, being evidently unaware of their having been hauled
> aground. The consequence was that she ran upon a shoal, and
> remained fast, nearly bow on to the broadsides of the French line-of-
> battle ships, which with the shore batteries and several gun-boats
> opened upon her a concentrated fire. This, from her position, she was
> unable to return. The result was that her guns were speedily dis-
> mounted, her rigging shot away, and a third of her crew killed or
> wounded; Captain Ferris, who commanded her, having now no alter-
> native but to strike his colours – though not before he had displayed
> an amount of endurance which excited the admiration of the enemy.
>
> A circumstance now occurred which is entitled to rank amongst
> the curiosities of war. On the French taking possession of the
> Hannibal, they had neglected to provide themselves with their
> national ensign, and either from necessity or bravado rehoisted the
> English flag upside down. This being a well-known signal of distress,
> was so understood by the authorities at Gibraltar, who, manning all
> government and other boats with dockyard artificers and seamen,
> sent them, as it was mistakenly considered, to the assistance of the
> Hannibal.
>
> On the approach of the launches I was summoned on deck by the
> captain of the Dessaix, who seemed doubtful what measures to adopt
> as regarded the boats now approaching to board the Hannibal, and
> asked my opinion as to whether they would attempt to retake the

ship. As there could be no doubt in my mind about the nature of their mission or its result, it was evident that if they were allowed to board, nothing could prevent the seizure of the whole. My advice, therefore, to Captain Palliere was to warn them off by a shot – hoping they would thereby be driven back and saved from capture. Captain Palliere seemed at first inclined to take the advice, but on reflection – either doubting its sincerity, or seeing the real state of the case – he decided to capture the whole by permitting them to board unmolested. Thus boat by boat was captured until all the artificers necessary for the repair of the British squadron, and nearly all the sailors at that time in Gibraltar, were taken prisoners!

The British sent a boat under a flag of truce to suggest an exchange of prisoners. Christie-Palliere refused, but he did agree to parole the young British lieutenant. This was a colossal mistake, as subsequent events were to show, but it was demonstrative of the Frenchman's respect towards his guest-prisoner. Cochrane returned to a hero's welcome at Gibraltar.

It was still a moment of extreme danger and anxiety for the British garrison in the port. A Spanish flotilla of six warships was on its way to rescue the three French craft. Saumarez, with just five ships, sailed into the attack as night fell. In the ensuing confusion two of the biggest Spanish warships of 112 guns destroyed each other, giving the British victory. Cochrane watched the whole show along with the garrison at Gibraltar.

A few days later he was formally court-martialled for the loss of the *Speedy*. Such court martials, with all their ceremony and pomp, automatically took place on the loss of a ship. Cochrane was acquitted with honour and on the same day was promoted to post-captain, reflecting his achievement at last in capturing the *Gamo*. However, the appointment was not backdated, so he was left at the bottom of the seniority list, well below many undistinguished colleagues of his own age and with no chance at all of being given a command in view of the huge surplus of officers to ships.

Cochrane's uncle Alexander and his father lobbied the crotchety old Lord St Vincent on his behalf. This proved counterproductive.

'The Cochranes are not to be trusted out of sight,' he thundered. 'They are all mad, romantic, money-getting and not truth-telling.' When he was told he must give young Cochrane a ship, St Vincent retorted, 'The First Lord of the Admiralty knows no must.' To Cochrane's former commander, Admiral Lord Keith, St Vincent wrote more reasonably: 'It is unusual to promote two officers [Cochrane and William Parker] for such a service – besides which, the small number of killed on board the Speedy does not warrant the application.'

Cochrane himself entered the fray, once again, typically, on behalf of his subordinate Lieutenant Parker, so valiantly injured in the capture of the *Gamo*. St Vincent's reply had been calculated to drive a man of his passion to fury:

> His reasons for not promoting Lieutenant Parker, because there were only three men killed on board the Speedy, were in opposition to his Lordship's own promotion to an earldom, as well as that of his flag captain to knighthood, and his other officers to increased rank and honours: for in the battle from which his Lordship derived his title, there was only one man killed on board his own flagship, so that there were more casualties in my sloop than in his line-of-battle ship.

This played on the popular perception that Nelson had won the Battle of Cape St Vincent, while Lord St Vincent had watched safely from his flagship. St Vincent was beside himself with this gross impertinence which, however accurate, was extraordinarily ill-advised of Cochrane. The naval establishment substituted its instinctive dislike of the young hero with real spite. The unfortunate Parker was despatched to the West Indies to take command of a ship that mysteriously failed to materialize and was a broken man on his return home.

Cochrane, a captain without a command, was made doubly redundant by the short outbreak of peace between France and Britain as a result of the Treaty of Amiens of March 1802 and returned to Scotland. Astonishingly, he decided to cross the Firth of Forth to study moral philosophy at Edinburgh under a famous pedagogue, Dugald Stewart. He took the opportunity of leisure to make up for his elementary schooling, but moral philosophy remains a remarkable choice for a fighting man, and one can only surmise that he was examining the ethical implications of his own profession. Cochrane was nothing if not a man of paradox: high intelligence and deep thoughtfulness underlay the popular image of a half-crazed warrior. His acute and overworking mind would lead him to a passionate interest in public affairs, in particular the politics of injustice, which later got him into so much trouble.

At about that time he first met the Radical leader, William Cobbett, on a visit to Hampshire, as well as another prominent Radical who was to become one of Cochrane's lifelong supporters, Mary Russell Mitford. She gave this description of him: 'he was as unlike the common notion of a warrior as could be. A gentle, quiet, mild young man, was this burner of French fleets as one should see in a summer day. He lay about under the trees, reading Seldon on the Dominion of the Seas, and letting children (and children always know with whom they may take liberties) play all sorts of tricks with him at their pleasure.' Dreamy, gentle, philosophical, young Cochrane appeared to be more a poet than a warrior, the embodiment of the Romantic movement then so fashionable, except that in reality he was a battle-stained hero, not a dandy, a poet, or a fop.

—◦◦◦—

In March 1803, war was renewed between Britain and France, and Cochrane promptly and predictably applied for command of a ship. He was just as promptly and predictably fobbed off. He then compiled a list of all the ships under construction and sent it to the Admiralty. St Vincent replied huffily that they had all already been allocated to other commanders. Cochrane took a coach down to London to see the crotchety First Lord personally. Once again the old disciplinarian, after refusing to see him for several days, stonewalled him. The incensed young officer played his last and only card, threatening to resign the service. This would have brought a storm of obloquy down upon the Admiralty – he was one of the few naval commanders with a genuine popular reputation.

The First Lord looked at him with icy thoughtfulness and told him that after all there was a ship available at Plymouth. Cochrane was exultant and travelled down on the first available coach. When he arrived at the great dockyard and saw her, his first words were 'she will sail like a haystack!' HMS *Arab* was a converted collier, a sluggish flat-bottomed hulk with neither speed nor manoeuvrability. He had been outwitted by St Vincent.

As soon as Cochrane took to sea with her, he discovered that her greatest problem was that she would not sail against the wind. Ordered to Boulogne, he found it impossible to return:

> With a fair wind, it was not difficult to get off Boulogne, but to get back with the same wind was – in such a craft – all but impossible. Our only way of effecting this was by watching the tide, to drift off as well as we could. A gale of wind anywhere from N.E. to N.W. would infallibly have driven us on shore on the French coast... I wrote to the Admiral commenting that the Arab was of no use for the service required, as she could not work to windward, and that her employment in such a service could only result in our loss by shipwreck on the French coast.

In a thunderous rage, when Cochrane managed to struggle back across the Channel, he intercepted an American merchant ship, the *Chatham*, on its way to Amsterdam, informing its startled and indignant captain that there was a British blockade of the river Texel. This was news as much to the Admiralty as to the Americans. Cochrane was promptly ordered north to protect the Shetland fishing fleet, which was odd, as the Shetlands had no fishing fleet to protect. He was, in effect, in a degrading exile for nearly 14 months aboard a wallowing and useless tub, far away from any action.

Cochrane has sometimes been interpreted as the creator of his own problems. In fact, it was the Admiralty which had taken the initiative in his persecution and he had manfully, if unwisely, risen to the bait. In time of war they were even further in the wrong to so ill-use one of their best commanders. There was no doubt of his naval skills, as the *Speedy* campaigns had shown, and really good captains were in desperately short supply. Because he had tweaked the noses of naval bureaucrats, challenged their system of prefer- ment and, above all, affronted the First Lord, the most exciting British seaman alive was left patrolling the empty northern extrem- ities of Britain in an old collier while the country's very existence was at stake – Napoleon was now preparing to invade. To the impa- tient young man, his career must have seemed almost over, at the ripe old age of 27, a commander of brilliance crushed by the system.

—◈—

Fate is nothing if not ironic and even capricious. Cochrane had secured his initial advancement largely through the connections of his aristocratic, if impoverished, family. He had then made his name through superb seamanship and captaincy, excoriating those of lesser talents who had ascended through favouritism, and been obstructed every step of the way. The man who had most come to hate him, Lord St Vincent, was himself a meritocrat who bitterly opposed preferment. The middle-class St Vincent despised Cochrane for his aristocratic hauteur and for his general lack of respect for authority.

Now, with the accession of a new Tory government under William Pitt, Henry Dundas, First Viscount Melville, was appointed in St Vincent's place. Melville was political jobbery and corruption personified. He was the political boss of Scotland who could deliver the whole country to Pitt through manipulation and appointment.

As a Scot, he took notice of the incestuous lobbying of Scottish families, in particular the Duke of Hamilton, on behalf of young Cochrane, and so the latter's fortunes took a remarkable new twist: he was appointed through favour by this corrupt old political boss to be commander of the *Pallas*, a brand new 667-ton frigate of 38 guns – 12 of them 24-pounders, 26 of them 12-pounders – with a crew of over 200. It was a dream come true. Melville, it seems, had the shrewdness to see that much-needed victories against the French could be won only by appointing the best commanders, however insubordinate, and not by exiling them to the Shetlands. Cochrane, bemused by this astonishing change in his fortunes, was forced to resort to the pressgang to recruit his crew – his old one on the *Speedy* had been dispersed – and he was ordered to attack enemy convoys crossing the Atlantic.

The young captain left Plymouth on 21 January 1805 and, after a month's training at sea, made his way to the Azores, where he could intercept ships making the Atlantic crossing. On 6 February he reported:

> We fell in with and captured a large ship, the Caroline, bound from the Havannah to Cadiz, and laden with a valuable cargo. After taking out the crew, we despatched her to Plymouth. Having learned from the prisoners that the captured ship was part of a convoy bound from the Havannah to Spain, we proceeded on our course and on the 13th captured a second vessel which was still more valuable, containing in addition to the usual cargo some diamonds and ingots of gold and silver. This vessel was sent to Plymouth as before. On the 15th we fell in with another, La Fortuna, which proved the richest of all.

When *La Fortuna* was taken, its cargo proved to be worth £132,000. Cochrane generously allowed the captain and cargo-manager, much of whose fortune this was, to retain 5,000 doubloons each; the crew was consulted and shouted 'Aye aye my lord, with all our hearts' – as well they might because they stood to gain so much. By the end of March 1805, four major prizes had been sent home.

Disaster then struck in an uncanny repetition of the events that had led to the capture of the *Speedy*. As one of the *Pallas'* masts poked above a heavy sea-mist one morning, the lookout called that he could see three masts approaching. Cochrane himself scrambled up the rigging and immediately recognized them as French ships of the line. He had no choice but to run. Even as the chase began, the wind blew up, the sea grew choppier and the mist dissipated. The water deepened into the troughs of an approaching gale.

The three ships had much more sail than the *Pallas*, and were soon gaining upon him. However, the gale was an advantage to him, too: the French could not aim their cannon properly as they bucked and surged under the heavy seas. The *Pallas* plunged furiously forward at full sail, its bows swamped under water with each breaking wave. Even so, the battleships still gained upon him, two approaching at half a mile's distance on each side, with one coming up behind.

However, Cochrane had trained his men perfectly, and he had a plan. He ordered his topmen up into the rigging. As the boat thundered through the spray and they clung to the spars for life, he gave them the signal to furl every sail at once. The French ships ploughing through the waters alongside could not fire because of the violence of the seas and because they were not yet within range. At exactly the moment the sails of the *Pallas* disappeared from view, Cochrane's helmsman turned hard over.

For the ship it was a moment of supreme danger. Still moving fast, but now broadside to the waves in these ferocious seas, the *Pallas* could easily have capsized, but Cochrane had calculated that, with no sails, the wind would be unable to assist the sea in turning the ship over. Even so, she 'shook from stern to stern in crossing the trough of the sea'. In effect, she had stopped dead in her tracks, and the French ships of the line, their sails billowing, shot past for several miles downwind, while the *Pallas* tacked off slowly in the opposite direction, against the wind.

> Before they had fairly renewed the chase night was rapidly setting in, and when quite dark, we lowered a ballasted cask overboard with a lantern, to induce them to believe that we had altered our course, though we held on in the same direction during the whole night. The trick was successful, for, as had been calculated, the next morning, to our great satisfaction, we saw nothing of them, and were all much relieved on finding our dollars and his Majesty's ship once more in safety. The expedient was a desperate one, but so was the condition which induced us to resort to it.

By May 1805, Cochrane had arrived off the island of Aix. He then embarked on a new kind of warfare – commando raids to destroy French signal positions:

> The French trade having been kept in port of late, in a great measure by their knowledge of the exact position of his Majesty's cruisers, constantly announced at the signal-posts; it appeared to me to be some object, as there was nothing better to do, to endeavour to stop this practice.
>
> Accordingly, the two posts at Point Delaroche were demolished, next that of Caliola. Then two in L'Anse de Repos, one of which Lieutenant Haswell and Mr Hillier, the gunner, took in a neat style from upwards of 100 militia. The marines and boats' crews behaved exceedingly well. All the flags have been brought off, and the houses built by government burnt to the ground.
>
> Yesterday, too, the zeal of Lieutenant Norton of the Frisk cutter, and Lieutenant Gregory of the Contest gun-brigantine, induced them to volunteer to flank the battery on Point d'Equillon, whilst we should attack in the rear by land; but it was carried at once, and one of fifty men who were stationed to three 36-pounders was made prisoner – the rest escaped. The battery is laid in ruins – guns spiked – carriages burnt – barrack and magazine blown up, and all the shells thrown into the sea.

Cochrane spotted a large French frigate, the *Minerve*, with 40 guns, which was twice the size of the *Pallas* nestling under the battery of Aix. This 'large black frigate' had been plaguing the British for some time. In addition, there were three French brigantines protecting this predator. Cochrane nevertheless ordered the *Pallas* to sail straight down the Aix channel towards it. The French, astounded by this medium-sized ship taking on such odds, in their best protected and most formidable anchorage at that, 'scrambled', in the modern phrase. But by then he had already put one of the brigantines out of action. Tacking backwards and forwards, he managed to avoid the notoriously dangerous shoals of the Aix channel and destroyed another brigantine, while also doing damage to the rigging of the *Minerve*. The French were unnerved by the rashness of this crazy ship in their midst.

Cochrane sailed the *Pallas* between the *Minerve* and the shore battery, both of which were pounding away ineffectually. He ordered his ship to close with the *Minerve*, in preparation for battle. This was done too sharply: the two ships collided, their masts locking with one another, and the guns of the *Pallas*, which had just loosed off a broadside, were knocked back momentarily. Under Cochrane's frantic direction, the British crew recovered far more quickly from the impact of the collision than the French, and let off another devastating broadside at point-blank range.

No more than three solitary pistol shots came back in retaliation. The *Minerve*'s captain, Joseph Collet, had been the only man not to flee below under the onslaught of fire, and he coolly raised his hat in salute through the smoke. Cochrane, only a few feet away, was deeply impressed by his gallantry: when he later found the same officer as a captive in the stable block of Dartmoor prison, he had him moved to better quarters.

Meanwhile, the young captain, for all the verve and nerve of his attack, was in greater danger than ever. His own ship was almost as crippled as the *Minerve* and two French frigates were now bearing down to the latter's help. Fortunately, a British ship, the *Kingfisher* under Captain George Seymour, was a little way off. Seymour was regarded as imprudent, and he had orders from Admiral Thornburgh not to proceed beyond a lighthouse above Aix. Seeing Cochrane's predicament, however, he decided to ignore these. He sailed south to escort Cochrane out. The two frigates – although each had more guns than the two British ships combined – had seen enough of the danger posed by the British and sheered off to go to the rescue of the crippled *Minerve*.

Cochrane returned to Plymouth a week later as even more of a popular hero. His tour in the Bay of Biscay had been a dazzling display of aggression, fearlessness and skill: a single ship had terrorized coastal France. No other British commander since Nelson had achieved what Cochrane had – taken the fight directly to the enemy – nor had any French commander done the same along the

British coast. He had punched down the Garonne River and intimidated a major French city, Bordeaux, and destroyed its naval defences; he had penetrated the very centre of French naval power at Rochefort, destroying its signals system; and he had crippled a major French ship twice his size and destroyed two brigantines. The effect upon French morale was overpowering: nowhere along the coast seemed safe from this marauder. The effect on the British war effort, at a time of despondency, was equally electric: here at last was a sailor worthy to succeed Nelson. In the highest personal compliment of his career following this attack, Cochrane was dubbed by Napoleon 'le loup de mer' – the sea wolf (or more literally the sea bass, which is a fast-moving and fast-feeding inshore fish).

—∿∿—

Cochrane's performance in the Bay of Biscay, coming after his exploits in the Mediterranean and off the Azores, clearly demonstrated he was the outstanding sea-captain of the time, but he had one colossal defect in the eyes of the Admiralty: he cared not a fig what they thought. So confident was he of his own abilities that he saw no need to ingratiate himself with his superiors or toe the line.

In 1807, he was given command of the *Imperieuse*, a 1,064-ton frigate, about twice the size of the *Pallas*, and even faster, with 38 guns and 300 men, many of whom Cochrane had arranged to be transferred from his previous ship. Among the new recruits was a 14-year-old boy, Frederick Marryat, the son of a rich MP and West Indies merchant. Marryat was later to become the first great novelist of the navy in Napoleonic times. He was vividly to describe his experiences under Cochrane. Cochrane took to raiding the French coast once again, capturing ship after ship with a languid professionalism that deeply impressed the young Marryat:

> The cruises of the Imperieuse were periods of continual excitement, from the hour in which she hove up her anchor till she dropped it again in port; the day that passed without a shot being fired in anger was with us a blank day; the boats were hardly secured on the booms than they were cast loose and out again; the yard and stay tackles

were for ever hoisting up and lowering down. The expedition with which parties were formed for service; the rapidity of the frigate's movements day and night; the hasty sleep, snatched at all hours; the waking up at the report of the guns, which seemed the only key note to the hearts of those on board; the beautiful precision of our fire, obtained by constant practice; the coolness and courage of our captain, inoculating the whole of the ship's company; ...when memory sweeps along those years of excitement, even now my pulse beats more quickly with the reminiscence.

Cochrane embarked on another of his spectacular raids inshore, against a French convoy guarded by small warships south of the Gironde. The convoy was protected by the formidable guns and defences of Fort Roquette. The French, hearing of his approach, had ordered the soldiers from the fort down to the beach. As they waited for the expected attack, Cochrane landed a raiding party further up which attacked the almost undefended fort, destroying its guns and blowing up the arsenal. On hearing the explosion, the French soldiers on the beach ran in the direction of the attack, abandoning the ships. Cochrane's boats silently pounced upon them, setting fire to seven merchant ships and gunboats.

Returning to the fleet, which was anchored off Rochefort, he encountered the *Atalante*, a battered British sloop which had been on station blockading the port for eight months. Its captain appealed to him: she was leaking so badly that she could barely stay afloat. The pumps could barely expel this. Cochrane protested to the commander of the squadron, Richard Goodwin Keats, who did nothing, and then to the authorities at Plymouth on his return there. In any gale, he declared, the *Atalante* was certain to sink. Soon enough word came that just this had happened and that the similarly unseaworthy *Felix*, whose commander had also been rebuffed by the ruthless Captain Keats, was also lost. Cochrane now saw the corruption, jobbery and indifference of the mediocre naval establishment in a different, more sinister light.

Cochrane was ordered to the Mediterranean to serve under Admiral Lord Collingwood, who sensibly respected his independence and sent him to command the Corfu squadron, patrolling the Ionian Islands. Collingwood, an exceptional and enlightened commander who had banned the use of flogging aboard his ships, then appointed him to harass France and Spain. The vigorous young captain resumed his old activities along the Spanish coast with gusto. As in the days aboard *Speedy*, he found it almost too easy – and he was now commanding a much bigger and better ship.

On 17 February 1808, the *Imperieuse* spotted a convoy some eight miles west of Cartagena and pursued the ships along the shore. It veered away when it spotted four gunboats, anchoring out of sight of land, and waited for them to leave their anchorage just after sunset. The predatory *Imperieuse* suddenly moved in among them, firing broadside after broadside, sinking two with all hands and boarding another. The fourth escaped to Cartagena, where the Spanish fleet was at anchor, and Cochrane prudently decided not to pursue it.

From the captured prisoners, he learnt that a large French ship filled with munitions was at anchor in the Bay of Almeria, and he decided to 'cut her out' – take her at anchor. The *Imperieuse* hoisted American colours, sailed in close to the French ship and sent out two boats with boarding parties. The French opened fire, but were successfully boarded although the leader of the boarding party, Lieutenant Caulfield, was killed as he jumped aboard. However, the wind suddenly died away, leaving the *Imperieuse* and its prize becalmed under a heavy fire from shore batteries just half a mile away. The battery damaged the hull of the prize, which Cochrane had skilfully placed between the *Imperieuse* and the enemy guns, and at 11 a.m. a light breeze took them out of range – not a moment too soon, as a Spanish ship of the line had arrived to help. The *Imperieuse* was, however, the faster ship, and got away.

—

The greatest of Cochrane's battles soon followed: the Battle of the Aix Roads in April 1809. Napoleon's Admiral Willaumez had liberated a large section of the French fleet from British blockades along the French coast, but found himself trapped by the British at Rochefort. The French fleet was a sitting duck for annihilation. It was vital to stop it escaping, but Admiral Lord James Gambier, who was dithering out at sea with the main British fleet, was simply too cautious a man to deal a fatal blow to the French and it was becoming increasingly likely that the French would escape. The Admiralty, which so disliked Cochrane, conceived of an extraordinary idea. The one officer with close knowledge of Rochefort and Aix Roads from his tour of duty three years before was Thomas Cochrane, who had long suggested invading the anchorage with fireships. Here, at last, was a use for this tiresome but fearless seaman. If Cochrane perished the Admiralty would be well rid of him; if he succeeded, it could claim the credit.

Cochrane was summoned to Whitehall, where he was received warmly, even effusively, by the new First Sea Lord, Lord Mulgrave, a red-faced Tory. Mulgrave was to the point, informing him that in spite of Gambier's reservations, 12 transports were being converted for use as fireships: 'You were some years ago employed on the Rochefort station and must to a great extent be acquainted with the difficulties to be surmounted. Besides which, I am told that you then pointed out to Admiral Thornburgh some plan of attack, which would in your estimation be successful. Will you be good enough to detail that or any other plan which your further experience may suggest?'

Cochrane was immediately interested, and launched into his own pet project for building 'explosion ships' to add to the fireships. Even Cochrane was taken aback by how seriously he, a mere captain, was being taken by the First Sea Lord. Now came the shock: Mulgrave told Cochrane that he was to command the expedition.

At this Cochrane was aghast: he knew the fury that giving command of so major a venture to so junior a captain would arouse, not just in Admiral Lord Gambier, but in all the senior captains serving with him. Despite his reservations, Cochrane's head was swimming with the opportunity as his carriage galloped with all speed to Plymouth to join the 12 transports and to meet up with William

Congreve, the inventor of a new type of explosive rocket, who was to take part in the attack.

Cochrane supervised the conversion of the transports into fireships as they arrived from England. The construction of fireships was an old technique. Five large trails of gunpowder were laid criss-cross on the deck. Wood and canvas were stretched between them. Up above, tarred ropes dangled down from sails also covered in tar. Chains were fixed to the sides with grappling hooks so that it would be difficult for a ship to detach itself. Resin and turpentine were poured all over the fireship to help it to burn. Finally huge holes were made in the hull to make it suck in air and feed the flames after the ship began to burn.

With the arrival of a further nine transport ships, Cochrane now had 21 fireships under his command. However, he was busier still on his own invention, explosion ships. The French would be prepared for fireships, but they would have no understanding of his new secret weapon, just approved by the Admiralty. The preparations for these were more elaborate still:

> The floor was rendered as firm as possible by means of logs placed in close contact, into every crevice of which other substances were firmly wedged so as to afford the greatest amount of resistance to the explosion. On this foundation were placed a large number of spirit and water casks, into which 1,500 barrels of powder casks were placed, several hundred shells, and over these again nearly three thousand hand grenades; the whole, by means of wedges and sand, being compressed as nearly as possible into a solid mass.

Admiral Willaumez had been replaced by Vice-Admiral Allemand, who had anchored the French ships in an apparently impregnable position. They were drawn up in two lines, between two small islands, the Ile d'Aix and the Ile Madame, which dominated the approaches to the Charente River. There were gun batteries on the Ile d'Aix and the Ile d'Oléron, a large spur of land to the west, as well as on the mainland.

Cochrane had already personally observed that the battery on Aix was in a poor state of repair, and its firepower grossly exaggerated. Moreover, his earlier reconnaissance had led him to discover a remarkable thing. The only clear line of attack upon the French would have to be between a large reef, around three miles wide, called the Boyart Shoal, which was uncovered at low tide, and the Ile d'Aix. Cochrane, crucially, had found out that 'there was room in the channel to keep out of the way of red-hot shot from the Aix batteries even if, by means of blue lights [flares] or other devices, they had discovered us'. In other words, the fort providing protection for the French fleet was no use at all.

However, Cochrane did not know that the French had their own secret defence – a 900-foot long boom made of wooden trunks, held together by chains and anchored to the sea floor. Allemand had also taken other precautions: he had stationed four frigates along the boom, as well as some 70 smaller boats whose purpose was to tow the fireships away from the main fleet should they succeed – which seemed unlikely – in breaking through the boom. The 10 French battleships in the frontline had lowered their sails in order to lessen their chances of catching fire.

On the morning of 10 April, Cochrane went to Admiral Gambier to seek formal authorization to put his plan into action. To his astonishment, Gambier refused, citing the danger to the crews of the fireships: 'If you choose to rush on to self-destruction that is your own affair, but it is my duty to take care of the lives of others, and I will not place the crews of the fire-ships in palpable danger.' Depressed and frustrated, Cochrane returned to the *Imperieuse*. The following day the wind got up from the west and a heavy sea began to run. Far from being deterred by this, Cochrane saw that it presented an opportunity: the sea would favour the British, especially as the tide came in, and the French would be less on their guard, thinking the conditions too dangerous for an attack. Of course, the swell would make navigation much trickier in the treacherous channel.

Gambier, meanwhile, had taken the time to reflect. His explicit orders were to allow Cochrane to make the attack and he could not continue to refuse him authority without risking injury to his own reputation. Cochrane returned on board the flagship to ask for permission and this time it was grudgingly given.

His ships would attack in three waves. The first would be his three explosion ships, the foremost of which he would command himself. The second wave would consist of the 21 fireships. Behind them were three frigates, Cochrane's former charge, the *Pallas*, the *Aigle* and the *Unicorn*, accompanied by HMS *Caesar* to pick up the returning crews of the explosion vessels and fireships; but they would not come close to the action at this stage.

There were two sobering thoughts. First, the French understandably regarded fireships as a barbaric instrument of war and would execute anyone they caught that could be identified as crewing them; the sailors were instructed to say, if caught, that they belonged to supply ships nearby. Second, although the flood-tide to shore in this heavy swell favoured the fireships' approach, it would make it very difficult for their crews, now in small boats, to return against the flow and reach the safety of the rescue ships.

Gambier, astonishingly, anchored his fleet nine miles away. It was such a distance that it could only be supposed he wanted to be able to make a break for it and escape if the French fleet came out after him. The fleet would be too far to exercise the slightest influence on the initial action and, worse, it was impossible for him to see what was really going on; even signals were liable to be misinterpreted at that distance.

Cochrane floated in on the flood-tide aboard the foremost explosion vessel – itself a desperately dangerous venture, as he and his men were sitting on top of tons of explosive: one lucky shot from the French and they would be annihilated. Besides Cochrane and Lieutenant William Bissell of the *Imperieuse*, there were just four seamen. Behind him a second explosion ship followed with Midshipman Marryat on board, commanded by a lieutenant. Cochrane had no idea that there was a boom but his ship navigated successfully down the channel at dead of night, in spite of the heavy swell, and approached as close to the distant huddle of the French fleet as he dared. He then lit the 15-minute fuse of the explosives, while his men were already aboard the getaway gig.

As soon as he jumped aboard, they rowed for all they were worth away from the explosion ship in the pitch darkness. According to press accounts, Cochrane, hearing barking, saw a dog – the ship's mascot – aboard and rowed back to fetch it. Certainly something delayed his departure and the fuse, for some reason, went off after only nine minutes. Cochrane's boat had barely managed to get clear of the ship again when it went up. He was saved by his failure to get further. If he had not gone back he would have been on the receiving end of the shower of debris that soared overhead and landed in an arc in the sea just beyond.

The explosion was awesome. Cochrane vividly described the scene:

> For a moment, the sky was red with the lurid glare arising from the simultaneous ignition of 1,500 barrels of powder. On this gigantic flash subsiding, the air seemed alive with shells, grenades, rockets, and masses of timber, the wreck of the shattered vessel; whilst the water was strewn with spars shaken out of the enormous boom, on which, on the subsequent testimony of Captain Proteau, whose frigate lay just within the boom, the vessel had brought up before she exploded. The sea was convulsed as by an earthquake, rising in a huge wave on whose crest our boat was lifted like a cork and as suddenly dropped into a vast trough, out of which, as it closed on us with a rush of a whirlpool, none expected to emerge. The skill of the boat's crew however overcame the threatened danger, which passed away as suddenly as it had arisen, and in a few minutes nothing but a heavy rolling sea had to be encountered, all having become silence and darkness.

The boom lay in pieces. The second ship passed through its broken fragments some 10 minutes later, and the decision was taken to detonate the explosives and abandon ship in the same way. Another tremendous roar shattered the peace of the night sky. The third explosion ship had, however, been pushed away from the scene by the *Imperieuse* because a fireship had come too close and there was a risk of all three blowing up together. Marryat was ordered to go aboard the fireship and steer it away, a heroic action, after which Cochrane asked him laconically whether he had felt warm.

To Cochrane's disappointment, the fireships were badly handled. As he rowed back to the *Imperieuse*, four passed him, being towed by small rowing boats towards their destination, but the towing boats of some 17 others had abandoned them about four miles out to sea, judging the risk too great, and most drifted harmlessly ashore.

The whole spectacle had been enough to cause havoc among the French fleet. Their first experience of the attack had been the ear-shattering explosion and conflagration aboard Cochrane's ship, followed by another even closer to hand. Then the night sky had been lit up by the spectacle of 20 blazing vessels, some close, others out to sea, in a massive attack to destroy the French fleet.

The French's first assumption was that the fireships coming towards them were also explosion vessels, and in the small space of water of the Aix anchorage, the ships of the line manoeuvred desperately to avoid them, while both wind and tide drove them relentlessly towards the shore. The flagship *Ocean* was the first to run aground. According to one of its officers:

> we grounded, and immediately after a fireship in the height of her combustion grappled us athwart our stern; for ten minutes she remained in this situation while we employed every means in our power to prevent the fire from catching the ship; our fire engines and pumps played upon the poop enough to prevent it from catching fire; with spars we hove off the fireship, with axes we cut the chains of the grapplings lashed to her yards, but a chevaux de frise on her sides held her firmly to us. In this deplorable situation we thought we must have been burned, as the flames of the fireship covered all our poop. Two of our line-of-battle ships, the Tonnerre and Patriote, at this time fell on board of us; the first broke our bowsprit and destroyed our main chains.

Some 50 of the *Ocean's* men fell into the water and drowned. In the confusion the French ships made towards the coastal mud-flats and the Palles Shoal off the Ile Madame; they got too close. The tide was on the turn and now ebbing fast: the *Ocean* was joined ashore by the *Aquilon*, *Tonnerre*, *Ville de Varsovie* and *Calcutta*. Soon there were seven ships with their hulls stranded like ducks' bottoms out of the water.

As the first streaks of light illuminated the morning sky, Cochrane looked on the scene with deep satisfaction. His victory had been far from perfect: he had been forced to blow up the explosion ships before they could reach the fleet but they had destroyed the boom that protected the French fleet. The fireship attack had been almost a disaster: but the confusion sown by the first two explosion ships and the four fireships that had reached the French fleet had been enough effectively to disperse the French fleet, run most of it aground, and place it at the mercy of the British. Complete victory lay in the offing, thanks to his imagination and the bravery of his crews.

At 5.48 a.m. he signalled triumphantly to the flagship, the *Caledonia*, some nine miles away: 'Half the fleet to destroy the enemy. Seven on shore.' Gambier signalled back with the 'answering pennant' – a bare acknowledgement. Cochrane, just outside the Aix channel, watched the floundering French fleet and waited for Gambier's ships to approach and give him the signal to attack with his small flotilla of frigates. He wondered why there was no movement by Gambier's ships, but watched delightedly through his telescope as four more French ships were beached.

At 6.40 a.m. he reported this to the *Caledonia*. The answering pennant was hoisted but still Gambier made no move. Cochrane's notoriously short fuse was now burning to explosion point: he had just taken in a ship laden with explosives at enormous personal risk to himself, narrowly escaped with his life, rowed back against a surging flood-tide and taken action to save his ship from a rogue fireship. He had seen his attack effectively incapacitate the entire French fleet. It was impossible for beached ships to fire any guns at all. Now that they could be picked off at will, Gambier and his huge fleet were still hesitant to come in and finish them off.

An hour later, at 7.40 a.m., Cochrane sent another signal: 'Only two afloat.' The reply was the answering pennant again and the fleet made no move. Whatever the explanation he gave at the subsequent court martial, Gambier's motives in refusing to attack the beached French fleet were probably mixed. He had been witness to the amazing fireworks of the night before. He heartily disapproved of the whole tactic of sending in explosion ships and fireships, and disliked the impulsive and reckless Cochrane. His captains had been almost mutinous about Cochrane's appointment.

How could the commander-in-chief even be sure that Cochrane was telling the truth and not seeking to entice the fleet into a dangerous engagement from which it might emerge badly damaged? Gambier's duty was the protection of the fleet, and he could not put it at risk on the word of an impertinent young captain. He decided, first, not to risk his ships in the confined waters of the Aix–Boyart channel under the guns of enemy batteries and, second, to teach Cochrane a lesson and show him who was in command. The Admiralty had ordered him to support Cochrane's fireship attack; it had not insisted that he risk any of his own ships.

This was to be one of the most contemptible acts of any commander-in-chief in British naval history. The ideal chance to move in and destroy the beached French fleet would be short-lived. The British ships would have the perfect chance to come in on the flood-tide before the French ships floated once again. It was a small window of opportunity.

Cochrane fumed in an agony of frustration and impotence. He signalled at 9.30 a.m.: 'Enemy preparing to move.' Gambier was later to claim that 'as the enemy was on shore, [I] did not think it necessary to run any unnecessary risk of the fleet, when the object of their destruction seemed to be already obtained'. There is a small possibility that he was telling the truth – in other words that he believed the French ships to have been incapacitated by their grounding – although any sailor with more experience than

Gambier would have realized that a ship beached by a tide was perfectly capable of floating off with little damage done.

It is perhaps true that there was a slight element of ambiguity in the first three signals – but only to the most obtuse commander. Cochrane claimed later that he then sent another signal 'the frigates alone can destroy the enemy' – which allowed no ambiguity, but was clearly impertinent. It was not, however, logged aboard the flagship. After the 9.30 a.m. signal, even Gambier could have harboured no illusions that the enemy was destroyed.

At 11 a.m. the Admiral ordered his captains aboard to confer – itself a time-wasting procedure. He at last ordered his ships inshore – and then, to Cochrane's astonishment, the fleet stopped some four miles out. Cochrane watched in utter disbelief: victory was ebbing away with the incoming tide. As he wrote:

> There was no mistaking the admiral's intention in again bringing the fleet to an anchor. Notwithstanding that the enemy had been four hours at our mercy, and to a considerable extent was still so, it was now evident that no attack was intended, and that every enemy's ship would be permitted to float away unmolested and unassailed! I frankly admit that this was too much to be endured. The words of Lord Mulgrave rang in my ears, 'The Admiralty is bent on destroying that fleet before it can get out to the West Indies.'

Having displayed so much courage the previous night, he now took what is said to have been the bravest decision of his entire career, because it involved both defying his commander-in-chief and taking on alone the might of the French navy – although to him the risk may have seemed small as the ships were at his mercy. However, they were floating off, and Gambier's prevarications had left it almost too late even for him to attack successfully.

In an action that compared with Nelson's raising the telescope to his blind eye at Copenhagen, Cochrane decided to raise anchor aboard the *Imperieuse* and drift, stern foremost, down the perilous Aix channel – that is, with his vulnerable rear exposed to enemy fire – and straight into the midst of a dozen warships. This required superb seamanship. The idea was not to let Gambier see what he was doing until the last moment, and to be able to claim that he had floated accidentally with the tide. The shore batteries on the Ile d'Oléron opened up, but the shells fell reassuringly far from the ship – as Cochrane had always predicted they would. The ones on the Ile d'Aix were so ineffectual that, according to a British gunner, 'we could not find above thirteen guns that could be directed against us in passing; and these we thought so little of that we did not return their fire'.

However, the huge flagship *Ocean* was now afloat again, as were four other ships, which immediately turned tail and made for the safety of the Charente estuary upon the *Imperieuse*'s backwards approach. The French were now so demoralized they were not prepared to take on even Cochrane's single ship. Cochrane wrote later, 'Better to risk the frigates or even my commission than to suffer such a disgraceful termination' of the engagement. At last, when he had safely emerged from the channel, he unfurled his sails, signalling at the same time to Gambier: 1.30 p.m., 'The enemy's ships are getting under sail'; 1.40 p.m., 'The enemy is superior to the chasing ship'; 1.45 p.m., 'The ship is in distress, and required to be assisted immediately'. He had cleverly outwitted his admiral: he could claim that he had not been responsible for the *Imperieuse*'s approach to the French fleet; and it was unheard of for a commander not to come to the help of one of his ships in distress, thus forcing Gambier's hand.

By 2 p.m. the *Imperieuse* was close enough to deliver a broadside into the 50-gun French magazine ship, the *Calcutta*, while her forward guns fired upon the *Aquilon* and her bow guns fired on the *Ville de Varsovie* – three ships at the same time. Captain Jean-Baptiste Lafon of the *Calcutta*, fearing that his explosive-laden ship would blow up, climbed understandably but ignominiously out of his stern cabin window and ran away across the mud – for which he was later shot by the French.

The *Imperieuse* itself came under fire. Marryat recalled graphically how a seaman in the forecastle was decapitated by a cannonball, and how another was blown in two while the spine still attached the two parts: the corpse, its reflexes still working, jumped to its feet, stared at him 'horribly in the face', and fell down. In fact, only three members of the crew were killed and 11 wounded throughout the whole engagement – another example of this 'reckless' man's meticulous care for the safety of his men. The *Calcutta* surrendered at 3.20 p.m. and Cochrane's men took possession.

Behind him, Gambier had at last been goaded into action. He sent in two battleships, the *Valiant* and *Revenge*, along with the 44-gun *Indefatigable*. The *Revenge* fired at the *Calcutta* before she realized it had already been occupied by Cochrane's sailors. The *Aquilon* and the *Ville de Varsovie* surrendered at 5.30 p.m. The *Caesar*, under Rear-Admiral Robert Stopford, had also joined the battle by then. At 6 p.m. the crew of the *Tonnerre* abandoned ship and set fire to her; an hour later it blew up, as did the *Calcutta*, which had been set alight by Cochrane's men, at about 9 p.m. Six of the French ships had, however, escaped up the Charente. Stopford sent in hastily converted fireships after them, but these were unable to prevail against the wind and he used them instead against other ships.

The fighting raged on through the following night. At 4 a.m., however, Gambier hoisted three lights aboard his flagship as a signal for the recall of the British ships. The two ships Cochrane had captured, the *Aquilon* and the *Ville de Varsovie*, were set alight by Stopford – although Cochrane had hoped to bring them back as prizes. As the *Indefatigable* sailed past, Cochrane tried to persuade her captain to join him in a final attack on the French flagship, the *Ocean*, but he refused. Cochrane set off in pursuit, accompanied by a flotilla of small boats.

Gambier thereupon sent him an astonishing letter, which had to be rowed all the way to his ship:

> You have done your part so admirably that I will not suffer you to tarnish it by attempting impossibilities, which I think, as well as those captains who have come from you, any further effort to destroy those ships would be. You must, therefore, join as soon as you can, with the bombs, etc, as I wish for some information, which you allude to, before I close my despatches. PS: I have ordered three brigantines and

two rocket vessels to join you, with which, and the bomb, you may make an attempt on the ship that is aground on the Palles, or towards Ile Madame, but I do not think you will succeed; and I am anxious that you should come to me, as I wish to send you to England as soon as possible. You must, therefore, come as soon as the tide turns.

Cochrane replied curtly: 'I have just had the honour to receive your Lordship's letter. We can destroy the ships that are on shore, which I hope your Lordship will approve of.' For four hours now Cochrane and his little boats had engaged the mighty *Ocean*, convinced that further successes could be obtained. At 5 a.m. a further letter arrived from Gambier unambiguously relieving Cochrane of his command:

It is necessary I should have some communication with you before I close my despatches to the Admiralty. I have, therefore, ordered Captain Wolfe to relieve you in the services you are engaged in. I wish you to join me as soon as possible, that you may convey Sir Harry Neale to England, who will be charged with my despatches, or you may return to carry on the service where you are. I expect two bombs to arrive every moment, they will be useful in it.

At last, after nearly 36 hours of exhausting battle, Cochrane obeyed orders and returned to the flagship. The battle-stained and exhausted young captain confronted the impeccably dressed and pompous non-combatant admiral who had done so little to help him, and had turned what should have been an overwhelming victory into half of one. Cochrane wrote that he:

begged his lordship, by way of preventing the ill-feeling of the fleet from becoming detrimental to the honour of the service, to set me aside altogether and send in Admiral Stopford, with the frigates or other vessels, as with regard to him there could be no ill-feeling: further declaring my confidence that from Admiral Stopford's zeal for the service, he would, being backed by his officers, accomplish results more creditable than anything that had yet been done. I apologized for the freedom I used, stating that I took the liberty as a friend, for it would be impossible, as matters stood, to prevent a noise being made in England.

Gambier replied huffily: 'If you throw blame upon what has been done, it will appear like arrogantly claiming all the merit to your-self.' Cochrane retorted: 'I have no wish to carry the despatches, or to go to London with Sir Harry Neale on the occasion. My object is alone that which has been entrusted to me by the Admiralty – to destroy the vessels of the enemy!'

Cochrane was peremptorily ordered to depart for Britain the fol-lowing morning, arriving at Spithead six days later. Even the French acknowledged the magnitude of the victory: 'This day of the 12th was a very disastrous one: four of our ships were destroyed, many brave people lost their lives by the disgraceful means the enemy made use of to destroy our lines of defence.' A planned French expedition to Martinique had been completely destroyed.

It had been the last great naval battle of the Napoleonic wars, a victory won largely by a single captain in a single ship, on a par with the Glorious Fourth of June, St Vincent, Copenhagen, the Nile and Trafalgar. Although fewer ships were destroyed thanks to Gambier's ineptitude, the Battle of Aix Roads had momentous effects. The French never stirred in force again, or threatened Britain seriously with invasion: there were no more great sea battles.

Cochrane, however, was far too junior and controversial to enjoy the thanks of the Admiralty or the government. On the return of the British fleet to Britain, it was Gambier who was granted the honours of victory. When Cochrane protested publicly, a court martial was held which was a travesty of justice. When Gambier was commended, Cochrane was considered disgraced. He furiously turned down an offer to command a flotilla in the Mediterranean.

At last, Britain's greatest living seaman was offered in 1814 com-mand of a ship of the line, in the war with America. Before he could sail, however, he was implicated, almost certainly falsely, in a spectacular stock exchange fraud and was sent to prison for a year.

Afterwards, Cochrane was forced abroad and was hired by the rebels in Chile to act as their admiral. He sailed down to Valdivia

along the southern cost, then an impregnable fortress consisting of
a finger of sea leading to the river Valdivia enclosed by land on
almost all sides, approached by a single narrow 1,200-yard channel.
The almost landlocked anchorage was covered on one side by no
fewer than four forts, and by one significant and four smaller forts
on the other side. In the middle of the channel was the fortified
island of Mancera. It would be suicidal for any ship to attack down
the narrow channel under the guns of the forts, which made the
harbour virtually unassailable.

Cochrane, on arriving off the coast, made a reconnaissance.
Hearing that three Spanish ships were expected in Valdivia – one of
which he knew had been delayed, another sunk off Cape Horn, and
a third in hiding – he hoisted a Spanish flag, coolly dropped anchor
off the port, and requested a pilot from the Spaniards. As soon as the
pilot's party arrived, they were taken prisoner and the pilot forced to
lead Cochrane into the entrance of the channel, where he was able
to ascertain the positions and strengths of the forts before sailing out
again, to the astonishment of the Spaniards on shore. From the same
pilot, Cochrane learnt that another ship was approaching the estuary, and this he captured, together with the 20,000 dollars aboard.
Cochrane sailed north to Concepcíon, where he picked up 250 soldiers from the local Chilean garrison before returning, at the end of
January 1820, to a position opposite Valdivia.

Cochrane decided that the impossible expedition to Valdivia
must proceed:

> Cool calculation would make it appear that the attempt to take
> Valdivia is madness. This is one reason why the Spaniards will hardly
> believe us in earnest, even when we commence. And you will see
> that a bold onset, and a little perseverance afterwards, will give a
> complete triumph.

He transferred his men from the crippled flagship, which he
feared would have been recognized in Valdivia, to two small companion ships, the brig *Intrepido* and the schooner *Montezuma*. He
made for a surf-strewn beach just outside the entrance to the

harbour, the Aguada del Ingles ('the English beach'), behind Fort Ingles, determining not to attack from the sea but from the land, immobilizing the forts that made it so dangerous to enter the land-locked stronghold by sea. But his ships would still have to come within range of Fort Ingles itself.

Once again raising the Spanish flag, his two small ships arrived off the beach. A Spanish-born officer told the commander ashore that they were escorts for a Spanish convoy which had been detached from the main fleet, and that they had lost their boats and so could not land. In fact the boats were in the water on the sea-ward side of the ships, in preparation for a landing. One, however, drifted free, and the suspicious Spaniards saw that the officer was lying.

The alarm was given and Fort Ingles opened fire at point blank range. Cochrane immediately decided to attack, sending officer Miller in charge of 44 marines. The boats set out for the beach, their oars snagged by a huge quantity of seaweed. They were pep-pered with musket shot from a force of 75 Spaniards ashore, but Miller led an ordered bayonet charge which soon dispersed the defenders on the beach. The 250 Chilean troops behind the advance guard were then landed safely.

When darkness fell, Cochrane decided to stage the attack on Fort Ingles. He divided his men into two forces, one in front and one creeping around the back of the fort. Those in front attacked, firing into the air and creating the maximum disturbance. The larger second party, under Ensign Vidal, crossed the ditch surround-ing the fort across an improvised bridge in silence and climbed the ramparts behind the Spaniards, who were concentrated to face the first assault.

The rear party attacked, with the furious cries of the Araucanian Indians of southern Chile. The garrison fled, and in so doing pan-icked the 300 Spanish reinforcements sent when news of the Chilean landing had reached the other Spanish positions. With frenzied bayonet charges, the Chileans turned a retreat into a rout, pursuing them to Fort Carlos, where the defenders were unable to close the gates before the Chilean attackers broke in.

The disorderly retreat, now swollen by the occupants of the second fort, continued to Fort Amargos and once again the Chileans
were so hard on the Spaniards' heels that they broke into the garrison, defeating the Spaniards. The ever-growing horde of fleeing
Spanish troops reached Corral Castle, where they at last succeeded
in keeping out the Chileans. This buttress was much better
defended, and could have withstood a prolonged siege.

As the exhausted but elated Cochrane surveyed the night's work,
he had succeeded in taking three out of the four forts commanding
the western approaches to the channel. But the Spanish fleet was
still protected by Corral Castle and Fort Niebla on the eastern
shore, and Mancera Island in the middle, which between them
could inflict a withering crossfire on any ship attempting to make
the passage. Cochrane could be satisfied, though, that he had captured part of the Spanish artillery on Fort Chorocomayo overlooking Corral Castle, and could bombard it at daylight.

He did not expect the Spaniards simply to give up, however. Yet
100 of their force had been killed and 100 taken prisoner – there
were only about 300 left, facing about the same number of
Chileans. Colonel Hayas, the commander of Corral Castle, was
sinking into an alcoholic stupor, realizing the position was hopeless.
Before daylight he ordered half of his men into the boats below the
castle to cross the harbour, and himself surrendered with the rest to
Miller. Cochrane had secured the whole western bank of the
'impregnable' harbour at Valdivia at a cost of just seven dead and 19
wounded, through the simple expedient of attacking from the land,
not from the sea.

The following morning his two small ships, the *Intrepido* and the
Montezuma, sailed into the channel under the fire of the smaller
eastern forts, and anchored off Fort Corral to ferry Chilean troops
across for an attack on the other side of the harbour. A moment
later, on Cochrane's orders, the frigate *O'Higgins* appeared and,
assuming that the large ship was bringing a wave of fresh troops,
Spanish morale finally collapsed. Fort Niebla and the other eastern
defences were abandoned as the Spanish troops evacuated upriver
to Valdivia. In fact the *O'Higgins* had only a skeleton crew aboard,

not even enough to man the guns, and no troops, and it was steadily sinking; it only just made it to the beach. But Cochrane had guessed accurately that it would inspire terror in the demoralized Spaniards.

He wasted no time. Two days later he sent the *Intrepido* and the *Montezuma* upriver towards Valdivia. Although the former ran aground, when Cochrane reached the town he found that the Spanish garrison and the army had fled, and the local notables were suing for peace. Cochrane had captured Ambrosio O'Higgins's Spanish redoubt, along with 10,000 cannon shot, 170,000 cartridges, 128 pieces of artillery, 50 tons of gunpowder and a ship – at a cost of seven dead.

—⁓—

Next Cochrane launched a daring raid to 'cut out' – seize at anchor – the Spanish flagship at Callao, the port of Lima and seat of the viceroyalty. At 10 p.m. the little force of 14 small boats set out from the *O'Higgins*, which was anchored just out of sight of the harbour, rowing through a small gap in the boom which Cochrane had noticed two days before. Just past the boom, the small and silent flotilla was challenged by a gunboat. Cochrane brought his boat alongside, saying he would surrender. The Spanish commander was suddenly faced by a boatload of armed men and surrounded by others. He yielded quietly.

The little armada now rowed past the bulk of a United States warship, the *Macedonian*. As one of Cochrane's officers noted, 'many of her officers hung over the bulwarks, cheered us in whispers, wishing us success, and wishing also that they themselves could join us.'

However, the sentries aboard a British ship, the *Hyperion*, loudly challenged Cochrane's boats, making him fear that the Spanish had been alerted. All remained silent elsewhere. Within a few moments, Cochrane's boat was alongside the *Esmeralda*, and he and his men were climbing the main chains from all sides. Cochrane himself was one of the first to reach the deck, but the sentries had heard the rattle of the chains and a blow from a musket butt sent him crashing back into his boat, severely injuring his back as the thole-pin, behind the oar, penetrated him near the spine. In agony, he climbed up again to shoot the sentry. Another sentry fired at him, although he succeeded in pushing his assailant overboard.

Cochrane's men streamed aboard, grappling with sentries and shooting at them from all sides. But they had lost the element of surprise, although most of the crew remained below deck. The Spanish admiral sounded the alert and gathered his marines on the forecastle, from which they rained a fusillade of shots down on the deck. Cochrane, along with Captain Guise, led an attack from the deck, but he was shot in the leg, and forced to pull back, directing the assault sitting on a gun. He had now been twice wounded, but was unbowed.

After a fierce firefight, with British sailors climbing up the rigging American-style to fire on the Spaniards below, the tide turned against the latter and many dived into the sea. Admiral Coig of the *Esmeralda* surrendered to Cochrane, but was himself injured by a stray shot shortly afterwards. Simply through staging a surprise attack at the very heart of Spanish strength, Cochrane had succeeded in capturing the Spanish flagship.

The difficult part was about to begin: getting the ship out of the harbour. As soon as he came aboard Cochrane had ordered men up the rigging to prepare for sailing. In charge of the ship with the loss of eleven dead and 30 wounded in just 17 minutes of intense fighting, he gave the order to prepare the sails – but not to move. He still wanted to capture two brigs which were nearby, and set other ships adrift:

> The two brigs of war are to be fired on by the musketry from the *Esmeralda*, and are to be taken possession of by Lieutenants Esmond and Morgell in the boats they command; which being done, they are to cut adrift, run out, and anchor in the offing as quickly as possible. The boats of the Independencia are to turn adrift all the outward Spanish merchant ships; and the boats of the *O'Higgins* and *Lautaro*, under Lieutenants Bell and Robertson, are to set fire to one or more

of the headmost hulks; but these are not to be cut adrift, so as to fall down upon the rest.

Some 300 yards away the main shore batteries and gunboats were blazing blindly away in the dark. It seemed only a matter of time before the ship was hit and became an incandescent target. Cochrane coldly assessed the nearby British and American ships which were leaving the harbour to get away from the fighting. He ordered the same signal lights as they were showing to be hoisted aboard the *Esmeralda*. He judged that the Spaniards would be terrified of sinking a neutral ship. He was right: the guns suddenly fell silent.

Cochrane, having given his orders and been immobilized by his wounded leg and the pain in his back, left for his flagship to have his bleeding staunched. He was furious to discover later that Captain Guise, who he had left in charge, had given the order to sail *Esmeralda* at full speed out of the harbour before, as Cochrane wanted, every vessel there was 'either captured or burned'. Guise claimed that the Chileans were plundering the ship and the English crewmen had broken into the liquor store and were drunk, and that anyway it was more important that the pride of the Spanish navy be attached to the rebel fleet than that it be exposed to further danger. Given the gallant conduct of the crews during the fighting, both stories seemed unlikely. When the Spanish guns opened up again the *Esmeralda* was safely away, along with two captured gunboats. A boat from the American ship, the *Macedonian*, which had cheered Cochrane on, went ashore at Callao the following day for provisions. The crew were lynched for suspected collaboration in the raid. It had certainly been one of the most daring and boldest raids in naval history.

The significance of the capture of the *Esmeralda*, coming after the loss of the Spanish stronghold of Valdivia in Chile, was enormous. Just as San Martin's crossing of the Andes had provided the key to the consolidation of the independence of Argentina and Chile, or Bolivar's crossing of the northern Andes had at last flanked the Spaniards in the north, so Cochrane's mastery of seapower in the Pacific was the turning point in the destruction of the last great redoubt of Spanish power on the continent, Peru. As Captain Basil Hall put it, the capture of the Esmeralda

> was a death-blow to the Spanish naval force in that quarter of the world; for, although there were still two Spanish frigates and some small vessels in the Pacific, they never afterwards ventured to show themselves, but left Lord Cochrane undisputed master of the coast.

With Cochrane in undisputed control of the sea the remainder of the Spanish fleet did not dare to stir out of Callao, which was blockaded by the Chileans, and food became increasingly scarce in Lima. Some 650 Spaniards belonging to the crack Numancia battalion deserted to the Chileans in the aftermath of the capture of the *Esmeralda*. News also reached them that the 1,500-strong garrison at the port of Guayaquil further up the coast had revolted against the Spaniards.

Control of the sea had permitted the Spaniards to dominate the western side of the continent. With its loss they were defenceless, particularly as Lima, surrounded by an inhospitable desert, was supplied from the sea.

—◦◦◦—

Brazil now recruited Cochrane for its own struggle for independence from Portugal.

His first skirmish with the Portuguese suggested that at last he had taken on too much. The 160-strong crew of the *Pedro Primeiro*, under his command, consisted of some English and American sailors, freed slaves and the 'vagabondage' of Rio de Janeiro. It led three other seaworthy ships proudly into battle, sailing through a gap in the Portuguese lines and cutting four ships off from the main fleet. When Cochrane ordered his ship into battle the three others kept their distance, and the *Pedro Primeiro* found itself on its own.

He soon noticed that only a few of his guns were firing, and sporadically. The two sailors directing the guns were trying to save on powder. Humiliated, the *Pedro Primeiro* had to retreat. In a fury, Cochrane, on returning to port, stripped the three ships of their British and American seamen and brought them all aboard the *Pedro Primeiro*. As with most occasions in his naval career, he was happiest commanding a single ship against far greater odds.

His next target was the Portuguese-occupied port of Bahia, 600 miles up the coast towards the equator. He resolved to reconnoitre in typically bold fashion. In June 1823, he sailed at night into the huge bay of Bahia, mapping the anchorage of the Portuguese fleet. When hailed by a nearby warship, he claimed to be a British merchant vessel. However, on that moonless night, the wind suddenly dropped and he was becalmed right under the guns of the Portuguese fleet and the shore batteries. Keeping his nerve, he allowed the ship to drift with the ebb tide downriver, skilfully using anchors to keep it clear of the rocks. Once again, luck seemed to be against him on his Brazilian campaign.

Appearances were deceptive however: the Portuguese, fearing that he was preparing fireships, were terrified of a repetition of the Battle of the Basque Roads (1809). Cochrane's reputation from both France and Chile had preceded him. When the Portuguese commander at Bahia, General Ignacio Madeira, learned that the mysterious interloper had been Cochrane's flagship, he was gripped with terror that the fleet, trapped in its anchorage, would be easy prey for fireships and explosion vessels.

> The crisis in which we find ourselves is perilous, because the means of subsistence fail us, and we cannot secure the entrance of any provisions. My duty as a soldier and as governor is to make any sacrifice in order to save the city; but it is equally my duty to prevent, in an extreme case, the sacrifice of the troops I command – of the squadron – and of yourselves...

Cochrane bombarded Madeira with psychological warfare, urging him to surrender, for fear that civilians might be killed. The garrison at Bahia was running short of supplies, as Cochrane's ships blockaded the port. It seemed astonishing that so large a Portuguese fleet should be so terrified of so small a flotilla. But on 2 July Madeira decided to evacuate the entire garrison and most of the civilian population in an attempt to escape the trap.

The 13 Portuguese warships were to accompany some 70 transport ships to the safer anchorage of Maranhao, 1,000 miles to the north. Cochrane's four ships worked like predators and began to pick off the transports one by one. The Portuguese warships preferred to keep their distance while even the armed troopships put up little resistance. Cochrane's men simply boarded one boat after another and, lacking the men to man them, had them dismasted so that they could travel no further and drifted back to the Bay of Bahia.

After thus disabling a large number of boats, Cochrane's small fleet sailed off in pursuit of the rest of the large, unwieldy convoy. When the *Pedro Primeiro* boarded the *Gran Para* along with several troopships, several thousand soldiers were immobilized. Cochrane was hoping to lure the Portuguese warships into attacking him, and then pull them away from the rest of the convoy in a futile chase into mid-ocean. But the Portuguese warships steered clear. The chase extended from 13 degrees south to 5 degrees north.

With around half the Portuguese transport fleet disabled, he attempted to launch a night attack on 16 July upon the warships themselves. But the mainmast of the *Pedro Primeiro* split into two and the ship was crippled. Because of the dark, the Portuguese did not realize this, and Cochrane was able to break off the engagement safely. Having captured half of the Portuguese garrison at Bahia, he was deeply frustrated at seeing the other half – and in particular the warships – sailing off into the hazy mists of the equator.

—✺—

Cochrane now staged one of the greatest hoaxes in naval history, eclipsing even his previous escapades of deception and masquerade. Taking advantage of the much greater speed of the *Pedro Primeiro* once its mainmast was repaired, and leaving his three lesser ships behind, he decided that, while he had lost the Portuguese fleet, he knew where it was headed from captured despatches, and could overtake it. In 10 days Cochrane's ships sped northwards towards Maranhao, arriving there on 26 July, well ahead of the sluggish Portuguese fleet.

He hoisted Portuguese colours, and awaited a brig sent out from shore to greet him. The Governor, Dom Agostinho Antonio de Fama, believed this to be the advance guard of the Portuguese evacuation force from Bahia. On boarding the *Pedro Primeiro*, the welcoming party was seized, and the captain despatched ashore with a message from Cochrane to the governor. This asserted that the Portuguese fleet had been completely destroyed, and that the *Pedro Primeiro* was the advance guard of a huge Brazilian convoy. Cochrane's message declared:

> I am anxious not to let loose the Imperial troops of Bahia upon Maranhao, exasperated as they are at the injuries and cruelties exercised towards themselves and their countrymen, as well as by the plunder of the people and churches of Bahia.

Cochrane's own ship was supposedly filled with such bloodthirsty men. However, the admiral said he was prepared to grant generous terms, which included the repatriation of the Portuguese troops in Maranhao to Portugal, giving them safe passage aboard merchant ships. In fact, Cochrane was desperate to get them out before the remainder of the Portuguese fleet should arrive to expose his bluff. He had only a single ship's crew to pit against the several thousand men stationed at Maranhao, the well-defended shore batteries, and the truncated, but still formidable force being brought in by Madeira.

To Cochrane's own astonishment, Dom Agostinho agreed to his terms without further ado. Cochrane's meagre force occupied the defences of Maranhao while the Portuguese garrison was evacuated and fled the port before the arrival of the rest of the Portuguese fleet.

When Madeira's fleet reached Maranhao they found, to their surprise and horror, that the place was under Cochrane's control, and desperately turned north towards the final Portuguese stronghold of

Para. But Cochrane had already despatched Captain Pascoe Grenfell, another former British officer, with a captured ship to repeat the trick. There the authorities refused to be deceived; but they knew that without the assistance of the two main Portuguese armies, one of which had left for Portugal, the other still on its way, they could not hold out long. On 12 August Para surrendered.

After just three months under the Portuguese flag, Cochrane had delivered the whole of northern Brazil to the young emperor. Of all Cochrane's escapades this, while by no means the most dangerous, was the most completely audacious and breathtakingly cheeky of his entire career. Cochrane returned to Rio to a tumultuous popular welcome and the embrace of the emperor.

His spell as commander of the Greek independence fleet against the Turks was less successful, however, largely owing to the poor quality of the Greek sailors. Cochrane died at the ripe old age of 84 in 1860, a pioneer of the steamship and other inventions.

Cochrane had been the last of the great naval heroes of sail, after Drake, Morgan, Raleigh, Rodney, Nelson and St Vincent. He was a master of seamanship second to none, a brilliant improviser and an excellent naval tactician. Throughout his rollercoaster career, he was a true naval professional, always rebounding from setbacks. Incredibly courageous, quick-thinking under fire, with an eye for the bold and unexpected strike and a complete disregard for the odds against him – the worse, the better – he also possessed the flamboyance and eccentricity of charismatic leadership. He led his men from the front, a tall figure with a shock of red hair. Yet there was method in his madness, and high responsibility: he always picked his targets with scrupulous care to achieve victory and avoid unnecessary losses to his men and even to the enemy. His men would follow him devotedly because he not only won battles but took care to protect their lives: he was much less of a disciplinarian than either Nelson or Wellington, who were both regarded as careless with the lives of their men in battle, because he did not need to be.

Cochrane possessed the mavericks' contempt for authority and penchant for insubordination to an almost comic degree, quarrelling with virtually all his superiors, convinced, often correctly, that he was in the right. He was essentially a one-man band, who barely got on with his fellow officers, and was not effective at coordination as a fleet commander, as his records in South America and Greece show. He was also a hopeless, if admirably idealistic, politician. However, if Nelson was the greatest fleet commander of all, Cochrane was the best captain, with Aix Roads, although smaller than Trafalgar, marking just as decisive a victory in containing the French. Cochrane was a military genius, the last great naval warrior of sail, who was always at the head of his men in the thick of the fighting.

Chapter 6

WELLINGTON, THE IRON DUKE: MASTER OF THE SUDDEN STRIKE

Like Washington, the Duke of Wellington's inclusion in this book as a maverick may raise eyebrows. Was he not the master of defence rather than offensive tactics, caution rather than boldness and risk-taking? In fact, Wellington was a stronger, bolder, more eccentric figure than he outwardly appeared.

The infant Arthur Wesley was born a child of privilege. His family hailed from the middling aristocracy of Ireland, which counted as the lower aristocracy of England. Arthur was born on 1 May 1769 at the family's Dublin house. Their country residence was Dangan Castle, a day's ride away. Much has been made of Arthur's having been born of a large family on an island which was somewhat looked down upon by its rulers – just like Napoleon. Yet Napoleon's highly strung personality had much more in common with that of Nelson. The young Arthur appeared anything but highly strung – in fact he was something of a dolt. He seemed an amiable, sometimes mischievous, slow-witted, dreamy dunce. A year younger than either Napoleon or Nelson, he was of a similar social background to Bonaparte although superior in pedigree to Nelson, in an age when this was hugely important. The boy trundled dreamily through his uneventful childhood as his family's fortunes subsided about him.

His elder brother Richard seemed to have everything he lacked: he was strikingly good-looking and highly intelligent. He was nine years older than Arthur, which placed him in a paternal, supporting relationship to the young brother rather than in sibling rivalry. Nevertheless, Richard once pointed his brother out to a friend as 'the biggest ass in Europe'. The elder boy was wafted into Harrow, then Eton, then Christ Church, Oxford – the cradles of the establishment.

Wesley was sent to Brown's seminary in the King's Road and then, in turn, to Eton. He was slow of speech, shy, with few friends, uninterested in either rowing or cricket, then in vogue at the school, and performed poorly academically. He enjoyed going on long solitary walks. The extraordinary mixture of ambition and introversion that made him one of the most peculiar of men in later life were already evolving.

With the family lacking the money to continue his education at Eton, he was sent to a tutorial establishment in Brighton. A friend of his wrote that he was 'extremely fond of music, and played well upon the fiddle, but he never gave any indication of any other species of talent. As far as my memory serves, there was no intention then of sending him into the army.'

He went on to study in Brussels, where his mother was living to save money, before attending a riding academy in the stolid middle-French town of Angers. Although still happy-go-lucky and idle, his mother detected a 'remarkable change for the better' in him. His older brother, now Lord Mornington and as an Irish peer permitted to sit in the House of Commons, secured for him an appointment to the 73rd regiment as an ensign in March 1787, at the age of 17.

Like most other officers, Wesley was the fortunate object of preferment, one of the commonest ways of elevating one's status in those days. He was first despatched as an aide-de-camp to the Viceroy of Ireland, Lord Buckingham, of the all-powerful Grenville clan, where he played the naughty boy. Dublin girls would not go to a party if 'that mischievous boy' attended, according to Lady Aldbury, who also turned him out of her carriage because she found him such dull company on one occasion. He would tweak the neck-cloths of his friends, and was dumped in mid-dance by a local beauty, possibly on account of a boorish amorous advance.

By the end of Wesley's playful time in Ireland, the features that were to become so famous had emerged. He was of medium height; his face was long, with a pointed, determined chin, a thin-lipped, haughty, aristocratic mouth, a formidable, aquiline but hawk-ended nose, a languid, still dreamy expression and prominent, contemptuous eyes beneath full brows and a high forehead. He was extremely neat and well turned out, dapper even, and certainly good-looking, although not so much as his older brother. However, his detached expression and slow diction did not make him immediately charismatic. He seemed an embodiment of the classical English gentleman, which he ardently desired to be, rejecting his long roots in Ireland.

With the declaration of war with France in 1793, Wesley asked to be sent as part of the army to Martinique in the West Indies, but was turned down – which saved him from the disease that decimated the troops that went there. He borrowed money from Mornington to buy a lieutenant-colonel's commission and was despatched to join the Duke of York's force in Flanders. In June 1794, he left Cork, reaching the barren, flat shores of Flanders later that month. His commander was Lord Moira. Thus at the age of just 24 – such was the unprepared state of the British army – he was placed in command of a brigade without having ever even seen a shot fired in anger.

He was not slow to show his mettle. Moira put him in charge of a force ordered to take Ostend, while the main reinforcements went off inland to join the Duke of York's army, which after the rout in Flanders was in headlong retreat along the Scheldt. No sooner had Moira departed than Wesley re-embarked his men and sailed to Antwerp, where he reinforced the Duke of York before Moira arrived by land.

In September 1794, Wesley was ordered to the aid of General Sir Ralph Abercromby to reinforce Boxtel and the Dommely River, which had been taken from the French. Abercromby had, however, blundered into the main French army and had to beat a hasty retreat. Wesley was given control of the rearguard where he arrayed his troops in line and coolly stopped the French advance, allowing the main force to retreat safely. Despite the failure of the campaign, he was commended for his courage in the engagement.

He was now ordered to a more exotic location – India. He left in June 1796 at the age of 26, some time before the Irish rebellion of 1798: he would otherwise have certainly been given a distasteful role in suppressing his fellow countrymen. He reached Calcutta after a sea journey of eight months. He stepped ashore opposite the elegant fortress of Fort St George along the fetid, disease-infested banks of the Hugli in February 1797.

Real opportunities for Wesley's advancement at last beckoned: with Britain and France at war the former decided on a more 'forward' imperialist policy of expansion in India at the expense of the local princes supported by the French. In addition, his brother, Lord Mornington, was appointed governor-general of India by his friend William Pitt. Around this time, Mornington decided that the family name was too plebeian and adopted the name of Wellesley, linked back to the female line of his grandfather. Arthur 'Wellesley' was soon promoted to full colonel, well in advance of longer-serving officers of his rank.

Mornington's first target was the state of Mysore, which was under the control of the most fearsome and effective of Indian princes, Tippoo Sultan, the 'Tiger', son of Hyder Ali, who had been a consistent thorn in the British side but had been kept behind his borders by the competent Lord Charles Cornwallis, Mornington's predecessor as governor-general. The Muslim Tippoo was a wise and enlightened ruler by contemporary Indian standards, showing considerable religious tolerance towards the Hindu majority and interested in economic and scientific advances.

Wellesley was placed under the command of General George Harris, the commander-in-chief at Madras. Given the rank of brigadier, he was ordered to march a contingent of the troops of a British ally, the Nizam of Hyderabad, the 250 miles from Madras to Mysore, and displayed unusual efficiency in provisioning troops and transporting the necessary artillery – two huge 24-pound cannon,

18 heavy 18-pounders and eight nine-pounders. Mornington himself had wanted to accompany the army into the field, but was dissuaded by Wellesley, who warned his brother that 'your presence will diminish [Harris'] post'. The offensive was two-pronged, with the force of 4,000 British and 16,000 Indian troops from Madras joining up with a smaller force under General James Stuart from the west coast of India.

After a long and slow march, the army advanced into Mysore, into which Tippoo had retreated while using his superb horsemen to harass the British and pursuing a scorched-earth policy; thoughtfully anticipating this, Wellesley had already secured his supplies. When they reached the Eastern Ghats range on 10 March 1797, the Indian cavalry attacked Wellesley's troops near Kelamangalam, but he led a counterattack which drove them off.

Meanwhile, Stuart's column had also beaten back an attack at Sedaseer in the Western Ghats, causing Tippoo to disperse his men. At Malavelly, Tippoo established two heavy guns to cover the main road and attacked with about 2,000 infantry, but they were repelled by ordered, linear fire from the infantry under Wellesley's command.

The British marched on to Seringapatam, Tippoo's stronghold located on a peninsula between two branches of the Cauvery River, which was dry at that time of year. The position was an immensely strong one. Harris' approach was to flank it from the southwest, before ordering his men to attack a grove near the village of Sultanpettah. It was badly handled, and Tippoo counterattacked in force, driving Wellesley's men north and then west. Wellesley's first real engagement had ended in failure. The following day he took the outpost with a much larger force, but his cocky self-confidence had been badly dented.

General Stuart arrived to the north of the Cauvery River and a concerted attack on the fortress was made on 26 April. Wellesley took part, clearing an area beneath the walls of enemy troops so that assault cannon could be brought forward. However, he was placed in reserve for the actual assault which was to be commanded by General David Baird, an old rival of Wellesley: it took place in classical fashion after breaches had been made in the walls on 4 May.

The attack was highly successful and Tippoo was killed. Wellesley, who arrived afterwards, found his body. The British lost some 400 killed or wounded to 9,000 on Tippoo's side, which were largely the result of a rampage of atrocities committed by British troops on storming the fortress, which revealed that the Indians were not the only ones to perpetrate horrific cruelties on their opponents. Wellesley, to his credit, was horrified.

Baird apparently asked to be relieved of his command as he was exhausted, although he later denied having said this. He was dismayed to find that he was to be replaced by his old junior rival, the pampered governor-general's brother who had played little part in the actual fighting. The failure to prevent the murderous rampage of his men, after the brilliant success of the assault, may have been the reason for his being relieved.

Wellesley was then appointed the senior military officer in the region, a vast swathe of the subcontinent, while the main armies withdrew, leaving a five-year-old Hindu prince nominally on the throne. The impecunious Arthur also secured some £4,000 in prize money. The young officer ruled his new fiefdom from the splendid comforts of Tippoo's palace and slipped into comfortable respectability.

It was not until 1803 that the fortunes of Arthur Wellesley, now a major-general, moved on apace. In March he was assigned to take advantage of the divisions between the five great Maratha princes of central India to extend British rule. Under General Stuart, he was given personal command of around 15,000 British soldiers and a force of 9,000 from Hyderabad. He marched this large army a full 600 miles under his customary iron discipline, carrying its own supplies. He managed to surprise the main Maratha force, now 200,000-strong, at Assaye near the rivers Kaitna and Juah, on 23 September.

Fearing that the Marathas would escape, Wellesley decided to attack without waiting for the reinforcements of a second British-led army under Colonel James Stevenson. It was a precarious position, but he managed to break the Marathas line and they fled, having suffered 6,000 casualties to Wellesley's 1,500. It had been a hard-fought battle, against overwhelming odds, which was decided by the greater discipline and steadiness under fire of the British-led force. Wellesley always considered it his finest battle and proof that old-fashioned linear tactics, coupled with disciplined last-minute volleys followed by bayonet attacks, could prevail. Wellesley's brigade-major said of him: 'The General was in the thick of the action the whole time, and had a horse killed under him. No man could have shown a better example to his troops than he did. I never saw a man so cool and collected.' Wellesley had shown a lightning readiness to seize opportunities, a decisive grasp of battlefield tactics and great courage. At last, he commanded the respect of his brother officers: the victory had undeniably been his.

In November 1803, Wellesley set out again alongside Stevenson to take on two Maratha armies at Argaum. Again he staged a frontal attack, bringing his own artillery to bear. Under his disciplined volleys the enemy ranks gave way. This time it was a walkover.

Following his successes, Wellesley was yearning to return to Britain and in March 1805 he set off, having received a knighthood from the British and amassing a fortune of over £40,000. He was worn out bodily, but recovered his health aboard the enforced idleness of the long voyage home and bracing sea air. His motto had been 'dash at the first fellows that make their appearance and the campaign will be ours'.

The campaigns had aged him; the youthful jollity and japes were things of the past. He had become a stern and incorruptible disciplinarian, methodical and careful to a fault in his preparation. He arrived in Britain in September. The country had just emerged from under the shadow of French invasion, and was only a month away from the divergent fortunes of the battles of Trafalgar and Austerlitz.

At 35, he was more or less unemployed, being sent to command a brigade at sleepy Hastings, but he was philosophical: 'I have ate of the King's salt, and therefore I conceive it to be my duty to serve with unhesitating zeal and cheerfulness, when and wherever the King or his Government may think proper to employ me.'

Although he had acquired a reputation for womanizing in India, on his return he was thrilled to hear that Elizabeth Pakenham, an old love, still longed for him. She had aged, too, and had become religious and serious-minded. Wellesley resolved to seek her hand without first meeting her again, now that he had established his position in society and earned significant wealth. However, when he met her after 12 years away he remarked to his brother, who had also returned from India, 'She is grown damned ugly, by jove.' He stuck by his promise and married her in Dublin in April 1806. She was sweet, domesticated and narrow-minded, and despised by most of Wellesley's newly glamorous circle. She was devoted to him, though, at least to begin with, and he cannot have been an easy man to get on with – he was reserved, commanding and had a roving eye for other women. They had two sons.

Wellesley secured election to parliament as part of Prime Minister George Grenville's faction – his old friend William Pitt having died. With the fall of Grenville and the accession of the Duke of Portland, he was offered the job of chief secretary for Ireland, which he dutifully fulfilled in that divided land until the summer of 1807, while pressing for another military command. At last, he was given the job of carrying out the land operation on Lord James Gambier's expedition to Copenhagen to cut out the Danish fleet, a job he performed with spectacular efficiency. He was now a respected military commander with a string of distinguished engagements behind him. Yet he was far from being a household name or Britain's top soldier.

⁓

Wellesley now seemed destined for an extraordinary adventure: to travel with Francisco de Miranda at the head of the expedition to liberate Caracas from the Spanish in South America; history would have been very different if he had embarked. However, with the French invasion of Portugal, he was given a new assignment. In July 1808 he spoke to a good friend: 'I am thinking of the French that I am going to fight... 'Tis enough to make one thoughtful; but no matter: my die is cast, they may overwhelm me, but I don't think they will out-manoeuvre me... I am not afraid of them, as everybody else seems to be.' The expedition was limited in scope and small in size, and seemed as doomed as other previous British military adventures on the continent: it consisted of 9,000 men sailing on 12 July 1808 and arriving a week later at La Coruña in northern Spain.

On arrival, he found to his dismay that the northern Spanish army under General Joaquín Blake had been defeated by Marshal Jean-Baptiste Bessières at Medina del Rio Seco. Meanwhile, General Pierre Dupont, with 15,000 men, had just taken Cordoba in the south and Marshal André Masséna had just occupied Valladolid in the centre. The new 'King' of Spain, Joseph Bonaparte, entered Madrid with 4,000 troops to take up his throne just the day after Wellesley first set foot on Peninsular soil. The news was all bad. Only the town of Zaragoza, it seemed, held out. It appeared that the French were invincible, moving relentlessly forward to occupy the huge, rugged Spanish interior. What possible impression could Wellesley and his puny force make upon them?

Wellesley's force sailed disconsolately further south to Oporto in northern Portugal. He did not know that an astonishing thing was happening even as he sailed: Dupont had moved beyond Cordoba to inflict a final defeat on the Spaniards, but the sullen people of the countryside had begun to resist the advance while others rose up behind him. After a few days the increasingly anxious general ordered a retreat to the Sierra Morena mountains: he was harried and ambushed on all sides. On 23 July 1808, he surrendered to the ragged Spanish 'army' of General Francisco Castaños.

The first triumph in the Peninsular War had been achieved by the Spaniards themselves. They were a people oppressively misgoverned for centuries. While the upper class had grown rich on South American gold and silver and refused to engage in the menial tasks of trade and industry, the social fabric of Spain was antiquated, unaffected by the economic and social revolutions that had taken place elsewhere in Europe. Many people were still living as peasants on harsh soils that barely afforded a living in many areas, but their swelling nationalism and resentment at the plundering, arrogant foreign invaders had reared its head for the first time.

Wellesley knew nothing of this. Further south there was discouraging news: a Russian fleet, which might be hostile, as well as several French vessels, were in the Tagus River. He decided it would be safest to make a landing from the Atlantic some 100 miles to the north at Mondego Bay, and from there to march on Lisbon.

When Wellesley's men at last went ashore, they were joined by a force of some 4,000 men from Gibraltar led by General Sir Brent Spencer. However, Wellesley learnt to his chagrin that he was soon to be reinforced by an army of some 16,000 under three senior officers, as he was considered too junior. General Sir Hew Dalrymple, an old buffer who had not seen active service for 14 years, was to arrive with General Sir Henry Burrard, an amiable officer of limited intelligence; they were to be followed by Sir John Moore, who had extricated himself and his men from the clutches of the King of Sweden and was preparing to embark from Britain. Wellesley promised to respect his seniors, but said privately 'I hope that I shall beat Junot [Jean-Andoche Junot, the French commander in charge of the invasion of Portugal] before any of them arrive, and then they may do as they please with me.'

It was brave talk, yet he must have feared that his first great opportunity was to be snatched away from him before his adventure had barely begun. Wellesley calculated that with the defeat of Dupont confirmed, the French armies in Spain would be too busy to threaten him from the east. He decided to move down along the coastal road to Lisbon with his 12,300 British troops and 1,500 Portuguese ones, so that no attack could deny him the possibility of naval support and evacuation.

He had little artillery and virtually no cavalry. His men made good progress in the intense heat of a Portuguese summer through fertile and well-provisioned countryside. Junot had sent General

Henri François, Comte de Laborde, with 4,000 men up the main road to Lisbon and instructed General Louis Henri Loison with another army across the river to reinforce him. On 15 August there was a first skirmish as the enthusiastic British advance guard routed a French patrol, only to pursue it straight into the main French army: two officers and 27 men were lost. Two days later Wellesley ordered a general attack on Laborde's small army for fear that he would soon be reinforced by Loison.

Wellesley divided his army in two, sending 4,000 towards the French rear which could also intercept Loison if he should arrive. Laborde issued a general order to occupy a ridge overlooking the Lisbon road, where he inflicted great damage on the advancing British before withdrawing to avoid being outflanked on both sides. The British lost some 500 men, the French around the same, but they retreated intact. The first little battle of the Peninsular War between two able generals had been a stand-off.

Learning that British reinforcements were being landed to the west at Vimeiro, Wellesley lengthened his position to protect them: there were now up to 17,000 infantry and 18 guns, as well as the 1,500 Portuguese. Wellesley decided to march for the defile of Torres Vedras, but Sir Henry Burrard had just arrived and assumed command: he ordered Wellesley to adopt a defensive position until further reinforcements arrived. Wellesley was incensed, believing he had a good opportunity to seize Lisbon, but had no choice but to obey. He took up a defensive position on a ridge to the east and on Vimeiro Hill, south of the village of that name.

Junot himself had arrived to take command of his 13,000 troops and 24 guns; his 70,000 remaining men were left in and around Lisbon to maintain order there. His aim was to drive the inexperienced British forces to the east. Wellesley sent his skirmishers forward along and down the sides of the ridge while placing his main forces intact behind it. The French came bravely forward under fire from their flanks and in front, unaware that a larger force awaited them on the reverse slope.

The British artillery opened up, using shrapnel, a shell which blew up in the air raining grapeshot on the men below, for the first time. At close range, the volleys were fired at 15-second intervals by the disciplined British soldiers who were drawn up in two lines of 800 men. After the volleys, a textbook bayonet attack decisively dispersed the French who were exhausted by the uphill walk under intense fire.

As they broke and ran, Wellesley's small cavalry was ordered forward where it at first put the French infantry to flight. But the horsemen went too far, to Wellesley's irritation, and came up against superior French cavalry before galloping back to the main British lines with a quarter of the men lost. Renewed French attacks on the left failed and by midday Junot's force was in full retreat: they had lost some 2,000 men, as well as 15 guns, to 700 British casualties. It had not been a major battle, but it was a successful one in which the British had fought creditably.

Wellesley rode up to Burrard, who had arrived on the battlefield, and urged him to finally march on Torres Vedras: 'We shall be in Lisbon in three days.' The cautious general flatly refused, and was reinforced in his dithering by Sir Hew Dalrymple, who arrived the following day. Moore, who arrived several days later, took Wellesley's view: 'Several of our brigades had not been in action; our troops were in high spirits and the French so crestfallen that probably they would have dispersed. They could never have reached Lisbon.' It was too late: the French had already entrenched themselves at Torres Vedras.

However, General François-Etienne Kellerman arrived under a flag of truce, bearing an offer from Junot to withdraw all French forces from Portugal. To Dalrymple and Burrard this seemed a vindication of their caution, although Wellesley fumed at 'Dowager Dalrymple and Betty Burrard'. In fact, Junot had shrewdly assessed that it would have been disastrous for him to remain at Lisbon. The British had assembled a fleet which could bottle up or attack the Russian and French ships in the Tagus and bombard Lisbon from the sea; and they had an army approaching from the north which could trap the French in an enclave surrounded on three sides by water. In addition, the people of Lisbon were highly restive and might stage an insurrection against the French.

The two generals reached agreement with Kellerman at the Convention of Sintra, then ordered Wellesley in to sign the terms. He read them with astonishment, describing them as 'very extraordinary' but obeying his superiors' orders in an untypical show of humility. The terms were surprising indeed: the French were to be evacuated by the Royal Navy to a French port, no less, and retain their arms and baggage and all their personal property; French troops were to be allowed to return to the fight from the port in which they were landed; those Portuguese who had collaborated with the French were not to be punished; and the Russian fleet was to be allowed to depart for the Baltic.

Wellesley promptly wrote to Viscount Castlereagh, Secretary of State for War, to disassociate himself from the agreement, but it was too late. News of the agreement signed by the three British generals arrived in Britain and joy turned to fury. Wellesley begged Castlereagh to relieve him of his post as he could not continue in a subordinate capacity to these two old gentlemen, and departed after making arrangements for the French withdrawal. After his spectacular victory and his bottling up of the French army in a trap where it faced certain defeat, he was now unfairly blamed for snatching defeat from the jaws of victory: his career seemed all but over. The enemies of the Wellesleys – of which there were many – closed ranks and attacked him.

In November 1808, an inquiry was set up at the Royal Hospital at Chelsea at which Dalrymple and Wellesley gave conflicting accounts. The army proceeded to exonerate all three officers. Parliament voted to thank Wellesley for the victory at Vimeiro. Dalrymple was dismissed as governor of Gibraltar while Burrard was retired to domestic duty. Wellesley himself retired to his duties in Dublin bitter and angry at what seemed a terminal setback to his career.

Command in the Peninsula now devolved upon the capable shoulders of Sir John Moore. Admiral Sir Charles Cotton, in charge of the British squadron off Portugal, insisted that the three generals had no right to decide naval dispositions and ignored the Convention of Sintra; instead he forced the Russian admiral to give up his ships to the British until the end of the war, a minor but significant victory.

Castlereagh determined that Britain should go on the offensive. After learning of the French defeat at Bayonne, he had agreed to despatch a fresh army of 30,000 troops to the Peninsula. In the event 14,000 infantry, 4,000 cavalry and 800 artillerymen were sent under Sir David Baird, Wellesley's old *bête noire*, to Corunna in northern Spain. There they were to link up with 20,000 of the 30,000 troops in Portugal under Moore's command. Quite quickly, Britain's commitment in Portugal had escalated to the status of major intervention.

The British and the Spaniards had both underestimated the enemy they were dealing with. Napoleon had always regarded Spain as a 'sideshow', a walkover on a par with the almost bloodless seizure of Naples. The disasters first at Bailen and then at Gerona, Valencia, Zaragoza and Vimeiro had brought him down to earth. He feared that failure might be contagious across Europe and was bent on a crushing revenge and re-establishment of French authority in the Peninsula.

Napoleon himself decided to take charge in the Peninsula. As he departed on his long journey, some 60,000 French troops were ordered to reinforce the army along the Ebro. Napoleon took a further 100,000 along with his best marshals – Lannes, Soult, Ney, Victor and Lefebvre. He set about totally annihilating the Spanish army's resistance and conducted a genocide of its allies within the civilian population – one of the most brutal ever mounted in history.

Moore had driven his main army towards the centre of northern Spain in order to link up with the Spanish in an astonishingly bold attempt to cut Napoleon's supply lines. Napoleon repaid the compliment by turning north-east to chase Moore's small army. Moore's army headed back to Corunna to be evacuated by the British navy once he realized his allies were decimated and his position was perilous. Napoleon turned his attention to Austria, leaving Marshal Nicolas Jean-de-Dieu Soult to complete the rout. Moore's force plundered the countryside as it retreated during the harsh winter, and arrived in Corunna intact. On 16 January 1809, Soult surrounded the port. The British had to fight their way out to sea, suffering 900 casualties and abandoning much of their supplies. Sir John Moore himself was among the dead, having been hit by cannon shot, and General Sir David Baird was injured. It became stuff of legend, Moore being immortalized as Britain's first land hero of the war.

There were many now in Britain who argued in favour of abandoning the Peninsula altogether. These included even Lord Grenville, who had so long resisted France. In addition the Duke of York, an appalling commander of men in the field but a good administrator, was forced to resign from the army in a scandal: his former mistress had been caught selling commissions and it was alleged that the Duke knew of her trade. With York departed, Moore dead and Baird wounded, that left Wellesley as the only promising field commander.

From Ireland, Wellesley pestered Castlereagh with his advocacy of a further expedition to Portugal. He argued that it would require only 20,000 to 30,000 troops to hold Lisbon, which he believed he could protect indefinitely. The Spaniards, meanwhile, had made clear that any further expeditionary force landing on their territory would be unwelcome, even though Cadiz, Seville, Castile, Granada and southern Spain remained free.

Wellesley won the argument and on 6 April 1809 he was authorized to lead a new expeditionary force to the Peninsula. He had been given a second chance to resume his controversial career. On 14 April, Wellesley embarked, but the captain told him the ship was sure to founder in a terrible gale. 'In that case,' replied Sir Arthur laconically in one of the curt soundbites that were increasingly becoming his trademark, 'I shall not take off my boots.'

On 27 April, he landed at Lisbon with 23,000 men – including 3,000 Hanoverians. Some 6,000 men had already arrived under Sir Rowland Hill, an amiable, outgoing personality – entirely unlike Wellesley – who was beloved of his men. They liaised with General William Beresford who had been placed in command of a considerable force of 16,000 Portuguese troops, with Captain Robert

Harvey as his chief aide. Wellesley did not waste time: the plight of
his army was precarious: in the north Marshal Soult had occupied
Oporto, Portugal's second city, with 23,000 men, while to the east
Marshal Claude Victor-Perrin was approaching the frontier with
Spain with 25,000 men; between these two was a small army under
General Pierre Lapisse. There were a staggering 250,000 French
troops altogether in the Iberian Peninsula.

The British had just one thing going for them: the incredible brutality of the French, combined with their unpopularity as invading
oppressors, which meant that the Spanish and Portuguese were
united in hatred of them. However, they were almost equally suspicious of the British, whose motives they suspected and who they
regarded as mere allies of convenience – leading in turn to considerable British distrust, mingled with contempt.

The Peninsular War thus was to become a three-way conflict in
which the bitter and continuing resistance of the Spanish and
Portuguese against the invaders, usually involving small-scale
attacks, was supplemented by a disciplined regular British force.
The British would not have prevailed without the local resistance
which was widespread and tied down enormous bodies of French
troops; equally, the partisans would eventually have been crushed
without the British, who posed the greater military threat.

Wellesley moved with the speed he had learnt in India. The
country in Portugal was somewhat different – a rugged one of hills,
woods and ravines, all of which grew more impassable the further
north he travelled. He assembled nearly 18,000 men at Coimbra on
the way to Oporto, reasoning that if he immediately defeated Soult,
he would prevent a junction of French armies that would otherwise
be larger than his own.

As he moved northwards, Wellesley routed a small French force
of around 4,500 men above Grija, and reached the town of Vila
Nova along the upper bends of the wide and beautiful Douro River.
He was now overlooking Oporto, an ancient and picturesque city
crammed down the opposite slope. It was the trading entrepôt of
the area, with its access along the river to the sea. It was also the
great wine-producing centre of the region, traditionally supplying

the British with enormous quantities, particularly now that trade with the rest of the continent had been blocked off.

Soult had little warning of Wellesley's arrival in Oporto. He promptly destroyed the single bridge across the Douro and ensured that all river craft were on his side. If an attack came, he thought it would be from the west, using fishing boats brought up by the British from the sea. Wellesley instead turned his attention eastwards, upstream along the river, where he found several unguarded boats, mostly for carrying wine. Wellesley is usually considered a defensive general but he was capable of great offensive boldness when necessary, as his campaigns in India showed.

Risking everything, he sent across a small force to seize a large enemy-held seminary on the opposite bank, and they managed to hold it against repeated attack. By that time Portuguese boats were ferrying the British across in increasing numbers. The French, who faced being attacked by the vengeful Portuguese in the narrow streets of the steeply descending riverside town, ordered a retreat to the east. The British had quickly captured nearly 1,300 prisoners and some 60 guns. Some 500 Frenchmen had been killed, for a loss of just 23 Britons.

To the east, Beresford and Harvey had repulsed another French force and occupied the town of Amarante on the old road from northern Portugal into Spain, thus cutting off Soult's retreat. Blocked off to the east, the French army swung north into the hilly and wooded country towards Galicia, abandoning their guns and provisions, in a desperate attempt to get away. They had several thousand troops in their way, many of them Portuguese insurgents, who responded to the routine raping of their womenfolk by castrating French soldiers and stuffing their genitals into their mouths, or nailing them alive to trees and doorways.

The British proceeded to march into Spain to take the battle to the enemy. Their intention was to liaise with the 30,000-strong Spanish army of General Don Gregorio de la Cuesta, a 69-year-old Spanish caudillo who trundled about in a huge coach drawn by mules and was bedecked by medals and a magnificent uniform. Cuesta, who treated Wellesley as a subordinate and the British as junior partners, proposed encircling Marshal Victor-Perrin's 23,000-strong army across the border. As Wellesley descended from Portugal with his 21,000 men, leaving Beresford and 4,000 to defend Portugal, they found that Victor-Perrin had withdrawn towards Talavera to the southeast.

Wellesley followed Victor-Perrin to Plasencia, the local capital, early in July 1809, and was now just 100 miles from Madrid. While Soult's forces held back for the moment, it was planned that the Spanish army should cross the Tagus to the northern bank and march eastwards to join up with the British at Talavera. To the south, another 23,000-strong Spanish army under General Francisco Javier Venegas was to engage the French forces in Madrid and stop them reinforcing Victor-Perrin.

Wellesley's chief problem was a shortage of supplies, for he insisted that his men should not plunder the countryside and antagonize the local population. However, he continued his march and on 16 July moved forward from Plasencia, reaching Talavera six days later. It was the height of a Spanish summer: the heat on the baking plains was intense and the dust kicked up by the marching army was choking. Even so, there was snow on the mountain range to the north, which extended nearly as far as the river at Talavera. The French were surprised by the British advance but quickly retreated east towards Madrid.

Cuesta, that 'desperate-looking lump of pride, ignorance and treachery' as one British soldier called him, ordered his army forward in pursuit, with Wellesley wisely refusing to follow. The Spaniards soon ran up against a force of 46,000 Frenchmen, a combination of Victor's army and King Joseph Bonaparte's reinforcements from Madrid. Venegas was nowhere to be seen: he had stopped at Aranjuez to the south. Cuesta was forced immediately to retreat to the British position behind him.

Wellesley, with his extraordinary eye for a good defence, had drawn up the British between the mountains and the river. He allowed the Spaniards to occupy the most protected front beside Talavera itself, while the British were in the exposed gap and the steep foothills of the mountains, the Cerro de Medellin, overlooking the valley. There were only 20,000 British and German troops and just 30 light cannon against the 46,000 French troops and their 80 cannon. On the evening of 27 July 1809, Victor-Perrin ordered his men to attack and they succeeded in taking the top of the Cerro de Medellin before a British counterattack led by Rowland Hill drove them back down.

On the following morning, the battle began in earnest. The French opened up with their guns. Wellesley ordered his men back over the brow of the hill and told them to lie down. The French infantry marched up the hill, but as they reached the top the British rose in good formation and fired volleys before Wellesley ordered them down the slope, routing the French with their superior forces.

There was a lull in the fighting before a general advance was ordered. On the British right, near Talavera, General Alexander Campbell repelled the French so successfully that he had to restrain his men from advancing too fast and breaking the already over-stretched British line. To the north, though, a British pursuit was counterattacked by the French, who killed half of them as well as their commander, opening up a huge gap in the British line which 15,000 French infantry moved quickly to occupy. The British reserves were hurried up.

Wellesley also ordered infantry down from the Cerro de Medellin to plug the hole, but there was a further danger: the French had scrambled up the rocky ravine to the north of the Cerro de Medellin to outflank the British where they were weakest. Cavalry were ordered forward to stop them, but many plunged to their deaths into a hidden gully. Even so, enough survived to halt the advancing French.

At this stage, on learning that Venegas was at last advancing from the south to threaten the capital, King Joseph and his commanders decided to cut their losses and withdraw. A particular horror of the battle now ensued when the long grass on the slopes of the Cerro de Medellin caught fire, leading to the burning alive of hundreds of wounded lying there.

The Battle of Talavera had been a victory of sorts, with 7,000 French dead and captured compared to some 5,000 British, Spanish and Germans, who had also taken the battlefield. It had been the first real feat of British arms in the whole of the Revolutionary and Napoleonic wars, a major battle won through the perfect deployment and redeployment of men and superb discipline throughout the battle. Wellesley had shown that he was not just a capable and lucky commander, as at Vimeiro and Oporto, but a first-rate one who was possessed of careful preparation and absolute coolness in the heat of the fighting. Talavera was anything but a decisive victory, but it was a start for an army that had previously been the laughing stock of Europe.

Victor-Perrin withdrew towards Madrid with just 18,000 men to defend the capital from the supposedly imminent southern attack from Venegas. The British and the Spanish armies also prepared to march on Madrid from the east. However, on 1 August, Wellesley learnt that Soult had been reinforced from the north by Marshal Michel Ney and Marshal André Masséna to 50,000 men; the French were marching on Plasencia having driven through the 3,000-strong Spanish force guarding the crucial Pass of Banos.

Wellesley learnt of the French concentration of forces in the nick of time and escaped to the southwest across the Tagus using the only available bridge, the Puente del Arzobispo. General Cuesta followed reluctantly and his rearguard was badly mauled by the French who captured most of the Spanish guns. Meanwhile, Venegas' army was also badly beaten at Almonacid de Toledo. Wellesley's force huddled in the barren hills south of the Tagus, quarrelling with Cuesta's troops, and they were in danger of starving as the Spaniards, took what little was available from the peasantry. After a few weeks, Wellesley, disgusted with the Spaniards, whom he blamed for failing to fight effectively at Talavera, decided to bolt back into the fertile land of southern Portugal. He had overreached himself in classical fashion and been forced back to his heartland.

The Spaniards were furious with what they saw as British abandonment. They staged a new, quixotic attack, but this was crushed at Ocana in November 1809 by 50,000 men against 34,000. The Spaniards fought bravely but lost 18,000 men and were routed. The governing junta were driven south by a French attack in January

(above) Clive of India: 'Heaven-born' warrior of speed, guile, surprise and self-aggrandizement.

(above) George Washington: Cautious but could move with rattlesnake speed.

The Death of Wolfe on the Plains of Abraham: Router of the French and founder of British Canada.

(left) Field-Marshal
Erwin Rommel:
General of speed and
surprise.

(above) Field-Marshal Montgomery: Tough, contrary and always his own man.

(left) Giuseppe Garibaldi: Rebel, privateer, guerrilla, land general, fight-aholic.

(right) Ulysses S. Grant: Modest, tongue-tied and an extraordinary warrior.

(left) Thomas Cochrane:
Fearless single-ship hero
and seaman extraordinaire.

(above) The Duke of Wellington at Waterloo: Master of concealed defence
and timing in offence.

The Death of Nelson, greatest hero of them all, from an eighteenth-century painting by Benjamin West.

General George S. Patton: Mad, bad and victorious.

General Douglas MacArthur: The great encircler.

1810 and fled to the safety of Cadiz, where it was overthrown by its fellow countrymen. The French were stopped outside the city as Spanish troops under Sir Thomas Graham held the isthmus to the great port. Some 70,000 French troops found themselves tied down in the south, besieging Cadiz.

—*w*—

Wellesley led his men back to the temperate valleys of Beira and Mondego in southern Portugal. There they recovered, engaging in fishing, shooting and horse-racing. By that time Wellesley had been awarded a peerage as Viscount Wellington, after a town called Welleslieu in Somerset. The new lord realized that he could make his position in Portugal virtually impregnable and, at the end of October 1809, he ordered his chief engineer, Colonel Fletcher, to start building lines of defence – the Lines of Torres Vedras – to safeguard Lisbon.

Wellington had to fight calls from England for the withdrawal of his army. He was accused of causing his men needless suffering after Talavera, which was partly true. The new secretary for war, though, was Lord Liverpool, a pleasant, deeply unimaginative mediocrity who was a staunch admirer of Wellington. The latter defended himself with uncharacteristic modesty and persuaded Liverpool of the need for a continuing presence in the Peninsula. He handed Wellington a free hand in Portugal.

In addition to the Lines of Torres Vedras, Wellington proved a genius in irregular warfare. He sought to integrate his Portuguese troops under General Beresford. In this the young Major Harvey, now assistant quartermaster-general with the Portuguese army, was the key. He was sent to organize a force of Portuguese guerrillas in Beira. These became highly effective guerrillas, usually under the command of priests. On one occasion, near Penamacor, Harvey's irregulars captured a heavy convoy, fighting off the 150 French irregulars accompanying it: no fewer than 53 cartloads of ammunition and tobacco were taken.

Another leader of irregulars was the ferociously disciplinarian Brigadier Robin 'Black Bob' Crauford, who flogged any man who broke ranks crossing a stream and who could get his men under arms from sleeping quarters in just seven minutes. Crauford's guerrillas guarded the Portuguese frontier, bringing reports of suspect French troop concentrations. 'The whole web of communication quivered at the slightest touch,' wrote one observer admiringly.

Wellington and his small army remained in the hill fastnesses of central Portugal while the imperial armies of the French blundered about the plains and plateaux, under constant and relentless harassment from the local population. Every day, on average more than 100 French soldiers were killed. While bungling and ill-equipped Spanish armies were always at the mercy of the French in the field, in the hills and mountains and backwaters it was the other way around.

Wellington was largely entrenched behind the Lines of Torres Vedras, although he did take on Masséna's huge force of 60,000 troops at a place of his choosing, near Coimbra, in October 1810. The French called off their attack after they had lost more than 4,000 men, but Wellington was in danger of being outflanked, so he once again withdrew behind the Lines. Over the course of the next year, Wellington continued to conduct a very bloody and strategic game of chess with the French.

In August 1811, Wellington was on the move once again with 45,000 men in the mountains behind the Agueda River and the French stronghold of Ciudad Rodrigo. The French reacted with alarm and alacrity, mustering an army of 60,000 men at Tamames to the east under Marshal Auguste de Marmont, Masséna's successor as commander of the French campaign in northern Spain. Wellington responded by retreating again into one of his strategic fastnesses some 15 miles south of Ciudad Rodrigo. When the French failed to follow he emerged from this safe position on to the plain, only to be very nearly surprised by a huge French force. He immediately returned to his usual caution.

While this game of cat and mouse continued, Rowland Hill marched some 8,000 men across the highest point of the Portuguese mountains – some 6,000 feet – through rain and gales in October 1811 and attacked a force of some 5,000 French soldiers near Merida, killing 800 and taking 1,500 prisoner for the loss of just seven men.

Wellington stayed on the alert in his defensive position, waiting for the opportunity to cross over into Spain: he seemed certain that the days of fighting to defend Portugal were over. Like the hawk his profile suggested, he scented the kill, awaiting the opportunity to push beyond its boundaries.

It was January 1812 before a less cautious, meticulously prepared Wellington was ready to attack Ciudad Rodrigo, which was now much less strongly defended: the fact that it was winter caught the French unprepared. When he reached the fortress he sent some 3,000 British soldiers to storm the first redoubt of San Francisco, losing just six men in the process. He then began a classic siege, digging parallel trenches in a zigzag to close in on the fortress, a process which lasted five days and nights under heavy mortar attack which killed some 500 men.

After just a week, though, Wellington decided to storm the fortress to forestall Marmont, who was hurrying to the rescue. He made two breaches in the walls with his light guns – his heavy ones had not yet arrived – and then prepared three simultaneous attacks, two of them feints. It was to be a difficult operation. The unit calling themselves Forlorn Hope – because they thought so few of them would survive to reap the fine rewards they had been promised – decided to enter the breach first. It was to be followed by a 500-strong force under Crauford, the army's leading disciplinarian, who declared: 'Soldiers! the eyes of your country are upon you. Be steady – be cool – be firm in the assault. The town must be yours this night. Once masters of the wall, let your first duty be to clear the ramparts, and in doing this keep together.'

Crauford himself was one of the first to be killed. After fierce fighting the British at last reached the top of the breach and within half-an-hour were rampaging through the streets of the citadel. They went on a wild plundering spree. The citadel had been seized at a cost of around 1,000 British casualties; the entire French garrison had been captured or killed.

Wellington considered attacking the French headquarters at Salamanca but decided against it, as Marmont could quickly summon reinforcements on the open plains. Methodical and cautious as always, except when an unmissable opportunity presented itself, Wellington decided to repeat his feat of taking a fortress at Badajoz.

On his arrival at Badajoz in mid-March 1812, Wellington found the fortress very nearly impregnable. The approaches had been mined, the walls reinforced, the two outlying forts (San Cristobal and Pardaleras) strengthened and an impassable moat created on the east side of the fortress. The siege works were dug on the south-east side of the fortress and as they approached the walls in torrential rain, the French opened up a ceaseless artillery barrage. Once again, news arrived that a large French army, this time under Marshal Soult, was approaching to relieve the fortress. Again, the cautious Wellington was driven into speedy action, ordering an assault on 6 April, long before the customary softening-up by artillery attack had been completed.

One of the bloodiest assaults in history followed, seemingly untempered by Wellington's usual concern for losses among his men; he had acquired an almost psychopathic ability to switch off his feelings when required, arguably a necessary trait for a great commander and a characteristic shared by Napoleon. The attack very nearly failed against the formidably murderous French defences which included *chevaux-de-frise* (obstacles to stop cavalry), hand-grenades and the moat: some 500 were also killed when the French exploded mines.

The British attacks, staged over the bodies of their dead and wounded comrades, were repulsed some 40 times in all, with the 'butcher' Wellington constantly urging them forward. The experience of Sergeant Anthony Hamilton was typical:

> Though the carnage in our ranks was very great, we continued our advance... Owing to the darkness of the night... we came unexpectedly upon the counter-scarp, and nearly half our party, myself among the number, were precipitated into the ditch below. Much bruised by the fall I lay a few minutes insensible, till on the arrival of the main body, the ladders were fixed... and the descent into the ditch quickly effected... Twenty-one officers of the regiment were either killed or wounded, and of the ten men of our company who volunteered for

the forlorn hope only myself and a man by the name of Cummings came back alive, both wounded.

Some 2,000 men were killed in these repeated assaults against murderous fire and defences. All appeared to be lost, but Wellington ordered one final assault on the castle. One participant records:

> When we first entered the [ditch] we considered ourselves compara-
> tively safe, thinking that we were out of range of their shot, but...
> they opened several guns... and poured in grape shot upon us from
> each side... Our situation at this time was truly appalling... When the
> ladders were placed, each eager to mount, [the soldiers] crowded
> them in such a way that many of them broke, and the poor fellows
> who had nearly reached the top were precipitated a height of thirty
> to forty feet and impaled on the bayonets of their comrades below.
> Other ladders were pushed aside by the enemy on the walls, and fell
> with a crash on those in the ditch, while [men] who got to the top
> without accident were shot on reaching the parapet, and, tumbling
> headlong, brought down those beneath them. This continued for
> some time, until at length, a few having made a landing [they]
> enabled others to follow.

At last this terrible final assault succeeded. While the 4,000-strong French garrison now retreated, another assault on the San Vicente fortress along the town walls followed. Terrible scenes ensued as the British soldiery exacted their revenge in a wild orgy of pillage almost without precedent in British military history. Only repeated floggings restored order, although it is disputed whether Wellington ordered any hangings. It had been an horrific victory: the British lost more than 4,500 men at Badajoz.

The siege shows Wellington in a new light; the careful husbander of resources and his own men's lives had been willing to risk all in a brutal act of blood-letting he believed to be militarily necessary. Wellington had shown himself to be more than just a supremely skilled and cautious defensive general: he could be a ruthless gambler with his men's lives when the stakes were high enough: the prim, hawk-nosed, laconic, precise master of dispositions in battle was also a man of almost sadistic steel.

Learning that Ciudad Rodrigo was now under siege from Marmont, Wellington lost no time trekking north to relieve the citadel. He then set about ordering a complex set of manoeuvres involving Spanish forces in various parts of the country – supporting General Francisco Ballesteros in Andalucía; occupying Malaga; leading a French force on a wild goose chase through mountainous Granada; and finally escaping to the coast. Admiral Sir Home Popham led a series of raids along the northern coast, while Rowland Hill tied down French troops in the west in Extremadura. All of this helped to prevent the French forces in Spain concentrating on defeating Wellington; in truth the French were far too widely splayed out across the Peninsula in provinces under the control of jealous rival commanders to inflict a decisive defeat upon the British, however enormous their superiority in numbers.

Wellington remained passive outside Ciudad Rodrigo, despatching Hill, his best raiding commander, in mid-May 1812 to take the bridge at Almaraz which commanded the route from Madrid to the Portuguese frontier and the main commercial links between the northern and southern Spanish armies. This he did brilliantly, destroying Fort Napoleon at one end of the bridge, causing its defenders to flee and blowing up the bridge and its fortifications.

In 13 June 1812, Wellington moved his nearly 50,000-strong army to Leon and then advanced on Salamanca, where Marmont had left a small force behind its fortifications. This held out bravely until 27 June. Wellington was given a superb Spanish welcome into the beautiful, liberal university town, the warmth embarrassing the soldiers and even the unflappable British commander himself, who was pulled from his horse, losing his dignity for a moment. He attended a *Te Deum* in the cathedral and a glittering ball given in his honour that evening.

He moved his cavalry out into the great plain of Salamanca to entice Marmont into battle on ground traditionally most favourable to the French, but he believed he could win. He waited for his foe to come to him, but Marmont was equally cautious. In the heat of the day, the two great armies of 50,000 manoeuvred in parallel across the plain as though on a giant parade ground and rested in the freezing nights. During this anxious time, Wellington was described by one observer as 'in the prime of life, a well made man five-foot-ten-inches (1.77m)in height, with broad shoulders and well-developed chest. Of the cruiser, rather than the battleship build, the greyhound, rather than the mastiff breed, he seemed all made for speed and action, yet as strong as steel, and capable of great endurance.'

Marmont manoeuvred skilfully, crossing the Duero River to push Wellington's forces back towards Salamanca and threaten his communications with Portugal. The plain was not in fact flat, being criss-crossed by a line of low hills that helped to conceal the movements of one army from another. By 22 July, Wellington's forces were drawn up just southeast of the city, along one of the ridges whose southern end was marked by a little hill called the Arapil Chico. Marmont moved forward to occupy a large hill due south of them, the Arapil Grande, from which he could observe the British position. Marmont, anticipating Wellington's response, was determined not to repeat the mistakes of previous French commanders by attacking frontally a well-entrenched British position, and instead decided to march his army westwards around the British southern flank – their right – to catch them at their weakest point.

Wellington, realizing what was going on, promptly responded by shifting his division to a position running eastwards along another spur of hills, thus creating a new line facing the marching French. Marmont, believing Wellington to be a defensive general who would never attack, assumed he was preparing his army for a westward march in parallel to the French to protect his line of communication back to Portugal, and spurred his men to march still faster westwards to outflank him.

While his officers ate their lunch in a farmyard, Wellington observed through his telescope the French marching across his new front, in contravention of the most basic rules of warfare. He could see that the enemy, hurrying forward, were strung out along a vast extended line, widely dispersed, and would not be able to concentrate in time to repel a concentrated British attack at a single point. Famously, he threw the chicken leg he had been eating over his shoulder, exclaiming 'By God, that will do!' He added, 'Marmont is lost.'

He ordered Ned Pakenham, his brother-in-law, to attack the French left, the vanguard of their moving line. Pakenham led his men against the vulnerable and exposed French line in a frontal charge across the plain where the startled French were advancing. An officer described the scene:

> We were going up an ascent on whose crest masses of the enemy were stationed. Their fire seemed capable of sweeping all before it... Truth compels me to say... that we retired before this overwhelming fire, but... General Pakenham approached and very good natured said, 'Reform', and in... a moment, 'Advance... There they are my lads; just let them feel the temper of your bayonets.' We advanced, everyone making up his mind for mischief. At last... the bugles along the line sounded the charge. Forward we rushed... and awful was the retribution we exacted for our former repulse.

Having destroyed this division, Pakenham raced westwards down the line to attack the next part of the dispersed French column. They were already under attack from another column of British infantry and cavalry combined and were caught in the act of forming squares: they were soon overwhelmed. The French units immediately behind simply broke and fled: in just an hour the French advance had been smashed and 2,500 prisoners and 12 guns taken.

'By God Cotton,' Wellington said to his cavalry commander General Sir Stapleton Cotton as his horses charged, 'I never saw anything more beautiful in my life. The day is yours.' However, Wellington's depleted forces on the left fared less well attacking the French rearguard, and were forced back. Seeking to follow up this advantage, the French commander General Bertrand Clausel – Marmont having been wounded – launched an attack with two fresh divisions against the British centre. Wellington immediately ordered his reserves, skilfully hidden behind the ridge, to reinforce his centre. These included a Portuguese brigade led by William Beresford, who was wounded in the chest. Wellington himself was grazed by a bullet in the thigh.

The British attacked again, reversing the French charge, and the French centre crumbled. As night began to fall the entire French army fled in headlong and disorganized retreat: some 13,000 French soldiers had been killed or taken prisoner, along with 15 guns. In the darkness the British were unable to pursue. The following morning the German auxiliary dragoons inflicted another huge blow on the French by breaking up a massed infantry square at the village of Garcia Hernandez. Still, the British decided not to overextend themselves by pressing forward; the French rallied at Valladolid and then Burgos.

It had been a superb triumph, the greatest of Wellington's career so far, an offensive action of brilliant improvisation and skilled manoeuvre that exceeded even those of Napoleon. On a smaller scale, it was comparable to Austerlitz as a perfectly executed victory. The French General Maximilien Foy remarked of his adversary:

> Hitherto we have been aware of his prudence, his eye for choosing a position, and his skill in utilising it. At Salamanca he has shown himself a great and able master of manoeuvres. He kept his dispositions concealed for almost the whole day: he waited till we were committed to our movements before he developed his own: he played a safe game: he fought in the oblique order – it was a battle in the style of Frederick the Great.

Wellington was now faced with the difficult choice of pursuing and attempting to destroy the retreating army of the north which, however, could be quickly reinforced by other French armies; or staging a largely symbolic blow by liberating Madrid, which was poorly defended.

He chose the latter course, which many believe to have been a mistake, for he could probably have destroyed the fleeing army. A part of his calculation was that after his great victory at Salamanca, the Spanish might at last unite their vast, shambolic armies for a great drive to liberate Spain from the French. Occupying Madrid would provide a favourable position for this.

The triumph of Salamanca reverberated around the Peninsula. Soult learnt of Wellington's great victory: he immediately raised the siege at Cadiz and also abandoned Seville to march to the safety of the more defensible Valencia in the east. Meanwhile, the wretched King Joseph Bonaparte and his chief general, Jean-Andoche Junot, with only 22,000 mostly ill-equipped and untried troops, 15,000 refugees and 2,000 wagons, set off for the long trek from Madrid to Valencia in the heat of the summer. Most of southern, eastern and western Spain – Extremadura, Andalucía and now Castile – had been liberated. It was a heady moment of glory for the unflappable British commander. It seemed only a matter of time before the French were chased from their remaining strongholds across the Pyrenees.

Wellington arrived in the capital to a rapturous reception on 12 August 1812. As so often, hubris was followed quickly by nemesis, triumph by bitter disappointment and an almost complete reversal of fortune.

In taking Madrid, Wellington had secured a huge propaganda victory, but by advancing into the Spanish heartland he had dangerously lengthened his own lines of communication with Portugal. Moreover, the French had been boxed into a region from which they could stage a united counteroffensive. The expected junction of the Spanish armies and general uprising did not take place.

As that glorious August of 1812 mellowed into autumn, Wellington showed signs of becoming almost deranged in impatience and frustration with his allies. Always a man who considered himself indispensable, reluctant to delegate to his subordinates and obsessed with detail, his celebrated laconic sang-froid and carefully chosen phrases now gave way to outbursts of blind anger. His portrait painted by Goya at this time gives him a hunted, harassed look, utterly unlike the cool self-confidence he preferred to project. Wellington was acutely aware that he was over-exposed to a major French offensive against Madrid once their armies united. He abandoned his usual prudence in an attempt to regain the initiative.

He decided to do what he should have done while his enemy was on the run after Salamanca and go in pursuit of the French army of Portugal, which had regrouped and launched a minor counteroffensive in the north. It was a disastrous miscalculation. As he approached, the French retreated leaving a garrison of veterans in the formidable castle of Burgos, capital of Castile.

Wellington, never one to leave a castle behind his lines if he could help it, felt he had no alternative but to besiege it. However, he had only three cannon, picturesquely dubbed Thunder, Lightning and Nelson. It was a hopeless task. Burgos was to be no Badajoz. Displaying again the ruthless disregard for his own men's lives that now characterized his sieges, he stormed the outer redoubt before attacking the main defences. Wellington's closest military protégé, Major Edward Somers Cocks, was killed. Wellington was rendered speechless by the news and was bent over with grief at his burial. Some 2,000 British soldiers were killed to 600 Frenchmen.

After three day's further futile siege he ordered his angry men to retreat to save his army, which was endangered by the approach of an 80,000-strong French force. Even so, Wellington would have been overwhelmed by the advancing army but for the reconquest of the Basque capital of Bilbao by a Spanish force, which compelled the French to pause and detach part of their army to the city. The Spaniards Wellington so often railed against had saved him this time.

Wellington ordered his army in Madrid similarly to save itself and abandon the city: King Joseph and Soult were approaching with their now combined force of 60,000. The British blew up the powder depots and the fortifications of the capital as they withdrew. Hill led the army out of Madrid and they marched at some speed to catch up with Wellington's army before reaching Salamanca, in mid-November 1812. The retreat was marked by atrocities comparable to those of the French. One officer remarked that 'many peasants lay dead by the roadside, murdered. The old trade was going on, killing and slaughtering while capturing our daily bread.'

At Salamanca, a witness remarked that Wellington reviewed his troops in clothes 'unaccompanied by any mark of distinction or splendour. His long brown cloak concealed his undergarments; his cocked hat, soaked and disfigured under the rain.' Another commented that 'he looked extremely ill'. He was also bad-tempered and issued a general censure of his men for their looting and ill-behaviour, which caused immense resentment.

The largest French army was approaching Salamanca from the south, and Wellington had no option but to resume the retreat, knee-deep in mud because of heavy rain, to the safety of Ciudad Rodrigo. Corpses and dead horses lined the route as disease took its toll. The French gave up the chase, but by the time they reached Ciudad Rodrigo, some 6,000 soldiers had been lost.

Wellington had been pushed back to the Portuguese border, his old fastness. Now, at least, his men could rest. They were desperately disappointed. Two large British armies had previously penetrated deep into Spain – the army of Sir John Moore and that of Wellington at Talavera – and twice they had been driven out. This seemed merely another rerun. It had been demonstrated yet again that the French could not advance into Portugal without endangering themselves, and that the British could not enter Spain and hold their ground. It appeared to be stalemate.

Yet the British had made significant progress. The French had been driven from Andalucía, Extremadura and Asturias; and the British remained in possession of the key frontier fortresses at Almeida, Ciudad Rodrigo and Badajoz. Wellington assuaged his wounded vanity by riding down to liberated Cadiz, where the provisional Spanish government was sitting. He was given titular control of all Spanish forces as well as British ones, but to his fury he discovered that in practice this amounted to little. The Spanish generals simply ignored his directives, Spanish armies remained as disorganized as before and some commanders were deeply offended by the decree. One, General Ballesteros, came out in open revolt against the British 'oppressors'.

Back at his headquarters on the northern frontier at Freneida, Wellington indulged in the long idle months of winter and spring 1813 in more agreeable pursuits than quarrelling with the Spaniards: 'He had at headquarters a pack of hounds from England and hunted two or three times a week with such officers of headquarters as chose to join in the chase... There was no want of foxes, but it was a difficult and rocky country to ride over. He went out shooting every now and then, but did not appear fond of it, as he was a very indifferent shot.' He was fastidious in appearance, wearing his celebrated 'Wellington boots' frequently, and cultivated soundbites loaded with his dry, sardonic wit: 'I don't know what effect they have on the enemy, but by God they frighten me' was his celebrated remark on receiving a batch of new officers sent to join his army.

During that long period of rest and recreation, the news of Napoleon's terrible retreat from Moscow filtered through. Wellington became increasingly convinced that 1813 would be the decisive year of the war. He had at last recovered his old bounce and self-confidence after the awful setbacks of the previous autumn.

—◈—

It was not until 22 May 1813 that Wellington at last recrossed the frontier with his re-equipped, rested and reinforced army. Wellington sought greater speed and manoeuvrability. Light tin kettles now replaced heavy iron ones, freeing the mules to carry three tents for every company. The men were also told not to bring their greatcoats – which would be a deprivation if they had to return in winter. It was the equivalent of Wellington burning his bridges: he did not believe they would have to. As they crossed the border, Wellington ostentatiously took off his hat and shouted, 'Farewell Portugal. I shall never see you again.' He had already remarked that there was 'scarcely any French army left, except that in our front'.

His army consisted of 80,000 men, including the Portuguese, and 20,000 Spaniards. The French in Spain had been depleted of 20,000 of their best troops to reinforce Napoleon's beleaguered northern armies: worse still, Napoleon had ordered Wellington's old adversary, the French army of Portugal, to hold down the mounting insurgencies in the Basque country, Navarra and Aragon. General Bertrand Clausel, the new northern commander, was a brilliant and energetic soldier, but even he proved unable to control the rebellions in the north.

Wellington's offensive had been brilliantly and meticulously planned through the winter and spring, utterly in contrast to the improvised and disastrous one of the previous autumn. He used as a forward base the Spanish port of Santander in the north, controlled by the Spaniards, where he assembled voluminous supplies and a siege train, no longer having to depend on the long supply line of retreat to Lisbon and giving his army a point of evacuation if necessary. His army moved forward in two giant columns, one under Hill heading for Salamanca and the other much larger one under Wellington himself and Sir Thomas Graham.

The second column crossed the Douro River with great skill, with Wellington himself supervising the operation from a basket slung over the cliffs, and then marched on to Valladolid, which King Joseph and Marshal Jean-Baptiste Jourdan had previously evacuated. The two British armies joined up at Toro and, instead of attacking the French stronghold at Burgos, bypassed it and did what they should have the previous year – they moved into the sparsely populated hills to the north of Burgos, threatening to surround it and cut it off from possible retreat to France. The French had to abandon the fortress without a fight and retreat further across the Ebro to the town of Vitoria.

There, at last, King Joseph decided to make a stand. Vitoria was approached from the west by a valley bounded on one side by the Zadora River and on the other by virtually impassable mountains. The French feared, though, that an attack might be mounted from the north as well as the west. On 21 June 1813, the battle began with a skirmish from the southeast. The French immediately rushed troops there, imagining this to be the main thrust of the British attack. In fact, the bulk of the British forces were concentrated to the southwest, on the other side of the river valley, under the nominal command of Lord Dalhousie but under the actual command of Sir Thomas Picton and, behind him, Wellington.

From the north there appeared out of the supposedly impassable mountains another body of troops. Wellington's artillery was pounding away. The French fought bravely under this three-pronged attack, battling continuously as all three advanced. Harvey, Wellington's aide, had two horses shot under him in the thick of the fighting. If the northern force under Graham had advanced with speed, the French would have been completely trapped: instead, they hesitated and the French troops, in full retreat, were able to make their escape across the Pass of Salvatierra, leaving most of King Joseph's baggage train in its wake. This was promptly plundered by the British troops, who swarmed into Vitoria in an undisciplined mass.

Some 8,000 French soldiers were killed or taken prisoner, and 150 guns were captured. About 5 million francs were left behind along with golden doubloons and Napoleon coins. Some 500 prostitutes of the French army were taken. Wellington, as usual, was incandescent at the indiscipline of his troops.

The French were now in total disarray. Clausel fell back to Zaragoza and then to France, while another French army withdrew from Aragon; only Catalonia remained under French control. The escaping and defeated French army from Vitoria headed straight for the French border, leaving a few garrisons behind at Pamplona, San Sebastian and Santona.

Vitoria had been one of the most beautifully planned of Wellington's battles. If not so skilfully fought as Salamanca, its swiftness made it one of his finest victories. He had regained his touch. His strategic skill had ensured that the French had never stood a chance, were wholly overwhelmed and were so assaulted from every direction that they had little idea how to regroup and react. Again, it had been a magnificently executed offensive attack rather than the kind of defensive one for which he was more famous. The escape of the bulk of the French army was regrettable, but not his fault. Wellington had not made the mistake of heading towards Madrid again.

However, the Peninsular War was not over yet; nor, in spite of Napoleon's defeat at the hands of the Russians, was the Emperor's hold on Europe: Wellington was acutely aware that the tide could turn again, particularly if developments on the eastern front allowed Napoleon to send fresh troops back into Spain. Wellington was offered the command in Germany, but refused: 'Many might be found to conduct matters as well as I can, both here and in Germany; but nobody would enjoy the same advantage here, and I should be no better than another in Germany. If a British army should be left in the Peninsula, therefore, it is best that I should remain with it.'

His next objective was to take San Sebastian, a hugely well-fortified fortress protected on one side by the sea and on the other by the Urumea River. The unreliable if courageous Graham was put in charge of the siege: once again, Wellington's caution was evident in his inability to bypass a fortress which he feared could threaten his flank.

The siege proved a disaster, with attacks being made at low tide between the sea and the fortress under intense fire. While this was being botched, Napoleon staged a counteroffensive into Spain under Soult, who had been ordered to supplant the ludicrous King Joseph. A huge army of 85,000 poured through two passes in the Pyrenees in order to fulfil Napoleon's desperate need to secure a victory in the Peninsula, to display his power in the European theatre and in particular to prevent the Austrians declaring war upon him again in the east.

Wellington was caught with his army spread out between San Sebastian and inland Pamplona. One of two immense French columns ran up against Wellington himself, with a much smaller but substantial force in a typically well chosen defensive position on a ridge at Sorauren. Wellington actually saw his adversary, Soult, when a spy told him to look: 'I levelled my glass exactly as he pointed, and there, sure enough, I distinctly discerned Soult with his staff around him, several of them with their hats off and in animated conversation... I saw his features so distinctly that when I met him in a drawing-room in Paris for the first time I knew him at once.'

The fighting ended when Soult attempted a breakthrough to San Sebastian, and the British chose their moment to attack down the hill: the French were routed and made their escape back to the passes of the Pyrenees, where they took up strong positions and impeded any further British advance. Some 13,000 French casualties and prisoners had been taken.

With Soult's army departed, the British siege of San Sebastian intensified and two breaches were made in the walls. The citadel was taken, followed by the towers. The usual horrors ensued, the British soldiers showing yet again that they were little different from the French when motivated by revenge and plunder and unrestrained by their officers.

On 7 October 1813, Wellington crossed the lightly defended Bidassoa, the Rubicon of France. It was an historic moment, a turning point in the entire Revolutionary and Napoleonic wars: for the first time the British were on French soil in force, not as at the beginning of the Revolutionary war in alliance with continental countries or counter-revolutionaries, not as a raiding party, but through their own military efforts. Instead of Napoleon invading British territory, as he had so often blustered and threatened, Wellington was invading the territorial mainland of France.

Wellington's emotions at this juncture can only be imagined. His army had been the first to penetrate France, which was still uninvaded from the east after so many bitter campaigns there by the far larger forces of Austria, Prussia and Russia. He was under no illusions that the war was over, but held out the hope that the terror, strife and suffering which had dominated all of Europe for nearly two decades might at last be approaching the beginning of the end. Yet there could be no certainty: Napoleon and France were far from beaten. Wellington had learned to his chagrin the dangers of over-confidence the previous year and had been appallingly humiliated on the retreat from Burgos.

On 31 October 1813, Pamplona surrendered at last, finally ending the threat of a fresh strike across Wellington's rear and permitting him to advance tentatively to the French Pyrenees. On 10 November, his 55,000-strong army moved forward up the mountain passes against the heavily fortified but lightly manned French positions above. The British and Portuguese displayed extraordinary determination and bravery. In spite of considerable casualties – more than 3,000 – they prevailed and drove the French from the passes. The latter lost over 4,000 men and 60 guns in the murderous fighting. This was the Battle of the Nivelle, the first fought by Wellington on French soil.

The British commander rudely, but wisely, decided to dispense with the services of his Spanish allies for fear that they might antagonize the French population needlessly through acts of brutality – which of course infuriated the Spaniards. He advanced across the Nive River towards Bayonne. However, Soult launched a desperate counteroffensive on 10 December against the British–Portuguese vanguard but failed. He staged a further one, this time against the extremely able Sir Rowland Hill, who struck back with force and drove the French back to Bayonne, giving them, in Wellington's phrase, 'a hell of a licking'. Altogether in both battles the French suffered some 6,500 casualties to 4,500 Anglo-Portuguese ones – an illustration of the intensity of the fighting. Now some 4,500 German troops fighting for the French deserted. Behind Wellington, Spain had been liberated and in 1814 the final French stronghold in Catalonia fell almost without a fight.

Meanwhile, Wellington remained stuck at St Jean de Luz for a while because of the weather and there established comfortable quarters. Not until the end of February 1814 did he decide to advance across the Adour River, below Bayonne, which was bridged with a magnificent pontoon. Hill staged a major diversionary attack against Soult at Bayonne itself. Completely surprised, the French commander abandoned the town.

On 27 March, the British attacked at Toulouse where Wellington's sure military touch seemed to desert him. The pontoon bridge across the Garonne River was swept away by a flood, which left part of his army stranded on the wrong side. Then, on 10 April, he attacked at three points, and his forces were routed at two of them. Even so, Soult was forced to abandon the city. When he entered Toulouse, Colonel William Ponsonby arrived to tell Wellington:

'I have extraordinary news for you.'

'Aye, I thought so. I knew we should have peace; I've long expected it.'

'No, Napoleon has abdicated.'

'How abdicated? Ay, 'tis time indeed. You don't say so! Upon my honour! Hurrah!'

He was cheered at dinner for 10 minutes, to his enormous embarrassment. The great campaign of so many battles, setbacks and so much bloodshed and savagery was over at last. Napoleon was exiled to the island of Elba.

What had been the significance of the Peninsular War? Many historians consider it a mere sideshow to more significant events in eastern Europe, as Napoleon himself often offhandedly remarked. Others, like Thomas Cochrane, believed it was a mistake in principle and that attacks from the sea against the supply lines from France to Spain would have achieved victory at a much lesser cost, although this certainly seems exaggerated: the French could have reinforced their sea defences and Pyrenean passes to maintain supplies; the French armies in Spain much of the time lived off the land.

Contrary to conventional wisdom, the significance of the war in Napoleon's overall defeat was colossal. First, it provided a huge boost in Britain's continuous and often lonely campaign against Napoleon: given that the string of naval victories had ended – largely because the French had chosen to no longer fight at sea – it completely reversed the common concept in Britain as well as in Europe of the British army as a group of incompetents officered by aristocratic dunderheads. Wellington won battle after battle against the most formidable fighting force in Europe, which had defeated such legendary professional armies as those of Prussia and Austria, as well as the nearly suicidal Russian conscript armies. If he had sometimes made serious misjudgements, Wellington had also displayed superb professionalism and his soldiers had shown discipline, courage and ability.

Second, the Peninsular War had been a colossal drain on French resources, with anything up to a third of a million soldiers engaged, many of them crack troops that Napoleon could ill-afford to spare from his other fronts, particularly in 1812–14. The drain on France's financial resources was equally acute. It was a deeply unpopular war in France, which had never felt itself threatened by Spain, as it had been by Austria and its eastern enemies. Enforced recruiting drives had been raised every year for nearly six years, most of them falling upon the peasantry, which had been one of Napoleon's main bulwarks of support: undoubtedly, this contributed to the Emperor's growing unpopularity within France itself.

—*∿∿*—

Wellington was given a dukedom in 1814 and became ambassador to France before replacing Lord Castlereagh at the Congress of Vienna. However, he was summoned back to military command in 1815 with the news of Napoleon's escape from Elba and takeover of Paris.

He was sent to Brussels to integrate British, Hanoverian and Dutch units but found that his new charges were an 'infamous army, very weak and ill-equipped, and a very inexperienced staff'. He divided the army into three corps, one under the youthful Prince of Orange, the second under the sturdy Rowland Hill, with himself in charge of the reserve. He had a total of just 92,000 men and 192 guns. Under entirely separate control was Gebhard Leberecht von Blücher's Prussian army of 120,000 men and more than 300 guns. Wellington had met Blücher in Paris and, unusually for the acidulous Irishman, got on well with a brother general.

He disposed of his forces with an eye to protecting the coast, which meant they were kept a considerable distance from Blücher's army. He felt that his first duty was to his own men, which meant preserving his line of retreat to the ports of Antwerp and Ostend so that he could evacuate his army in the event of a defeat. He was concerned that Napoleon might come up around his west flank towards Tournai and threaten the coastal area, cutting him off. In spite of this worry, he privately believed that Napoleon, if he did come, would move towards Mons in the centre and keep his options open.

Wellington did not really believe Napoleon would attack at all. In fact he wanted to invade France as early as 1 May 1815 to surprise Napoleon. Tsar Alexander I, however, declared that an invasion from all sides should take place on 1 June. The British commander basked in complacency in the almost carnival atmosphere of Brussels, to which British society had flocked in early summer, but Napoleon was already preparing to take the attack to the allied forces.

Napoleon crossed the border into Belgium with his army on 15 June and appointed Marshal Ney to command the 1st and 2nd Corps on his left flank, while Emmanuel, Marquis de Grouchy commanded the 3rd and 4th Corps on the right. Ney was ordered to seize the hamlet of Quatre Bras just beyond the intersection of the main east–west Roman road and the north–south road to Brussels. Wellington was blissfully unaware of his approach, a major failure in allied intelligence, although Lieutenant-Colonel Colquhoun Grant, one of his intelligence officers, had tried to warn him on 14 June; another officer failed to pass the message on.

On 15 June, at just before 6 p.m., Wellington first heard the news that the French were attacking Prussian forward posts. He chose not to react, but to wait for further evidence of the size and whereabouts of the French force: the attack was much further to the east than he expected and could prove to be a feint.

Some German historians have alleged that he learnt much earlier of the attacks, but chose not to come to the help of the Prussians. There is no documentary evidence for this. Blücher sent a message calling for help, but Wellington had already left for a ball given by the Duchess of Richmond. There he 'affected great gaiety and cheerfulness', but an observer remarked, 'I had never seen him with such an expression of care and anxiety on his countenance.'

He was not neglecting his duties: he simply did not yet know how to react to an attack whose direction and intensity he could not guess.

That same night, Ney disobeyed the admittedly ambiguous order from Napoleon to take Quatre Bras and bedded down for the night. A small Dutch force commanded by Prince Bernhard of Saxe-Weimar-Eisenach, and sent there by the Prince of Orange's chief of staff in defiance of orders, had entrenched itself there. At nearly 9 p.m., Wellington was told by the Prince of Orange of the French concentration outside Quatre Bras. He affected calm, but summoned the Duke of Richmond and said tersely, 'Napoleon has humbugged me, by God, he has gained 24 hours' march on me.'

It was too late to send reinforcements to Quatre Bras. He decided to make a stand further back towards the village of Waterloo. After snatching three hours' sleep, he breakfasted leisurely, then rode forward towards Quatre Bras, which he found to be peaceful. He ordered some troops down to support the Dutch in their outpost and then he sent a letter to Blücher, declaring 'I do not see much of the enemy in front of us, and I await news of your Highness and the arrival of troops in order to determine my operations for the day. Nothing has appeared on the side of Binche, or on our right.'

He rode to meet the Prussian commanders at the village of Brye. Blücher reported to him that he had concentrated three corps around the village of Ligny nearby, to the southeast. The accounts of the meeting are contradictory: General Karl von Müffling, Prussia's liaison officer, claimed that Wellington, on being asked to lend support to the Prussian stand at Ligny, said 'Well, I will come, provided that I myself am not attacked [at Quatre Bras].' Another German officer claims that Wellington agreed simply to block the French at Quatre Bras and send the bulk of his forces to Prussia's aid. This seems highly unlikely, as he was hurrying most of his troops forward to the exposed position at Quatre Bras and could not spare many for Ligny; he still could not be sure where the main thrust of Napoleon's attack would come – at Quatre Bras or Ligny – and his army was weaker than that of Blücher. He did not know that Napoleon intended to attack both at once.

Privately, he considered Blücher had blundered in his decision to meet the French at Ligny: 'If they fight here they will be damnably mauled.' This was open ground in front of a hill. Meanwhile, in the west, Ney still hesitated to attack Quatre Bras because he was not sure of the enemy's strength. Owing to the incompetence of Napoleon's chief of staff, Soult, clear orders did not reach him until mid-afternoon to take the village and then wheel about and fall upon Blücher's exposed eastern flank and rear, while Napoleon attacked from the front. The Prussians would thus be annihilated between two fires.

On the morning of 16 June, Napoleon ordered his men forward against the exposed Prussian front at Ligny for the first of three battles over three days that collectively became known as the Battle of Waterloo. Napoleon declared 'the intention of His Majesty is that you attack whatever is before you and after vigorously throwing them back, join us to envelop this corps'. However, he believed the Prussians to have only 40,000 men when in fact they had double that; General Karl von Bülow's corps of 32,000 stationed at Liege was also on its way, although in the event it arrived too late for the battle.

Napoleon ordered a devastating artillery barrage upon the exposed Prussian positions, followed by a cavalry attack by Grouchy on the right, as well as an infantry attack. Soon, the French had captured the villages of St Amand and Sombrette. The 73-year-old Blücher, who had put himself at the head of a cavalry charge, had his horse shot under him and narrowly escaped being trampled to death. He was rescued, while command temporarily devolved to August von Gneisenau, who anxiously waited for reinforcements from Wellington that did not come. He later wrote 'on the 16th of June in the morning the Duke of Wellington promised to be at Quatre Bras at 10am with 20,000 men... on the strength of these promises and arrangements we decided to fight the battle'. As we have seen, the Germans had no reason to believe they would be reinforced unless Wellington felt himself secure at Quatre Bras.

At 2 p.m., three miles to the west, Ney's army had at last launched a major attack while Wellington was desperately trying to bring up the men being hurried along the Brussels road to hold the village of Quatre Bras. Ney had delayed attacking, believing the Dutch defending force to be greater than it actually was, while Wellington's army was largely concealed behind the brow of a low hill.

As the Dutch frontline gave ground under the French assault, Sir Thomas Picton and 8,000 troops arrived. He pushed them back for a short while before more French troops were committed and the Anglo-Dutch force were pushed back again. A force of cavalry under the Duke of Brunswick arrived and charged, but he was mortally wounded. Wellington, mounted on his horse Copenhagen, was nearly captured by a French counter-charge. He galloped into a British square yelling 'Lie down 92nd', and the men let him pass over, jumping up again to discharge volleys at the pursuing French horsemen, who veered away. Further French charges followed – in one case right into an incomplete square of the 42nd Highlanders, who closed it and trapped and killed the cavalrymen inside.

Ney's 40,000-strong army just kept on coming, counter-charging the reinforcements as quickly as they could be brought forward. Meanwhile Napoleon, realizing that Ney had not yet broken through Quatre Bras, instructed General Jean-Baptiste Drouet, Comte d'Erlan, who commanded Ney's 22,000 strong reserve, to stage the flank attack he had planned against the Prussian right which he believed would deliver a decisive victory. Ney had been right to press his attack on Quatre Bras: for we now know that if he had veered off to the right to help Napoleon, the British would have felt free to reinforce Blücher.

However, Napoleon's last-minute change of orders proved very nearly disastrous, for it deprived Ney of the reserve support he needed to overwhelm the British position. D'Erlan, misunderstanding his orders, moved to reinforce the French right rather than to attack behind Prussian lines: this panicked the French right, which mistook his men for enemy troops. This delayed Napoleon's own advance which had been going well, but he coolly ordered d'Erlan to march back upon the Prussian west flank and attack it.

Ney, preoccupied with his intense firefight at Quatre Bras, was incensed when he learnt that Napoleon had detached his own reserves, and issued a counter-order to the confused d'Erlan to come back to support him at Quatre Bras: he threatened to have the unfortunate officer court-martialled. D'Erlan was about to attack from the west at Ligny and rout the Prussians when he received the new order: he felt he had no choice but to march back to Quatre Bras, arriving after the fighting there had died down. The 22,000 troops which could have decided either battle were thus marching backwards and forwards all afternoon.

Back at Quatre Bras, the French had charged again, almost breaking one infantry square, that of the 69th, and then attacking the 33rd. The 69th were forced to take refuge in a wood, but another infantry division was brought up in the nick of time. As dusk had started to fall, it became apparent that Wellington had narrowly held the allied position with casualties on each side about evens, at 4,000 each. It had been an equal battle, to the relief of the British, who had been taken by surprise.

Not so at Ligny. Realizing that no help would be forthcoming from Ney or d'Erlan, Napoleon ordered a bayonet attack against the Prussian centre, which had backed up the incline known as the Heights of Bussy. The Prussians counterattacked, but by then the French were in control and had beaten them off. With darkness falling, the Prussians were able to withdraw in good order, but they had suffered a major defeat: some 16,000 men and 21 guns had been lost, compared to the 12,000 French losses with no guns. A further 10,000 Prussians deserted in the demoralized aftermath. Only nightfall had prevented a complete Prussian route.

Von Gneisenau decided to withdraw the Prussians to safety in the east, which would have left Wellington's army stranded and heavily outnumbered facing the French, but the battered old Blücher dragged himself from his sickbed just in time to prevent this. The decision was made to retire to Wavre, 18 miles to the north, giving the defeated Prussians the option of either supporting Wellington should the fight be renewed, or of retreating down their lines of communication eastward.

Napoleon had thus won the bloody Battle of Ligny, although not to the point of destroying the Prussian army, while his forces had been fought to a standstill at Quatre Bras. He was deeply frustrated: he had caught the Prussians virtually unsupported by the British and should have inflicted a decisive defeat. Ney's failure to take Quatre Bras, plus the mix-up over d'Erlan's army, had cost him a spectacular victory. He blamed Ney, but he might have been cheated of the victory at Ligny anyway if the British had been able to drive Ney back and reinforce the Prussians: he owed a great deal to Ney for keeping the British engaged.

Napoleon consoled himself with the thought that complete victory could be achieved the following day, now that the Prussians were badly mauled and licking their wounds. Wellington faced the terrifying prospect that the French would move forward through the territory abandoned by the Prussians and outflank him. He was a deeply worried man: in the small hours, he paced about, mulling his limited options. By 7 a.m., he seemed to have decided that, with the Prussian retreat to Wavre, the game was about up: 'As he [Blücher] has gone back, we must go too. I suppose in England they will say we have been licked.' It seemed that the battle had been won by Napoleon by default. However, he had one cause for consolation: Napoleon had lost the element of surprise. Wellington considered withdrawing to the defensive position near Waterloo which he had carefully mapped out before being dragged into the battle at Quatre Bras.

Two hours later, Wellington told Blücher's emissary that he would make a stand at Mont St Jean, his reserve position, if the Prussians promised to send 'even one corps only' in support. Inexplicably, the French had not attacked his vulnerable position at Quatre Bras in the early morning. By 11 a.m. Wellington's forces were retreating cautiously north, completing the task an hour-and-a-half later, with Wellington's second-in-command, Henry Paget, Lord Uxbridge, and his cavalry bringing up the rear. What had happened to the French? It seems that Napoleon had an acute attack of piles during the day, and possibly of cystitis, which would have given him a severe fever and pain. Grouchy, one of his key commanders, was refused access to him throughout that night.

At around 9 a.m. he rode to the battlefield at Ligny in self-confident fashion, perhaps so as to diminish the pain, talking to his commander and men. Grouchy rode up and asked for orders. Napoleon snapped back: 'I will give them to you when I think fit.' The Emperor's problem, quite apart from his embarrassing and painful ailments, was that he had no certain knowledge of the disposition of the allied troops: he believed Blücher and the Prussians to be in full retreat.

He now made another near-fatal mistake. Abandoning his old tactic of attempting to divide the two armies and falling upon one with a superior force, he summoned a meeting of his generals at around 10 a.m. and informed them he intended to split his own army into two, sending Grouchy in pursuit of the Prussians with 33,000 men and launching his own force of 70,000 men in a frontal attack against the retreating British and Dutch army. Both Ney, who had patiently awaited orders all morning from his position in front of Quatre Bras, and Soult remonstrated. Napoleon told the latter angrily: 'Because you have been beaten by Wellington, you think him a great general! I tell you Wellington is a bad general, the English are bad troops, and this affair is nothing more than a picnic.' Napoleon appeared to think that the Prussians were much further away than they actually were, and therefore believed that the British and Prussian forces could not combine for at least two days.

Still Napoleon did nothing, accepting the advice of his artillery commanders that the ground was too wet to move his guns forward; possibly, he felt he was in no shape personally to command the attack that day, but did not want to delegate the responsibility. At last, at 1 p.m., he ordered his forces to Quatre Bras to find that Ney, lacking specific instructions, had ordered his men to have lunch. Only after a further delay did the two forces combine and move forward, with both Ney and Napoleon seeking to engage the British rearguard, but getting bogged down in mud.

By 6.30 p.m. Wellington had completely escaped, drawing up his forces into their new positions on Mont St Jean, 15 miles to the north. He was entrenched in one of his classic defensive positions, skilfully chosen, along a low, long ridge overlooking a broad and shallow valley. The bulk of his army was sheltered behind the brow of the hill on its reverse slope, which protected them from enemy artillery and concealed their true size and dispositions: it was one of Wellington's favourite tactics.

In the approach to the ridge, Wellington ordered various sizeable buildings, such as Hougoumont chateau and La Haye Sainte farmhouse to be heavily reinforced to slow the French attack. He placed his men in a double line behind the ridge, with instructions to form squares if attacked by cavalry. These were supported by British artillery in clusters along the right. The cavalry were in the centre behind the infantry. However, still intent on securing his line of retreat, Wellington sent some 13,000 men to Hale, nine miles away. They were never to fight at all. It never occurred to Wellington to take the offensive against Napoleon: he was in his element in defence and only had 67,000 men to the French 74,000. A British attack would have been suicidal. This was almost certainly the right tactic, even if it was not heroic.

Having made his dispositions he returned to his headquarters at an inn in Waterloo just to the north. The rain was torrential. He had heard nothing from Blücher and made preparations to retreat to Brussels if no aid from the Prussians was forthcoming. Finally, at 3 a.m. he received a message from Blücher's headquarters in Wavre:

> I hereby inform you that, in consequence of the communication made to me to the effect that the Duke of Wellington will tomorrow accept battle in the position from Braine l'Alleud to La Haye, my troops will be put in motion in the following way: Bülow's corps will start very early at dawn from Dion-le-Mont and advance through Wavre by way of St Lambert, in order to attack the enemy's right wing. The second corps will immediately follow the fourth [Bülow's] corps; and the first and third corps hold themselves ready likewise to follow thither. The exhaustion of the troops, which in part have not arrived (namely, the tail of the fourth corps), makes it impossible to advance earlier. In return, I beg you to inform me betimes when and how the Duke is attacked, so that I may be able to take measures accordingly.

The order had come after a tense meeting of the Prussian high command at which Blücher had favoured a march to Wellington's aid and von Gneisenau had opposed it as being too risky. In fact, Blücher had already been reinforced by von Bülow, which more than made up for his losses at Ligny, and the Prussians believed that the French had sent a force of only 15,000 men to attack them at Wavre, so they could easily afford to spare the troops. Still, the cautious von Gneisenau resisted his master, distrusting the British and instructing General von Müffling to 'find out accurately whether the Duke has the fixed intention to fight in his present position, or whether possibly nothing but "demonstrations" are intended, as these can only be in the highest degree compromising to our army'. This delayed the despatch of the First, Second and Third Prussian corps until midday the following day.

Napoleon rode up to an inn called La Belle Alliance in the morning. There he learnt that Grouchy had progressed only six miles towards Wavres and had bedded his army down at Gembloux. Nervously, he went for a walk at 1 a.m. The night made an eerie spectacle, with countless small fires in the rain marking the positions of the two huge armies as the fateful dawn approached.

Still suffering from indecision, Napoleon woke at around 10 a.m. on 18 June before issuing orders to Grouchy to abandon his march on Wavre, and instead outflank Blücher by interposing himself between the British and Prussian armies and preventing reinforcements from the latter reaching Wellington. Grouchy misinterpreted the badly drafted orders and continued to move forward to Wavre even when he began to hear cannon fire in the direction of Waterloo to his left. Napoleon was incensed when he heard.

He decided to observe the battle from behind La Belle Alliance, delegating operational command to Ney, which scarcely suggested he had lost his confidence in him. Meanwhile, Wellington had jovially ridden up with his staff officers from Waterloo as though about to attend a meeting of hounds. His attitude masked a desperate anxiety as to the course of the battle, which he believed hinged on whether the Prussians would fulfil their promise to arrive. He expressed contempt for Napoleon: 'That fellow little thinks what a

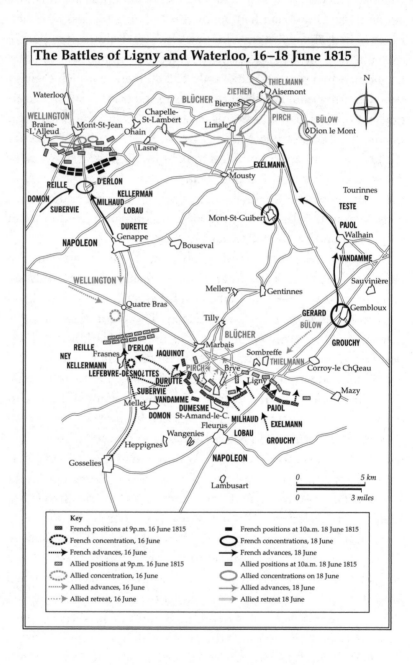

The Battles of Ligny and Waterloo, 16–18 June 1815

Waterloo

WELLINGTON
Braine-
L'Alleud   Mont-St-Jean

BLÜCHER
ZIETHEN   THIELMANN
Aisemont
Bierges

Chapelle-
St-Lambert
Ohain   Limale   PIRCH
Lasne   BÜLOW
                                                   Dion le Mont

N

REILLE   D'ERLON
DOMON   KELLERMAN
     SUBERVIE MILHAUD
               LOBAU
            DURETTE
NAPOLEON   Genappe

EXELMANN
Mousty

Tourinnes

TESTE
PAJOL
Walhain

VANDAMME

WELLINGTON

Quatre Bras

Mellery   Gentinnes
Tilly
BLÜCHER
Marbais

Bouseval

Sauvinière

GERARD   Gembloux
BÜLOW
            GROUCHY

REILLE
NEY   Frasnes D'ERLON JAQUINOT
KELLERMANN
   LEFEBVRE-DESNOËTTES
              DURUTTE
        SUBERVIE
Mellet VANDAMME
DOMON   DUMESME
        St-Amand-le-C.
         Fleurus
    Wangenies
Heppignes

PIRCH   Brye
        Sombreffe
           THIELMANN
        Ligny   Corroy-le-Château

                      Mazy

MILHAUD
PAJOL
EXELMANN
LOBAU   GROUCHY

Gosselies

NAPOLEON

Lambusart

0   5 km
0   3 miles

Key

French positions at 9p.m. 16 June 1815
French concentration, 16 June
French advances, 16 June
Allied positions at 9p.m. 16 June 1815
Allied concentration, 16 June
Allied advances, 16 June
Allied retreat, 16 June

French positions at 10a.m. 18 June 1815
French concentrations, 18 June
French advances, 18 June
Allied positions at 10a.m. 18 June 1815
Allied concentrations on 18 June
Allied advances, 18 June
Allied retreat 18 June

confounded licking he'll get before the day is over. He was a shabby fellow. I was never a believer in him, and I always thought that in the long run we should overturn him... His whole life, civil, political and military, was a fraud.' But he often expressed private admiration for Napoleon as a general.

After resting for a while, Napoleon at last gave the order to advance with a concentrated burst of artillery fire against the most advanced British position, the chateau at Hougoumont, at around 11.30 a.m. The British soon replied. The Battle of Waterloo had begun. Napoleon's brother Jerome was delegated to launch the first attack on the British position, which was defended by a few hundred men under the heroic James Macdonnell; it covered a small valley which would shelter a French column from British artillery. If it was captured the French would be able to pour troops on to the ridge above.

Soon Jerome's men were surging forward from the French side of the valley of death, where a total of 140,000 men faced each other, and surrounded the walls of the garden around Hougoumont. Fierce fighting lasted an hour-and-a-half, while both the main armies watched without moving, before the French at last succeeded in breaking down the main gate, but Macdonnell counterattacked and drove them out, killing all of those remaining within the compound. The buildings caught fire. Wellington coolly wrote instructions to Macdonnell:

> I see that the fire has communicated itself from the hay stack to the roof of the chateau. You must however still keep your men in those parts to which the fire does not reach. Take care that no men are lost by the falling in the roof or floors. After they will have fallen in, occupy the ruined walls inside of the garden, particularly if it should be possible for the enemy to pass through the embers to the inside of the house.

The battle around the chateau raged all day, the gallant defenders holding out in their outpost against far superior forces. Hougoumont was never captured: a colossal total of 10,000 men died in the struggle, most of them French.

At around 12.30 p.m. Napoleon's main battery on a hill just in front of La Belle Alliance opened up with its 75 guns, followed by a major infantry attack of 16,000 men under d'Erlan. The British counterattacked with infantry volleys and a cavalry charge which was badly mauled. Both sides disengaged with some 10,000 losses between them after just half-an-hour. General Picton was killed and Sir William Ponsonby cut up with lances. Lord Uxbridge admitted that mistakes had been made in the cavalry charge.

Napoleon could now observe Prussian troops approaching from the east, although he misinformed his troops that these were French reinforcements so as not to discourage them. Of Grouchy there was nothing to be seen. He ordered a full-scale attack on La Haye Sainte farmhouse to break the British centre before the Prussians arrived. Ney, receiving the order, inexplicably commanded his cavalry forward in a massed attack on the narrow ground between Hougoumont and La Haye Sainte. It seems that Ney had mistaken a redeployment of the British line by Wellington as the beginning of a retreat.

The British were incredulous: an attack by massed cavalry without infantry support against British lines was unheard of, particularly uphill. Ney admittedly had little sight of the main British lines over the brow of the hill. As the cavalry charged up, packed tightly together, the British formed impregnable squares and the horses shied away while the soldiers' volleys simply mowed them down. The Duke of Wellington took part in the fighting on his white charger Copenhagen, taking refuge in a square when attacked.

Uxbridge's cavalry counterattacked from their own position behind the infantry, driving the broken lines of French cavalry back. However, the latter reformed and charged again and again – a total of 12 times in all, each time breaking ranks as they swarmed around the impregnable squares, each time being driven back by British gunfire and cavalry counter-charges: it was magnificently brave, but utterly foolhardy.

The Duke was wondering what was holding up Blücher's Prussians, for without them he might still lose the battle and he was desperately hard-pressed. He did not know the difficulty of the terrain they were crossing, nor that Napoleon had sent 16,000 men under Georges Mouton, Comte de Lobau, to intercept them.

Von Bülow's corps, the freshest of the Prussian troops, reached Plancenoit, where they were intercepted by Lobau's force. The Prussians initially repelled the French and Napoleon was forced to divert two more battalions to this sideshow.

On the main battlefield, the intensity of French artillery fire was making inroads into the British. At around 5 p.m., Ney ordered seven infantry columns forward to seize the key British position of La Haye Sainte, which was in fact largely defended by Hanoverians. There the defenders held out valiantly, but owing to a serious British oversight they had not been resupplied with ammunition and now had no choice but to give up before an overwhelming French assault. Only some 40 members of the 360-strong garrison escaped the carnage on the farm. Ney's infantry were threatening to blast a path right through the centre of the allied lines.

At that moment, the 20-year-old Prince of Orange gave orders for the body of Hanoverians still holding the line to attack the French infantry. As the infantry was overwhelmingly superior and supported by cavalry, this was madness, but the order was insistently repeated and, gallantly, Christian von Ompteda led the attack. His men were wiped out, severely weakening the allied line in yet another place.

The battle seemed all but over: against the massed French infantry attacks the British line was barely holding, with Wellington ordering a few Brunswickers to plug the gap left by von Ompteda. He desperately sent an emissary to the nearest Prussian commander, General Hans Ernst Karl von Zieten, but he refused to come to Wellington's aid and instead marched to reinforce the Prussians at Plancenoit. Wellington had made the mistake of dispersing his forces along too broad a front and had insufficient men to redeploy towards the disintegrating centre.

What he did not know was that Ney, fighting furiously with his usual courage at the head of his men at La Haye Sainte, also had no more reinforcements. Napoleon angrily informed his couriers that he could spare no more. In fact, Napoleon had 14 regiments of the crack Imperial Guard, which he was anxious to keep in reserve at all costs. He now roused himself from his vantage point on a hill at Rossome like some tired old general and moved forward a few hundred yards to the inn at La Belle Alliance itself.

There he could see little of the fighting through the dense columns of black smoke clouding the valley. Instead, he could see Plancenoit, where he feared the Prussians were outflanking the French right and threatening to cut his communications and getaway route to Paris. He was furious with Ney for having attacked frontally without specific orders and thus endangering the battle. He had little idea that Ney was on the verge of victory.

Napoleon decided to send two further reserve battalions of the precious Imperial Guard towards Plancenoit and retain three on the plateau where he was standing. Thus the Prussian diversion in fact kept much of Napoleon's most elite forces from reinforcing Ney at exactly the moment when he could have broken through.

An extraordinary altercation was taking place to the east where Ludwig von Reiche, chief of staff to General von Zieten, was suddenly intercepted by a staff officer from Blücher, ordering von Zieten to go to the aid of von Bülow at Plancenoit as 'things were beginning to go badly there'. Von Müffling, the Prussian liaison officer with Wellington, rode up and desperately urged him to send the corps to Wellington's aid instead or the day would be lost. Von Reiche was undecided until von Zieten himself decided to disobey Blücher's order and go to Wellington's assistance.

The Prussians moved forward and supported Wellington's weak left flank, but were only minimally involved in the battle, as just one brigade was engaged. They lost only one of their officers, along with eight wounded. Napoleon spotted von Zieten's corps and told his men that they were in fact General Grouchy's army, come to the battle at last: it was a bare-faced lie, but understandable in the circumstances. Cries of 'Vive l'empereur' broke out. Ney shouted, 'Courage, France is victorious.'

Napoleon decided at last to send the Imperial Guard into the battle: it was 7.30 p.m. and the sun was beginning to descend through the thick smoke. A French victory seemed all but inevitable. To the intense joy of the French, it was observed that Napoleon himself was leading the Imperial Guard into battle. This turned to dismay when, supported by some of his generals but not by others, he veered aside. His brother Jerome exclaimed, 'Can it be possible that he will not seek death here? He will never find a more glorious grave!' Napoleon sought the shelter of a small quarry on the side of the road.

The exhausted and valiant Ney took command again – but instead of moving the Imperial Guard up the narrow road towards von Zieten's approaching Prussians, he preferred the more open ground to the left, the scene of so many cavalry charges. This had become deep in mud and was exposed to enemy artillery fire. Ney's horse was shot from under him for the fifth time that day: still he picked himself up and urged his men on.

Wellington, exposed on his horse on the ridge, observed the move and ordered reinforcements from his infantry. General Peregrine Maitland's five-deep squares, supported by artillery, waited behind the brow of the hill, holding their fire until the French reached it. Wellington screamed in his high-pitched voice, 'Now, Maitland, now is your turn. Up guards, make ready, fire!'

The French frontline recoiled in astonishment. A second British line commanded by Sir John Colborne marched in perfect order around the flank of the French. Under fire, the 'immortals' – the Imperial Guard so jealously husbanded by Napoleon – wavered.

The French cavalry counter-charged the British, who for a moment were held in check. The French retreat stopped, and they reformed temporarily with fresh regiments coming up from behind. Wellington (who had just seen his second-in-command Lord Uxbridge shot in the knee, prompting the famous exchange 'By God, Sir, I've lost my leg.' 'By God, Sir, you have') yelled at Colborne: 'Don't give them time to rally.' Colborne's troops charged.

The Imperial Guard, also cowed by the threat of von Zeiten's Prussians to their right, retreated. This caused panic through the French infantry behind them. As the French line wavered, Wellington raised his hat and waved in a prearranged signal and his reserve army charged forward in the centre, while some Prussians advanced on the right down that bloody, muddy slope with its tangle of men and limbs. Wellington himself charged forward as the British cheered but he upbraided them: 'No cheering my lads, but forward and complete your victory.' The wounded Uxbridge shouted, 'Don't expose yourself so,' but Wellington took no notice, in marked contrast to Napoleon's earlier behaviour.

To the southeast, von Bülow's troops were still fighting to take Plancenoit. As the British surged forward into the valley, at long last the final Prussian corps arrived to reinforce von Bülow, and the village was captured. Von Müffling wrote: 'The enemy was dislodged from Plancenoit; cannon and prisoners were taken, and the remainder got into the same confusion with the same mass, which, near La Maison du Roi, was just rolling along the high road. Had it been possible to take the village an hour sooner, the enemy could not have retreated on the high road to Genappe.' Napoleon had been right to be concerned at this flanking movement: he and his army would have been surrounded had it worked. The British cavalry attacked the French infantry as they retreated from Plancenoit, also routing the remainder of the French cavalry and capturing their guns.

As the main body of French soldiers streamed before the British attack across the valley of death, a squad of fresh Imperial Guards formed around their Emperor to protect him – their prime purpose – and retired in good order, fighting bravely. With Blücher's forces on the left now joining in the general British charge on the right, the French retreat turned into a rout and Wellington called off his exhausted men.

Although the Prussians have frequently tried to claim all the credit for the rout, it is clear that this was caused almost entirely by the British, joined by von Zieten's limited force – and then by the main Prussian force only after the capture of Plancenoit. The battle was won. After it, Wellington rode to meet Blücher at La Belle Alliance, where the gruff old Prussian soldier told him in his halting French, 'Belle affaire', and Wellington greeted him with exhausted and relieved cordiality.

Wellington rode back in the moonlight across the killing ground, accompanied by the screams and moans of the wounded and the looting and stripping of bodies. It was an eerie, spectral and dreadful scene. Wellington was utterly drained and depressed. Reaching the inn at Waterloo, he remarked: 'Well, thank God, I don't know what it is to lose a battle; but certainly nothing can be more painful than to gain one with the loss of so many of one's friends.' He made his most celebrated observation: 'Next to a battle lost, there is nothing so dreadful as a battle won.'

At a lonely dinner he said that 'the hand of God almighty has been upon me this day'. He fell asleep on the floor until 3 a.m. when he composed a victory despatch of great professionalism and cool detachment. He summarized the role of the Prussians generously and fairly:

> I should not do justice to my feelings or to Marshal Blucher and the Prussian army, if I did not attribute the successful result of this arduous day, to the cordial and timely assistance I received from them. The operation of General Bulow, upon the enemy's flank, was a most decisive one; and even if I had not found myself in a situation to make the attack, which produced the final result, it would have forced the enemy to retire, if his attacks should have failed, and would have prevented him from taking advantage of them, if they should unfortunately have succeeded.

He told Thomas Creeley, a Whig observer: 'It has been a damned serious business. Blucher and I have lost 30,000 [actually nearer 23,000] men. It has been a damned nice thing – the nearest run thing you ever saw in your life.'

The horrors of the day were not over yet. Four miles behind La Belle Alliance, the tens of thousands of French soldiers streaming into the village of Genappe were funnelled into a single bridge across the river some eight feet wide. Men trampled each other underfoot and slashed at each other with their sabres to get across. The Prussians caught up, attacking the French rearguard. Several hundred perished – although the river was only three feet deep and could have been forded.

Napoleon and a small protective guard forced their way through, although his lavishly equipped carriage, with its gold dinner set service and lavatories, its folding bed, writing desk and his diamond-studded uniform worth some 200,000 francs, had to be abandoned. He escaped across the bridge on his horse. As he reached Quatre Bras on that spectral ride, he saw 4,000 bodies stripped of their clothes by looters, a grotesquely macabre sight in the moonlight. Then it was on to Charleroi, where the bridge gave way and still more French soldiers were drowned. Behind him, the retreating Emperor had left some 40,000 dead and wounded along with 10,000 horses and 160 guns.

—◌◌◌—

The most celebrated battle in history was, perhaps, something of a fraud. It had not been fought at Waterloo, but at Mont St Jean. Wellington chose the name because it had a British ring.

Napoleon had been the French commander in little more than name: while the dimwitted General Grouchy had all but ignored the Emperor's orders, Ney had a much greater claim to the role. The battle dealt the final blow to Napoleon; but the Emperor was already a defeated man, with scant hope of survival in spite of his reckless adventurism in returning to take power in France: inexorably, large allied armies were advancing on him from all sides. Napoleon eventually made his way to Rochefort, and considered escaping to the United States, but he surrendered on 15 July 1815. He spent the remainder of his life under British-supervised exile on the Atlantic island of St Helena.

The battle had been lost by Napoleon, not won by Wellington. Wellington had exuded complacency before the battle in the face of so dangerous an opponent as Napoleon and the battle revealed a string of failings. He believed that the main French attack would come to the west; despatched part of his forces to counter that imaginary thrust; failed to support the Prussians adequately at Ligny (although his forces were hard-pressed at Quatre Bras); stretched his forces along too extended a line at Mont St Jean; showed little urgency in redeploying his troops along the line to where the danger was greatest; and kept inadequate reserves to resist the main French thrusts which, true to Napoleon's recent tactics, were in massed columns, not lines.

Yet Wellington had also displayed true leadership in battle, unlike Napoleon, remaining in the thick of the fighting throughout, never losing his cool judgment and detachment and knowing exactly when to strike as the tide of battle turned. His tactics had been defensive and unimaginative, although his choice of terrain displayed his old meticulous brilliance: a more imaginative general might have taken advantage of the French weakness and his own reserves to turn the tide sooner – although that would have been risky. The final charge was certainly perfectly executed and a master stroke. His conduct was ultimately vindicated by victory – by the narrowest of margins, and particularly through the luck of the main Prussian force arriving at the last minute, which helped to panic the French. Wellington's most famous and most significant battle was far from being his best.

The key factor at Waterloo was Napoleon's own incompetence. It was not just that he made mistakes: it was that he failed in virtually every respect to exercise either the courage or ability of even a mediocre military commander. His fever and piles do not explain this: he had frequently been ill in battle, yet excelled. The only explanation is that his overthrow the year before – which had driven him to attempt suicide – and his months of exile at Elba had changed him as a man. At Waterloo he showed himself to be cowardly, indecisive, poor at man-management, remote, haughty, unyielding, unwilling to listen, inept and, as Wellington had observed, extraordinarily lacking in his old flexibility and ingenuity in tactics. His inertia after Ligny prevented a crushing defeat of the Anglo-Dutch forces, which were tamely allowed to escape. At Waterloo itself, far from the battle, he was little more than a spectator, and the few decisions he made himself were almost always damaging.

In order to bring the Napoleonic era to a close, Wellington painfully reassembled and disciplined his army for the march on Paris in two columns: one British, the other Prussian under Blücher. Wellington officially told Louis XVIII to fall in with the march of his victorious army, something the king's adviser Talleyrand unsuccessfully advised him not to do for fear of being seen as a puppet of foreign powers by the French people. Paris soon capitulated.

There was no doubt about who the real masters of the city were: Wellington was head of an army of occupation of more than 1.2m troops altogether in France, occupying 61 departments. Napoleon's army was exiled to the provinces and demobilized. King Louis was treated as a powerless figurehead, while the Duke made the major decisions. He also set about stripping Paris of the art treasures, including the famous horses of San Marco in Venice, which had been plundered by Napoleon from all over Europe. He restored them to their former owners.

Under the Second Treaty of Paris of November 1815, the army of occupation was to be reduced to 150,000 and remain for five years, while France was required to pay 700 million francs in reparations. The country's frontiers were restored to those of 1790. Napoleon's second defeat had achieved the humiliation France had been spared on the occasion of the first. Wellington remained as proconsul with his usual indifference to what people thought of him. An attempt was made to blow up his house and then to shoot him in the Champs-Elysées in 1816. He dallied with his girlfriends, in particular the devoted Lady Shelley, Lady Webster, Lady Caroline Lamb and the Caton sisters.

Wellington remained attractively outspoken, as befitted a man who needed no favours from anyone else. Of the Prince Regent he declared: 'By God, you never saw such a figure in your life as he is. He speaks and swears so like old Falstaff, that damme, if I was not ashamed to walk into a room with him.' Of Napoleon's exile he remarked: 'Buonaparte is so damned intractable a fellow there is no knowing how to deal with him. As to the means employed to keep him there, never was anything so damned absurd.'

Only in November 1818 did the only Englishman ever to have ruled France resign his post and return to join a British cabinet, having left behind a weak French administration which ruled until 1820, when the country returned to more reactionary rule. Later he was to become the mostly undistinguished prime minister of one of the last administrations before the Great Reform Act, fighting to resist the tides of change.

—◆—

Wellington was a superb defensive general, often successfully employing his favourite tactic of hiding his troops behind the brow of the hill he was defending, luring the enemy forward, and then rising up to surprise the enemy army – which he exhibited at Torres Vedras, Coimbra and Waterloo itself. By contrast, his sieges of fortresses, while perhaps necessary, were deeply conventional, crude and bloody, not least in the cost to his own men – at Ciudad Rodriguez, Badajoz, Burgos and San Sebastian.

But that was not all there was to him. He could be lethally offensive as well, as at Vimeiro, Oporto and Vitoria. At Salamanca he displayed the intuitive brilliance of a genius who spotted the opportunity presenting itself before his eyes in a flash, winning his greatest and most resounding victory. Even at the largely defensive battle of Waterloo, Wellington's timing in launching his famous charge down the slope was faultless.

Underneath the mask, he was a maverick in his enormous courage in the thick of battle, best exhibited at Waterloo itself when he seemed to court danger as an example to his men; as his coolness under fire; his effortless skill at manoeuvre; in his larger-than-life public persona; and his disdain for the odds against him all showed. He was also a maverick in his concern for the welfare of his men (while also sneering at them, remarking when he saw soldiers bathing, 'I didn't know their skins were so white') and his superb selection of subordinates such as Rowland Hill, William Beresford, William Stewart, Robert Harvey, Ned Pakenham, the savage Robin Crauford and Lord Uxbridge. Wellington had enjoyed the unfair patronage of his brother in youth, but later revealed he had huge determination and the maverick's ability to return from major setbacks.

Discipline, command and control under Wellington were finely oiled machines, but behind the façade of the Iron Duke lay an eccentric and complex individual driven compulsively to succeed, not just on the battlefield, but at diplomacy, statecraft and then politics. Raised in straitened circumstances, he also proved shrewd enough to leave his dynasty in extremely comfortable circumstances. He was a military genius, one of the last warriors.

Chapter 7

GARIBALDI THE GUERRILLA: UNIFIER OF ITALY

How did an ill-educated merchant seaman from a humble background, with no social connections, rise to become the man who unified rigorously class-ridden Italy, one of the major centres of civilization in the world? With the possible exception of George Washington, Giuseppe Garibaldi was also the first guerrilla leader before Mao Tse-tung to achieve power. It was a phenomenal achievement, a social leap that surpassed the other mavericks in this book who, although mostly outside the nobility, all had some social standing or professional background.

Giuseppe Maria Garibaldi had neither. He spent the first 40 years of his life in such disreputable professions as a merchant sea captain, an outlaw, a rebel condemned to death, a mercenary in the paid service of two foreign states, a privateer and a guerrilla leader. The sheer romanticism of Garibaldi's career has obscured the reality that for most of it he was little more than a pirate at sea and a bandit on land.

Garibaldi was born on 4 July 1807 in Nice, a sleepy sun-baked little port which had just been taken over from Napoleonic France by the Savoy dynasty, the Dukes of Piedmont, who had also gained the kingdom of Sardinia (for simplicity's sake, although not strictly accurate, I will refer to the Piedmontese royal family from here on, as this was the possession that mattered on the Italian mainland). He must have been aware of the tumult of the Napoleonic wars in Europe, although he was only eight when they ended, because he lived in a hotly contested region. He was brought up speaking French, learning Italian from a clergyman who taught him at his elementary school. His background has an eerie similarity to that of Napoleon Bonaparte, raised in French-occupied Corsica nearby, although Napoleon's family was much higher up the social scale: it seems as though buccaneering adventurism was in the blood of the people at this hinge between France and Italy (as Rousseau famously observed).

Garibaldi's family hailed originally from Liguria, a province further down the coast of Italy. His father was the captain of a small vessel, a tartane, and his mother was a devout and kindly Catholic. They had six children, two girls who died in infancy and four boys, of whom Giuseppe was the second. The boy showed little interest in his studies, preferring gymnastics, fencing and swimming. He absconded on a boat with friends on one occasion and seemed set on following his father as a merchant sailor, taking a course in seamanship after his elementary education and becoming a trainee seaman at the age of 14.

By the age of 16 he was on his first long sea voyage to the Black Sea. He then accompanied his father to Rome to provide wine for pilgrims celebrating the Papal Jubilee. The visit made a profound impression on him and he called Rome 'the capital of the world'. In his late teens, he sailed up and down the Mediterranean and then out into the Atlantic for the first time when he was 20, visiting the Canary Islands. On another trip to the Black Sea he saw hostile action: his ship was three times captured by pirates and he despised his captain for not resisting. Falling ill, Garibaldi spent three years in Constantinople, making a living teaching Italian and French. Little is known about this lengthy sojourn in one of the most colourful ports in the world: he had several dalliances, one with Luisa Sauvaigo – 'one of those creatures who have convinced me that women are the most perfect of all beings'. He was clearly very attractive to women, although he was not above visiting prostitutes. By the age of 25 he had become a first mate aboard a ship of 20 men.

He was small – around five-foot-five (1.65m), well-built, stocky with distinctive flowing long blond hair merging with a full beard, which later reminded some of a lion's mane and others of idealized images of Christ. His most distinctive features, though, were his level brown eyes, with a calm, far-seeing, almost otherworldly gaze, and a nose that flattened out at the base, again reinforcing the lion image. His imperturbable and distant but friendly expression impressed others. He was a typical sailor, getting arrested for brawling in a port street and catching venereal disease in the many brothels sailors haunted. There was nothing at all in this tough, ill-educated young man's life that distinguished Garibaldi from the other experienced sailors that thronged the insalubrious ports of the Mediterranean – except that he had become addicted to reading when on his own, often under a street lamp in port.

In 1833 a party of French intellectuals came aboard his little ship as passengers: they were adherents of the theories of Saint Simon, who had argued that the middle classes would soon wrest power from the idle landed classes in Europe. One of these men, Emile Barrault, made a profound impression on the young sailor; his later friend, the great French novelist Alexandre Dumas, says he was struck by the thought of 'a man who, by becoming cosmopolitan, adopts humanity as his country and, by offering his sword and his blood to every people that struggles against tyranny, becomes something more than a soldier: he becomes a hero'.

Soon after, Garibaldi began to learn of the ideas of the radical Italian intellectual, Giuseppe Mazzini, who belonged to the secret society, the Carbonari, which espoused the idea of ridding Italy of its foreign oppressors, the Austrians in the north, and uniting its many small states to create a unified republic. Although a republican and anti-monarchist, Mazzini was no leveller and opposed socialism all his life, founding the Young Italy Movement. Garibaldi, who had previously shown no political interest whatsoever, wholeheartedly endorsed his message.

At this point, Garibaldi was called upon to do five years of compulsory military service, but was openly disrespectful of the King of Piedmont in a tavern and came under police surveillance. An uprising was planned by Mazzini's followers in Savoy and Genoa. However, the first failed to materialize. Garibaldi, politically naive as he was, went enthusiastically to join the 300 that were supposed to assemble in the piazza in Genoa, only to find no one there. Failing to report for duty aboard his ship, he was condemned as a deserter and came under open suspicion of being part of the plot. He fled across the hills from Genoa to Nice, an arduous undertaking on foot, where he had time to see his father for the last time, and then on to the anonymity of the bustling port of Marseilles.

There he found that he and two others on the run had been condemned as 'agents of a conspiracy... enemies of the fatherland and state... and category one bandits'. He was sentenced to 'ignominious death' *in absentia*, probably as an example, but perhaps because he was more deeply involved than surviving papers relating to the matter suggest. After a year of living clandestinely in Marseilles, he boarded a ship to Rio de Janeiro, under an alias, Giuseppe Pane.

—◊—

Rio was a city of around 140,000 inhabitants, including a few hundred Italian exiles into which Garibaldi could blend. On arrival after a journey of two months, members of Young Italy welcomed him as a wanted suspect with a death sentence on his head – he had acquired a reputation as a revolutionary he had done little to justify. He grandly declared that he would set up branches of Young Italy in Montevideo and Buenos Aires as well as Rio, and wrote to Mazzini, who had barely heard of him, letting him know that he had acquired a 20-ton schooner called the *Mazzini* to act as a privateer to attack Piedmontese and Austrian shipping. In fact, in order to earn a living, he used the ship to transport pasta up the coast. There was no call to arms from Mazzini, so Garibaldi languished with his few friends.

In 1837, he at last found a cause to fight for: the southern Brazilian state of Rio Grande do Sul was in open revolt against the central government and Garibaldi offered his little 'privateer' in the uprising's service. This was agreed by the hard-pressed rebel forces and, styling himself captain, Garibaldi set off with 12 men to challenge the might of the Brazilian government that had given him refuge. Rio Grande do Sul's wealthy landowning plutocracy was not exactly oppressed, and he was fighting for separatism – exactly the opposite of what he was to fight for in Italy. It is hard not to conclude that far from championing emancipation and liberty, he was seeking a living doing what he instinctively knew he was best at – fighting.

The little boat soon captured an unarmed cutter off the coast of Rio, followed by a slightly bigger 24-ton ship, before sailing south towards Uruguay. There, the angry Brazilian government asked the Uruguayans to arrest him and despatched a warship to capture his ship but he managed to slip away in a storm. Putting out to sea again after finding supplies, the crew saw a large cutter. It seemed as though there were only three crew on deck – but as it drew closer a score more appeared, with guns: the boat was Uruguayan and ordered Garibaldi to surrender. Fearing being captured and handed over to the Brazilians, he attempted to escape, fighting off a boarding party with cutlasses. The crews exchanged fire. The helmsman was killed while Garibaldi was shot in the neck, with the bullet lodging just below his right ear.

The ship escaped into the huge estuary of the river Plate and then up the Paraná to the port of Gualeguay. There, a rich merchant looked after him, while his crew dispersed. He gradually recovered, while being placed under house arrest, and learnt to ride with gaucho cowboys, an experience that was to stand him in good stead. He wrote at the time: 'I came into this world to be a right pain in the ass for half of humanity, and I have sworn to keep being one. I have sworn it, by God! To devote my life to upsetting others, and I have already achieved something, but it is nothing compared with what I hope to do, if they let me do it or they cannot obstruct me.'

He was beginning to acquire considerable notoriety. Violating the conditions of his house arrest, he attempted to flee, but was caught and brought back, bound over a horse's saddle. He was then flogged and hung by his wrists from a beam, before spending two months in the local prison. After being released, as he had done nothing wrong in Uruguay, he went to Montevideo to meet up with Italian friends in hiding, and then travelled on to his initial destination of Rio Grando do Sul, in whose service he had enlisted, declaring 'war is the true life for a man'. It seemed a grandiose remark for a more or less total failure, who had captained a small-armed merchantman, lost his ship, and been badly wounded, tortured and imprisoned, but it certainly reflected his indomitable spirit. He set off on horseback for the nearly 300-mile overland journey to the separatist republic's 'capital', Piratinim, a largely mud-hut structure. There, he met the rebel leader, Bento Gonçalves, a tall, impressive-looking man whom Garibaldi later considered fatally indecisive.

The real capital of the state, Porto Alegre, was under siege by rebels: it was situated at the end of the giant Lagoon of Ducks. The lagoon's entrance, 150 miles away from the port, was in the hands of the Brazilian navy and guarded by two forts which ensured that supplies reached Porto Alegre. Garibaldi ordered two small cutters to be built in a boatyard off the lagoon, one of 18 tons, the other of 15 tons. They captured one small supply ship while another escaped. This provoked the Brazilian navy, commanded by a British soldier of fortune, Admiral John Pascoe Grenfell, to use his fleet of 30 ships, 1,000 men, 90 cannon and two steamships to convey merchant shipping through the lagoon.

Frustrated in trying to capture more merchant ships, the cutters staged foraging and nuisance raids along the coast of the lagoon, capturing two other small cutters, while building two more of their own. At the boatyard, Garibaldi was suddenly attacked by 150 Brazilian soldiers led by Major Moringue, a much feared commander. Barricading himself in the boatyard along with 11 others, Garibaldi ordered his men to fire: Moringue's men tried to climb on to the roof and set fire to the building, but were driven off in a hail of shots from below through the roof. The Brazilian's arm was badly wounded and six of his men were killed.

Garibaldi decided to attack the port of Laguna, north of Porto Alegre, from the Atlantic: to do this, two of the cutters had to be transported across land to a network of swamps and down to the sea. It proved a herculean task: with the use of 200 oxen, the boats were carried to carts which had been lowered into ditches, then raised with great effort, and pulled across boggy land. When two cutters reached the sea, disaster followed: Garibaldi recklessly ordered them out in the teeth of a storm. He climbed the mast of his own cutter to find a landing place, only for the boat to be capsized by a giant wave; he was hurtled into the sea, but managed to swim to the shore. Sixteen of his best men were lost, including two of his closest lieutenants. Recovering from the tragedy, Garibaldi took charge of the other cutter, which had survived the storm. He sailed this provocatively close to the Brazilian flotilla of a brigantine and four cutters, before fleeing back into shallow waters with two cutters in hot pursuit: the latter were attacked and captured in an ambush by rebels armed with guns waiting on the banks.

With three ships now at Garibaldi's disposal, hundreds of rebels were transferred to surround Laguna; the rest of the Brazilian flotilla fled and the port surrendered, along with valuable supplies. Garibaldi now had a fleet of six ships. The Brazilians responded by sending 15 ships. For several days Garibaldi skilfully played mouse-and-cat games along the coast, entering shallow waters where he could not be followed, or sending one ship to distract the Brazilian navy while his others got away. However, he was sickened when, having been ordered to take a town which had joined the Brazilian side, his forces went on a rampage of 'threats, beatings and killings'. Along with his incorruptibility, Garibaldi's most attractive trait was his humane behaviour in war – which was unusual in South America, doubly so for a bandit, rebel and self-styled privateer.

The full imperial might eventually arrived opposite Laguna – 16 ships, 900 men and 30 cannon. Garibaldi's small forces proved no match and after a needless slaughter, he retreated by night from the port. Fleeing into the interior he won a major battle in December 1839 but was routed the following month. Garibaldi led some 70 survivors on a punishing, forced march for four days through forest and then across a freezing plateau to avoid capture. It was his first major experience of land warfare, and for a man accustomed to the tiny deck space of small ships, he proved astonishingly adaptable.

The Brazilians assembled some 4,300 soldiers against 3,400 rebel forces on the plain in front of Porto Alegre. However, the rebel leader Gonçalves decided not to attack, to Garibaldi's disgust. Hard-pressed, the rebels attacked San Jose de Norte, one of the forts overlooking the entrance to the Lagoon of Ducks. The surprise attack routed the defenders, but the rebels went on a looting rampage, while Admiral Grenfell brought up three ships to bombard the fort. The rebels were forced to flee. Garibaldi, by now thoroughly disillusioned, left for Montevideo in 1841. After a further defeat, the rebels reached an agreement with the Brazilian government, securing a degree of autonomy, but not separatism, and an amnesty. Garibaldi had emerged as a glorious failure.

—⁕—

Garibaldi settled in Montevideo, earning money as a teacher. However, Uruguay was now at war with Argentina. The intrepid seaman was asked by the Uruguayans to lead an expedition to come to the relief of the rebel Argentinian port of Corrientes, 600 miles up the Paraná River, which was under threat from Buenos Aires. Although the governor of the province of Buenos Aires, General Juan Manuel de Rosas, was effectively its brutal military dictator, it was far from clear who was in the right in this war of national interests. Garibaldi can hardly have been said to have been performing an idealistic role in taking sides: Uruguay was the smaller country, but it was tacitly backed by powerful European countries – Britain and France.

Garibaldi had three major ships, a 250-ton corvette with 18 cannon, a 160-ton brigantine with 11 cannon and a 71-ton schooner with five cannon. As his flotilla reached the mouth of the Paraná, a seven-ship Argentinian squadron, under another British paid admiral, William Brown, appeared, but his flagship, the *Belgrano*, ran aground. Garibaldi went upstream under cover of fog, while Brown pursued them mistakenly up the Uruguay River, with three more of his ships running aground. However, soon the Argentinians were in full chase with their larger force. He decided to engage in battle on 16 August 1842. Brown fired from a distance, using the superior range of his cannon. Garibaldi's ships were reduced to hulks. He embarked with what remained of his men on a small vessel and blew up his ships to save them from capture. The survivors walked across wetlands for three days until they reached Corrientes province, where they were safe.

Soon afterwards Garibaldi was recalled to Montevideo, which was now itself under siege after the Uruguayans had been massacred at the battle of Arroyo Grande, losing virtually their entire navy. However, the Argentinians were unable to launch a bombardment because the British and the French had threatened retaliation. So they imposed a naval blockade on supplies reaching the city, while the Italians, British and French formed 'legions' of volunteers to help the Uruguayans.

At the Battle of Tres Cruces on 17 November, Garibaldi personally led his forces in a bayonet attack. He also commanded a fleet in defence of the strategic Isla de los Ratos, opposite Montevideo. On 30 April 1844, Admiral Brown led a flotilla of three ships – two brigantines, one equipped with 16 cannon, and two schooners – against Garibaldi's two small ships armed with one cannon each. Just as defeat in the uneven contest seemed imminent, the British intervened between the two sides and the island was saved.

With his small navy, Garibaldi began attacking merchant shipping again, which aroused the ire of the Brazilians, who behaved with antagonism towards Garibaldi and the Uruguayans. Moving further north, Garibaldi's small fleet harassed neutral shipping, capturing supplies and even three Argentinian ships.

In mid-1845, the great powers, Britain and France, at last interceded. They proposed recognizing Uruguayan independence and ending the Argentinian attacks. The allies disarmed Brown's fleet, and sent the admiral packing back to Europe, returning his cutters to Argentina. However, the intervention was controversial, and the United States and Brazil objected to European military intervention.

The allies decided to open up the Uruguay and Paraguay rivers by sea, in a joint maritime expedition with Uruguay. This was led by Garibaldi, who was now receiving fulsome attention in British

and French newspapers. This formidable force, including two brigantines, five schooners and 10 small boats, possessed 40 cannon
and more than 300 men. It went up the river Plate in August 1845.

On the Uruguay, Garibaldi's fleet captured the wealthy settlement of Gualeguaychú and then broke past the enemy stronghold
of Paysandú, finally reaching its destination of Salto on 6 October.
After a setback he occupied the town, with its 10,000 population,
at the end of November. The Argentinians counterattacked with
artillery and laid siege with 700 men.

General Medina of the Uruguayan army set out to relieve
Garibaldi with 500 men. Garibaldi sallied out to meet him in the
flattish plain near the river with some 300 men. On the other side
of a small rise, he was ambushed by a hidden army of 1,200
Argentinians, three-quarters of them cavalry with lances. He was
by the hamlet of San Antonio de Salto, five miles from safety in the
town itself. Garibaldi feared that his men would be cut down if they
tried to fight in the open and took refuge in a small factory nearby.
An Argentinian line in classical formation marched forward and
discharged a volley at some distance. Garibaldi's men withheld
their fire and then cut the line down at point-blank range, before
charging with bayonets, which sent the Argentinian infantry fleeing. However, the much larger Argentinian cavalry staged repeated
attacks against Garibaldi's entrenched position. Thirsty and
exhausted, by nightfall their plight seemed hopeless. Garibaldi
arranged a withdrawal in a well-defended column under cover of
darkness, under fierce attack, until they reached the shelter of a
wood and retreated to the town. More than 40 of his men had been
killed and the same number wounded.

Garibaldi's heroic defence under attack quickly became the stuff
of legend, not just in Montevideo but in London and Paris. After a
successful raid against the besieging force in May 1846, he returned
in triumph to Montevideo to resume control of the navy, which
staged successful raids against merchant shipping at the mouth of
the Paraná. In June 1847 he was appointed commander of the army
garrison in Montevideo, but stood down quickly when patriotic
groups objected.

By this time he was tired and angry about the continuing rivalry between Uruguayan politicians. He applied to return to Italy, but was initially rejected by the reactionary government of King Charles Albert of Piedmont. However, he soon learned that the king was being forced to enact reforms, and in January 1848 Garibaldi felt sufficiently confident to send his wife Anita to Nice. In April, Garibaldi himself followed. He had been away for a decade. The war between Uruguay and Argentina would last four more years, with Brazil entering on Uruguay's side until the Argentinian dictator Manuel de Rosas finally gave up in 1852.

—⁊⁊⁊—

The movement to expel the Austrians from Italy and unite Italy under a republican government had been gaining momentum while Garibaldi was away. In 1846, Pope Pius IX, 'Pio Nono', was elected, a beacon for liberal reform in the Papal States. There was a growing clamour, not just from Giuseppe Mazzini's republicans, but from moderates, for a general capable of leading Italy to independence. Even the King of Piedmont, for whom Garibaldi was still an outlaw under sentence of death, subscribed to an appeal for a sword for the returning hero. Meanwhile, the 'year of revolutions', 1848, had occurred in which Louis Philippe had been toppled from the French throne. In Austria, an uprising triggered off insurrections in Venice and Milan, and the Austrian garrisons were forced out. The Piedmontese king, Charles Albert, ordered his troops to occupy these cities. There had also been insurrections in Sicily, causing the Bourbon king, Ferdinand II, to grant major constitutional freedoms in 1849, prompting both the Pope and Charles Albert to grant further concessions.

The following year there was a reaction: the Pope withdrew from the war with Austria and Ferdinand II counterattacked the moderates. Meanwhile, largely ignorant of these developments, Garibaldi was approaching Italy at a leisurely pace, arriving at Nice on 23 June 1848 to a tumultuous reception. The hero declared himself willing to fight and lay down his life for Charles Albert, who he now regarded as a bastion of Italian nationalism.

Mazzini and the republicans were horrified, regarding this as out-right betrayal: did it reflect Garibaldi's innate simple-mindedness, his patriotism in the war against Austria, or was it part of a deal with the monarchy? Charles Albert had pardoned Garibaldi, but to outward appearances he was still very wary of the general and the Italian Legion he had amassed of 150 'brigands'. The two men met near Mantua, and the king appeared to dislike him instantly. He suggested that Garibaldi's men should join his army and that Garibaldi should go to Venice and captain a ship as a privateer against the Austrians.

Garibaldi, meanwhile, met his former hero Mazzini for the first time, and again the encounter was frosty. Seemingly rebuffed on all sides, Garibaldi considered going to Sicily to fight Ferdinand II of Naples, but changed his mind when the Milanese offered him the post of general – something they badly needed when Charles Albert's Piedmontese army was defeated at Custoza by the Austrians. With around 1,000 men, Garibaldi marched into the mountains at Varese, commenting bitterly: 'The King of Sardinia may have a crown that he holds on to by dint of misdeeds and cowardice, but my comrades and I do not wish to hold on to our lives by shameful actions.'

The King of Piedmont offered an armistice to the Austrians and all the gains in northern Italy were lost again. Garibaldi returned to Nice and then across to Genoa, where he learned that, in September 1848, Ferdinand II had bombed Messina as a prelude to invasion – an atrocity which caused him to be dubbed 'King Bomba'. Reaching Livorno he was diverted yet again and set off across the Italian peninsula with 350 men to come to Venice's assis-tance, but on the way, in Bologna, he learned that the Pope had taken refuge with King Bomba. Garibaldi promptly altered course southwards towards Rome where he was greeted once again as a hero. Rome proclaimed itself a republic. It was an amazing progres-sion for a man who just a year before had been fighting a small South American war in defence of remote Montevideo. Garibaldi's Legion had swollen to nearly 1,300 men, and the Grand Duke of Tuscany fled Florence before the advancing republican force.

However, Charles Albert of Piedmont, who had been defeated by Austria, abdicated in favour of his son Victor Emmanuel II, who now sought peace with Austria. The Austrians marched southwards to place the Grand Duke of Tuscany back on his throne. King Bomba also regained control of all of Sicily. Worse still, Prince Louis Napoleon, nephew of Bonaparte, had seized power in France and responded to an appeal from the Pope to restore his lands, despatching an army of 7,000 men under General Charles Oudinot to the port of Civitavecchia to seize the city. Garibaldi was appointed as a general to defend Rome.

An Italian observer, Count Emilio Dando, described the extraordinary appearance and behaviour of Garibaldi's Legion, which differed little from that of the guerrillas he had led in South America:

> Garibaldi and his staff officers wore scarlet 'blouses' and caps of all shapes and sizes without any badges and without bothering with any military decorations. They mounted on American-style saddles and were keen to show their contempt for everything that regular armies care about and impose with great severity. Followed by their orderlies, who all came over from America, they disperse, gather together, and rush here and there in a disorderly manner, and are active, reckless, and untiring. When the troop halted to rest and make camp while the soldiers collected the weapons, it was wonderful to watch them leaping down from their horses and personally attending to them, even in the case of the general.

The republicans had around 9,000 men, and Garibaldi was given control of more than 4,000 to defend the Janiculum Hill, which was crucial to the defence of Rome, as it commanded the city over the Tiber. Some 5,000 well-equipped French troops arrived on 30 April 1849 at Porta Cavallegeri in the old walls of Rome, but failed to get through, and were attacked from behind by Garibaldi in a bold attack reminiscent of his defence of Montevideo. He led a baton charge and was grazed by a bullet slightly on his side. The French lost 500 dead and wounded, along with some 350 prisoners, to the Italians, 200 dead and wounded. It was a famous victory, wildly celebrated by the Romans into the night, and the French signed a tactical truce.

However, other armies were on the march: Bomba's 12,500-strong Neapolitan army was approaching from the south, while the Austrians had attacked Bologna in the north. Garibaldi took a force out of Rome and engaged in a flanking movement across the Neapolitan army's rear at Castelli Romani; the Neapolitans attacked and were driven off, leaving 50 dead. Garibaldi accompanied the Roman general, Piero Roselli, in an attack on the retreating Neapolitan army. Foolishly leading a patrol of his men right out in front of his forces, he tried to stop a group of his cavalry retreating and fell under their horses, with the enemy slashing at him with their sabres. He was rescued by his legionnaires, narrowly having avoided being killed, but Roselli had missed the chance to encircle the Neapolitan army.

Garibaldi boldly wanted to carry the fight down into the kingdom of Naples, but Mazzini, who by now was effectively in charge of Rome, ordered him back to the capital to face the danger of Austrian attack from the north. In fact, it was the French who arrived on the outskirts of Rome first, with an army now reinforced by 30,000. Mazzini realized that Rome could not resist and ordered a symbolic stand within the city itself, rather than surrender, for the purposes of international propaganda and to keep the struggle alive, whatever the cost. On 3 June the French arrived in force and seized the strategic country house, Villa Pamphili. Garibaldi's wife, Anita, now dressed as an officer with her hair cut short, joined him and helped to set about inspiring the troops.

Garibaldi rallied his forces and fought feverishly to retake the villa up narrow and steep city streets, capturing it, then losing it again. By the end of the day, the sides had 1,000 dead between them. Garibaldi once again had been in the thick of the fray, giving orders to his troops and fighting, it was said, like a lion. Although beaten off for the moment, the French imposed a siege in the morning, starving the city of provisions and bombarding its beautiful centre.

On 30 June the French attacked again in force, while Garibaldi, at the head of his troops, fought back ferociously. But there was no prospect of holding the French off indefinitely, and Garibaldi decided to take his men out of the city to continue resistance in the mountains. Addressing a huge and emotional crowd in St Peter's Square, he told them:

> Fortune, which today has betrayed us, will tomorrow smile on us. I am leaving Rome. Those of you who wish to continue the war against the foreigner should come with me. I cannot offer you pay, quarter, or provisions; I can only offer you hunger, thirst, forced marches, battles, and death. Those of you, who have Italy's name not only on your lips but in your hearts as well, must follow me. Once you have passed through the gate of Rome, one step backward will mean death.

Mazzini fled to Britain while Garibaldi remained to fight for the cause. He had just 4,000 men, divided into two legions, and faced some 17,000 Austrians and Tuscans in the north, 30,000 Neapolitans and Spanish in the south, and 40,000 French in the west. He was being directly pursued by 8,000 French and was approaching Neapolitan and Spanish divisions of some 18,000 men. He stood no chance whatever. The rugged hill country was ideal, however, for his style of irregular guerrilla warfare, and he manoeuvred skilfully, marching and countermarching in different directions, confounding his pursuers before finally aiming for Arezzo in the north. But his men were deserting in droves and local people were hostile to his army: he was soon reduced to 1,500 men who struggled across the high mountain passes to San Marino, where he found temporary refuge.

The Austrians, now approaching, demanded that he go into exile in America. He was determined to fight on and urged the ill and pregnant Anita to stay behind in San Marino, but she would not hear of it. The pair set off with 200 loyal soldiers along the mountain tracks to the Adriatic coast, from where Garibaldi intended to embark for Venice which was still valiantly holding out against the Austrians. They embarked aboard 13 fishing boats and managed to sail to within 50 miles of the Venetian lagoon before being spotted by an Austrian flotilla and fired upon.

Only two of Garibaldi's boats escaped. He carried Anita through the shallows to a beach and they moved further inland. The ailing Anita was placed in a cart and they reached a farmhouse, where she died. Her husband broke down into inconsolable wailing and she was buried in a shallow grave near the farmhouse, but was transferred to a churchyard a few days later. Garibaldi had no time to lose; he and his faithful companion Leggero escaped across the Po towards Ravenna.

At last Garibaldi was persuaded to abandon his insane attempts to reach Venice by sea and to return along less guarded routes on the perilous mountain paths across the Apennines towards the western coast of Italy. After a few days they sailed up to Porto Venere near La Spezia, where the local governor told him he was not welcome to stay and offered to send him into exile. Garibaldi put up no resistance. He was given safe passage to visit his family in Nice for an emotional reunion with his mother and his three children – but lacked the courage to tell them what had happened to their mother.

Then he was shipped around the Mediterranean, where one government after another refused to receive him, before he arrived finally in Tangiers. There, hosted by the kindly Italian consul, he was able to recover over the following six months and reflect on the immensity of his fate.

—∿∿—

Garibaldi found a ship to take him to the United States, where he intended to resurrect his old life as a sea captain. His fame was still a commodity: he was received sympathetically in New York and supported financially. He made a pathetic attempt to seek engagement as a humble seaman at the port and was turned down as too old. However, friends took him on a trip to the Caribbean and then across Nicaragua down the Pacific coast of Latin America to Lima, where he was given command of a ship at last. He sailed for Canton in China, and then to Australia and New Zealand. He travelled back from Lima to New York, then to London in February 1854, finally reaching Genoa in May. His exile had certainly been an enjoyable one.

His readmission suggested a change in policy under the Turin government of Count Camillo Benso di Cavour, the greatest Italian statesman at the time, who believed that the old warrior might still be of great use to the cause of Italian unity. Cavour permitted him to return to Nice. His mother had died but he was reunited with his three children. There he had an affair with a wealthy English-woman, Emma Roberts, whom he nearly married.

He decided to become a farmer and found his ideal bolthole on the rocky islet of Caprera off the coast of Sardinia. Yet his desire for the unification of Italy did not wane. In August 1856, he met Cavour, who had greeted him warmly. Cavour was a master diplo-mat: he had entered into negotiations with Napoleon III of France under which the Italians would provoke the Austrians into declar-ing war on them, and then the French would rush to their assis-tance. In return for giving Savoy and Nice to France, Piedmont would gain Lombardy, Venice, Modena, Parma and Emilla – effec-tively all of northern Italy. Who better, in the wily diplomat's view, to provoke Austria than Garibaldi, who could be disowned by Piedmont if necessary?

Garibaldi was quietly permitted to recruit a 3,000-strong corps of volunteers called the Cacciatori delle Alpi (Alpine Hunters). In response, the Austrian army crossed the Ticino River in April 1859. The Piedmontese, with an army of 60,000, declared war at this affront, as did the French with 120,000 men along the border against an Austrian army of 170,000. In June, Napoleon defeated the Austrians at Magenta. Garibaldi had been sent to Lake Maggiore and surprised the Austrians at Sesto Calende, before bril-liantly defending Varese against a superior Austrian force, although he was beaten off in an attack against an Austrian fort at Laveno. After occupying Brescia, he then rescued a force from a trap at

Lonato. By then, Garibaldi's volunteers numbered 12,000 men. However, Napoleon, finding the war unpopular in France, concluded an armistice with the Austrians under which only Lombardy would go to Piedmont.

———〰———

By 1860, Garibaldi, while still a legendary figure, had become something of an institution; he was a man in his fifties who was now taking the King of Piedmont's shilling and had been reduced to becoming a leader of irregular volunteer forces. He no longer seemed to be a republican, accepting the continued division of Italy and the presence of Austria in the north. He toured military hospitals and considered retiring to his isolated island.

Mazzini, though, had not entirely lost faith in his friend and urged him to go to the assistance of the Sicilians. They were thought to have been smouldering in resentful hatred of King Bomba by the time he died in May 1859. He was succeeded by his son, the more amiable, but equally obtuse, Francis II. Mazzini's lieutenant, Francesco Crispi, visited the island and reported that it was on the brink of open revolt: in April 1860 a few small uprisings were brutally put down with the Bourbons' customary savagery. Garibaldi, while appalled at this, was unwilling to embark on a venture unless it had a reasonable chance of success and unless it was backed by his new master, the King of Piedmont. He thus showed his cautious, realistic, conventional streak under the colourful exterior.

At last, he agreed in principle and appealed to the King for regular troops, but was refused. He decided to enlist volunteers, and the King did nothing to stop him. By the end of April 1860, Garibaldi had assembled 1,000 men, but heard that the opposition in Sicily had been contained and decided to abort the project. Famously, Crispi, almost certainly falsely, claimed that messages in code he alone could read said the report was mistaken: the revolt had been suppressed in the Sicilian capital of Palermo, but was continuing in the provinces – which was untrue. Thus, preparations for the technically illegal expedition were revived.

During the night of 5 May, 40 men climbed aboard a small boat in Genoa harbour and seized two merchant steamers, expelling those of the crew that did not want to remain. Garibaldi arrived dressed to kill in his trademark poncho, a red shirt and a neckerchief. After the engines had been started, which took some time, the 1,000 volunteers boarded the vessels. They reached the far southwestern tip of Sicily at Marsala on 11 May, where two British warships were in port protecting their own country's interests – the lucrative trade in fashionable Marsala wine.

A warship was hastily despatched from Trapani, the provincial capital just to the north, which hesitated to fire at Garibaldi's disembarking men for fear of provoking the ire of the British, and contented itself with a few token rounds. Garibaldi was proclaimed dictator of the island in the local municipal hall. The troops billeted in town and departed next day, led by Garibaldi on a white horse he named Marsala, into the mountainous and impoverished interior. They travelled to Salemi, where they received a noisy welcome, and 1,000 more raw recruits flocked to their banner.

The Bourbon army in Sicily consisted of 25,000 men, all but 5,000 of them in the capital, Palermo. The viceroy of Sicily, Prince Castelcicala, ordered reinforcements from the mainland. Major Michele Sforza, with a force consisting of 800 men, 40 cavalry and a couple of cannon, spotted Garibaldi's army in the rugged area outside Salemi, on a 1,200-foot terraced hill across a valley. Sforza attacked, but was driven off by guns and bayonet charges from above. Even more to his surprise, he was chased by the insurgents under Garibaldi up another hill. It was hard fighting and on being asked to withdraw, Garibaldi is said to have made the immortal remark, 'Here we will either create Italy or die.'

Withdrawing to Calatafimi, the Bourbon soldiers were ordered by General Lago to return to Palermo as news of Garibaldi's 'victory' spread like wildfire and Sicily erupted in open revolt. Under attack, the soldiers took four hours to fight their way through one town. Meanwhile, Garibaldi wasted no time in deciding to march on the Bourbon stronghold of Palermo. Expecting supporters there

to raise the city's population against the Bourbon cause, he discovered that they had been decimated by Swiss mercenaries.

Garibaldi could no longer risk attacking directly, and instead
marched around the city along appalling mountain roads during the
night, taking up a strategic position on a mountain called Cozzo di
Crasto. Then, on the night of 26 May, Garibaldi's forces marched
by night along a back road towards the barely defended city, where
they were intercepted by a small but fierce force, but fought their
way through the narrow working-class Fieravecchia districts.
Intense urban fighting broke out between ordinary people backing
the rebel forces and the Bourbon soldiers, as Lago hurriedly reinforced his forces from the other side of the city. After three days of
this, Lago organized his troops to attack the area around the royal
palace, but Garibaldi personally led a counterattack and bloody
mayhem reigned in the narrow streets.

Lago sought talks with Garibaldi aboard a British warship in port,
the *Hannibal*, and tried to persuade him to surrender in exchange
for safe conduct and pardons for his men. Garibaldi refused and
spoke passionately from a balcony about the need to fight on, infus-
ing his supporters with new determination. As barricades continued
to be erected against the Bourbons all over the city, it became
apparent to Lago that most of the populace wanted to tear his men
apart. It was his turn to seek a safe conduct from Garibaldi so that
they could return to their ships. The taking of Palermo aroused
almost unprecedented enthusiasm for the freedom fighter from
around the world, particularly in Britain and France.

However, the war was far from won: back in their stronghold in
Messina, eastern Sicily, the Bourbons had 22,000 men under
General Tommaso Clary. Garibaldi's forces were reinforced by
boatloads of volunteers from the north – some 3,500, along with
8,000 rifles and 400,000 cartridges. A further 3,000 followed soon
afterwards. Volunteers from Sicily were harder to find, and
Garibaldi's attempt to introduce conscription proved to be an
unpopular failure. He sent two reconnaissance detachments into
the interior, but found that all the Bourbon units had withdrawn
to the east.

Clary sent a force to take Milazzo, a strongly defended fort commanding an isthmus on the road between Palermo and Messina, and Garibaldi was forced to attack this obstacle. A fierce battle lasting all day ensued between forces of about 5,000 on each side. It was brought to an end when Garibaldi sent one of his ships to bombard the royalist Bourbon soldiers from the sea; they sued for peace and were allowed to evacuate by boat. According to Russo, Milazzo was the battle which decided the fate of Sicily. Garibaldi had lost 800 dead to the royalists' 150 but Clary, wary of being trapped in Messina, concluded that Sicily was no longer defensible and withdrew his remaining 18,000 troops to the mainland.

Garibaldi was now eager to launch an attack on the Italian mainland to liberate Naples. King Francis II decided not to make a stand on the plain of Salerno with his huge army, but to abandon the area and move to more defensible Capua in the north. Garibaldi took the new coastal train at Amalfi and arrived in this modern fashion at Naples station to a tumultuous welcome from an immense crowd. He declared that he was liberating the city 'in the name of all Italians and humanity'.

However, he was no administrator, and had little idea of how to restore working government to all of southern Italy. Moreover he was by now quarrelling bitterly with Cavour, who feared that he might try to set himself up as a military dictator and then march on Rome.

Garibaldi moved northwards towards the Bourbon army of 50,000, which had taken up its position at Caserta, a city within the Capua region. There, a couple of probing attacks by the Bourbons against Garibaldi were successful. Near the Volturno River, the Bourbon general, Giosué Ritucci, attacked on 2 October 1860 with 30,000 men to Garibaldi's 30,000, many of them ill-trained volunteers. The royalist forces broke through, but failed to follow up their advantage owing to a delay in bringing up their left flank and Garibaldi's lines closed up again. The battle raged without decision for 10 hours.

Abandoning his vantage point overlooking the battle, Garibaldi descended and ordered a frontal assault. During the battle, when Garibaldi was travelling in a carriage, he was nearly killed by

Bourbon troops who had infiltrated behind his lines: his coachman was killed and a reporter from the British *Daily News* with him was injured. Some 2,000 of Garibaldi's troops were killed, wounded or imprisoned, as against 1,300 royalists, but the former had gained the field. Garibaldi's victory was indecisive, though, and his way to Rome from the south was effectively blocked.

He also lost control of the political situation as Naples and Sicily voted overwhelmingly to unite with the north of Italy under Victor Emmanuel II, the King of Piedmont – a vote Garibaldi had been seeking to delay. The King himself was advancing at full speed down the eastern coast of his new provinces with his forces to take possession of Naples. He met Garibaldi cordially at Volturno, then proceeded on his way to take over Naples; his ministers pointedly ignored the general they had feared might become the independent military strongman of southern Italy. 'They wanted to enjoy the fruits of conquest but drive away the conquerors,' Garibaldi said bitterly. Later he remarked: 'Men are treated like oranges: once all the juice has been squeezed out of them, the skin is thrown away.'

He took a boat back to his simple island farm at Caprera. He had been the dictator of southern Italy one day and was a peasant farmer the next. He travelled to Turin to denounce the government in the assembly. Victor Emmanuel II made him meet Cavour, but the two men refused to shake hands. It was an historic encounter between the three founders of modern Italy: the constitutional monarch of old Italy; the representative of the newly dominant middle classes; and the general who had liberated southern Italy by force. The former two had prevailed as advocates of constitutional order, while Garibaldi, although wildly popular, had only the authority of force, as a *generalissimo*.

In 1861, remarkably, an emissary from President Abraham Lincoln of the United States offered him a generalship in the Union army in the American Civil War. He agreed – provided that he was appointed commander-in-chief and that Lincoln would guarantee the abolition of slavery. Lincoln could promise neither (his position at the time was to allow no *new* slaves) and nothing came of the offer.

Instead Garibaldi continued to agitate for the liberation of Venice and Rome, and travelled north, at one point considering staging a landing in the Balkans to precipitate unrest in the Austrian army as a way of loosening its grip on Venice. However, as a group of his enthusiasts approached Austrian-controlled territory in the north, they were arrested by the Piedmontese government, which was anxious not to provoke the Austrians.

Garibaldi's common-sense and pragmatism, which had stood him so well in the past, deserted him, and he travelled to Palermo, where he gave his backing to a group of 3,000 young volunteers seeking to liberate Rome. In August 1862, without authorization – indeed, in open defiance of the Piedmontese government, although Garibaldi believed romantically that the King privately supported him – he landed with his volunteers in two ships at Melita and Calabria: Rome was the target.

The Piedmontese government reacted belatedly, despatching seven battalions of troops down to the Aspromonte, the wooded mountains where Garibaldi had drawn up his troops in a defensible position. Quite how Garibaldi proposed to take southern Italy and Rome against not just the local opposition, but that of his old backers in Piedmont, is not clear. Perhaps he hoped to precipitate a change in heart by the government, which would join him in a new war of liberation.

As the royalist troops approached on 29 August, Garibaldi ordered his men not to fire, but a scattered volley from the royalists wounded him in his thigh and, more seriously and painfully, in his ankle bone. When their commander fell to the ground, the volunteers surrendered; there were a dozen dead on both sides.

Garibaldi was arrested, his followers rounded up, and he was transported by boat to La Spezia prison, where he was kept in the commandant's quarters. On 5 October, the King pardoned the rebels, but Garibaldi's recovery from the wound in his ankle was slow and painful.

After a stay at his farm on Caprera, he visited London, where he was greeted by a crowd of 500,000 and was given a dinner by the prime minister, Lord Palmerston. He was feted in high society – but not by Queen Victoria, who called him a 'revolutionary leader'. Returning to Italy, Garibaldi obtained permission from the King to lead a group of volunteers against the Austrians, who were now at war with both Prussia and Italy. The Prussians did well, the Italians less so, and Garibaldi was wounded yet again, although he staged a successful counterattack at Bezzacca. Peace was soon concluded and Venice was ceded to the Italians through the intervention of Napoleon III. Garibaldi had been denied the chance to liberate the city militarily, one of his two final ambitions.

———◦◦◦———

In 1870 the Franco-Prussian war broke out. Napoleon was defeated at Sedan and taken prisoner, and a republic was proclaimed in Paris. The French troops in Rome were withdrawn and the Italian army marched into the capital: it had at last joined a united Italy – in Garibaldi's absence. He had volunteered to fight for the French and travelled to Tours, where he was offered command of the Second French Corps, which grew from some 5,000 men to 20,000 in three months, facing 40,000 Prussians along the southeastern front: it was Garibaldi's first experience of the massed modern warfare that was to dominate Europe for the next three-quarters of a century. His 23-year-old son Ricciotti carried out a superb attack.

Garibaldi himself tried to storm Dijon, but was repulsed and counterattacked. Soon afterwards, he occupied the city after the Prussians withdrew, in freezing winter. He successfully defended it, narrowly avoiding capture just before the armistice to end the war was signed. It had been his last battle. He was briefly sucked into French politics by ardent republican admirers and went to Geneva to mount an anti-clerical tirade at a left-wing international conference for peace and freedom. He also supported most of the programme of the First International – earning the renewed ire of Mazzini, a republican but never a socialist. More palatably, he travelled to liberated Rome to advocate an extension of the franchise as well as vaguely socialist ideals.

Although increasingly arthritic and unwell, the old goat also bore three more children by Francesca Armosino, his personal maid. In 1882 he staged a final triumphal procession down to the south of Italy to Palermo, where he was revered almost as a holy person, people reaching out to touch him or his carriage – partly because he had survived death so often. Back at Caprera on 2 June 1882, he died suddenly following a short illness. His ashes were burnt humbly on his beloved island.

—◆—

Giuseppe Garibaldi was a scarcely believable character. He was one of the ultimate mavericks, a rebel all his life who is now rated as the father of his nation. He was a man who obeyed no one, listened to no one, lived freely and acted on his instincts. He was extraordinarily courageous, incredibly cool under fire (many observers described the calm that overtook him in the heat of battle, giving orders, his eyes gazing into the near distance, assessing the situation) and had a natural flair for seizing opportunities, whether by sea or by land. He was a brilliant guerrilla commander: if many of his battles were skirmishes, others included the defence of Montevideo's walls, savage house-to-house fighting in Palermo and Rome, a small set-piece battle at Calatafimi in Sicily and a much larger one at Volturno, both of which he won. Indeed, there seemed to be no kind of fighting to which he could not turn his hand and usually win.

If the first part of his career, as a mercenary, was hardly world-changing, the second – the liberation of Sicily and all of southern Italy – was an epic which paved the way for Italian unity, although others completed it. The third stage of his career, when he abandoned his usual judgment and embarked on a quixotic one-man war often in opposition to his own king, might seem wasted, and resulted in an uncharacteristic string of defeats. Perhaps all he really sought to do was to keep the flame alive until all of Italy had been united and freed from the foreign yoke – something he lived to see. He was a superb practitioner of public relations, being one of the most famous men in the world when only a guerrilla leader. However, Garibaldi was no ruthless killer of political opponents: he was humane towards his enemies, beloved by his men and enjoyed the trust of many of his lieutenants, although he often quarrelled bitterly with his contemporary commanders and his superiors.

Like so many of the other mavericks, his career was one of vertiginous ups and downs, from which he would recover and fight undaunted; like so many of them, he ended up in a position of considerable political power – ruler of southern Italy – for which he was entirely unsuited, being a poor politician. Above all, he was a natural fighter, hurling himself into the fray whenever he could and suffering five serious wounds and many near misses.

His biggest defect was his limited intelligence – in contrast to his gimlet eye in battle – which made his ideals seem confused and led him to blunder into political minefields: he was no Washington and Mazzini called him 'stupid'. Yet who was the stupider? Mazzini, whose short-lived Roman republic failed? Or Garibaldi, who understood he must work with the King of Piedmont in order to gain the unification of all Italy – royalists, bourgeoisie, radicals, ordinary people and even early socialists?

As the very embodiment of the independence struggle in Italy, he was an early example of the triumph of the common man, equipped only with good sense, professional soldiering ability and personal charm: the very vagueness of his political ideals made it possible for so many to follow him as the symbol and father of his nation. He was certainly one of the greatest and most fearless warriors in history, a military genius and a maverick commander, fearing no one.

Chapter 8

GRANT: AMERICAN HAMMER

To outward appearances, Ulysses Simpson Grant is surely an improbable maverick. Small, with a stubby beard and narrow eyes, he was as physically unimpressive as it was possible for a commander to be. He was also a timid, wooden speaker. As a strategist, he is unfairly associated with unimaginative tactics of direct assault on the enemy, but he was the winning commander in the American Civil War, a war which, unusually, was distinguished by four other great commanders: his subordinates General William Sherman and General Philip Sheridan, General Thomas 'Stonewall' Jackson and most glamorous of all, General Robert E. Lee. Looked at a little more closely it becomes apparent that behind Grant's gruff, shy, cautious exterior, he was not what he seemed to be at all, but a tactical innovator and a brilliant commander-in-chief like Washington and Wellington.

Ulysses Grant was born on 27 April 1822, the son of a tanner from Georgetown, Ohio, but descended from a distinguished Pilgrim Father family. He started out as an indifferent student at West Point military academy, where he snobbishly derided its alumni as 'from families that were trying to gain advancement in position, or to prevent slippage from a precarious place'. Grant graduated an undistinguished 21st in a class of 39: he was scrappy, slack on parade and did not keep his coat buttoned or his musket clean. He was a superb horseman, though, jumping a hurdle of six feet six inches, a record in those days.

He served at St Louis and then at New Orleans in the 4th Infantry with, as he put it, the job of provoking a war with Mexico. He opposed this policy as 'one of the most unjust ever waged by a stronger against a weaker nation' – an early expression of his independence and fairness of mind. He acquired experience of combat, fighting at Palo Alto, Resaca, Monterrey and Mexico City during the subsequent American–Mexican war. At Palo Alto he saw 'a ball struck close by me killing one man instantly, it knocked Capt Page's under jaw entirely off and broke in the roof of his mouth... the splinters from the musket of the killed soldier, and his brains and bones knocked down two or three others'. Grant was not deceived by mock heroics:

> A great many men, when they smell battle afar off, chafe to get into the fray. When they say so themselves they generally fail to convince their hearers... and as they approach danger they become more subdued. The rule is not universal, for I have known a few men who were always aching for a fight when there was no enemy near, who were as good as their word when the battle did come, but the number of such men is small.

At Monterrey he rode Cossack-style, clinging to one side of his horse for protection from bullets, while at Mexico City he captured a clock tower and erected a howitzer on it, helping to destroy the city's defences. However, Grant continued to hate the war and blamed the south for starting it with the object, in his view, of acquiring new slave states so that the north could not enforce the abolition of slavery.

He resigned his commission to live with his adored wife Julia, and cultivated a modest 80 acres near St Louis which he worked along with two slaves. He moved to St Louis after failing to make a sufficient living and tried to become an estate agent, an entrepreneur, a debt collector and a clerk in a company selling hides and saddles. He chain-smoked cigars and acquired a reputation as a virtually penniless drunk with four children.

On 11 April 1861, when Fort Sumter was attacked by the Confederates, the Civil War began. Grant, whose one real skill was waging war, promptly volunteered for the Union cause. He was 'elected' colonel of a regiment in Missouri – as an experienced former soldier he was an obvious choice – to make a demonstration against the Confederates at Belmont. He took 3,000 troops on a steamboat downriver, landed his men and attacked the Confederate camp. After routing the enemy, he was surrounded and had to cut his way down to the river bank again.

The soldiers on both sides were inexperienced volunteers – some 400,000 on the Union side against some 250,000 Confederates. Grant was one of the few trained fighters and disciplinarians among them:

> My regiment [the 21st Illinois] was composed in large part of young men of as good social position as any in their section of the State. It embraced the sons of farmers, lawyers, physicians, politicians, merchants, bankers and ministers, and some men of maturer years who had filled such positions themselves... The Colonel, elected by the votes of the regiment, had proved to be fully capable of developing all there was in his men of recklessness [i.e. indiscipline]. When there came a prospect of battle the regiment wanted to have someone else to lead them. I found it very hard work for a few days to bring all the men with anything like subordination; but the great majority favoured discipline, and by the application of a little regular army punishment all were reduced to as good discipline as one could ask.

Keeping good order was all-important to Grant. He placed his sharpshooters at the back of his forces to deter deserters from escaping and he tended to appoint loyal yes-men to his staff rather than strong personalities, but they carried out his orders – and William Sherman, his chief protégé, was to develop into a highly independent spirit.

Grant was described at the time as 'small, with a resolute, square thinking face':

> He sat silent among his staff, and my first impression was that he was moody, dull and unsocial. I afterwards found him pleasant, genial and agreeable... Among men he is nowise noticeable. There is no glitter or parade about him. To me he seems but an earnest business man. He liked to eat cucumbers in vinegar, corn, port, beans and wheat cakes, oysters and well-cooked beef. He had no servants, just a tent, camp bed, a table and a couple of chairs. His uniform was that of a private, on which he pinned his stars of rank.

Unlike some of the mavericks he did not deliberately court danger. No one doubted his courage if he came under fire, but he regarded himself as too indispensable to take unnecessary risks. Grant himself gave this description of a near-miss at the Battle of Shiloh:

> When we arrived at a perfectly safe position we halted to take account of damages. McPherson's horse was panting as if ready to drop. On examination it was found that a ball had struck him forward of the flank just back of the saddle, and had gone entirely through. In a few minutes the poor beast dropped dead; he had given no sign of injury until we came to a stop. A ball had struck the metal scabbard of my sword, just below the hilt and broken it nearly off; before the battle was over it had broken off entirely. There were three of us; one had lost a horse killed, one a hat and one a sword-scabbard. All were thankful it was no worse.

Grant's big break came with the Battle of Fort Donelson in February 1862, when he was a brigadier-general under the command of Andrew Foote. He went up the Tennessee River in steamboats with 18 regiments totalling 27,000 men. At the fort, the Confederate garrison of 18,000 sought to make a breakthrough:

> [Our] men had stood up gallantly until the ammunition in their cartridge boxes had given out... I saw the men standing in knots talking

in the most excited fashion. No officer seemed to be giving any directions. The soldiers had their muskets but no ammunition, while there was tons of it close at hand... I directed Colonel Webster to ride with me and call out to the men as we passed, 'Fill your cartridge boxes quick and get into line; the enemy is trying to escape and must not be permitted to do so.' This acted like a charm. The men only wanted someone to give a command.

Grant insisted on an unconditional surrender, which soon followed, and took 14,000 prisoners, although casualties had been higher on the Union side.

Two months later, on 6 April 1862, Grant was camped by a church called Shiloh on the Tennessee River when his 35,000-strong army was ambushed by General Albert Sidney Johnston's force of 40,000. It took him several hours to get to the scene of the fighting, one of pandemonium and butchery. He did not yield ground but sought reinforcements.

Grant was eventually forced backwards, but he coolly organized a battery of 50 guns. Johnston, however, had been killed and the Confederates had suffered 30,000 casualties, while Grant's army was reinforced by 25,000 men in the morning (he had spent the night under a tree, with a leg injury). By 2 p.m. on 7 April, the Confederates decided to retreat. Grant had suffered some 13,000 casualties. It had been the bloodiest battle of the war so far. Soon Grant was excoriated as having been drunk at the scene of the battle, and as a butcher. But he had won.

———*ᐯᐯᐯ*———

Grant's emergence as a leader had been unexpected: he seemed to be an unimaginative minor commander, despised for his homespun ways. A visiting congressman sniffed: 'for five days he has had neither a horse nor an orderly or servant, a blanket or overcoat or clean shirt; his entire baggage consists of a toothbrush'. Yet Grant had shown extraordinary bravery and an eagerness for the fight. He was therefore ordered to Vicksburg fort, which controlled the

Mississippi, the artery dividing the Confederacy. In late April 1862, David Farragut's squadron of Union ships had run past the fort and forced the surrender of New Orleans, but President Lincoln realized the key importance of taking Vicksburg itself:

> See what a lot of land these fellows hold, of which Vicksburg is the key. Here is the Red River, which will supply the Confederates with cattle and corn to feed their armies. There are the Arkansas and White Rivers, which can supply cattle and hogs by the thousand. These supplies can be distributed by rail all over the Confederacy. Then there is that great depot of supplies on the Yazoo. Let us get Vicksburg and all that country is ours. The war can never be brought to a close until that key is in our pocket... We may take all the northern ports of the Confederacy and they can still defy us from Vicksburg. It means hog and hominy without limit, fresh troops from all the States of the far South, and a cotton country where they can raise the staple without interference.

Vicksburg seemed an impregnable obstacle to the seizure of the Mississippi. It was on a crag some 250 feet above the river and included a community of some 3,000 people; moreover, there were key Confederate bases near Vicksburg, and their 12 guns nicknamed the 'Twelve Apostles' overlooked the water.

In addition, Vicksburg was a railhead in a war where rail links were crucial for the first time, greatly aiding an army's speed of movement. The American Civil War was the first great war which was dominated by the need to defend railways as lines of supply. The Unionists, in particular, had quickly become extremely reliant on the railways to feed through supplies, but this revolutionary solution could actually hinder as the tracks were uniquely vulnerable to an attack which could cut the line of supply to a huge army.

In December 1862, Grant came down overland to Vicksburg, in parallel with the railway, while William Sherman came down the Mississippi in boats. The railway, and Grant's line of supply, were repeatedly cut by Confederate cavalry attacks, and then Sherman was beaten off when he tried to attack the fortress of Vicksburg

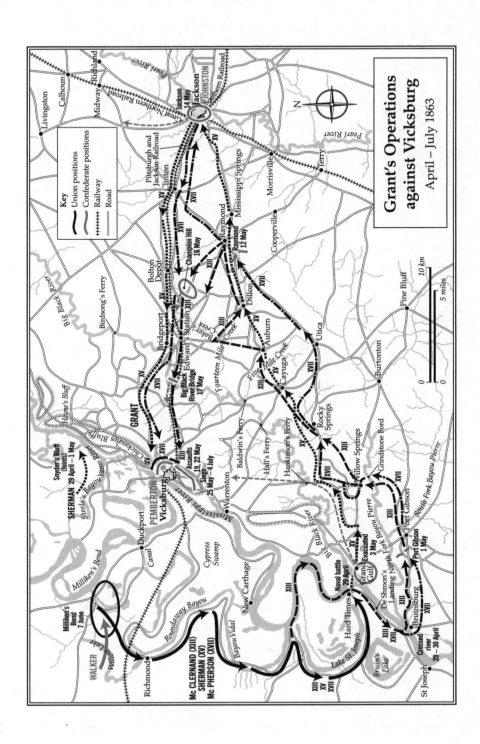

Grant's Operations against Vicksburg
April – July 1863

itself. Grant's army marched 180 miles, fighting five battles, taking 6,000 prisoners and 90 cannon; meanwhile, the Union side now controlled the river approach to Vicksburg.

Grant surprisingly ordered Sherman's fleet to sail south, past the garrison of Vicksburg by some 30 miles, while Grant's army arrived at the same spot overland. Sherman and his boats were then ordered to attack from the north in a feint, which allowed Grant to cross the river to the east bank and then encircle the fortress, cutting off its railway link and resupply line to Jackson in the east. It was a completely unexpected move which took the enemy by surprise. Grant formed virtually a 360-degree circle around the whole of Vicksburg, which seemed an almost suicidal manoeuvre because it put his army between the two Confederate forces at Vicksburg and Jackson.

In fact, he had divided his troops and immediately sent one group to Jackson, taking the Mississippi state capital by surprise, destroying the forces there, burning the buildings and severing Vicksburg's lines of communication.

He now had to dig in for a long, grim war of attrition against the citadel, twice attacking and being driven off by the forces of General John Pemberton, a man who told his men grimly: 'You have heard that I was incompetent and a traitor; and that it was my intention to sell Vicksburg. When the last pound of beef, bacon and flour, the last grain of corn, the last cow and hog and horse and dog shall have been consumed, and the last man shall have perished in the trenches, then, and only then, will I sell Vicksburg.'

Grant's surrounding army was reinforced from about 40,000 to 70,000. Women and children fought starvation in caves in the hillside as shells burst around them: they ate rats, cane shoots and bark after the horsemeat, mules and dogs ran out. On 4 July 1863, yet another terrible day of siege dawned, but Pemberton finally bowed to the inevitable and surrendered, with some 32,000 prisoners, 170 cannon and 60,000 muskets. It was the most decisive victory so far in the Civil War.

Grant generously pardoned the prisoners on the grounds they were 'tired of war'. Lincoln wrote to Grant: 'My dear General: I do not remember that you and I ever met personally. I write this now as a grateful acknowledgement for the almost inestimable service you have done the country.' Lincoln admitted that he would have pursued an alternative strategy at Vicksburg and commended Grant's superior knowledge of the art of war: 'I now wish to make the personal acknowledgement that you were right I was wrong.' Although the siege itself had been a terrible, classic affair, the manoeuvring before it had been brilliant and a magnificent *coup d'oeil* on Grant's part.

———

The American Civil War, although seemingly a baffling strategic quiltwork of marches and countermarches on three widely distributed fronts, was in fact a simpler affair than it appeared. It was staged, unlike in Europe, over a vast and mostly uninhabited territory whose only natural barriers were rivers, wetlands and the ragged southern end of the Appalachians: the many towns, narrow fronts and boundaries of the European wars were largely absent in America. The strategic stage – particularly after Vicksburg had effectively cut off states west of the Mississippi – was a box, bounded by that great river in the west and the sea in the south and east. In the north, on the western flank, there was great fluidity in the frontline; in the northeast the two opposing capitals of Washington and Richmond glared at each other across a relatively short strip of territory. To the west stood the Shenandoah Valley where the main armies had been concentrated in a hitherto unimaginative and bloody eyeball-to-eyeball confrontation, each seeking to secure the other's capital – a classically stupid objective in warfare.

Grant and Sherman's expedition to Vicksburg, which in fact had been hugely important, was regarded in Washington as a sideshow. A succession of incompetent, political and unimaginative Unionist generals had served in this slugfest. These included General Winfield Scott; General George McClellan, the supposed 'American Napoleon' who requested ever more supplies and men ('sending reinforcements to McClellan is like shovelling flies across a barn', Lincoln said); General Ambrose Everett Burnside, with his enormous sidewhiskers (hence the word 'sideburns'); General Joseph Hooker, who studiously ignored Lincoln and impressed no one; General George Meade, an old-style field general; and General Henry Halleck, who required his commanders to conform to strictly staff college lines and was patently a political opportunist.

McClellan, the least bad, attempted to show some initiative by landing his army at Yorktown (famous as the site of the British defeat in the American War of Independence), outflanking enemy lines and then marching on Richmond from behind. The first battle of the war, on the eastern front at Bull Run in July 1861, had been a fiasco, with both sides retreating from the other. McClellan took charge with his landing at Yorktown in 1862, but not before Lincoln, fearing that his capital of Washington had been stripped of defenders, insisted that 40,000 troops were kept back along with the 20,000 still in Washington. Lincoln and McClellan fell to quarrelling about the Yorktown expedition:

> There is a curious mystery about the number of troops now with you. When I telegraphed you on the 6th, saying you had over 100,000 with you, I had just obtained from the Secretary of War a statement, taken as he said from your own returns, making 108,000 with you and *en route* to you. You now say you will have but 85,000 when all *en route* to you shall have reached you. How can the discrepancy of 23,000 be accounted for...? Once more let me tell you it is indispensable to you that you strike a blow. I am powerless to help this.

McClellan at length landed with some 120,000 men at Yorktown, shipped in by an armada of nearly 400 boats. He faced just 55,000 men but would not attack. When he did move against Yorktown, he found the enemy had understandably left, faced with such odds. With characteristic dithering, he decided at length to march on Richmond. Here, the Confederates, now with 83,000 to McClellan's amassed force of 200,000, struck back in June 1862 with a series of offensives known as the Seven Days' Battles: some 16,000 Union men were killed to 20,000 Confederates in this ferocious week-long frontal assault, a tribute to Confederate resistance against an overwhelmingly superior enemy.

Having won this grim war of attrition on points, McClellan abruptly decided to call it a day and retreat, to be shipped back to the old frontline between Washington and the Potomac River, leaving Richmond untaken – a blow which might have decided the Civil War there and then. This face-to-face confrontation, based on huge armies well-supplied (but vulnerably so) by railways, was to provide a foretaste of the fierce confrontations in the Franco-Prussian war and, later, in the First World War. Such a head-on attritional confrontation should have been found unnecessary in the vast strategic canvas of southeastern America.

The incompetence of the Union commanders in the east was matched by the brilliance of the two Confederate commanders. General Robert E. Lee, a cousin of George Washington and a West Pointer who once wrote that 'duty is the sublimest word in the language', had been offered the job of commander-in-chief of the Union armies by Lincoln, and declined: 'I declined the offer stating as candidly and courteously as I could, that though opposed to secession and deprecating war, I could take no part in the invasion of the southern States.' As a Virginian he would not fight against his own state.

Lee was a master of the duplicities of war, manoeuvring the same 10,000 men in and out of an area of woods to give the impression he had an immense army on one occasion. He had also cleverly sent General Thomas Jackson on a marauding expedition up the Shenandoah Valley, in a thrust to the northwest, which prevented McClellan being reinforced in his campaign to take Richmond. At Malvern Hill, Lee's inferior army was beaten back, bloodily, by McClellan's superior forces, but Lee pressed the attack the following day and McClellan gave up.

General Thomas Jackson, another West Pointer, who had served in Mexico and become professor of philosophy and artillery at Lexington, brilliantly led the offensive through the Shenandoah Valley with 17,000 men, which has been compared to Napoleon's drives for its speed of marching, countermarching and manoeuvring

– 'mystify, mislead and surprise' was his dictum. On one occasion his men covered 30 miles in 24 hours while marching a total of 170 miles over 14 days; on the way, he captured 3,000 prisoners and routed 12,500 soldiers in five battles. Jackson earned the unfair nickname 'Stonewall' from a supposed comment that a Confederate general used to describe his imperturbability as bullets flew about him: in fact, he was one of the most brilliantly mobile generals in history.

After the confrontation with McClellan at Richmond in June 1862, Lee marched his forces into Maryland towards the old eastern frontline that divided the two sides. At Harper's Ferry, on 15 September, Jackson took 11,000 prisoners, while at Antietam on 17 September, Lee's force of some 45,000 faced an enemy twice as big, and another bloody gridlock ensued, with losses of a horrendous 12,000 on each side. Lee retired across the Potomac, but the ever-cautious McClellan did not follow. In November, McClellan was superseded by the bluff Burnside, who sensibly attempted to decline the post on the grounds that he lacked the intellectual capacity.

In the meantime, Lee encamped at Fredericksburg with 72,000 men across the Rapahannock River. It was not until December that the reluctant Burnside landed a force there, across pontoon bridges into a heavily defended river bank overlooked by a ridge. In the ensuing battle, the Union side lost nearly 13,000 men to 5,000 Confederates in a particularly senseless frontal slaughter.

Learning nothing, the following morning General Hooker and his Union army crossed the same river at Chancellorsville, with the same result. The Union forces lost 11,000 men and 6,000 prisoners, the Confederates 10,000 and 2,000 prisoners, although they had an army half the size. In addition, though, they lost General Jackson, who was felled in the assault.

Characteristically, Lee responded aggressively, crossing the Potomac with an army of 75,000 men and taking the battle north to the enemy. As Lee approached Gettysburg on 1 July 1863, he unexpectedly ran into the force of the newly appointed commander of the army of the Potomac, General Meade. Lee ordered an attack on both flanks and sent 15,000 men up a slope to attack the Union centre. They were repulsed, the first denting of the Lee legend, and he withdrew across the river after three days of carnage with some 28,000 casualties or captured. Meade, instead of pursuing Lee across the Potomac and attacking again, did nothing.

Gettysburg was just another appalling bloodbath on this north-eastern frontier, but it was to become a massive Union symbol through Lincoln's address on the occasion of the dedication of the war cemetery there:

> Fourscore and seven years ago, our fathers brought forth upon this continent a new nation, conceived in liberty and dedicated to the proposition that all men are created equal. Now we are engaged in a great civil war, testing whether that nation – or any nation, so conceived and so dedicated – can long endure. We are met on a great battle-field of that war. We are met to dedicate a portion of it as the final resting place of those who have given their lives that that nation might live. It is altogether fitting and proper that we do this. But, in a larger sense, we cannot dedicate, we cannot consecrate, we cannot hallow, this ground. The brave men, living and dead, who struggled here, have consecrated it, far above our power to add or to detract.

Although eloquent and economic in its turn of phrase, it is something of a mystery why this address acquired the mystique it has since enjoyed.

In the southwest, Grant decided to make for another railhead, Chattanooga, following a terrible mauling that another Union general, William Rosencrans, had received at nearby Chickamauga at the hands of the Confederate General Braxton Bragg on 18–20 September 1863. Chattanooga was key to keeping open the main Confederate east–west supply line across the Appalachians. Bragg occupied an impregnable position at the top of Missionary Ridge and Lookout Mountain, some 400 feet above Grant's Unionist troops, with the Tennessee River behind them. On 25 November, after two days of inconclusive fighting, part of Grant's force moved forward to take the frontline of the Union's defence at the bottom of the rocky slope, with the main Confederate force watching complacently from above. They then began to march up the escarpment.

Grant was surprised, as were Bragg's men, at this seemingly suicidal advance up a slope to an entrenched enemy. It was led by Arthur MacArthur, the father of the Second World War hero Douglas MacArthur (see Chapter 12). More troops followed suit as the Union generals grasped the opportunity. They succeeded in storming Missionary Ridge and broke the centre of the Confederates' line of defence. Bragg and his army fled back to Chickamauga.

—⁓—

The hour of Grant, the loner, the outsider, had come: in March 1864 he was appointed lieutenant general and effective commander of the Union forces, in a war that had been characterized by astoundingly cautious and politicized commanders. Grant was as modest and tongue-tied as ever on his appointment: his speech, however, as he finally made the grade, fitted the man. Facing Lincoln, he read his three-sentence response:

> Mr President, I accept the commission, with gratitude for the high honour conferred. With the aid of the noble armies that have fought in so many fields of our common country, it will be my earnest endeavour not to disappoint your expectations. I feel the full weight of the responsibilities devolving on me; and I know that if they are met, it will be due to those armies, and above all to the favour of that Providence which leads both nations and men.

Then Grant, rather than heeding Sherman's sound advice to move to the Mississippi Valley, accepted Lincoln's insistence on another great push on the eastern flank towards Richmond in a frontal assault.

In early May 1864, in the Spotsylvania County scrubland, Grant engaged in an unimaginative frontal assault, known as the Battle of the Wilderness, along a 12-mile-wide front with twice as large an army as Lee, although the latter was encamped across the Rapidan River in a better defensive position. After he had lost 14,000 men,

Grant relentlessly decided to press on for Richmond but the two forces engaged again, on 8 May, this time for a long-winded battle in the town of Spotsylvania. The fighting was furious, unceasing and murderous. By the time the battle reached its indecisive conclusion, the Army of the Potomac had lost 31,000; there were no figures of Confederate casualties, although they were certainly less.

General Philip Sheridan, a dashing young commander, was sent to stage a flanking attack against the Confederate's railway supply route. Meanwhile, Grant and his men were forced to Cold Harbour on 3 June, where they lost 3,000 men in less than half an hour, and a further 7,000 by nightfall. Even Grant regretted the losses. He suddenly wheeled about and attacked at Petersburg to the west of Richmond, losing a further 10,000 men, while Confederate losses were around 5,000.

Lee responded with his usual sangfroid, regarding attack as the best form of defence and sending an army of 20,000 men up the Shenandoah Valley for a potentially lethal strike at Baltimore and then Washington. They stopped on 11 July within sight of the dome of Capitol Hill. Grant rushed up two relief divisions of men by sea, which arrived just in time. Lincoln himself watched from a rampart on Fort Stevens as a small battle ensued before the Confederates departed.

While Grant had been inching his painful and bloody way forward on the eastern front, momentarily diverted by Lee's expedition to capture Washington, Sherman was in the west. He resolved to march to Atlanta, Georgia – the junction of five railways, a huge industrial centre and the gateway to Georgia, the 'granary' of the Confederacy. Sherman's army was some 100,000 strong, compared to the Confederates' 62,000 protecting Atlanta.

Sherman's army marched for 130 miles across difficult mountainous terrain and many rivers, employing marching, countermarching and flanking manoeuvres to protect his army along the way. He rarely ventured into a direct attack on the enemy during the journey, preferring to lure the Confederates into attacking him on more easily defensible ground. It was a masterful strategy that allowed him to remain close to his vulnerable, single railway supply line during the march. It also disheartened the Confederates, who found their offensives rebuffed while incurring a greater number of casualties.

Finally, as he approached Atlanta, the Confederate General Johnston managed to force him into a more open battle near to Kennesaw Mountain on 27 June 1864. The Union lost 3,000 soldiers to the Confederates' 800; in subsequent fighting, Sherman lost another 10,000 to 11,000 on the Confederate side. However, at last, Atlanta fell. Soon afterwards it was burnt to the ground – 1,800 buildings in all, possibly with greater destruction than Sherman intended.

Sherman then embarked on his famous march through Georgia to the sea, abandoning his supply line to pillage off the land. He divided his remaining 60,000 men into five corps, with foraging parties across the front and along the sides – they were a plague of locusts on a broad, marauding, murderous rampage. Sherman's tactic was to place his enemy on 'the horns of a dilemma', to make it unclear what his objective was – Macon, Augusta, Savannah or Charleston, and then Columbia or Charlotte, or Fayetteville, then Raleigh or Goldsborough or Wilmington. In fact, he marched more than 400 miles to Goldsborough.

Sherman's tactics, approved by Grant, were to lay waste to the countryside in order to instil terror in the very heart of the south, to impress upon them the hopelessness of their cause and to demoralize the southern armies by threatening their families in their homes. Sherman justified this speciously:

> I, too, had the old West Point notion that pillage was a capital crime, and punished it by shooting, but the rebels wanted us to detach a division here, a brigade there, to protect their families and property while they were fighting... This was a one-sided game of war, and many of us... kind-hearted, fair, just and manly... ceased to quarrel with our own men about such minor things, and went in to subdue the enemy, leaving minor depredation to be charged up to the account of the rebels who had forced us into the war, and who deserved all they got and *more*.

Over the course of 32 days they laid waste to 300 miles of ground, leaving behind them naked smokestacks, burned culverts, shattered trestleworks and wailing humanity. On the railroads every rail was twisted beyond use, bridges were destroyed and depot buildings were burned. For the economy of powder they had sabred hogs and knocked horses between the ears with axes. They killed every dog that looked as though it could be used to track runaway slaves, and either took or destroyed all the livestock.

It was a terrifying and implacable strategy dictated by Grant and Sherman. The march of destruction ended with Sherman's arrival at Savannah at Christmas 1864, but by now the south had realized that it could not win and its sufferings could no longer be supported.

With Grant's blessing, now General Sheridan moved down the Shenandoah Valley, waging a war of terror and scorched earth. Burning barns lit the night sky – about 2,000 of them, along with 70 mills filled with wheat and flour. In Raleigh County about $25m worth of property was destroyed, including 50,000 bushels of corn, 100,000 bushels of wheat, 450 houses and 30 barns. In total, Sheridan reckoned that he had inflicted $100m (about $400 billion at today's values) worth of damage while also destroying 200 miles of railway in Georgia.

Lee was beginning to sense the end as he was situated between the two pincers of Sherman in the south and Grant in the north:

> I have been up to see the congress and they do not seem to be able to do anything except to eat peanuts and chew tobacco, while my army is starving. I told them the condition the men were in, and that something must be done at once, but I can't get them to do anything, or they are unable to do anything. When this war began I was opposed to it, bitterly opposed to it, and I told these people that unless every man should do his whole duty, they would repent it, and now they will repent.

In early 1865, Sherman set off northwards across the Carolinas – something it was said could not be done in winter, with its swollen rivers and swamps. Sherman's men were even more ruthless than they had been in Georgia. At last his army was close enough to join up with Grant's forces outside Richmond. Grant was determined to forestall a breakout by Lee, and launched an attack on Petersburg to the south of Richmond.

The game was over: Confederate President Jefferson Davies and his supporters evacuated Richmond, followed soon by Lee's remaining army, which moved eastwards and then southwards to join General Johnston's other remaining Confederate army in North Carolina. On 9 April 1865, Lee saw that Sheridan's cavalry was in front of him, along with an indeterminate number of infantry. He had just 10,000 men to the enemy's 50,000. He considered staging a breakthrough and taking to the hills to fight a guerrilla war. Then he decided the war was over: guerrilla fighting would 'bring on a state of affairs it would take the country years to recover from'. He added: 'How easily could I be rid of these and be at rest. I have only to ride along the line [to be shot] and all will be over. But it is our duty to live.'

At a house on the edge of Appomattox village, the tall, well-dressed 58-year-old Confederate general met the small, 42-year-old Grant, dressed in a rough smock. At 3.45 p.m. on Palm Sunday, they both signed the Confederate surrender documents. In total, some 360,000 Union men had died and some 260,000 Confederates, but the American Civil War was finally over. On 14 April, Lincoln was assassinated. Four years later he was followed as president by the shambling, humble, understated, cigar-chomping, hard-drinking figure of Ulysses Grant.

—~~~—

Ulysses Grant won the 1868 presidential election at the age of just 46, the youngest president in his country's history. Originally believed to be a hardliner towards the South, he supported amnesty for Confederate leaders, promoted the rights of black people and fought the Ku Klux Klan. The Grants entertained lavishly at the White House, holding state dinners consisting of 29 courses accompanied by nine French wines. He lodged both his father and father-in-law (who hated one another) in the building, and held a splendid wedding for his daughter Nelly in 1874.

Re-elected overwhelmingly in 1872, he was knocked off course by the sudden economic panic the following year. He was accused of doing too little to alleviate the depression, while a welter of accusations of corruption, such as the 'whiskey ring' of 1875 in the Interior, War and Navy Departments, reached as high as Grant's private secretary, although not to the president himself. 'Failures have been errors of judgement, not of intent,' he protested lamely.

From 1877 the former president travelled the world for two years and was entertained by Queen Victoria and Bismarck. Two years later an attempt was made to secure him a third term and he won 300 votes in the Republican convention, but the nomination went to James Garfield. Soon after, Grant was swindled by a business partner and had to write his widely praised memoirs to survive financially, while also securing a pension from Congress. He died of throat cancer on 23 July 1885 and was buried in an immense mausoleum in New York.

—⁓—

Grant's relentless determination for victory was on display throughout his career. He was a bulldozer, crushing all obstacles before him. It would be easy to say he does not qualify for the maverick label: most were characterized by their skills for negotiating obstacles, not battering them down. Easy, but wrong. For Grant was both a conventional and unconventional general, as the situation required. A pragmatist, he was a modernizer in war: 'war is progressive', he claimed. His manoeuvre at Vicksburg, which took the enemy entirely by surprise and split its forces, was one of the greatest feats in military history.

As soon as he assumed overall control he combined the unimaginative frontal attack he was ordered to by his political masters with Sherman's unconventional flanking attack to the south behind enemy lines. Without the brutal determination of his attack from the north on the main Confederate front, it would have been easy for Lee to mop up Sherman's forces; without Sherman's attack from the west, Lee might have overwhelmed Grant in the north. It was a pioneering strategy of the hammer and the sickle. Without Grant's farsighted decision to send Sheridan down the Shenandoah, that spear into the heart of Union territory might still have been able to turn the tide of war.

Grant's overall grasp of tactics was brilliant. Until he took control of the Union's forces, it was by no means certain that the war would be won. It would be hard to think of two men that less resembled each other physically and in manner than Grant and the Duke of Wellington, yet both had the same overall grasp of the battle-field, the imagination to try unconventional tactics and the grim ruthlessness to practise murderous conventional ones in the interests of victory.

Grant had most of the characteristics of the mavericks: he was courageous under fire, and cool and rational on the battlefield; he had a superb eye for opportunities as they occurred and immense skill in manoeuvre; and he had a well-run staff and superb subordinates like Sherman and Sheridan. Also, he was highly intelligent and was insouciant towards the rule book. Furthermore, he showed concern for his own men, although he was prepared to sacrifice them in vast numbers in the pursuit of victory. His career was marked by a long and major setback, and he showed determination in rising again.

Unlike many of the mavericks, he had a deeply, psychotically brutal streak in the interests of victory – he fought with relentless ferocity on the eastern front, wearing his enemy down through sheer attrition, while despatching Sheridan and Sherman to pursue inhuman scorched-earth campaigns in the Shenandoah Valley and in Georgia. This ruthlessness paid off: he delivered victory. He used an extraordinary combination of brilliant, indirect manoeuvres and sheer brute force.

Grant completely lacked charisma and he was eccentric. He tended to fight only when the odds were on his side – which sets him apart from the other mavericks. Like so many of the others he tried to be a capable administrator, becoming President of the United States, although a poor one – and he was an appalling businessman. Yet he showed genius in his grasp of tactics, which won the Civil War.

Chapter 9

ROMMEL: THE DESERT FOX

For those who abide by national stereotypes of ramrod-straight Prussians or the cruel, we-will-obey German, it comes as a surprise that the most charismatic, often disobedient, dashing, daring and unconventional – if not necessarily the best – senior general of the Second World War was Erwin Rommel. He personified military bravery, leadership, heroism and romantic warriordom, and was admired by his fellow countrymen and respected by his enemies.

In the First World War he was a young commander of brilliant and fearless aggressive skills; in the Second, along with Heinz Guderian, he was the master of the *blitzkrieg* tactics that won the Battle of France within weeks and, with only a small force, he repeatedly out-witted the British in North Africa until the iron will of Montgomery and the huge US reinforcements arrived to tilt the balance. In 1944, quicker than most Germans, he realized that his country could not win the war and the tragic, operatic, *Götterdämmerung* end that ensued was at one with his entire romantic career. No other Second World War commander's star shone as brightly – not that of crotch-ety Montgomery, or braggart Patton, or the politically astute Eisenhower – although MacArthur's came close.

This is not to say that Rommel lacked faults: he was too much the prima donna who refused to delegate, a defect made worse by his own penchant for leading from the front – which meant he was often hard to reach or uncertain of the deployment of his forces.

Also, he could be too impetuous – although usually he calculated the odds carefully before making what to others seemed an impossibly bold strike. Certainly, his own men did not accuse him of endangering their lives unnecessarily. He was one of the greatest offensive commanders in history – a man whose skill and brilliance struck terror into the hearts of his enemies. He led from the front and was rarely constrained by orders from his commanders in the rear including, on occasion, from Hitler, to whom he was personally close until the very end.

Erwin Johannes Eugen Rommel was born on 15 November 1891 in Heidenheim, about 50 miles east of Stuttgart, of Swabian stock (usually a level-headed and unemotional people). He was the son of a schoolmaster who had been a cavalry officer, while his mother was of higher social origins as the daughter of a local politician. He was not particularly strong in youth, although vigorous exercise later made him so, but he suffered from recurrent severe stomach problems. He was hugely independent, interested in mathematics, skiing and adventure. In 1910, at the age of 18, he became a cadet at Danzig for a modest infantry division and was quickly promoted to corporal, then sergeant and by 20 was a lieutenant. In Danzig he fell in love with Lucy Mollin, a beautiful girl from an aristocratic West Prussian family, whom he soon married. For once it was, by all accounts, happiness ever after, with the two devoted to the end of his life.

The world which Rommel now inhabited was the most ferocious military caste system since the Mamelukes in Egypt. The Prussian army was a steel first forged in the fires by Frederick the Great, officered by the cream of the aristocracy and manned by the peasants of Prussia who, it was said, had little else to do in that flat, cold, barren land. The army's prestige was such that it attracted the brightest brains, and it made a virtue of firmness and discipline: in a society which despised trade, the professions and civilians, to be a senior officer in the Prussian army was the very height of prestige.

However, the army was far from rigid: the brains at the top were flexible and subtle enough continually to seek to improve it as a fighting machine. The Napoleonic wars, when the flexibility of the

French army's mobile attacks convincingly demolished the old line strategies of the Germans, had persuaded it to adopt the new tactics. The chief architect of these was that magnificent old warhorse Gebhard Leberecht von Blücher, his chief of staff General August von Gneisenau and then General Gerhard von Scharnhorst.

The Prussian War Academy was founded in 1810 by Carl von Clausewitz. The military caste owed its allegiance directly to the Kaiser and the army had the sacred duty of being 'guardians of the store' in times of danger, including civil strife, for which the Kaiser could declare a state of siege. Kaiser Wilhelm I was discreet, but his successor, Wilhelm II, revelled in his military authority. The Prussian army glorified war and honour. Rather like the Japanese samurai of old, it was an affront for an officer not to punish any slight made against him by a civilian, and officers who did not do so could be stripped of their commissions: many shot themselves to avoid this fate.

Field-Marshal Helmuth von Moltke's interpretation of Clausewitz's Doctrine of War made him the disciple of his theory that a super-concentration of force would smash its way through enemy defences and overcome everything in its path. This was applied in the Franco-Prussian and Austro-Prussian wars. Even though this sometimes failed, the German high command remained committed to the theory, with terrifying results when total war was made possible by conscription and mass mobilization.

According to Field-Marshal Helmut von Moltke, the first German chief of staff and great protagonist of the Franco-Prussian wars:

> Eternal peace is a dream and not even a beautiful one. War is a link in God's order of the world. In war, the noblest virtues of man develop: courage and renunciation, devotion to duty and readiness for sacrifice, even at the risk of one's life. Without war the world would sink into materialism.

With the coming of the First World War, a plan of astonishing boldness and aggression was adopted by the German chief of staff,

General Graf von Schlieffen, utterly at variance with Clausewitz's and Moltke's teaching. The French had fortified their 150-mile border with Germany with strategic fortress bases at Epinal, Tourn and Verdun; the Vosges mountains and the thickly wooded hills and valleys of the Ardennes blocked the rest. Although French tactics were originally based on simply defending the fortresses, a new French commander-in-chief, Marshal Joffre, had come to power in 1912 advocating the Clausewitzian doctrine of a massive attack through the centre 'with all forces united'. The British had agreed to serve as part of the French left wing, although their commander, Sir John French, wanted to occupy Antwerp and retain his forces' autonomy, as well as deter a German strike through Belgium. For this is what the Schlieffen Plan was – a giant cartwheel through Belgium and round to the left, trapping the French forces from both behind and in front.

It was an incredibly bold strategic plan, but unfortunately Schlieffen was succeeded by Moltke, the dimmer nephew of the victor of the Austrian and Franco-Prussian wars, who decided to send back divisions from the Belgian front to the southern flank, including six ersatz crack divisions, so that 25 German divisions faced 18 French divisions, which encouraged the German commander, Prince Rupprecht of Bavaria, to go on the attack at Lorraine where he found his way blocked by the French fortress defences.

Meanwhile in the north, Moltke weakened the attacking force through Belgium by a further 11 divisions, some to go to the Russian front, some to face Antwerp and the Channel ports, leaving him with just 13 divisions against the 27 French and British divisions. Worse, German supplies ran out after the destruction of barges along the Meuse, with only one railway line being left open. Thus while the Germans were unexpectedly stalled in the north – the scene of their surprise attack – the French were stalled in the south.

Joffre promptly assembled a new 6th army to fight on the other flank, only to find that the Germans under Kluck had broken through; but Moltke mistakenly advised Kluck to pass east of Paris, instead of the eminently more sensible western route originally planned, and the French attacked at his exposed flank from Paris. The Germans rushed troops from their northern armies to resist, and the British struck in between the two vulnerable German forces, winning the Battle of the Marne and forcing the Germans into retreat.

Moltke was replaced by Falkenhauser, who laid siege to Antwerp to prevent supplies and reinforcements reaching the British, and then sought to sweep down to the coast. The Belgian army blocked him and flooded the coastal districts. The war settled into a long grim one of attrition through trench warfare – Neuve Chapelle, Champagne, Verdun, the Somme, Arras, Ypres and Passchendaele.

Only with the collapse of Russian resistance in the east in 1917 did the odds change, with the Germans rushing divisions to the western front for a huge Clausewitzian concentration of force along the frontier, spearheaded by their new commander, Erich von Ludendorff, chief of staff to Field-Marshal von Hindenburg, victor of the Russian front (who was largely a figurehead).

The Germans now had 193 divisions against 173 Allied divisions on the western front. Ludendorff's attack was to come between Arras and La Fère, a 60-mile front, splitting the French and British armies. His offensive was a general one on too broad a front, and, although it broke through in the south, it was blocked at Arras. Ludendorff launched a further offensive at Armentières and to the south near Rheims, where he was successful, but nowhere decisively so and he now had an indented front susceptible to counterattacks from almost anywhere. On 8 August Field-Marshal Haig launched the first great tank attack of the war, with 450 of these awkward vehicles routing the Germans at Amiens.

Luendorff was demoralized and sought a negotiated peace: the Germans were relentlessly pushed back towards the Hindenburg line by British, French and American pressure and, although they could probably have held it, the collapse of the German economy after years of sea blockades and the capitulation of Turkey and Austria, as well as the advance of Italian armies in the south, caused a revolution within Germany that forced the Kaiser out of office and an armistice was signed on 11 November.

Despite the carnage and the eventual failure of German tactics, Rommel had a glorious First World War. In August 1914, Rommel was in charge of a platoon that was sent to the Meuse front at Bleid, where he personally led a surprise attack on an entire French position and then engaged in vicious house-to-house fighting in what was to widen into the Battle of Longwy. After this baptism of fire the young officer was engaged in almost continuous fighting, always rushing ahead of his troops, seizing the initiative, and sometimes ignoring cautious orders from behind.

By early 1915, at the age of 23, he was appointed company commander of troops bogged down in the trenches near Verdun. On 29 January, he led his men into a large French concentration in woods and held the position heroically in spite of lack of support: he was awarded the Iron Cross, First Class. According to his biographer, General Sir David Fraser: 'Rommel by this time was a famous regimental personality, his name a byword... He had a "feel" for battle, for the enemy's likely plans and reactions, for what might or might not work... it infused utter faith in the men he led. "Where Rommel is," they said, "there is the front."'

Subsequently, he was transferred to the High Vosges region of the Alsace, where he led raids against the much less entrenched French positions, 3,000 feet up, in a more mobile kind of warfare at which he excelled. In October 1916 his 'Mountain Battalion' was transferred to the even higher and more spectacular, if bitterly cold and snowbound, mountains of Romania. At the battle for Mount Cosna he commanded the whole battalion. He was wounded but performed spectacularly, bursting through the Romanian uphill lines to conquer the summit, while suffering only 30 dead and 500 wounded.

Soon afterwards he was sent to the Italian front to capture Mount Matajur near Cividale, which he did in a daring attack behind enemy lines, going round the mountain and outflanking the Italians, catching them in an encirclement. He took 9,000 prisoners and lost just six dead and 30 wounded. He crossed the strategic Piave River and advanced remorselessly, but to his disgust was transferred in January 1918 to become a staff officer on the Western Front.

—∿—

The ensuing years of instability following the Treaty of Versailles only momentarily unsettled the German officer class from their self-appointed role as guardians of Germany's destiny. In 1919 a new chief of staff emerged who was nothing short of a political and military genius: Hans von Seeckt, a hero of the eastern front. Monocled, moustachioed and severe-looking, he was the very model of the Prussian officer class. He wrote: 'War is the highest summit of human achievement; it is the natural, the final stage in the historical development of humanity. The Reich!... The army should become a state within the state, but it should be merged in the state through service; in fact it should itself become the purest image of the state.'

A man of high culture and intelligence, von Seeckt subtly pursued his own ends. He did two things: first, he ensured that the German army, which had been virtually disbanded under the provisions of the Treaty of Versailles, lived on in the guise of a vast trained militia, with its officers becoming NCOs (no limit had been placed on militia at Versailles); second, he decided to ditch the disastrous trench mentality in favour of mobility, and in particular tank warfare. In 1921 he published his *Basic Ideas for the Reconstruction of the Armed Forces*, arguing that 'The whole future of warfare appears to me to be in the employment of mobile armies, relatively small but of high quality, and rendered distinctly more effective by the addition of aircraft, and in the simultaneous mobilisation of the whole defence force, be it to feed the attack or for home defence.'

The next two decades were to see the uneasy marriage between an overweening Prussian warrior caste and a lower middle-class of nationalist politicians that resulted in the Third Reich. It was into this background, and in particular von Seeckt's commitment to mobile warfare, that Erwin Rommel rose as a young officer from a relatively humble background, on his own merits. He was a passionate admirer of Hitler, but more especially a disciple of the other greatest German general of the war, and his only superior as a tank commander, Heinz Guderian. The general was the creator of the German Panzer forces, which many more traditional German officers treated with suspicion (the same was true in Britain, the United States and France).

After the First World War, Rommel had been put in charge of a machine-gun company and later appointed to instruct at the Infantry School at Dresden, before being promoted to lieutenant-colonel and battalion commander where he enjoyed ski operations. In September 1934 he met the newly appointed German chancellor, Adolf Hitler, on a routine tour, and insisted that the Schutzstaffel – the SS – not be present as his men would provide protection. In 1937 he was given the job of liaising between the army and the Hitler Youth, but fell out with its fanatical commander, Baldur von Schirach. At the age of 47 in August 1939, on the eve of the invasion of Poland and the Second World War, he was promoted to major-general as commander of the Führer's special guard of honour. Rommel's first command was highly prestigious and marked him out as a coming man, but it was hardly a martial commission – although the Führer insisted in being taken dangerously close to exposed positions.

Poland was ideal for a tank invasion: with a front with Germany of 1,250 miles, plus another with German-occupied Czechoslovakia of 500 miles in the south, it was incredibly exposed. It was also largely flat and passable, except for lakes, forest and soft sand in some areas. Poland's 20 armoured divisions and 12 obsolete cavalry brigades were largely deployed west of the Vistula to protect its industrial heartland.

Two German armies thrust in from the northwest, while the main armoured thrust was at the centre of Gerd von Rundstedt's forces, the 10th Army, which came from the south. Guderian's armour was attached to the 1st Army in the north, which drove to the isolated German province of East Prussia, and then turned south to Brest-Litovsk on the Bug River. Meanwhile, the other armies enveloped the main Polish armies, and Guderian's vast sweep denied the Poles the chance of withdrawing into the mountains to the southeast in order to carry on resistance. As much of

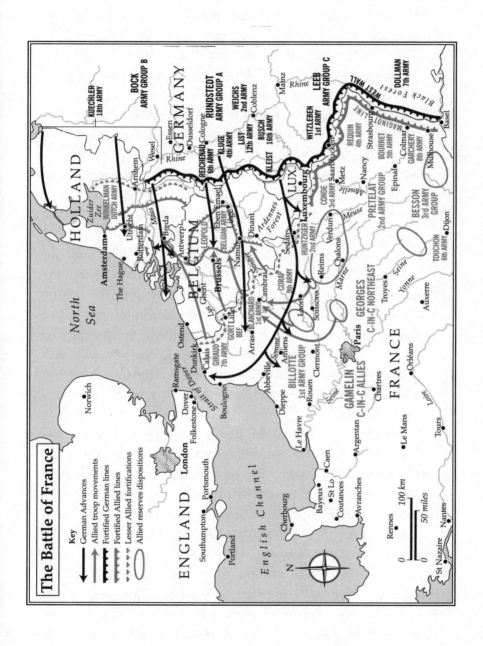

The Battle of France

Key

- German Advances
- Allied troop movements
- Fortified German lines
- Fortified Allied lines
- Lesser Allied fortifications
- Allied reserves dispositions

the Polish army slipped over the Vistula to defend Warsaw, the main German forces moved in a still wider sweep to the Bug. The Polish Poznan army on the west of the Vistula struck against the exposed rear of the German force, and a furious battle ensued. The 100,000 Polish troops surrendered on 19 September. In less than three weeks, around 700,000 Poles were wounded or taken prisoner by the Germans, at a cost of some 14,000 Germans dead.

It was the first massive display of *blitzkrieg* – 'lightning war' tactics. It was designed to throw the enemy off-balance through sustained air attacks, coordinated with ground attacks moving much faster than in the past, enveloping defences, positions and armies before the enemy had the time to react. Like Napoleon's attacks in Italy and central Europe, the sheer speed of the offensives and the envelopment completely disoriented the enemy.

Once Poland was subdued, the next target was France, and, this time, Rommel was to be involved in the action. Hitler wanted the offensive to start in the second week of November 1939 – belying Allied wishful thinking that he would seek peace in the west to free himself to attack the east – but it was repeatedly postponed. The plan was highly unimaginative: it was to be a frontal attack through Belgium, including Guderian's armoured units, while von Rundstedt carried out a smaller flanking attack through the wooded and hilly Ardennes.

General Erich von Manstein, von Rundstedt's chief of staff and perhaps the most intelligent officer in the army, argued that the main thrust should come through the Ardennes to wrongfoot the Allies, who would be expecting the attack through Belgium in the north, where Britain's crack troops would be concentrated. Von Manstein feared that the war would then get bogged down in Flanders, First-World-War-style. Guderian, the Panzer commander, advised him that it was possible to lead a large armoured force through the supposedly impassable Ardennes. However, he was blocked by the commander-in-chief, General Walther von Brauchitsch, and his chief of staff, General Franz Halder, who finally decided to get rid of him by appointing him commander of a corps on the eastern front.

On the occasion of paying his respects to Hitler before his departure, von Manstein went behind his superiors' backs and outlined his idea for staging the main offensive through the Ardennes. When a staff officer carrying details of the original plan was forced to land in France in a snowstorm, it was feared that it might have been intercepted. Hitler decided quickly to go for von Manstein's new plan. Operation Sickle Strike was born, involving a massive push through the Ardennes to catch the French and British armies arrayed to meet the German attack through Belgium in the rear.

The Germans were organized into 10 Panzer armoured divisions, nine motorized divisions (including SS) and 119 infantry divisions. The operation began on 10 May 1940 with a diversionary attack through Belgium and Holland, which was so violent it convinced the French and British that it was the main attack. Airborne attacks were staged at the fort of Emael and Rotterdam. General Maurice Gamelin, the Allied commander, rushed his forces into Belgium to meet the challenge. Hitler was overjoyed.

Even as the French and British forces rushed to meet the challenge, long columns of tanks and armoured vehicles were crawling through the narrow roads of the Ardennes screened from the air by woods. There were three armoured divisions under Guderian, then four more motorized ones, with von Rundstedt in overall control. Altogether there were 1,800 tanks, encountering nothing more than French forest rangers – the Chasseurs Ardennais. Behind them were two weak armies who were not expecting the enemy.

On 12 May, two days after the German attack on Belgium and Holland, the German columns poured out of the Ardennes. Commanded by Rommel, the 7th Panzer division, known as the 'ghost division' for the stealth with which it had arrived, forded a weir across the Meuse. The following day his tanks crossed over heavily, hastily erected pontoon bridges, while another crossing was made by Guderian. Rommel's tank was hit and he was wounded in the head by a splinter. Within a day all three of the advance Panzer divisions were across the river. Guderian's superior, Paul von Kleist, ordered him to consolidate the bridgeheads until infantry arrived.

Guderian took no notice – an unprecedented act of insubordination in the German army – and drove 50 miles west to the Oise the following day. The French flailed in front of the Germans, wondering whether these fast-moving tanks would go north or to Paris. Even Hitler now ordered a two-day delay. Guderian promptly resigned as commander, but was ordered back and told he could conduct 'strong reconnaissance'. He instantly pushed on with his full force just as fast as before, reaching Amiens on 20 May, and then the sea at Abbeville, slicing the Allied armies in half.

Rommel, to the north, broke through the French line with a loss of just 15 German dead and charged forward to Arras. On 21 May, two British armoured divisions attacked Rommel's front so violently that he thought he was facing five divisions. Although Guderian had by now isolated Boulogne and Calais and had reached Gravelines, just 10 miles from Dunkirk, Hitler's two-day delay permitted the British to strengthen their defences around the port, their last avenue of retreat.

On 20 May the British high command had taken the decision to evacuate their expeditionary force. They did not believe that General Maxime Weygand, the new French commander, could trap the exposed German front along the corridor to the coast: they turned out to be right. Hitler had been assured by the ever-boastful Hermann Goering that the Luftwaffe could prevent any evacuation by the British, and he was also concerned, rightly, that his tanks would get bogged down in the waterlogged region around Dunkirk.

Over the next few days 337,000 Allied soldiers were evacuated, about a third of them French. Only six British and two French destroyers were sunk in nine days of ceaseless air attack. A vast array of small boats – merchant ships and fishing vessels – helped to carry off the evacuees. Both Guderian and Rommel had been cheated of a large part of their prey by Hitler's uncharacteristic caution. But Rommel's hero, Hitler, came to visit his protégé, saying, 'We were all very worried about you.'

The remaining 66 French divisions attempted to regroup along the 'Weygand line'. Guderian attacked with six divisions along the Aisne, being briefly held up by forces under Marshal Jean de Lattre de Tassigny. German mobility continued to astound as it attacked Weygand's base line. Rommel now performed a brilliant stroke: the French had blown up the road bridges across the Somme, but left two rail bridges along narrow embankments that led across water-logged fields. Rommel captured the bridges before dawn, pulled up the rails and ordered his tanks across while under heavy shelling.

Within two days he had advanced nearly 50 miles, splitting the French 10th Army in two. On 8 June 1940, after another 40-mile hike, he reached the banks of the Seine, south of Rouen, and crossed before the French could organize themselves. On 10 June he made directly for the coast, cutting off the left of the French 19th Army, which surrendered (five divisions in all). Guderian, attacking across the Aisne on the same day, encountered much greater opposition from French armour, but penetrated nearly 20 miles in three days and a further 40 miles after that. By 17 June, the French army behind the useless Maginot Line of defence was trapped. The French asked for an armistice, which was signed on 21 June.

The extraordinary duo of Guderian and Rommel had, almost between them, won the Battle of France: it had been their startling journey through the Ardennes, boldness, imagination and mobility that had defeated a much larger French army and sent the British packing. The feint attack in Belgium and Holland was the second great manoeuvre that had permitted their forces to attack round the back, then to defeat the French both in the north and the south: it had been one of the greatest and fastest military feats since ancient times. Had it not been for the caution of the high command, and even of the usually impatient Hitler, they would probably have caught the British as well and possibly brought about a swift end to the war. Their extraordinary feats were based on their fearlessness, speed, aggression, improvisation and generalship, and also on their supreme skill in using tank mobility and independence of action. Moreover, they had shown reckless insubordination towards their superiors, even to Hitler himself at times, which would normally have resulted in their dismissal or worse – but they were saved by the irrefutable brilliance of their victory.

By contrast the French had dispersed 1,500 of their 3,000 tanks among the infantry, and 700 among their cavalry and mechanized divisions, a throwback to the tactics of the First World War, and had only 800 tanks allocated to their mobile divisions. The British, who had invented the tank, had just nine armoured divisions. The Mark II and Mark IV Panzer tanks were inferior to the British ones in armour and had just one gun turret which could only fire straight ahead, but they could be mass-produced easily, there were more of them and they moved faster. The Germans had lost just 27,000 men to the French 90,000. Rommel exulted to his wife, '...reached here without difficulty. The war has become practically a lightning Tour de France. Within a few days it will be over for good.'

—*﬚*—

Rommel was feted as a popular hero in Germany, a trusted confidant of the Führer, and he was wildly popular with his own troops. He was soon approached to come to the rescue of the beleaguered Italians in North Africa. There, in December 1940, General Archibald Wavell's British Army in Egypt had led a 'raid' against the Italians, which had pushed them 60 miles from the border with Egypt. In three days the British under General Richard O'Connor had captured 38,000 Italians. Soon Bardia, just across the Libyan border, had fallen, and then Tobruk on 21 January 1941. With the Italians still reeling along the coast road, O'Connor with just 3,000 men took the gamble of crossing the supposedly impenetrable desert by the shorter route to the south. He covered the 170 miles to Beda in 36 hours, reaching it ahead of the Italians, and then captured another 90,000 of them.

Within weeks Hitler despatched Rommel with an 'Afrikakorps' of just two divisions – the 15th Panzer and 5th Light, which was all he could spare from the impending invasion of Russia. Meanwhile, the British forces were depleted by the decision to launch a mistaken expedition to Greece. Hitler entertained Napoleonic delusions for a 'Plan Orient' in which Rommel would invade Egypt, cross Syria, Iraq and Iran and join up with the northern armies in Russia to seize the oilfields.

Rommel moved fast, encircling the British vanguard at Melili and thus capturing the arc of the peninsula of Cyraenaica. He failed to capture the fortress of Tobruk in two disastrous assaults in April 1941 and he had also overextended his lines of communication and was forced to stop at the Egyptian frontier. In this he also showed an extraordinary inability to delegate either to his Italian allies, in particular his nominal commander General Ettore Bastico, or to his own Afrikakorps commander, General Ludwig Crüwell. In June, Wavell launched Operation Battleaxe which attacked Rommel's front along the coastal strip. Rommel, the master of tank warfare, proved that he was also a master of the anti-tank guns which wrought havoc on the British. Wheeling around south into the desert, he outflanked them and drove them back. Wavell was replaced by Claude Auchinleck as British commander in North Africa following this setback, while General Alan Cunningham became commander of the 8th Army.

On 18 November the British went on the offensive, and this time were cunningly lured by Rommel through a weak initial defence on to carefully screened anti-tank guns, which decimated the British armour. The British lost some 200 tanks. Five days later the British withdrew and Rommel went on the offensive, staging a daring raid south across the desert to sever the British supply lines behind them. Meanwhile, behind Rommel, the now encircled British forces surprised him by breaking through his rear to link up with the besieged garrison at Tobruk: it was Rommel who was now overstretched, and he had to return beyond Tobruk to Bazale and then beyond that to Benghazi.

The British launched a new offensive on 27 December 1941, but once again Rommel used his anti-tank guns to great effect and outflanked them, trapping a huge number of tanks. Meanwhile, he himself had been reinforced and wasted no time in launching a further offensive, again from the southern desert flank, pushing the British all the way back to Gazala again. Rommel's lightning movement, his capacity for improvisation and his ability to deceive and trap the enemy were all demonstrations of pure military genius.

The most remarkable episode was about to come at the Battle of Gazala. With around 18,000 killed and wounded, 440 tanks and 300 aircraft lost to the British, and 38,000 men, 340 tanks and 300 aircraft to the Germans and Italians, battle honours were about even up to now. On 27 May 1942, Rommel suddenly attacked with another of his wide flanking movements on the desert side, but failed to cut the British off and reach the coast: he took up a defensive position in the British minefields and the latter, thinking they had the 'desert fox' trapped at last, attacked – only once again to be lured on to his anti-tank guns and artillery. Rommel personally led his men with ferocious courage. Further to the south his forces were attacking the Free French brigade at Bir Hacheim; once they had done this they turned north, relieving Rommel. The British forces were outflanked.

Auchinleck broke off from this fierce engagement and made for the Egyptian border, with Rommel seemingly speeding in pursuit – but then he sprang another surprise. He suddenly turned back towards Tobruk and broke through its weak defences, capturing the part of the British army that had sought refuge there as well as its South African defenders. It was a huge blow to British pride. Rommel then turned his attention to chasing the British back along the coast as far as Alam Halfa, threatening the Nile Valley itself at the point where the Qattara Depression approaches the sea and makes a natural defensive point. Auchinleck himself took charge and managed to hold the line against Rommel's repeated thrusts. In effect, the British position in North Africa was in danger of collapsing altogether through the brilliant fighting skills, offensive and counteroffensive efforts of one man.

At this stage, Prime Minister Winston Churchill, desperate for a victory there, replaced Auchinleck with Harold Alexander and appointed Bernard Montgomery as the commander of the 8th Army. Montgomery won the defensive battle of Alam Halfa, then the offensive battle of El Alamein (see a full description in Chapter 10). Rommel knew he had to withdraw or face encirclement and total defeat, but Hitler issued a grim order that 'Not a step is to be yielded... as to your troops you can show them no other road than victory or death.'

'The Führer must be a complete lunatic,' said Rommel, wandering in the desert. He ignored the order and withdrew, saving the German and Italian armies. Rommel's 2,000-mile retreat to Tunis, along a thin corridor of land virtually controlled by the British and while being chased by a superior force, was a remarkable achievement. In the end, Rommel was defeated largely through shortage of supplies and reinforcements. He was ordered home in March 1943.

Despite his successes against the odds, Rommel was sick and disappointed, feeling let down by his masters in Berlin who had failed to support him sufficiently. Like some great knight at a medieval pageant he had jousted with his British enemies, winning most of the tournaments, but lost the last against a much better armoured enemy with a longer lance. Rommel now openly opined that the war was lost and even that Hitler must abdicate; he also believed that the persecution of the Jews should end. Rommel's stance was all the more remarkable in that Rommel, not a member of the Prussian military aristocracy that despised Hitler, had been his admiring protégé. When Rommel saw Hitler in March 1943, the Führer was ranting about sending Rommel on an expedition to retake Casablanca, to the general's incredulity.

Instead, in August 1943, Rommel was appointed commander-in-chief of German forces in North Italy, headquartered near Lake Garda. His time there was uneasy: Rommel was in charge of Operation Alaric which was to infiltrate 20 divisions of German troops through the Alps into Italy in anticipation of an Allied invasion, but without upsetting the Italians, still nominally allies. He believed that Germany should make a stand in northern Italy to defend the Alpine passes, rather than further south, as the eastern and western fronts were much more crucial to Germany's survival. He was overruled and was subsequently moved to the position of inspector of western defences in December 1943, and then commander of Army Group B defending western Europe.

Although feeling sidelined, he had needed a rest and benefited from the tour. Moreover, he had a massive popular following in Germany and his military skills were simply too valuable for him to be left to one side. The figure of Rommel, in desert gear, often clad in shorts, with his trademark peaked hat and dark glasses against the sand and sun of the desert, and his sun-baked, weatherbeaten face, had become an enduring symbol of German military prowess.

—◈—

As the apprentice had dazzled in the desert, what of the sorcerer himself? General Heinz Guderian was given his chance of covering himself in further glory with Operation Barbarossa, the invasion of Russia on 22 June 1941 – a theatre Hitler correctly regarded as infinitely more important than Rommel's in North Africa. Guderian and General Herman Hoth were given command of the Panzer divisions in Army Group Centre, pushing through along Napoleon's old invasion route into Russia to meet at Minsk, 200 miles inside the border. Some 300,000 Russians were captured by the pincer-movement after putting up little resistance in the first encirclement battles.

However, Hitler had made the colossal strategic blunder of dispersing the overwhelming force he enjoyed against three different military objectives several hundred miles apart – Leningrad in the north, Moscow in the centre, and the oilfields of the Caucasus in the south. Guderian rushed forward, crossing the Dniepar at three points on 10 July, without waiting for the infantry, and reached Smolensk on 16 July. He had travelled 400 miles in less than a month, and was only 200 miles from Moscow. Another pincer with Hoth's forces at Smolensk trapped 180,000 more Russian soldiers (in marked contrast with Napoleon's advance, when the Russians escaped his attempted entrapment).

Hitler then abruptly decided to prioritize the attacks in Leningrad in the north and Kiev in the south, at the expense of Moscow. Guderian's Panzers were ordered to Kiev; he decided to disobey orders, and engaged enemy positions south of the Moscow road at Roslavl as a pretext for not joining the Kiev offensive. Hitler dithered for nearly three weeks, then Guderian flew down to convince him of the need to take Moscow: it was Napoleon's indecisiveness outside Moscow all over again.

At length, a compromise was reached: it was agreed that Guderian should go to help in the southern offensive against Kiev commanded by von Rundstedt, but then veer back to Moscow if circumstances permitted. The Russians meanwhile sought to break through and part the two German armies, but Guderian moved with such speed that they closed the gap and surrounded Kiev on 26 September 1941, taking some 665,000 Russian prisoners – the largest number before or since in battle.

Guderian was then ordered back towards Moscow, this time with mixed feelings, for the window of opportunity afforded by the weather was past. As the weather began to deteriorate, the German plight began to resemble that of Napoleon's army.

The Germans had around 80 divisions, 14 Panzer and eight motorized, and 1,400 aircraft; the Russians had 90 divisions, some 800,000 men and 770 tanks, but only 364 aircraft. Guderian rushed forward, breaking through the Russian lines and penetrating just 20 miles from Moscow before being stopped by heavy resistance and intense cold. The Russians counterattacked out of the city on 5 December, driving Guderian's forces back and dividing them from the German 4th Army. It was this hitherto undefeated commander's first major setback. On 20 December 1941, an enraged Hitler dismissed Guderian, along with several other commanders, for preparing to withdraw his Panzer divisions from this impossible position. The Germans staggered through the grim winter until Hitler resumed operations directed at the southern oilfields, away from Moscow and towards what was to become his nemesis: Stalingrad. Guderian was no longer around to point out his mistakes.

It took the cathartic defeat at Stalingrad to persuade Hitler to send for Guderian once more, appointing him inspector of Panzer troops. Guderian was shocked at the post-Stalingrad transformation in the Führer when they met in February 1943: 'His left hand trembled, his back was bent, his gaze was fixed, his eyes protruded but lacked their former lustre, his cheeks were flecked with red. He was more excitable, easily lost his composure and was prone to angry outbursts and ill-considered decisions.'

Guderian set about seeking to modernize German tank production to 1,000 a month, one of them the crack new Panzer Mark IV. As punishment for his failure to take Moscow, and possibly for his insubordination beforehand, he was reduced to the role of an administrator now.

—⁓—

In western Europe, Rommel set about his new tasks with characteristic energy. He found to his dismay that only 1.7 million mines had been laid; four months after he took over, 4 million were in place. His tactics, which Montgomery predicted, to meet the expected Allied landings in western Europe were characteristically bold: he wanted to bring his tanks down to the water's edge to meet the invader.

However, there was a bitter dispute between Rommel and von Rundstedt, his immediate superior, as to where the landing would take place. Convinced in part by elaborate Allied deceptions, von Rundstedt expected attackers to make for Calais. Hitler, however, believed the landing would be in Normandy so two Panzer divisions were allocated there. Von Rundstedt argued that the Panzer and the reserves must be kept back from the beaches until they could be certain where the attackers were landing, to which Hitler grudgingly agreed. Rommel instead argued that the tanks should be down on the beaches, even if half of them were on the wrong ones, to prevent the enemy establishing a foothold; he also feared that as the tanks rushed to intercept the landing forces, they would be highly exposed to Allied airpower.

When the landings took place on 6 June 1944, Rommel was away on sick leave (actually attending his wife's birthday party) and he had to be driven at speed from Ulm, arriving at 10.30 p.m. The 21st Panzer division were only ordered into action on the following morning, by which time the Allies had got from the beaches and were approaching Caen. The British were able to beat off the Panzer attack. When the SS Hitler Youth Panzer division attacked the Canadians west of Caen, they did considerable damage, but failed to push them back to the sea.

After this, Rommel was deeply disillusioned with Hitler, to whom he had once been so close. At around this time he was approached by some of those conspiring in the bomb plot to kill the Führer, but he opposed assassination and suggested instead that Hitler be seized by rebel Panzer units and forced to abdicate. He would then be put on trial for crimes against humanity and the German people. Even von Rundstedt had asked him to eliminate Hitler: 'You are young and popular with the people. You must do it.' At a six-hour meeting to discuss the plot in February 1944, Rommel, who was seen by the conspirators as a possible head of state or chief of staff after Hitler's overthrow, is reported to have said, 'I believe it is my duty to come to the rescue of Germany.'

Rommel's idea was to conclude peace with the Allies and with their help defeat the Russians – a wildly unrealistic objective. By the first week of July 1944, Rommel had decided to seek a cessation of hostilities on his own initiative in his sector of France. He thought that the war could not be won and Hitler 'must make a political decision' to step down. If not, 'I open the western front. There will be only one important matter left – that the Anglo-Americans reach Berlin before the Russians.'

Events moved fast. On 15 July he wrote boldly to Hitler: 'The troops are fighting heroically everywhere, but the unequal struggle is nearing its end. It is in my opinion necessary to draw the appropriate conclusions from this situation without delay. I feel it my duty as the commander-in-chief of the army group to express this clearly.' Two days later, in one of the great ironies of history, his staff car was shot up by British fighter aircraft, his driver was killed and he was so badly injured that he was at first thought to be dead.

Three days later a bomb exploded at Hitler's headquarters, injuring but failing to kill him. One of the conspirators in the plot confessed under torture that Rommel had been implicated. 'Tell the people in Berlin that they can count on me,' he is said to have remarked, although this was ambiguous and evidence obtained under torture can scarcely be considered reliable.

Wilhelm Keitel, the new German commander-in-chief, was shaken by the report. He informed Hitler, whose fury at this supposed Brutus-like betrayal by his subordinate knew no bounds. Rommel must pay the ultimate price – but in secret, because he retained such a following among the German people. An officer was despatched to bring him a box of poison capsules and the assurance that he would be given a state funeral and his family looked after well. On 14 October 1944, having surrounded Rommel's house with SS men, the officer delivered the capsules and the message. Rommel said goodbye to his wife and son, who departed by car. About 15 minutes later his wife was rung to say he had died of a cerebral embolism from the head injuries he had sustained in the car crash. Von Rundstedt gave his funeral oration.

As for Guderian, the bomb plotters had tried to recruit him into their ranks, but entirely failed. After the plot, the loyal Guderian was appointed chief of staff. He behaved cravenly, instituting the Nazi salute into the army in place of the regular salute, describing the July conspirators as 'a few officers, some of them on the retired list, who had lost courage and, out of cowardice and weakness, preferred the road of disgrace to the only road open to an honest soldier – the road of duty and honour'.

He also sent out an order: 'Every general staff officer must be a National Socialist officer-leader, that is not only by his knowledge of tactics and strategy, but also by his attitude to political questions and by actively co-operating in the political indoctrination of younger commanders in accordance with the tenets of the *Führer*.'

Finally, in March 1945, Guderian tried to persuade Joachim von Ribbentrop, Hermann Goering and Heinrich Himmler on the need for an armistice with the west – but none, including Guderian, dared broach the subject with Hitler. Guderian in the end had shown himself to be a great tank soldier and a master of the Panzer attack, but no more than that. In its way, the fate of this gifted but simple soldier was even more tragic than that of Rommel, for he did not retain his honour in spite of his military heroism, or ultimately rise to the occasion and seek to serve his country as events required.

Rommel's tragic demise was part and parcel of the man. A professional soldier to his fingertips, fearing nothing and no one, he had even dared to challenge the Führer when he judged this to be in Germany's best interests. No democrat, he was a product of the officer caste which regarded itself as even above the head of state in protecting the nation. But his rugged suntanned good looks in the desert, his absolute fearlessness and his devil-may-care skills in handling his ships of the desert – all combined to make him unique and popular in Germany.

The manner of his dying was just as brave. He was politically naive but seen as a respected rallying point for the July conspirators (even though he had supported Hitler for so long). On the face of it, so fearless a man would not have killed himself just to avoid torture if he was innocent: by taking the pills he apparently gave as clear an indication of his guilt as was possible – the guilt of putting Germany first and trying to rid it of the monster that was bringing about its destruction. Yet he told his wife on their last meeting that he had not been implicated but that he believed he would be eliminated even before the matter came to trial.

Rommel fits all too smoothly into the maverick bracket. Incredibly courageous and cool under fire, he grasped opportunities with astonishing speed, was a superb tactician who regularly took on greater odds, was good at choosing subordinates and getting them to execute his orders, and was an often reckless innovator at tank tactics. Although obedient to his superiors while young, in the breakout from the Ardennes in the Battle of France, he and Guderian showed no particular regard for their orders (which makes the latter's cravenness in 1944 all the more remarkable). His undoing was his readiness in the end to do his duty and take on his own godlike supreme commander, the Führer. He was enormously liked by his men as delivering great victories, and had a huge popular following – although perhaps no exceptional intelligence outside warfare. He had great stamina and ability to roll with the punches, in spite of often poor health, although his career was less of a rollercoaster than one moving rapidly and steadily forward, like a tank – until it drove over the landmine of the July bomb plot.

Chapter 10

MONTY: THE DESERT RAT

Bernard Law Montgomery is today regarded as a rather dull figure, a conventional general with a military moustache whose main achievement was a frontal attack against a German position at El Alamein (a view reinforced by his adoption of the title Montgomery of Alamein), essentially a sideshow in the Second World War. He seemed reminiscent of the rather raffish, dapper cads portrayed in postwar films by David Niven and Terry Thomas: a character with a whiff of disreputability about him. This was not only a matter of his appearance – moustached, twinkle-eyed, mischievous, debonair – but of his own deliberate creation. For Montgomery, like most of the mavericks, was a natural rebel; his modest deportment camouflaged an extremely tough, ruthless and abrasive interior, to the point of nastiness. Far from being part of the military establishment, which he became after the Second World War, he was initially opposed to the peacetime generals, who in turn distrusted him.

The classic adage is that good generals in peacetime are not good generals in war, and vice versa. Montgomery emerged entirely because of the failure of Britain's peacetime generals to adapt to war; he was a natural warrior who could shine only in war. The postwar image of Montgomery as a conventional general – assiduously cultivated by himself when he became part of the establishment – was fabricated.

Montgomery was born on 17 November 1877 in Kennington, London. He was a tough, strong-willed little boy from a large family, the fourth of nine children. His father was a clergyman, the vicar of St Mark's at Kennington Oval, who was later appointed Bishop of Tasmania, possibly the most remote and undistinguished appointment in the British empire, but one calculated to induce a sense of superiority towards the locals and inferiority in his children towards fellow Britons. Although Montgomery spent his formative years in Tasmania (from 1889 to 1901), in his autobiography he says virtually nothing about this strange, beautiful and wild land: perhaps, in spite of its exotic nature, he was so confined to the small-town respectability of being a bishop's son, he experienced little of it except colonial gentility and stuffiness. What he does admit to is an almost venomous dislike of his mother, who was obviously just as strong-willed as himself and clearly a no-nonsense and powerful figure, as the bishop's wife, in this tiny southern enclave in the middle of nowhere.

At an early age, Montgomery was sent to the prestigious St Paul's School, London, where he excelled at games but was academically backward. However, he took pride in his emergence as a tough and fierce fighter at school. He wrote:

> When I went to school in London I had learnt to play a lone hand, and to stand or fall alone. One had become self-sufficient, intolerant of authority and steeled to take punishment. By the time I left school a very important principle had just begun to penetrate my brain. That was that life is a stern struggle, and a boy has to be able to stand up to the buffeting and set-backs. There are many attributes which he must acquire if he is to succeed: two are vital, hard work and absolute integrity.

He managed to get into Sandhurst, where he soon became a lance-corporal. He was a keen sportsman, but he was also a natural thug and was soon in trouble. Hazing was commonplace amongst the cadets but Montgomery often found himself at the centre of the mêlée. On one occasion he set fire to the tail of a colleague's shirt as he was undressing. The victim was hospitalized but refused to blame his fellow cadet. Nonetheless, Montgomery was reduced to the ranks.

Having just avoided expulsion, he joined the Royal Worcestershire Regiment, which was one of the less glamorous corps, recruiting from among those, such as Bernard, without much money. At the age of 21 he arrived at Peshawar on the northwest frontier of India. There, rather like George Orwell, he took an intense dislike to the pettiness of colonial life. On arrival it was custom to visit the officers' mess of each unit within the garrison, where a whisky and soda was thrust into one's hand. Life revolved around the tedious rituals of deference to the senior officers, alcohol and dining.

While impressed by the character of the Indian soldiers, he was less impressed by his compatriots. On one notable occasion, he was interviewed by an outside examiner who specialized in transportation. At the time the battalion was wholly reliant on pack mules and carts. 'Question no. 1: How many times in each 24 hours are the bowels of a mule moved?' Montgomery got the answer wrong but impertinently asked why it was important to know such matters. It was symptomatic of wider ills within the Indian corps.

Montgomery soon realized that, amongst the officers, military matters counted for little: it was a way of life rather than a profession. The communal unit of a battalion seemed to matter more than the whole. When a battalion arrived at a new station the first question the commanding officer would ask was 'How does the general like the attack done?' and the attack was conducted accordingly. In addition, the study of war was minimal.

Returning to Britain in 1913, Montgomery discovered things were not much better at home, despite the impending mobilization for war against Germany. Rather than planning how to fight the war, Bernard was commanded to get his sword sharpened and his hair cut. When he asked whether he needed to take money with him, he was told that all would be provided for him.

Once in France, his first experience of war provided all the necessary evidence of the poor preparation. On 26 August 1914, his brigade was camped outside the village of Harcourt. A forward battalion, camped on a hill overlooking a valley, was attacked by Germans at short range while they were preparing breakfast. They rapidly retreated down the hill. Rather than preparing an organized assault, the commanding officer ordered an immediate attack on the hill position. After a rush up the incline, an inevitable retreat was called. 'If this was real war,' Montgomery later wrote, 'it struck me as most curious and did not seem to make any sense.'

His battalion was involved in close fighting on 13 October 1914, and once more Montgomery learned the lessons of poor preparation the hard way. Leading an attack on the village of Meteren, he was surprised by a trench full of Germans:

> In my training as a young officer I had received much instruction in how to kill my enemy with a bayonet fixed to a rifle. I knew all about the various movements – right parry, left parry, forward lunge. I had been taught how to put the left foot on the corpse and extract the bayonet, giving at the same time a loud grunt. Indeed, I had been considered good on the bayonet-fighting course against sacks filled with straw, and had won prizes in man-to-man contests in the gymnasium. But now I had no rifle and bayonet; I had only a sharp sword, and I was confronted by a large German who was about to shoot me. In all my short career in the Army no one had taught me how to kill a German with a sword. The only sword exercise I knew was saluting drill, learnt under the sergeant-major on the barrack square.
>
> An immediate decision was clearly visible. I hurled myself through the air at the German and kicked him as hard as I could in the lower part of the stomach; the blow was well aimed at a tender spot. I had read much about the value of surprise in war. There is no doubt that the German was surprised and it must have seemed to him a new form of war; he fell to the ground in great pain and I took my first prisoner!

Later that day Montgomery was shot in the chest, but a soldier ran to his aid, dressed his wound and himself was killed, falling on top of the young lieutenant who was only rescued several hours later. He was assumed to be dying and a grave was dug for him.

However, he recovered, and went on to become a staff officer. He returned to the front in 1916, where he had early experiences of communications difficulties between the front and rear of his brigade: a pigeon had been assigned to the job!

In addition, Montgomery also learned to despise the generals. He complained that a general was never seen on the frontline and that the higher staff were out of touch. He remembered an anecdote concerning General Douglas Haig's chief of staff, who decided to visit the Passchendaele Ridge and see the country before returning to Britain. When he saw the mud and the ghastly conditions under which the soldiers had fought and died, he was horrified and said: 'Do you mean to tell me that the soldiers had to fight under such conditions?' And when he was told that it was so, he said: 'Why was I never told about this before?'

Thus, when Montgomery joined the staff college at Camberley after the war, this rebellious figure at last turned his attention to a complete overhaul of the way war was run. He studied the major figures in military history and by 1930 he was tasked to rewrite the manual of military training. Like General Douglas MacArthur and General George S. Patton, he was seen as a visionary staff officer. His attitude towards toughening and training his men was uncompromising.

Montgomery turned 50 when the first rumblings of the Second World War began. He was far from the famous leader he was to become, but he enjoyed a reputation for hard work and dedication. He was promoted to major general and fought the Arab rebellion in north Palestine, which he hugely enjoyed, but fell ill in May 1939, and was repatriated. He then took charge of the 3rd Division, which was to be part of the British Expeditionary Force to France, just before war was declared on 3 September 1939.

He was caustic about the state of the British army at the beginning of the Second World War, and particularly about the incompetence of the War Office under Leslie Hore-Belisha – 'admirably equipped and organised to fight the 1914 war and with the wrong officers at the top'. He went on:

In September 1939 the British Army was totally unfit to fight a first class war on the continent of Europe. It had for long been considered that in the event of another war with Germany the British contribution to the defence of the West should consist mainly of the naval and air forces. How any politician could imagine that, in a world war, Britain could avoid sending her army to fight alongside the French passes all understanding.

Hore-Belisha declared grandly that 'our army is as well if not better equipped than any similar army'. This, after years of German rearmament, was plain foolery. Montgomery was also scathing about the commanders of the British Expeditionary Force, who held a regimental attitude and skills learned in the previous war.

Montgomery was further astounded at the total absence of co-operation or intelligence between the British, French and Belgian armies. In his view the Battle of France was 'lost really almost before it began'. He was even more critical of the British government: 'It must be said to our shame that we sent our Army into that most modern war with weapons and equipment which were quite inadequate, and we had only ourselves to blame for the disasters which early overtook us in the field when fighting began in 1940.'

Montgomery took part in the retreat to Dunkirk in May–June 1940, and, returning to Britain, served under Claude Auchinleck, then under Harold Alexander and Bernard Paget. At last fighting generals were replacing the peacetime generals. He became a passionate advocate for rigorous training of the raw recruits. Weak officers were to be weeded out while the young soldiers were to be prepared for any eventuality. Large-scale exercises were organized to instil a sense of urgency into the yawning British army.

Montgomery also took part in defence planning. He found himself in opposition to the accepted doctrine that every inch of the southern coast had to be defended. He thought that this only offered a thin line of defence. Instead, he created small teams of troops ready to counterattack and repel the invaders should they arrive at the beaches. Attack was the best form of defence: 'my idea of the defence was that it must be like a spider's web; wherever

Germans went they must encounter fresh troops who would first subject them to heavy fire and then attack them'.

—␣␣␣—

On 8 August 1942, Montgomery was appointed to lead the 8th Army in North Africa. He was 53, but still a man of energy, quick wit and dedication to his profession. He was also mischievous, insubordinate, irascible and intolerant – enough to impress the high command that he should lead the most important firefight then underway between British, German and Italian troops. Critical and impatient, he had always seemed a warrior, not a pen-pusher, and now he was to be given the chance of displaying his abilities – or being exposed as a hollow boaster.

Technically, the desert was not strategically important, but for struggling Britain it was enormously significant in boosting morale and impressing the United States. Also, it was a romantic and glamorous theatre, particularly because of the speed with which the forces duelled across a vast area.

In fact, the size of the desert was deceptive: the battle space was much more confined than in Europe. It was a fight along the narrow strip of coast between Alexandria, the British base, and Tripoli, the Italian base. Only one road ran along the coast, even if for a vast distance, and penetration into the desert was often suicidal, even for cars, let alone tanks, which were liable to get bogged down and certainly could not be supplied or rescued.

In 1940, General Rodolfo Graziani's Italian army had some 200,000 men at Tripoli, which could be easily resupplied from Sicily, just across the Mediterranean Sea. The British, under General Archibald Wavell, had some 63,000 troops at Alexandria. In September of that year, the Italians staged a massive offensive, covering a distance of almost 1,000 miles along the coast in three days and pushing 60 miles into Egypt, but they were hugely over-stretched. The British counterattacked and chased them to Beda Fomm, nearly halfway back to Tripoli, capturing 130,000 prisoners. The British troops then raided inland into the desert itself and tried to encircle the enemy.

However, many of Wavell's troops were sent to fight in Greece, while at the same time German General Erwin Rommel arrived with two small Panzer divisions, the Afrikakorps, to buttress the remaining 70,000 Italians. Rommel immediately took the offensive against the now over-extended British. He captured Benghazi and surrounded, but did not take, Tobruk which was being held valiantly by Australian troops. He had recouped virtually the entire Axis losses by April 1941.

Rommel's great advantage – tanks – was countered when the British were strongly reinforced with tanks from the Mediterranean, which they controlled. The war for control of the air was also fierce and the British counterattacked with Operation Battleaxe in June 1941. The air assault failed against Rommel's huge arsenal of anti-tank guns and heralded a counterattack from the Germans.

As a result, Wavell was sent off to India in July 1941 and replaced by General Claude Auchinleck – himself from India. After a pause, Auchinleck tried to relieve Tobruk in Operation Crusader in December. He found that the Germans, having been depleted of supplies, had diverted some of their forces towards the invasion of Russia, but the same would soon happen to him as the British had to send troops to the Asian theatre. Their supply lines became once again overstretched and in January 1942 Rommel launched another attack, driving them back to Gazala, not far from Tobruk. A ferocious battle ensued and, in June, Auchinleck was forced back to Alam Halfa, over the Egyptian border and near El Alamein. The Alam Halfa ridge dominated the area between the sea and the forbidding, impassable Qattara Depression. For many, Auchinleck's retreat was a stroke of brilliance, but not all saw it this way.

When Winston Churchill, the prime minister, flew to Cairo in August 1942, along with the chief of staff, Alan Brooke, it was decided to dismiss Auchinleck which, as Churchill wrote, was like 'shooting a noble stag'. He was succeeded by the hugely competent Harold Alexander, while command of the 8th Army passed to the potentially lethal Montgomery, a close friend of Alexander.

Almost immediately, Montgomery had an embarrassing confrontation with Auchinleck, who refused to countenance any alternative to his own scheme, even though his command was coming to an end: if Rommel were to attack, the 8th Army would retreat further into Egypt; and if Cairo looked beyond saving the army would retreat southwards. Montgomery could not agree, but kept his peace. Instead, he planned to take the fight to the Germans.

He went to see the deputy chief of staff, General John Harding, and told him that he wanted his own version of Rommel's Afrikakorps. This would be a mobile armoured division, cobbled together from the various tank formations around Egypt and buttressed by the expected 300 Sherman tanks from America. He appointed a chief of staff, Francis 'Freddie' de Guingand, and travelled to the headquarters of the 8th Army. He was not impressed by what he saw:

> The sight that met me was enough to lower anyone's morale. It was a desolate scene; a few trucks, no mess tents, work done mostly in trucks or in the open air in the hot sun, flies everywhere. I asked where Auchinleck used to sleep; I was told that he slept on the ground outside his caravan. Tents were forbidden in the 8th Army; everyone was to be as uncomfortable as possible, so that they wouldn't be more comfortable than the men. All officers' messes were in the open air where, of course, they attracted the flies of Egypt. In the case of the mess of senior officers which I was inheriting, a mosquito net had been erected round the table; but it didn't shade one from the sun and the flies, once inside, could not get out.

Montgomery was also frustrated by the distance between the 8th Army site and the Air Force HQ which was situated near Burg-el-Arab, miles away on the coast. It seemed to him that the army and air force were fighting two separate battles. Despite these problems, he set out the key strategy of the campaign. There was to be no retreat. Recalling the story of the Spartans at the famous Battle of Thermopylae, the 8th Army would stand its ground: 'we would fight on the ground we now held and if we couldn't stay there alive we would stay there dead'.

There was no time to lose, as Montgomery believed an attack by Rommel was imminent and that the Germans would attempt to outflank the 8th Army in the south. He therefore strengthened his divisions in the south on the Ruweisat ridge and the Alam Halfa ridge already prepared by Auchinleck. He also studied his rival. He knew that Rommel preferred the opposition to rush forward and then be broken by his anti-tank artillery. Instead, he planned to fight a static battle where Rommel would have to move forward towards his enemy. Montgomery chose El Alamein as the place where he could set out his defence. Here, he would dig the tanks into the sand and wait for the arrival of the enemy. Churchill approved his plans.

On 31 August 1942, Rommel attacked, wheeling around to the south as expected, before running up against the entrenched forces on the ridges and being bombarded from the air. His supplies soon ran dry. Montgomery had rebuffed the attack and now had to take the offensive against a powerful enemy which had inserted itself between the sea and the vast Qattara Depression to maintain momentum; he was determined to seize the initiative. By October the British had 11 divisions, five of them armoured, with just over 1,000 tanks, including the Shermans, 900 guns and 530 aircraft. The Germans, in their strong defensive position, had five divisions, including two armoured, and the Italians had six divisions, two also armoured. The Germans interspersed their own troops with the Italians, who had no enthusiasm for the war, to make them stand fast. Rommel himself had flown to Germany and only returned a day after the British offensive had begun.

Montgomery, in his thorough, merciless way, had resolved to send the enemy packing back to Tripoli, as had happened before, and to get behind the city, surround it and destroy it. Montgomery's strategy was to attack with infantry and blast two corridors through the enemy lines so that the tanks of the 10th armoured division could break through and encircle the Germans and Italians. In out-flanking the enemy infantry, he expected the German tanks to rush forwards and attack the British armoured vehicles which by now would have got through the corridor. Montgomery would then

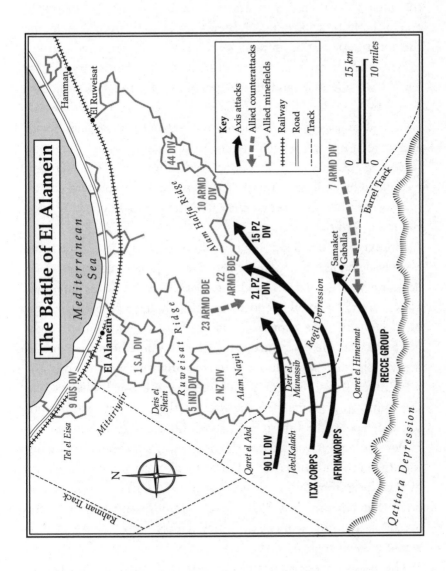

The Battle of El Alamein

Key

Axis attacks
Allied counterattacks
Allied minefields
Railway
Road
Track

Mediterranean Sea

Hamman
El Ruweisat
44 DIV
10 ARMD DIV
Alam Halfa Ridge
15 PZ DIV
22 ARMD BDE
23 ARMD BDE
21 PZ DIV
1 S.A. DIV
El Alamein
9 AUS DIV
Tel el Eisa
Miteiriya
Ruweisat Ridge
Deis el Shein
5 IND DIV
2 NZ DIV
Alam Nayil
Qaret el Abd
Jebel Kalakh
Detr el Munassib
Ragil Depression
Samaket Gaballa
7 ARMD DIV
Barrel Track
Qaret el Himeimat
RECCE GROUP
90 LT. DIV
ITXX CORPS
AFRIKAKORPS
Qattara Depression
Rahman Track

N

0   15 km
0   10 miles

entice them on to anti-tank guns, which was a classic German tactic. Montgomery's other tactic was to attack not through the south – the usual way of crossing through the desert and getting behind the enemy – but directly in a massed formation through the north. Accordingly, he set up a massive feint attack in the south, including the construction of bogus pipelines and dummy lorries and guns.

At midnight on 23 October 1942, some 450 British guns bombarded the German and Italian positions. By the following day, both the corridors had been opened. Montgomery sent in the armoured divisions: these reached the edge of the vast minefields and were also being bombarded in the air. They wanted to retreat. Furiously, Montgomery ordered them forward. The Germans responded by concentrating their forces along the northern coastal road where they now feared the main thrust would come, leaving the Italians to the south.

Montgomery decided to change the plan and not to attack the fiercely defended northern section. He withdrew his forces while deciding where to attack and this 'retreat' alarmed his superiors. However, he had merely bought time in which to prepare the final offensive, which he named 'Operation Supercharge', for the night of 31 October. He postponed this slightly because of 'stage management problems'. While furious but static fighting continued in the north, four British armoured divisions broke through massively in the south on 2 November: the Italians there, bereft of transport, surrendered. As the British raced to cut off the retreat, Rommel, on Hitler's orders, retreated along the northern road at full speed. Thus Montgomery had shown the skill to break with traditional tactics by attacking from the north, instead of the south as expected, and once that advance was blocked to improvise and switch to the south – a lightning manoeuvre which a more conventional general would have missed.

The main operation would have three distinct phases, two of which had already been successfully completed. The first was the battle for position. This was followed by 'the dog-fight... a hard and bloody killing match'. Only then could Montgomery contemplate the third phase, 'the break-out'. This final phase would be complicated and involve deception and courage. Rommel would expect such a manoeuvre but could not predict where it would come from. It was a huge success.

Thus there ensued a chase down the coastline as the British pursued Rommel's retreating army. The 630 miles from El Alamein to Tobruk were covered in a week, with a further 560 miles more in the next five days – in spite of heavy rains bogging down the 8th Army on two occasions. Montgomery himself was nearly captured by a German rearguard at Mersa Matruh. The chase continued past Benghazi to Rommel's old standfast point at El Agheila. Here, Montgomery was determined to prevent a stand between the sea and soft sand and salt flats that were impassable to the south; he sent forward the New Zealand brigades who brilliantly fought their way forward around the German positions. With the British 7th Armoured Division advancing, the Germans retreated into the New Zealanders. The battle was almost won: some 60,000 Axis troops had been killed or captured, leaving only 40,000 and some 80 tanks.

Montgomery's forces then pressed on to Tripoli, which they reached on 23 January 1943. In front of this was a formidable defensive position, the Mareth Line, originally built by the French, between the sea and the bottom of the Mahatma hills, to the west of which was the legendary and impassable 'sand sea'. Montgomery's long-range desert group found a way through these soft and shifting sands. He sent 27,000 New Zealanders and 200 tanks through this route, while his main force attacked on the seaward side; the Germans were also under constant air bombardment. The enemy was outflanked and outfought from in front, and collapsed.

In all nearly 300,000 were taken prisoner in a massive encirclement, one of the greatest of the Second World War. Montgomery provided the epitaph on the 8th Army 'brotherhood':

> We were a 'brotherhood in arms'. We did what we liked. What mattered was success, with only a minimum of casualties. I was the head of the brotherhood. I was pretty tough about mistakes and especially mistakes which cost lives; I would allow no departure from the

fundamentals of the master plan. But I let subordinate commanders do as they liked about details and didn't fuss about the wrong things. Until we had burst through the Gabes gap and emerged into the plain of Tunisia, it was a private war run by the 8th Army; we made our own plans and adjusted the time factor to suit the problems. Alexander let me run this private war in my own way and supported me to the hilt; we gave him success all along the road and he was content to leave well alone.

—◦◦◦—

Montgomery's next campaign was in Sicily, in rivalry with the American General George Patton, in 1943. His 8th Army was still unconventional; as he wrote: 'The men in back areas discarded all possible clothing and some even took to wearing the wide-brim Sicilian straw hat. I was not particular about dress so long as the soldier fought well and we won our battles.'

Montgomery's role in the mainland Italian campaign, however, was limited: assigned with the 8th Army to land and capture the toe of Italy from Sicily, he did so successfully; but he was at a loss to understand his army's purpose, as the American 5th Army, under General Mark Clark, had simultaneously landed at Salerno, much further to the north.

On 14 September, Clark asked for help as his forces were under intense attack. Montgomery veered his army northwards, marching nearly 300 miles in 17 days, through appalling mountains and easily defensible country while the enemy blew the bridges in their path. However, Clark had the problem in hand when Montgomery's forces arrived. Next, he was ordered southeast across the Apennines to the ports of Taranto, Brindisi and Bari, and then northwards up the Adriatic coast to Foggia and Tremoli in appalling rains and winter weather. Montgomery was rightly perplexed at the strategic purpose in this.

On Christmas Eve 1943, he was ordered back to Britain to take charge of preparing the British armies for the invasion of France. He threw himself into his new command with his customary workaholic zest. At the same time he assiduously toured the country, explaining the plan to officers and ordinary soldiers, and even had his own personal train, called 'Rapier', for the task. He toured England, Wales and Scotland, visiting every formation which was to take part in Operation Overlord on 6 June 1944.

Montgomery, under US General Dwight Eisenhower's overall command, was then made commander of the invasion forces which were made up of the British 2nd Army under General Miles Dempsey and the US 1st Army under General Omar Bradley. They were later joined by the 1st Canadian Army and 3rd American Army under Patton. Montgomery's plan was to threaten the enemy on the eastern flank, near Caen, to ease the pressure of enemy troops on the western flank. He launched four separate attacks on the town; all were repulsed. By 26 June 1944, meanwhile, some 25 Allied divisions were in France, and another 15 were on the way from Britain, facing 14 German divisions, and eight out of Germany's total of 12 Panzer divisions.

On 7 July, 2,500 bombs were dropped on Caen, but the British still failed to secure it. On 18 July, British armoured divisions attacked in force and nearly 200 Allied tanks were destroyed. After the euphoria of the first couple of days, it seemed that Operation Overlord had bogged down; the British at Caen were facing a huge concentration of enemy armies, while the Americans to the west were blocked by difficult terrain and overgrown stone walls known as 'bocages'. By the end of 18 July, some 100,000 British and American soldiers had been killed or wounded. Opposite the Americans, who had lost two-thirds, there were 190 tanks and 92 infantry battalions.

On 25 July, Operation Cobra, the breakout, was launched, with spectacular results in Patton's sector; to the northeast the Germans counterattacked on 7 August with eight divisions and 1,400 tanks. There followed the massive battle of the Falaise Gap between 10 Allied and 10 German armoured divisions. This gave the Allies their opportunity. As the Americans swung around to the south, and the Canadians to the north, they encircled the advancing German forces. The Germans lost 50,000 and 200,000 were captured; yet some 30,000 men and 25,000 vehicles escaped, largely through Allied delays in closing the gap.

Hitler grimly and sensibly hung on to the Channel ports that were essential to providing supplies for the Allied armies as they moved towards Germany; stupidly, the Allies did nothing to secure them. On 25 August, Paris fell. Montgomery proposed that all 40 of the Allied divisions should be concentrated in a massive hammer-blow northwards between Paris and the sea, aiming straight for the huge German industrial complex of the Ruhr. He reasoned that with the Ruhr taken, Germany would fall quickly. However, Montgomery had been bitterly criticized for failing to use the forces at his disposal to occupy the Channel ports and the Scheldt estuary to ease the Allies' colossal supply problems. Eisenhower took the opportunity to reject Montgomery's northern thrust in favour of Bradley's 'broad front' strategy of attacking Germany along the length of its border. In Montgomery's view this would fatally dis-perse Allied troops for the purely political reason of giving the American commanders (Bradley himself and, in particular, Patton) victories they could call their own as they advanced further south.

Montgomery had a tense meeting with Eisenhower on 10 September aboard the latter's aircraft, where he laid his cards on the table: 'There are two possible plans – Bradley's and mine. It is essen-tial to back one of them.' Eisenhower only half-heartedly approved Montgomery's plan for the thrust towards the Ruhr, called Operation Market Garden, as part of the wider offensive along the whole German border. The result was the worst disaster in Montgomery's career. Operation Market Garden consisted of two operations: the seizure of the bridges at Eindhoven and Nijmegen across the Meuse; and the capture of the bridges at Arnhem across the Rhine. It was to be accomplished by the hitherto redundant airborne divisions – the American 82nd and 101st would take the Meuse bridges while the British 1st Airborne attacked the Rhine bridges.

The first part went smoothly as the Meuse bridges were only lightly defended. The second, by the 1st Airborne commanded by General Roy Urquhart, also set off promisingly, with a landing sev-eral miles away from the objective so that the defenders were taken by surprise. 'Our arrival,' said Urquhart, a lion of a man, 'was deceptively peaceful, in fields near woods, as 300 gliders were unloaded with equipment, while the 1st Parachute Brigade landed nearby.' Urquhart, an extraordinarily brave, competent but headstrong soldier, immediately decided to set off towards the bridges. He did not know that nearby the 9th and 10th Panzer divisions were recuperating after the battles of Normandy, with much more firepower than his own lightly armed forces. Field-Marshal Walter Model, Hitler's trusted 'fireman', had got wind of the landings and was soon ordering his forces into action as well as summoning up reinforcements. Urquhart, meanwhile, drove straight into the German frontline.

The British were unsupported and overextended: the relief force was 30 hours behind schedule, encountering huge resistance along the way and being pounded by German fighters. Meanwhile, Major-General John Frost's forces had seized the north end of Arnhem bridge and fought heroically for three days and three nights, as Urquhart's brigades fought in the narrow streets of the town and the nearby woods to keep the encroaching Germans at bay. Urquhart transmitted the message back to headquarters: 'No knowledge elements of Div in Arnhem for 24 hours. Balance of Div in very tight perimeter. Heavy mortaring and machine gun fire followed by local attacks. Main nuisance SP guns. Our casualties heavy. Resources stretched to utmost. Relief within 24 hours vital.'

No fewer than 35 planes had been shot down trying to bring in supplies. Finally, Urquhart decided on 23 September to withdraw and reached the other side of the river after a terrible evacuation under fire on the night of 25 September. He was bitter, all the more so at the lavish and inappropriate dinner offered by his commander, General Brian Horrocks. Just 2,400 of the original 10,000 troops dropped to seize the Arnhem bridges survived, while German casualties were around 6,000–8,000. Montgomery took responsibility:

> The airborne forces at Arnhem were dropped too far away from the vital objective – the bridge. It was some hours before they reached it. I take the blame for this mistake. I should have ordered Second Army and 1 Airborne Corps to arrange that at least one complete

Parachute Brigade was dropped quite close to the bridge, so that it
could have been captured in a matter of minutes and its defence
soundly organised with time to spare. I did not do so...

The 2nd S.S. Panzer Corps was refitting in the Arnhem area, having limped up there after its mauling in Normandy. We knew it was
there. But we were wrong in supposing that it could not fight effectively; its battle state was far beyond our expectation. It was quickly
brought into action against the 1st Airborne Division.

As after Normandy, so again after Arnhem, I was bitterly disappointed. It was my second attempt to try to capture the Ruhr quickly.
Bill Williams used to tell me that the Germans could not carry on the
war for more than about three months after they lost the Ruhr. But
we still hadn't got it.

And here I must admit a bad mistake on my part – I underestimated the difficulties of opening up the approaches to Antwerp so
that we could get the free use of that port. I reckoned that the
Canadian Army could do it *while* we were going for the Ruhr. I was
wrong.

Montgomery himself rightly laid some part of the blame on
Eisenhower: he believed that if Operation Market Garden had succeeded, the war in Europe would have been over by the winter of
1944, and he may well have been right. It is hard not to conclude
that the mistake was an overall strategic one, not a tactical one,
and that both Eisenhower and Montgomery were deeply at fault.
Eisenhower showed little enthusiasm for the Operation and had
dispersed his troops along the front, thus denying Montgomery the
overwhelming resources needed to make a success of Arnhem and
the breakthrough to the Ruhr. Montgomery should not have
pressed ahead without the resources that he needed, which he must
have known would have made it a gamble.

It was surely over-ambitious to seek to take both sets of bridges –
across the Meuse and the Rhine – in one thrust. If the first forces
were delayed – and they were after taking the Meuse bridges – the
second would inevitably fail without reinforcements. It was not
Montgomery's finest hour, combining impatience and, perhaps,

wounded vanity. Montgomery's daring as a commander cannot be faulted and was in keeping with the other mavericks. This was a bold roll of the dice, but he failed disastrously – the ultimate test of command – because he did not ensure the gamble was adequately backed up.

His verbal battles with Eisenhower continued unabated – and in this he was surely right. For just as Montgomery can be blamed for seeking a British success in the north, Eisenhower – in an American election year – was bent on delivering an untarnished American success further south. At a conference in Maastricht, on 7 December 1944, the atmosphere was sour.

Montgomery continued to press his convictions that the Ruhr had to be taken. In addition, he suggested that the Allies force a mobile war upon the Germans. As their stock of tanks and transport was declining, and the availability of oil depleted, a fast mobile campaign would find the enemy lacking. This strategy would also indicate a campaign to the north, rather than the south where it would be easier for the Germans to establish defensible positions.

The Battle of the Bulge was the result, which is largely told in Chapter 11. Montgomery performed skilfully and imaginatively in commanding the northern sector around the German attack and by 16 January 1945 the battle was over. But the fight with Eisenhower was not: one letter he wrote ended, 'very upset that my letter may have upset you and I would ask you to tear it up. Your very devoted subordinate Montgomery.'

Gradually, Montgomery convinced Eisenhower that the main thrust into Germany should be in the north – even though the latter would not abort Patton's southwards thrust and the broad front strategy along the Rhine. Moreover, the route north had required huge supplies of ammunition and food.

The next offensive in Montgomery's sector was Operation Nij Veritable, which went east of Nijmegen and into the Reichswald Forest at the beginning of February 1945, in the area just south of Arnhem. Soon the entire west bank of the Rhine was in Allied hands. There were now 85 divisions and 4 million men fighting just

26 German divisions as Operation Plunder was being prepared with a general crossing of the Rhine on 23 March 1945.

However, before that the US 9th Armoured Division had found an unguarded railway bridge at Remagen below Cologne, and Patton took another near Oppenheim, still further south. The result was a gradual great encirclement by the US 1st Army – Patton's 3rd was despatched in southern Germany right around the Rhineland largely, before Montgomery could cross the Rhine.

Montgomery then urged Eisenhower to make for Berlin at speed; but he ordered his forces to stop at the Elbe River, in accordance with the agreement at Yalta to allow the Russians to take Berlin; Patton was similarly stopped at Pilsen before getting to Prague.

Montgomery, dispirited, led his forces northwards towards the Baltic, arriving on 2 May at Weimar and Lubeck, and saving Denmark from Russian occupation with only six hours to spare. At Lüneburg Heath the previous day, Montgomery had learned that Hitler was dead and had been succeeded by Admiral Karl Dönitz. On 3 May, a German delegation headed by Admiral Hans-Georg von Friedeburg, commander of the German navy, arrived to discuss surrender with Montgomery, provided that he would protect them from the Russians, which he refused to do in the already agreed Soviet sector.

The following day the Germans returned to sign with the full authority from Dönitz and Wilhelm Keitel, the German army commander. The surrender was signed with Montgomery at 6.30 p.m. in a tent. Friedeburg poisoned himself soon afterwards.

But the problems were hardly over. Montgomery was now in charge of a large swathe of northern Germany and administered it with his usual rigorous efficiency. There were over 1.5 million German prisoners of war and 1 million wounded to care for despite the scarcity of even the most basic medical provisions. One million refugees had flooded his section in terror from the Russians. Transportation and administration had all been destroyed and there were fears of famine and widespread disease. 'Here was a pretty pickle!' he exclaimed.

In addition, Montgomery was injured when his aeroplane crash-landed in August, and remained ill most of the following winter. After nearly a year of acting as proconsul he was appointed chief of the imperial general staff in June, where he presided with his usual brisk efficiency, but he proved overly tetchy, refusing to sit in the same room as his old enemy, RAF chief Lord Arthur Tedder.

Nonetheless, he was showered with honours, becoming Viscount Montgomery of Alamein in 1946. He also became chairman of the Western Union's commanders-in-chief committee in 1948, with the aim of coordinating a European response to the Soviet threat, but quarrelled with the French commander, Marshall Jean de Lattre de Tassigny, and, at his political masters' bidding, refused to commit British troops to a common defence. Instead, he played a formative role, with his old sparring partner Eisenhower, in setting up NATO in 1951, which was dominated by the United States and provided the pillar of western European security against the Soviet Union for 40 years.

He retired in 1958 and died at the ripe old age of 88 in 1976. He was given a state funeral at St George's Chapel, Windsor.

———

Peppery, contrary, prickly, always self-justifying, dismissive of lesser mortals and offhand, almost casual, in manner, Montgomery's character might not seem the stuff of heroes. But he was a remarkable general: he was instinctively courageous; he was a cool commander with a brilliant and quick grasp of the battlefield; he seized opportunities and would always go for the jugular; and he was quick to change tactics and manoeuvres, as at El Alamein, resulting in a superb victory. He had stamina and made his way from middle-class origins to the top entirely on merit. He had no hesitation in taking on superior odds – although he preferred to even them or overwhelm the enemy if he could.

He was good with his subordinates and a devotee of training and morale for his men – although he was little fussed about spit-and-polish. He was a master of command, control and meticulous preparation, and showed the highly direct intelligence, in getting straight to the point, of the very best commanders.

Above all, he was deeply insubordinate throughout his life, always questioning his superiors and contemporaries, dismissing the abilities of men like Auchinleck and quarrelling bitterly with Eisenhower and Patton; and he was no respecter of traditional tactics. His ascent through the army was perhaps less of a roller-coaster than those of the other mavericks, and charismatic leader-ship and communication skills were almost entirely absent, except in his beret, badges and bomber jacket. In spite of this, the image of this snappy little terrier – Monty – became the most enduring of any British commander in the war.

Montgomery's victory at El Alamein was a superb one, whether or not built on Auchinleck's defensive foundations, and showed a masterful ability to change plans entirely halfway through the bat-tle on an enormous scale – something no lesser general would have been capable of. In northern France in 1944 he was blemished hugely by the failure at Arnhem. His concept of advancing towards the Ruhr was absolutely right and would have shortened the war by at least six months; subsequently, he commanded faultlessly on the northern flank of the Battle of the Bulge and secured the defeat of German forces further north. His grit and determination were what was required in a British military machine previously overstuffed with staff generals. He was one of the last warriors, a wild one, a true maverick.

Chapter 11

PATTON: THE BULLDOZER

At first glance, General George Smith Patton seems more of a martinet than a maverick. For much of his life he was an obscure provincial general and not a world-shaker at all. He was certainly the most charmless of the men described in this book. He was ingratiating towards his superiors and brutal towards his subordinates – the classic attributes of the bully. He has been acclaimed as a role model for all that is least attractive about the American leadership style: self-promoting, an advocate of victory at all costs, and a despiser of cowards and losers. He was also a humourless, foulmouthed racist – even in the US press he was compared to Hitler.

He has been the model for a host of Hollywood characters, including his own biopic, *Patton*, starring George C. Scott, as well as the brutal but effective training sergeant in *The Dirty Dozen*, starring Lee Marvin; and he was satirized mercilessly in Joseph Heller's *Catch 22*. Yet as an American Second World War hero, he is regarded, particularly in military circles, as second only to Douglas MacArthur. How does he qualify as a man who changed the course of history, a maverick, a military genius?

The answer lies in his extraordinary achievement in the Battle of France in 1944, when from this unpromising background there sprang a fully-fledged warrior of speed and decision, the only effective western practitioner of German *blitzkrieg* tactics, a master of manoeuvre and accomplishment who achieved with his tanks what his hero Napoleon accomplished with men and horses.

Patton's early career mirrored, with a somewhat eerie precision, that of his contemporary MacArthur. His pedigree, in American terms, was in fact slightly grander: he was descended from an early settler, Robert Patton, who arrived in Fredericksburg, Virginia in 1771. Patton's grandfather, George, served in the American Civil War at Shenandoah and was killed at Winchester, while his brother was killed at Gettysburg. George's father, also called George, had a military upbringing but became a lawyer, and then took over the huge estate brought into the family by his wife, Ruth. She was the daughter of a successful businessman who led a somewhat colourful life, marrying a Mexican woman and becoming known as Don Benito before becoming the first mayor of Los Angeles, with huge vineyards in California.

Patton was born on 11 November 1885 in California. As a boy he was from the first unashamedly martial in his interests, a fine horseman, an outdoor type, and a slow learner suffering, it was later discovered, from dyslexia. He spent a year at Virginia Military Academy, which both his father and grandfather had attended, and then in 1904, with assiduous pulling of strings, obtained entry to West Point, where he suffered the inevitable initiation rites and ill-treatment of 'plebes' – freshmen. He found his classmates depressingly low-born, 'not gentlemen... they are just very respectable middle class fellows', whom he considered languid and lazy.

Unlike MacArthur, Patton was a mediocre student, obtaining 71st place in English (although criticizing his fellow cadets for not using good grammar) and, surprisingly, just 30th place in drill out of 152. He was also unpopular as acting first corporal in summer camp, bossing his fellow cadets; he was demoted to sixth corporal. His nickname was 'Quill' – meaning someone who reports his classmates to higher authority. Although he was an excellent fencer and horseman, he graduated a mediocre 46th out of 103 in June 1909.

He joined the cavalry, a suitably elite military calling. Posted to dreary Fort Sheridan, north of Chicago, Patton immediately sought to ingratiate himself with its commanding officer, Captain Francis Marshall, whom he rated a 'gentleman' in contrast to other officers. To his subordinates, Patton was harsh and demanding. While at this dull post, he decided that 'for so fierce a warrior, I have a damned mild expression', and began to practise a stern, furious look in front of the mirror which was to survive as the image of Patton in later life.

By cultivating his superiors, Patton secured a transfer to the influential Fort Myer, outside Washington, DC, which was staffed by gentleman officers who played polo. Patton soon ingratiated himself with the Secretary of War, Henry Stimson. His superb horsemanship won him a place in the Olympic Games in Stockholm, in 1912, securing fifth place in the Pentathlon.

At last active service beckoned: Mexican rebels under Pancho Villa crossed into New Mexico, at first slaughtering some 17 Americans and then 24 more at Columbus, including 14 US soldiers. Patton volunteered to act as personal aide to John 'Black Jack' Pershing, who had been ordered to command a 'punitive expedition' into Mexico. This consisted of 15,000 men – two cavalry brigades and a brigade of infantry, as well as half a dozen already obsolescent early aircraft called the Curtiss JN-215, or 'Jennies'. For a year his force wandered about the Sierra Madre mountains trying to find Villa, without engaging.

In April 1917, Patton and a party of 14 in three vintage cars set out to find Villa's right-hand man, 'General' Julio Cardenas. They found his uncle whom they tortured nearly to death, but failed to find out anything. On a second visit to the house where Cardenas was believed to be, Patton vividly recorded killing a man who was trying to escape. Another man tried to flee but was cut down by gunfire. To approach the house, Patton seized the herdsmen as human shields – not a heroic act – but found only cowering women and a body. Cardenas himself was dead along with two of his men. The bodies were loaded as trophies on to the bonnets of the three cars and driven to Pershing's headquarters.

At the late age of 31, Patton had seen his first action, albeit one which had involved torture, using innocent people as human shields and overwhelming firepower. It was far from being a glorious encounter, but he became a momentary celebrity to bored journalists who had reported the non-story of the Mexican war so far.

Soon he was back at humdrum duties: 'I did absolutely nothing but take a bath,' he wrote in one diary entry, while in another observing that it was windy and rainy. To be fair, it was hardly his fault that the nation was not at war. His only achievement was a cosy one of married life with a dutiful wife, Beatrice, who, however, was later to resent his overbearingly intolerant nature. One suspects she must have been a saint, putting up with quite a lot. She certainly bankrolled him.

—◦◦◦—

Patton got his first big break when America entered the First World War. Pershing was appointed by President Woodrow Wilson to a mighty command: a 2 million-strong expeditionary force to Europe. Patton was chosen to accompany his old patron aboard his ship, the *Baltic*. In London, he was accommodated in the Tower of London before travelling to Paris, where he did dull staff work. In September 1917, Pershing moved his headquarters close to the front at Chamonix, appointing Patton post-adjutant in charge of headquarters, but he was struck down with jaundice.

In hospital he remained determined to go to the front, and had to choose whether to become an infantry major, or a major in the completely new medium of tank warfare. Patton chose the latter, arguing that tanks were similar to cavalry. Tanks, although largely untried, had the advantage of keeping him from serving in the grubby trenches, attracted a lower level of casualties, and would get plenty of press publicity. At the Battle of Cambrai in late 1917, some 500 British heavy tanks and infantry had advanced seven miles in four hours – a rate unheard of in the trench-war stalemate.

Patton's new command was to be 144 French light tanks, which he preferred to the heavy ones as they were more mobile. He treated his crews to his usual exacting standards of discipline, mitigated by the care he took to see that they had good food and accommodation. Patton's orders were stark and brutal:

No tank is to be surrendered or abandoned to the enemy. If you are left alone in the midst of the enemy keep shooting. If your gun is disabled use your pistols and squash the enemy with your tracks. By quick changes of direction cut them with the tail of the tank. If your motor is stalled and your gun broken... You hang on, help will come... You are the first American tanks [in combat]. You must establish the fact that American tanks do not surrender... As long as one tank is able to move it must go forward. Its presence will save the lives of hundreds of infantry and kill many Germans.

At 5 a.m. on 12 September 1918, a huge Allied offensive got under way at Saint-Mihiel, consisting of 160,000 troops of which Patton's force was a small but key part. He soon left his observation post and, showing the extraordinary personal bravery and involvement in battle that were to become a trademark, walked forward to help encourage his men as they tried to pull tanks out of a bog. A little further on, in the smoke and rumble of battle, he encountered the young and glamorous General Douglas MacArthur on a hill wearing his customary scrambled-eggs cap and long scarf, and carrying a cane. MacArthur, several years Patton's senior, had graduated at the top of West Point, and the hitherto undistinguished Patton must have gazed on him with a mixture of admiration and envy. They talked without listening to one another under the shellfire, each silently daring the other to seek shelter first, which neither did, in an almost childish game of chicken.

Patton soon walked forward, ahead of his tanks, to the village of Essey, but he was forced back from the next village, Pannes, because the infantry refused to follow and only one tank still had petrol. Soon, thanks to Patton's efforts, fuel was brought up and the tanks continued to advance in this sector, with the infantry just behind. With an attrition rate of two tanks destroyed, five broken down, 40 bogged down and 30 out of petrol, 100 tanks moved forward the following day and encircled 150,000 Germans who, admittedly, were not putting up much resistance.

Patton eagerly took part in the next offensive on 25 September, himself helping to dig tanks out of the mud under intense shellfire. Ascending a hill he came under machine-gun fire, where he experienced a near-mystical experience, as he admitted wanting to run:

he seemed to see 'my progenitors... in a cloud over the German lines looking at me'. He exclaimed aloud, 'It is time for another Patton to die.' The men around him were cut down; he was shot in the thigh. Bleeding profusely, he believed he was near death, but was bandaged by his orderly and lay for an hour while tanks dispelled the machine-gunners. He was in hospital for a month, where he was promoted to colonel. The armistice was announced before he could see further action.

———∞———

Patton returned to serve on temporary duty in Washington, DC with the peacetime rank of major, where he began to write talented papers about the virtues of tank warfare. He was one of the earliest to understand their importance. His great insight was that tanks should not any longer act in support of infantry, which would merely delay them: they should go on ahead and cut enemy lines, breaking a hole through which the infantry could pour. He also wrote a manual for tank operations and supported the Christie M1919 prototype, which could cross a seven-foot wide trench, climb earthworks and travel at speeds of up to 60 miles an hour. He also played polo and bought a new car.

In 1925 he was sent to the idyllic posting of Hawaii where, however, his reputation for strictness and discipline in that sleepy backwater earned him demotion. After attending the prestigious Army War College, he joined the 3rd Cavalry back at Fort Myer. There, he stood at the head of a cavalry unit ordered to disperse the Bonus Marchers of penniless ex-servicemen in Washington: under the orders of the army chief of staff, MacArthur, Patton on his white horse whacked veterans on their bottoms. He then carried on to their camp on the Anacostia River, where they were dispersed and their tents set on fire.

Patton was again sent to Hawaii, but turning 50, with no war in sight, plunged into a mid-life crisis and began to have romantic flings, including an incestuous one with his niece, the 21-year-old Jean Gordon. He quarrelled furiously with his long-suffering wife, Beatrice, whose considerable wealth underpinned his social pretensions.

Soon, however, war was raging in Europe. In the spring of 1940, Patton met the commander of US armour, Adna Chaffee, and other officers in the basement of a high school. They formulated a project to set up a new 'armoured force'. Patton was appointed to command a brigade and was made brigadier general and then commanding general of the entire 2nd Armoured Division. On 14 April 1941, Major-General Chaffee, who had cancer, retired and Patton became the leader of the corps. He seized his moment.

In February 1942, after the United States had entered the Second World War, Patton, who was eager for active command, was appointed to command a desert-training centre for tank warfare, to his disappointment. A site known as Little Libya was chosen 200 miles east of Los Angeles. The men were made to live in tents, run a mile in 10 minutes, and march eight miles in two hours every day, in the intense heat, which appealed to Patton's stern disciplinarianism, and maybe a latent sadism, on the grounds that the tougher the men, the more likely they were to survive the war. Some 60,000 men passed through 'Camp Indio' in just four months, establishing Patton as the greatest trainer the American army had ever had.

In July 1942 he was at last appointed to combat duty: to command part of the task force in the three-pronged invasion of North African territory held by Italian, Vichy French and German forces. Flying to London, he found Dwight Eisenhower, the invasion's overall commander, gloomy: 'not as rugged mentally as I thought; he vacillates and he is not a realist'. He also considered Eisenhower too pro-British – 'I am not, repeat not, pro-British' said Patton. He agreed with Eisenhower that 'we both feel that the operation is bad and mostly political' – designed to assuage the immense pressure for an attack on France, which Winston Churchill and the British high command believed would take much longer to prepare. Patton's sector was to be in the west: the invasion of North Africa from the Atlantic into Morocco, and to take Casablanca. The central and eastern task force, launched from Britain, would head to Oran and Algiers.

On 8 November 1942, after several days' bad weather, a landing was staged by Patton's 24,000 men and 10 ships. Meanwhile,

Algiers was captured after a day and Oran after two days of stiff fighting. Patton landed some time after his troops, as his own landing craft had been destroyed in an accident, and he angrily kicked and pulled his troops out of the beachhead foxholes they were digging, which he labelled 'graves', exhorting them to advance: he behaved more like a sergeant-major than a general, but perhaps there was something to be said for that.

After three days of fighting the Vichy commander surrendered Casablanca, and Patton conceded a generous armistice. However, he remained in Casablanca, hundreds of miles from the main action, organizing an American base and hosting the historic Casablanca conference of January 1943. In March, however, he received the call from Eisenhower: an American army, the US 2nd Corps, had been badly mauled by Rommel's Afrikakorps, with losses of 6,700 killed, wounded or taken prisoner, as well as 200 tanks destroyed. Patton was appointed the 2nd Corps' new commander to restore it to effectiveness.

Soon he was on the offensive, taking the villages of Gafsa and Gabes. Some 30 enemy tanks were also destroyed at El Guettar. However, the Americans were blocked at Maknassy Pass. Patton's British commander, General Harold Alexander, ordered him to pursue retreating Germans, but this too stalled, with Patton complaining bitterly of lack of sufficient air cover.

However, Patton had proved himself and was appointed joint commander for the Allied invasion of Sicily, the other being General Bernard Montgomery of Britain, an almost equally cussed personality. In Sicily, at last, he would be in the vanguard of the major Allied offensive against the Germans.

—⁓—

The strategic and tactical arguments about the Sicily invasion had raged for months: while the British were firmly in favour of striking at Italy, the 'soft underbelly' of the Axis, the Americans preferred an immediate invasion of France from Britain. The British argued this would take months to prepare and the time was not yet right.

The British believed that Mussolini was a ripe fruit, about to drop, while others argued that the presence of huge numbers of German troops across this rocky, easily defensible peninsula made the scheme dangerous and of little strategic value (such value as there was lay in opening up a second front in Europe, diverting German resources from Russia and, when it came, from the invasion of France).

As it turned out, the British were right to think that Mussolini could easily fall. However, there was also a bitter dispute about the shape of the intended invasion. The eighth plan – no less – put forward by headquarters in London was for the main landing to be made just south of the port of Siracusa, on the southeastern side of the triangular island, extending around the Pachino peninsula, westwards towards Gela, where the main airfields were located.

The American 3rd Army was to land at Trapani on the far west of the peninsula, and march to the capital of Palermo: the Allied forces were to converge in a massive pincer on Messina, where German forces were concentrated. The whole island would then have been conquered. Montgomery considered this madness. He wanted his forces to be concentrated just south of Siracusa, which would allow them to take the port and ensure supply. In the end, he carried the day. Patton, who was not consulted and had vigorously approved the original plan, was dismayed. He wrote nervously in his diary: 'The US is getting gypped. The thing I must do is retain my self-confidence. I have greater ability than these other people and it comes from, for lack of a better word, what we must call greatness of soul based on a belief – an unshakeable belief – in my destiny. The US must win – not as an ally, but as a conqueror.' He rushed off to issue one of his characteristically bombastic calls to arms, which probably attracted as much ridicule as admiration, ending: 'in case of doubt, attack!'

On 10 January 1943, the invasion got under way. As Montgomery predicted, German resistance proved exceedingly tough: the airborne landing was a disaster, with pilots dropping into the sea and several aircraft being shot down. The British airborne paratroop operation to seize Primasole Bridge south of Mount Etna went badly wrong, when Germany's 1st Paratroop Division counterattacked.

However, the seaborne landing went perfectly. Many Italians welcomed the invaders, treating them as liberators. Patton's men landed among high surf. He strode ashore in his carefully pressed clothes, tie and polished riding boots, with his pearl-handled pistol strapped to his side, as shells exploded in the water around him. He walked among his men ashore, yelling 'Kill every one of the goddam bastards', while under air attack as well as artillery bombardment.

There followed one of the most controversial incidents in a controversial career. Montgomery's priority was to push up the eastern coast towards Messina in order to cut off the possibility of German retreat from the island. To this purpose, he had assigned Patton to take the road west that encircles the enormous bulk of Mount Etna, while he took the coastal road to launch a joint assault on the strongest point just opposite the toe of Italy. However, he was blocked by fierce resistance outside Augusta, up the coast from Siracusa, which he finally took before encountering even stiffer resistance from German troops. At that point Montgomery decided to split his army in two, one continuing to fight along the obstructed coastal road, and another along the inland road west of Etna, which had been assigned to Patton's US forces. He ordered Patton to support his rear along the embattled coastal road, an order confirmed by Alexander as commander-in-chief for North Africa.

Patton, eager for glory and furious at being asked to play second fiddle, in particular to the hated British, decided to strike out on his own. Disingenuously, he asked Alexander for permission to send part of his force to take Agrigento, a town of no strategic importance whatever to the west along the south coast of the island, away from the fighting. Alexander agreed and Lucian Truscott, Patton's most trusted commander, was despatched to do the job while Patton quietly ordered Omar Bradley, commanding 2nd Corps, to prepare for a thrust northwards towards the Sicilian capital of

Palermo. Flying to North Africa and back, Patton claimed to have secured Alexander's agreement to strike at Palermo, although Alexander insisted that this was no more than an agreement, in principle, eventually to take Palermo.

On his return on 18 July 1943, Patton immediately ordered Bradley forward on to seize Palermo on the northern coast, again an objective of no strategic value but of great symbolic importance. In a remarkable display of the value of Patton's spartan training, the 3rd Division under Truscott managed to move at five miles an hour – the 'Truscott trot' – along the largely unguarded mountain road to Palermo. They covered 100 miles in just three days. The city, largely unguarded and taken by surprise, quickly surrendered. Rather late in the day Alexander clarified his orders on 19 July, insisting that Patton delay his planned attack on Palermo and support Montgomery's embattled force on the coastal road to Messina. Patton's chief of staff, Hobart Gay, knowing his master's wishes, withheld the order until Palermo had fallen, saying it had been garbled in transmission.

Montgomery later complained, with characteristic British understatement, although it must have galled him furiously: 'The US army, once on shore, was allowed to wheel west towards Palermo. It thereby missed the opportunity to direct its main thrustline northwards in order to cut the island in two as a preliminary to the encirclement of the Etna position and the capture of Messina.' Montgomery clearly felt that, had Patton been supporting him, they would have broken through and cut off the German and Italian armies retreating into Messina, if not actually capturing the strategic city. But Patton was more interested in his image as conqueror of Palermo and thereby, by implication, of Sicily. He rushed down to Agrigento to boast to American journalists of his triumph in capturing 44,000 and killing or wounding 6,000 Italians.

He also proposed moving along the northern coast and inland towards Messina – something he viewed as 'a horse race' with the hated Montgomery and the British, whom he regarded as the real enemy: 'The prestige of the US Army is at stake. We must take Messina before the British. Please use your best efforts to facilitate the success of our race.' However, he encountered the same ferocity of German resistance as Montgomery had on the eastern coast of the island.

Frustrated, he sought to stage landings further along the coast, but had only limited numbers of landing craft. His subordinates, Bradley and Truscott, both objected that such landings would expose the men unnecessarily, while the land forces were too far away to help the men on the beaches. The landing was costly in terms of US casualties, and cut off a few German troops, but at least it was not repulsed.

To his delight, however, a limited American force under Truscott got to Messina a few hours before Montgomery's army, through far fiercer resistance. 'What in hell are you standing around for?' Patton asked the war correspondents and photographers he had speedily brought in. In fact, the real victory belonged to the German and Italian commanders: realizing that they would inevitably be overwhelmed, they staged a superb rearguard fight on two fronts. This mini-Dunkirk across the Straits of Messina permitted 40,000 Germans and 70,000 Italians, along with nearly 10,000 vehicles and some 50 tanks, to escape the trap that was closing in from two sides. Montgomery, ever the realist, regarded the inappropriately named 'Operation Husky' – in one of the warmest spots in Europe – as a defeat.

Patton was forced to suffer the consequences. In charge of 200,000 troops at the end of Operation Husky, he was told that most of his 11th Army would now be placed under the control of General Mark Clark's 5th Army, leaving him with just 5,000 men. Effectively, his superiors had decided to punish him for disobeying orders. Yet he was too popular with the American public, thirsting for a genuine US hero and victory in battle, to dispense with.

Patton was too intelligent not to sense what was happening; his frustration and pent-up rage had long begun to get the better of him. Some of his biographers believe, charitably, that he was a psychological timebomb waiting to explode, and not a calculating personality at all: he certainly had acquired enemies, not in the least in the American high command.

The hammerblow was dealt in November 1943 when journalist Drew Pearson, clearly at official instigation, recounted two stories of Patton's brutality towards his own troops during the last advance on Messina. On 3 April he had encountered a private, Charles Kuhl. The official report described the incident: '[Patton] came to Pvt Kuhl and asked him what was the matter. The soldier replied, "I guess I can't take it." The general immediately flared up, cursed the soldier, called him all types of a coward, then slapped him across the face with his gloves and finally grabbed the soldier by the scruff of the neck and kicked him out of the tent'. On 10 April, he met Private Paul Bennet and much the same happened, except that Bennet had indeed been seriously ill and had resisted transfer from the front.

The first private was found to be suffering from malaria, Bennet with a fever. Yet Patton was completely out of control, issuing an amazing directive:

> It has come to my attention that a very small number of soldiers are going to the hospital on the pretext that they are nervously incapable of combat. Such men are cowards and bring discredit on the army and disgrace to their comrades... Those who are not willing to fight will be tried by court-martial for cowardice in the face of the enemy.

He went on to denounce 'cowardly bastards', and suggested 'we'll probably have to shoot them some time anyway'. The incident was covered up but not forgotten.

Omar Bradley – safe, uninspiring Bradley – was chosen to oversee Operation Overlord, the Allied invasion of France. In January 1944 Patton was appointed to command the US 3rd Army, based at Knutsford in rural Cheshire. He had been recalled to the task his superiors thought him best at: training troops, around 100,000 of them in all. As usual, he placed huge emphasis on the three 'd's – discipline, dress and drill.

He was undoubtedly a superb trainer, a kind of glorified, British-style regimental sergeant-major on a colossal scale, and it has to be borne in mind that the US army, which was shambolic in many places, needed training much more than the British. Patton's legendary image was further enhanced by his own personal appearance in his impeccable uniform, with his American-football-style helmet, tie, cavalry trousers and shiny boots, along with his perpetual scowl and set expression.

To Patton's further frustration, he was used by the British War Office in the massive deception to make it look to the Germans as though the D-Day landings would come from Dover to Calais. Patton nearly blew his cover when silly remarks he made at a Women's Institute gathering in Knutsford were reported in the press. The 3rd Army was put in reserve until after D-Day, not arriving in Normandy until July 1944. On landing, he told correspondents he would 'cut the guts out of those Krauts and get the hell to Berlin'.

At last, on 27 July, he was ordered into battle to take Avranches in the Gulf of St Malo, which he speedily did. The US forces were ready for breakout: for Patton it was a personal breakout – he at last had shed the dark cloud hanging over his career from Sicily, his continuing reputation as no more than just a great trainer of American troops, and the suspicion and ridicule that had dogged him all his life.

He had achieved the purpose for which he had worked all his life – command of a major army, with plenty of his favourite weapons of tanks, in a huge theatre of operations ideal for tank warfare, as north-central France was. He was fortunate, too, in that the spearhead of the invasion of Normandy to his north was engaged in furious fighting with the bulk of the German tank army, while he had a largely open field of play. He secured his rear in Brittany, although Brest took a long time to fall on his southern flank, and ordered the 3rd Army forward to the Seine to cut off the German retreat, and to the Loire to create a diversion. Wade H. Haislip's corps reached Le Mans in just a week and William Walker's corps penetrated still further forward.

Patton was ordered to send his forces at Le Mans up north to help close the 'Falaise Gap' from the south, and trap the Germans by barring their only escape route out of Normandy. Patton wanted to drive to the Einse, instead, and then turn north, trapping even more Germans, but was overruled by Bradley, Montgomery and Eisenhower.

A frustrated Patton met Bradley, his old subordinate, commenting acidly that his motto seemed to be 'in case of doubt, halt'. Bradley gave his grudging permission for Patton's armies to start their eastward advance, capturing Dreux, Chartres and Orléans, which would make possible a giant envelopment of German armies. Bradley, on Montgomery's orders, at last persuaded Patton to resume his march to the north and close off the Falaise pocket with the Germans trapped in it – only to be frustrated by delays caused by General Leonard Gerow, commanding the US army 5th Corps. Patton reacted vehemently, unfairly blaming Montgomery for the delay: 'Let me go on to Falaise, and we'll drive the British back into the sea for another Dunkirk.'

Hitler at last gave the order to withdraw and Patton was unable to seal the pocket until 21 August: some 50,000 Germans were killed, wounded or taken prisoner, but 10,000 escaped. It was reminiscent of Messina again – but this time the fault did not rest with Patton. The US army promptly ordered Haislip from Oreux to the Seine, which he was to cross and then follow downstream to prevent the German army crossing in their retreat. However, Bradley ordered him to send no more than one division across. Patton's concentrated armoured columns, supplied by infantry, moved with great speed across the river then towards the Meuse between Metz and Nancy in an effort to make a dash for the Rhine, which Patton wanted to be the first to cross. He ran out of petrol on the Meuse at the end of August.

While Patton fumed as the Germans retreated across the Meuse, Montgomery was arm-twisting Eisenhower. Montgomery wanted a massive thrust to the north, rather than promote Patton's drive to the south. Eisenhower characteristically pursued both plans, and the battle was dispersed along the front, to both Montgomery's and Patton's fury. As a consolation prize, Montgomery was given some inadequate US support for a limited thrust to the Ruhr – Operation Market Garden.

As a result, Patton kicked his heels as his force now advanced painfully slowly, while Market Garden proved a disaster. After the euphoria of the summer, the front was in danger of bogging down to a First World War confrontation. With extraordinary intuition, Patton realized in November 1944 that a division near Bastogne on the Luxembourg border was exposed 'as it is highly probable that the Germans are building up east of them'. On 16 September, Hitler had spelt out his plan for Operation Autumn Fog – a daring counterstroke across the woods and the villages of the Ardennes to relieve Antwerp and, to the north, his V2 rocket bases, dividing the British and Canadians in the north from the US forces in the south. Two Panzer armies were involved, with nine land divisions and two parachute divisions between them. However, they had only a quarter of the forces they needed, and conscripted many Czech and Polish conscripts.

The consequences of Eisenhower's dispersal of his army across the entire German border were becoming apparent: there were only four US divisions across the entire 900-mile front, two of them resting after battle, and one completely inexperienced. On 16 December, the Germans attacked, and they only encountered serious resistance to the south. Bradley, the commander of the front, was in Versailles visiting Eisenhower and enduring miserable weather. It was initially thought that the attack was simply a minor diversionary one.

At last Eisenhower ordered a division to the north and telephoned Patton to send one which was at that moment tied up in the south. Patton resisted at first but then, realizing the gravity of the situation, changed his mind. The German spearhead was aimed towards the town of Bastogne. Montgomery was given charge of the forces north of the spearhead, Patton to the south. At a conference on 19 December, Patton promised he would attack on 22 December with his three divisions. Patton's strategy was to strike northeast, cutting off the enemy's supply line, and to then advance and bag the German army in the spearhead: this was

rejected because his superiors wanted him to relieve the beleaguered army at Bastogne.

Patton agreed to send his forces, under John Milliken, to aid the
101st Airborne at Bastogne, while arguing that it was necessary to
try and close the pincer behind the Germans. Montgomery's more
relaxed view was that the German cause was hopeless in the face of
some 19 American and British divisions. The 101st Airborne
division was still holding out heroically as Milliken's men trudged
through the heavy snow, without air support, in atrocious weather.
On 22 December the Germans asked General Anthony McAuliffe,
acting commander of the 101st, to surrender and received the
immortal answer 'We surrender? Aw, nuts.'

Perhaps in confirmation of that very word, Patton had asked his
chaplain, James O'Neill, to provide 'a good prayer for the weather'
(an episode satirized in Joseph Heller's *Catch 22*). The unfortunate
O'Neill, wondering whether it was ethical to seek celestial interven-
tion for an air attack against the Germans, reluctantly obliged.
Patton ordered the prayer distributed to 250,000 men in the 3rd
Army, and the heavens duly obliged on 23 December, permitting
massive bombing of the German positions outside Bastogne. On
Christmas Day 1944, Patton observed, 'Lovely weather for killing
Germans, which seems a bit queer, considering whose birthday it is.'

On 26 December the 3rd Army broke through, reaching
Bastogne, although further fighting continued for three days. The
Germans launched another short-lived offensive in the Saar region,
but Montgomery's armies in the north launched their own attack
on 3 January 1945: Hitler was forced to order a withdrawal of the
four main Panzer divisions for fear they would be cut off. What
became known as the Battle of the Bulge was over, with 19,000
American dead and 15,000 made prisoner, compared to around
100,000 German casualties altogether. Patton and Milliken had
performed superbly – but received little praise.

Undaunted, in February 1945, Patton resumed his advance
towards the Rhine through the Eiffel region to the well-defended
Siegfried Line, capturing Trier. General William Hodge's men
reached the Rhine on 7 March 1945, crossing the bridge at

Remagen, and, on 22 March, Patton's men crossed a pontoon – a day before the hated Montgomery. The next day he followed, writing characteristically that he had stopped 'in the middle to take a piss in the Rhine, and then picked up some dust on the far side'.

His 3rd Army was then ordered to the south to free Czechoslovakia. Berlin was to be left to the Russians, to Patton's disgust. He got as far as liberating Pilsen, near Prague, before the Germans surrendered. He asked: 'I wonder how the dead will speak today when they know that for the first time in centuries we have opened Central and Western Europe to the forces of Genghis Khan. I wonder how they feel now that they know there will be no peace in our times and that Americans, some not yet born, will have to fight the Russians tomorrow, or 10, 15 or 20 years from tomorrow.'

On his return to the United States in June 1945, Patton had a hero's welcome. He was then given the job of running the occupation in Bavaria and quite rightly sought to keep competent officials in their posts, even though some had been Nazis. Asked by the press about this, he responded: 'more than half the German people were Nazis and we would be in a hell of a fix if we removed all Nazi party members from office. The way I see it, this Nazi question is very much like a Democratic and Republican election fight... Now we are using [former Nazi party members] for lack of anyone better until we can get better people.'

Towards the end of 1945 he decided to return to the United States for Christmas, but on a return journey from a shooting party just before he was due to leave, he was badly injured in a car accident. After a fortnight of paralysis, with Beatrice beside him, he died of heart failure, aged just 60, on 21 December 1945.

———

George S. Patton, it might seem, was the most deeply unlovable personality even among the contrarians in this book. Perpetually glowering – the Patton look precluded a smile in the photographs – he was an aggressive spartan devoted to the art of war and killing as many of the enemy as possible, and a swearing racist who often seemed an ogre rather than a military genius. A recent biographer, Alan Axelrod, has sought to defend him on the grounds of his psychological shortcomings, in particular his fear of being thought cowardly, but this is a thesis that is difficult to accept, in view of his conspicuous bravery.

More plausibly, he was somewhat deranged – he astounded the British commander Alexander in 1943 by answering a compliment that he would have made a greater general than Napoleon with the answer, 'But I did.' He also believed he had been a Roman legionnaire and had fought against the Turks. At the age of 18 he argued: 'I belong to a different class, a class perhaps almost extinct or one which may have never existed yet as far removed from these lazy, patriotic, or peace soldiers as heaven is from hell.' It is hard not to conclude that he was a little unhinged.

Yet there seems a more prosaic possibility, one that applies to others in this book. Patton was a loner, with a narrow range of interests – specifically warfare – at which he was supremely knowledgeable and professional. Dyslexic and awkward as a child, friendless and shy, falling instantly for the first girl who seemed interested in him, gangly and much too direct in speech, he was almost certainly looked down upon by those who were more obviously cleverer than he in military life. Patton was one of nature's awkward squad, aware that he was different but possessed of great intelligence, determination and formidable courage, and, in two areas, training and tanks, a military genius.

Above all, he had the extraordinary drive and determination to overcome his handicaps – even though he was overlooked time and time again, through a lack of opportunity rather than his own faults. He was one of the greatest pioneering practitioners of mobile warfare in history, proving to be superb in its execution when at last – just once – he was given the stage.

In spite of Patton's late-starting career, sometimes crazed views and often outspoken stupidity, as well as his (almost unique amongst the mavericks) obsession with spit and polish, he ticks most of the maverick boxes: he was courageous under fire, was an instant decision-maker on the battlefield, made his way up with merit and showed extraordinary resilience and strength in the face of innumerable setbacks. He seized the opportunities he was offered, he was a superb tank tactician, an enthusiastic and early practitioner of public relations – perhaps to excess – was unafraid of superior odds, always questioning his peers and superiors, and was no devotee of conventional tactics. His military bluffness, however, probably concealed a limited intelligence except in army matters, as seemed evident from his frequent blunders.

Chapter 12

MACARTHUR: THE LAST AMERICAN HERO

Douglas MacArthur was a child of the nineteenth century, and in many ways his attitudes and fighting style were geared more to that period than the one in which he rose to military prominence. An extraordinary figure – towering, patrician, arrogant, with a colossal intellect – he was an early master of the importance of public relations and he was fearlessly brave, always happiest being seen on the frontline.

Like so many of the mavericks, save, perhaps, Washington and Grant, he was vain. However, he demonstrated his skill as a commander and fighter again and again in the First World War, his campaign to regain the Philippines and his master stroke at Inchon in the Korean War. MacArthur, described by Winston Churchill as 'the glorious commander' and by Richard Nixon as one of the 10 most influential figures of the twentieth century, has gone down in history as the archetype of the tough-talking, corncob-pipe-chewing, right-wing American martinet. Yet, although he was a brilliant general, he was first and foremost an inspired proconsular political leader with an instinctive grasp of the importance of public relations and of leadership in the Far East that dwarfed his political faults in the United States. The very qualities of imperiousness and decisiveness that made him a failure on the American political stage produced astonishing results in Asia.

After 1945, he laid the foundations of modern Japan and of strategic stability in the Far East. Liberal American historians have been unable to reconcile themselves to the idea of a genuinely far-seeing soldier, while conservative historians always viewed MacArthur's attempts to reform Japanese society with intense suspicion. MacArthur, in the end, was assassinated in a political cross-fire between right and left. A man who only attained greatness in his seventh decade, he displayed an uncanny ability to foresee disaster – and was usually found to be arguing for the more moderate course. He was a dove in hawk's clothing.

----*◦✑✑◦*----

Douglas MacArthur was born in Little Rock, Arkansas, on 26 January 1880. His early military career was overshadowed by his distinguished father – Arthur – a hero of the Civil War who had also fought Chief Geronimo in the Frontier Wars. Douglas had been bought up in this Wild West environment before excelling at West Point, graduating with marks of 98 per cent, the highest recorded since Robert E. Lee. After West Point he worked at his father's headquarters at the Pacific Coast Command, San Francisco, before a short tour of the Philippines. It was the first time Douglas had left his native shores, and he had plenty of time to consider the exciting challenges ahead. It was also here that he first saw action, killing two men on a foraging excursion into the jungle, and only narrowly missing death: 'the slug tore through the top of my campaign hat and almost cut the sapling tree immediately behind me'.

He was to return to the Far East soon afterwards, when his father took him as an aide-de-camp on his strategic tour in October 1905. Arthur MacArthur thought he was doing his son a favour by taking him on a fantastic voyage of discovery. It was not clear that he was. The already almost insufferable lieutenant, top of his class at West Point, son of one of the foremost commanders in the US army, was now exposed to some of the most exotic luxuries available to anyone outside royalty. Returning to the United States, his swollen head grew bigger still: as a youth gilded for greatness, in 1906 he was appointed aide-de-camp to President Theodore Roosevelt himself. The young lieutenant behaved like the crown prince at some oriental court. Arrogant, with his head in the clouds, he neglected his studies at the elite School of Military Engineers in Washington, DC to which he had been assigned.

Befriended by one of the four greatest presidents of the twentieth century, rubbing shoulders with the most powerful men in America, an interlocutor with emperors and kings, the finest graduate from West Point since General Robert E. Lee, the gilded youth was brought sharply down to earth by his superiors. In 1907, he was appointed to a junior post in Milwaukee where, back in the real world of a provincial army posting, he seemed to go rapidly downhill. He neglected his duties to spend time with his parents. He was next appointed commander of the most junior company in Fort Leavenworth, Kansas – the very same company his father had commanded in 1885. It seemed a total comedown – an obscure outback command, almost in disgrace.

By now he was 28 years old, no longer the most promising young man in the American army and regarded by many of his new brother officers as a snobbish dandy. Yet the new role would prove to be his making. For long a stuffed shirt, he became again a western cowboy, one of the guys, an officer in the saddle, a leader of men and a good comrade. He was a superb junior officer, performing the jobs of quartermaster and engineer officer among others and writing a field manual. Above all, he excelled in getting the most out of his men. At about that time, however, he received news that his mother was seriously ill. Then disaster struck. His father died aged 69 at the 50th annual reunion of his old regiment – the 24th Wisconsin.

After a brief reprise in Washington, MacArthur was sent on a secret mission to Mexico in 1914. At that time, the United States was provoking its neighbour into war and he was commanded to reconnoitre and obtain 'all possible information which would be of value in possible operations' – including a major US attack on Mexico. It was a James Bond-style mission, undoubtedly devised to test the young soldier. In Veracruz he found the US army was virtually devoid of transport and decided that the answer was to steal locomotives from the ample rolling stock lying idle in the city. Wearing military uniform, so as not to be shot as a spy, he got three Mexican railway men to lead him to the Jamapa River and, skirting the town of Alvarado while lashed to one of the men to prevent him running away and betraying him, he finally found three locomotives in good condition.

On the return journey to report the find, things went wrong: they were intercepted by bandits, who opened fire: MacArthur shot two of them. A few miles further on they ran into a band of 15 armed men. According to MacArthur, three bullets went through his uniform and one of his Mexicans was injured in the shoulder, but he killed four bandits and the rest fled. They grabbed a railway handcar to get away and were attacked by three men on horseback, one sending a bullet through MacArthur's shirt. He fired back and shot a horse from under one of his assailants which fell on the line ahead of the railcar. At daylight, after a hazardous river crossing, MacArthur returned exhausted. Already a captain, he was promoted to major. It was the first indication of the superhuman courage of the talented young officer.

—⁓—

Back on the general staff in Washington, he found himself under orders from an earnest, highly intelligent young patron, the Assistant Secretary of the Navy, Franklin D. Roosevelt, who was preparing plans for mobilization in case the United States was sucked into the war that had broken out in Europe. MacArthur was commended by his superiors as 'a high-minded, conscientious and unusually efficient officer, well-placed for posts requiring diplomacy and high-grade intelligence'. He got on well with the new Secretary of War, Newton D. Baker, who said he had a 'swift and uninhibited mind'. Baker appointed MacArthur as his 'press censor' – his public relations officer.

By all accounts he performed brilliantly at the job, his laconic intelligence and courtesy winning over the hard-bitten journalists who were accustomed to being treated brusquely by haughty army officers. This experience was pivotal to one of MacArthur's greatest advantages in later life. Long before most of his contemporaries, he understood the importance of image, of manipulating the news, of ensuring he was cast in the best possible light and of suppressing his mistakes in public.

On 6 April 1917, the United States declared war on Germany. Having endured two years of its merchant ships being sunk by U-boats, the sinking of the *Lusitania* was the final straw. On 19 October 1917, MacArthur set sail across the U-boat-infested Atlantic with the 27,000 men of the Rainbow Division. They ran aground 40 miles off St Nazaire, but landed shortly afterwards in cold rain. At the age of 37, after a glittering launch to his career and an equally inglorious setback, destiny had given MacArthur a fresh chance. A senior officer, with a solid reputation at headquarters, he now possessed a considerable operational responsibility. However, he was to endure several months of frustration before he saw action, training his raw men behind the lines, near the US headquarters of Chaumont, in the dreary cold of a French winter with inadequate clothing and blankets.

Mindful of his training in public relations, he established his own extraordinary style, which he put into practice when he was at last permitted to accompany his troops on their first engagement along-side the French – a night attack on German lines in February 1918. It was relatively small-scale stuff, entirely typical of the Western Front, and involved crawling forward from the frozen squalor of the trenches across no-man's-land, detonating a hand grenade to signal the attack, and a quick and savage occupation of enemy trenches, ended by a hand grenade thrown at the last German outpost. In the morning, his men retired with 600 enemy prisoners, including a German colonel, and MacArthur was greeted by French soldiers offering absinthe and cognac; he was awarded a French Croix de Guerre and an American silver star.

Apart from his utter fearlessness, his extraordinary attire was the most unusual thing about the raid: he wore a turtleneck sweater, riding breeches and cavalry boots. On his head was what was to become his famous 'scrambled eggs' cap – a battered parade-ground hat – instead of a helmet. In his mouth was clamped an elegant cigarette holder. In his hands, instead of a gun, was a riding crop. The outfit was topped off by a four-foot scarf – a present from his mother. When he returned, with mud camouflage on his face and a hole torn by barbed wire in the seat of his riding breeches, he looked even more extraordinary. He was to be dubbed at once by the press as the 'Beau Brummel of the American expeditionary force'.

After his first experience of the front, he was confident enough to lead the Rainbow Division into an engagement on the night of 9 March 1918. As the Germans opened up with 40 batteries, he climbed up a scaling ladder: 'The blast was like a fiery furnace. For a dozen terrible seconds I felt they were not following me. But then, without turning around, I knew how wrong I was to have doubted for even an instant. In a moment they were around me, ahead of me, a roaring avalanche of glittering steel and cursing men. We carried the enemy position.'

Later that same month, as he recovered, the Germans embarked on their last full-scale offensive of the war: to capture Paris. The Rainbow was rushed to help the French in their defence of the city. For 82 days, the division was in almost constant combat. The German offensive now reached its crescendo and to meet this the Rainbow was moved west to join the French 4th Army defending the road to Chalons. Here he formulated a new tactic to meet the German advance: he would vacate his forward trenches, leaving only a handful of 'suicide squads' to put up token resistance and warn of the German advance. Then the French guns would fire further back with deadly accuracy on the Germans as they moved forward to occupy the French forward trenches. The Germans attacked on 15 July: as they took the trenches, 1,000 guns opened up on them, pinning them down. They were repulsed and the Germans' last great attack of the war was over.

Taking refuge in a nearby chateau, MacArthur discovered ample food that had been left behind on the German retreat. A shell cut through the courtyard next to where he was about to dine. 'All of Germany cannot make a shell that will kill MacArthur,' he remarked. 'Sit down, gentlemen, with me,' he instructed the officers lying flat on the floor.

The American advance was now pinned down by fire from a ridge of hills known as the Côte de Châtillon. His commanding officer arrived. 'Get me Châtillon, or a list of 5,000 casualties,' he told MacArthur. 'All right general, we'll take it' was the reply. He moved forward in a pincer under relentless fire. Of the 1,450 men and 25 officers that led the assault, only 300 men and 10 officers survived when the hills were taken. MacArthur himself was badly gassed again in the attack. Baker dubbed him 'the greatest front-line general of the war', and recommended him for the Medal of Honour; instead he was awarded a second Distinguished Service Cross.

Following the Armistice on 11 November 1918, the Rainbow Division was ordered into Germany as part of the occupation force. In the Rhineland, MacArthur occupied the castle of Sinzig, 25 miles south of Bonn, where suffering from post-battle exhaustion and the after-effects of gas, he fell desperately ill with a throat infection, and then again with diptheria. But he and his men had at last reached paradise. There he had held court in a ragged brown sweater and civilian trousers. A portrait painter called and painted him by candlelight.

Unlike many fellow officers, who immediately faded into obscurity, MacArthur's battlefield successes had been too well reported for him to suffer a similar fate. The new army chief of staff, General Peyton C. March, offered him the prestigious job of superintendent of West Point with a mandate to revitalize the institution. An astonished and delighted MacArthur accepted and took up his new duties in June 1919. He and his mother moved into the superintendent's mansion 20 years to the day after he had first arrived at the prestigious academy. An authentic war hero, he looked a decade younger than his 39 years.

MacArthur's unusual personality soon imposed itself on the stuffy academy and he proposed a radical set of changes: more subjects in the curriculum; more contact with the outside world; abolition of the elaborate social routine of summer camp in favour of training under regular army officers; and the introduction of compulsory games for all cadets. He only partly succeeded, however. He slammed up against the 'privy council', as he called it, which was the 12-man academic board of greying old conservative military pedagogues (on which he had only two allies) who regarded him as their servant, rather than as their leader. Then MacArthur really began treading on toes. He proposed practical steps to ban 'hazing' – the bullying of young cadets from which he himself had suffered; he introduced a new code of conduct; and he shut down the 'beast barracks' where young cadets arrived for their initiation rituals.

General John 'Jack' Pershing, his venerable commander, and most of his clique of senior officers swore by the old ways and could not stand MacArthur. They were determined to get him out before he further undermined their cherished institution. To add salt in the wound, MacArthur then fell head-over-heels in love with, and married, Pershing's former mistress, the immensely wealthy Louise Brooks – a vivacious, spoilt rich kid who took absolutely nothing and no one seriously. Pershing was beside himself with rage. In 1922, he took his revenge by cutting short MacArthur's term as West Point superintendent by a year and sending him to the Philippines to take up the comparatively lowly post of commander of the military division of Manila. His first task was to map the torrid Bataan Peninsula at the mouth of Manila Bay.

MacArthur's career now seemed headed towards respectable mediocrity amid the dull provincialism of stodgy, sub-colonial American expatriate society in a peaceful tropical outpost. It was to his credit that he chose not to dwell on the setback in his fortunes, but threw himself into his mundane tasks with his usual energy and vigour, professing himself honoured to perform on his father's former stage. Moreover, he personally believed in the possibility of the Philippines becoming a battleground in a future war with Japan. The army high command had ostensibly sent him to Bataan with the intention of finding out whether, in the event of a Japanese invasion overwhelming the thinly defended Philippines, it would make a suitable defensive holdout until a relief force could be organized.

On his return to the United States there was a further disappointment: he was posted to command the 4th Corps in Atlanta, Georgia, another provincial backwater. In the deep south, there remained simmering resentment of Arthur MacArthur's Civil War record. When he attended a church service, MacArthur was humiliated to see three-quarters of the congregation walk out in protest. He immediately demanded a transfer, and was sent to command the 3rd Corps in Baltimore, Maryland, a more agreeable backwater. In spite of his comparative youth, he chafed for a more challenging role. This came unexpectedly in September 1927 when he was offered the job of president of the American Olympic Committee for the 1928 games. With his passion for athletics, he instantly accepted. With his difficult marriage to Louise now over, he returned once more to the Philippines, but the world was soon shaken by the 1929 Wall Street Crash and he was recalled to take care of more pressing matters at home.

In the summer of 1930 he was offered the job of chief of engineers – the highest tribute from President Herbert Hoover, himself an engineer. MacArthur's task was to embark on public works projects to mop up some of the unemployment resulting from the crash. To everyone's astonishment, he refused. He was holding out for the highest stakes of all: chief of staff. In August 1930 he was awarded the post.

MacArthur cut a dash from the moment he arrived in Washington. He surrounded himself with bright young officers of which two – Dwight Eisenhower and George Patton – were to ascend to much greater prominence. He was easygoing, loquacious and enjoyed intellectual challenge. He was no stickler for military convention, occasionally wearing a Japanese kimono at his desk, and sometimes sported a jewelled cigarette holder. He was denounced as a poseur by officers irritated at these affectations. They were the trademark and props of an actor, which would have been intolerable in a less talented man, but they were part of the showman in MacArthur, the public relations practitioner who realized that modern society craved something out of the ordinary.

He had taken office at a time of appalling economic crisis: as war clouds loomed once again abroad, the cry was for the US's tiny military to be much further reduced. The armed forces consisted of just 132,000 men, fewer than those of either Greece or Portugal, and little more than $300m was spent on defence. Its equipment included only 12 postwar tanks, 50 calibre machine-guns and First World War mortars. The US armed forces ranked just 16th in the world. President Hoover sought to cut them further in order to balance his budget and spend more on job creation.

In response, MacArthur introduced plans for national industrial mobilization and general manpower mobilization in the event of war. He based the defence of the United States on his 'Four-Army plan'. He set up the independent air arm which eventually became the US Air Force. He established a school for an independent armed land force which was the embryo of the armoured divisions. In contrast to the romantic who had sauntered through the killing grounds of the First World War in cavalry boots and riding crop, all of this was visionary and modernizing after years of stagnation under less imaginative stuffed-shirt generals. He laid the foundations for the huge military machine that was to win the Second World War.

The Great Depression had further impact when some 10,000 'bonus marchers' arrived in Washington in 1932. They were veterans from the First World War and they had a legitimate demand: made jobless in the Depression, they wanted to redeem immediately a bonus of around $1,000 payable on their deaths or in 1945, whichever came first, which had been approved by Congress in 1934. Legislation had been introduced in Congress to permit them to obtain this. Their leader was Walter Waters, from Oregon, an eloquent former sergeant who had served in France. The demonstrators staged daily marches to the Capitol, the White House and other government buildings.

At last the bill passed the Congress' House of Representatives, but was rejected in the Senate, which was righteously angered by this attempt to coerce through mob rule. Congress then adjourned for the summer. The President appealed for the bonus marchers to go home, and offered them the money to do so. Franklin D. Roosevelt, now the liberal governor of New York State, did the same. Many of the marchers took up the offer and drifted away but a hard core of around 8,000 remained. Tempers frayed and acts of violence became common, along with petty criminality. MacArthur had much less time for men 'abandoning the plea for justice and adopting in its place threat and coercion' and was convinced that communists had taken control of the marchers. He even took the precaution of ordering reinforcements to Washington.

On the afternoon of 26 July, Waters went to see Patrick J. Hurley, the Secretary for War, and found MacArthur with him. Both were in intransigent mood, MacArthur furiously pacing the room. Hurley told Waters bluntly, 'we are interested only in getting you out of the district and we have plenty of troops to force you out'. Waters asked that his supporters be allowed to retire with dignity if confronted by the army, not be driven out 'like rats'. MacArthur impatiently gave him that assurance, but it was clear that the armed forces commander had decided that the moment of truth had come.

On the morning of 28 July, a handful of the marchers reoccupied a building that they had previously evacuated. The police went in at lunchtime to get them out and a scuffle ensued, in which several policemen were slightly injured. This was still small-scale stuff, but the police had become jittery and, when marchers moved on the Capitol, as usual, fighting broke out and the police opened fire, shooting two marchers, one of whom died.

At this stage the police, fearing they were losing control, asked MacArthur to use his troops. The order had to come from the White House and Hoover refused unless the police request was made in writing. This the police chief did, saying that unless the army intervened it would be 'impossible for the police department to maintain law and order except by the free use of firearms'. That was MacArthur's cue. He ordered the 16th Infantry Brigade to cross the Memorial Bridge from Fort Myers. A young commander, George Patton, headed the tanks.

MacArthur put it with characteristic bluntness: he was going 'to drive the veterans out of the city. We are going to break the back of the BEF.' It was as though he were talking about an enemy army, not a ragged group of unarmed American demonstrators. He cited orders from Hoover in his support; no such orders had yet been issued.

The cavalry advanced on the marchers with the flats of their sabres exposed. The infantry was behind them with their bayonets drawn. Tear gas was poured down on the demonstrators, to be met by desultory volleys of stones and the waving of sticks as they retreated. MacArthur was taken aback: the 'communist revolution' did not occur: these desperate men did not fight back, or make a stand to be mown down. Sadly, dispiritedly, they retreated before the overwhelming show of force. Only a few were hurt, no one was killed – which said as much for their peaceful intentions as for the army's excellent discipline.

After reporting to Hoover and Hurley, MacArthur held a triumphal press conference, but the major consequence of the whole affair was the precise opposite to the one MacArthur had intended. Public opinion was appalled. Furthermore, Hoover had proved himself incapable of responding to the giant challenges raised by the Depression. MacArthur watched with grim apprehension as Roosevelt was swept to power at the expense of Hoover and the Democrats seized control of both houses of Congress. To MacArthur it almost seemed that the very forces of communism and revolution had won at the ballot box.

Roosevelt, a patrician who had worked with MacArthur in the past, made an unlikely revolutionary. He proclaimed a New Deal for America and this included a radical reduction of the military budget. MacArthur was incensed but outmanoeuvred. Roosevelt, having utterly neutralized MacArthur, could have seized the chance of being rid of him when his traditional four-year term was up. However, for reasons that are still unclear, he gave MacArthur a further year in office and then offered him the post of governor-general of the Philippines where a Filipino, his old friend Manuel Quezon, had just been elected president of what was in effect an independent government. The post would get MacArthur, with his troublesome penchant for meddling in politics, out of the way and into a gilded cage.

However, MacArthur had also been offered the job of running the Philippines armed forces, which were still American-led, by Quezon. This offered the prospect of an active retirement in his beloved Philippines. Telling Roosevelt he could not resign as a soldier, he accepted Quezon's offer. Roosevelt was furious. MacArthur, the best-known general in the army, would remain on active service and a rallying point for political opponents. Roosevelt said farewell with grace, however, meaning not a word of it: 'Douglas, if war should suddenly come, don't wait for orders to come home. Grab the first transportation you can find. I want you to command my armies.'

As he travelled to Manila in 1935, MacArthur had plenty of time to reflect on the twists of fate. He had enjoyed one of the most brilliant careers in American military history, becoming chief of staff at the age of 50. Now he was prematurely and effectively retired at just 55: a man of vigour and intelligence, still at the height of his powers, he was now acting as a mercenary for a foreign government. Moreover, while still enjoying the respect of those that worked for him, and probably believing he had saved the US army from virtual extinction during the Depression years, his professional reputation was in ruins. The verdict of many, as he well knew, was that one of the youngest chiefs of staff of the American army had also been one of the worst.

In the Philippines, MacArthur was left starved of funds from Washington to create his guerrilla army. He took refuge in impressing his boss, Manuel Quezon, and accepted the extraordinary rank of field marshal which no American soldier had ever held before. He sported a self-designed uniform of black trousers, a white tunic regaled with gold braid and medals, and a cap laden with gold braid surmounted by an American eagle. All of this made him an object of derision among Americans, some of whom thought he had gone mad, but it seemed to impress Quezon. Meanwhile, MacArthur's personal life improved with his marriage to Jean Fairclough in 1937 and the birth of their son, Arthur, a year later.

With the outbreak of war in Europe in September 1939, neither MacArthur nor the US government could have been under any illusions about the approaching danger. Yet as MacArthur showered requests for military assistance upon Washington he was met with a blank refusal. Part of the trouble was that MacArthur was no longer an American general. Another part was that the Americans not only considered the Philippines indefensible but felt that if they entered the war, they would concentrate their main effort on Europe. Nothing happened.

Another year-and-a-half passed. By May 1941 the demoralized MacArthur wrote to the new chief of staff that he would return home if no help was offered. The Japanese then occupied part of Indochina after bludgeoning the Vichy government in France to allow them in: they now threatened all of Indochina. Roosevelt's reply – after first placing MacArthur in charge of a unified Philippine defence – was to freeze Japanese assets in the United States and to declare an embargo on oil, iron and rubber exports to Japan. The British and the Dutch joined the embargo. The Japanese were surprised by the vigour of the American response, and were left with no alternative but ignominious retreat or an invasion of Malaysia and the Dutch East Indies to obtain these resources.

The Philippines were in the way. On hearing the fateful news, MacArthur said to his chief of staff, 'I feel like an old dog in a new uniform', but Quezon was overjoyed by MacArthur's new appointment as US commander in the Far East, concluding that the Philippines at last had the active support of the United States. MacArthur took the view that the Japanese invasion would come in April 1942 after the monsoon: he had nine months to prepare. American supplies were still slow in coming – just 6,000 new troops arrived in December 1941 out of a promised 50,000, along with a handful of dud mortar shells and a few tanks. The promised aircraft never arrived.

At 4 a.m. on 8 December 1941, MacArthur was awoken by the news of the Japanese attack on Pearl Harbor. He was told that 'considerable damage' had been inflicted and that an invasion of the Philippines 'in the near future' was a strong possibility. MacArthur

read his bible for a while in shock. Like other American comman-
ders, he had believed Hawaii to be virtually impregnable: the
Japanese could not risk an assault there, and could not cross the
Pacific without being detected.

As numbed officers congregated in MacArthur's office, his new
air commander General Lewis H. Brereton said it was his intention
to attack Formosa by air. MacArthur had not arrived but Richard
Sutherland, MacArthur's acerbic chief of staff, told Brereton to
wait. Brereton, a timid man, made no real attempt to persuade
MacArthur. 'Our task is defensive, but stand by for orders,'
MacArthur told him. Meanwhile, reports came in of an attack on a
seaplane and two patrol boats in Davao by Japanese aircraft.
Fighters also strafed a radio station on the north of Luzon.
MacArthur did not hear of these attacks until 10 a.m., three hours
after they occurred. Brereton had sensibly scrambled his B-17s into
the air in case of a dawn attack, but they were now running short of
fuel and had to land. By 10 a.m. the uncharacteristically indecisive
MacArthur at last issued the order authorizing the air force to
attack Formosa. While the B-17s were refuelling, Brereton also
ordered all his P-40 fighters to land for refuelling at Iba airfield –
whereas he should have taken the precaution of keeping at least
half in the air while the others refuelled, or made them land south,
out of Japanese range.

Why had MacArthur delayed so long in giving the order to
attack? There are suggestions that he thought the Japanese might
consider the Philippines neutral under Quezon's Commonwealth
government and would therefore not be attacked. His own orders
were clear: not to initiate offensive action against the Japanese
from the Philippines – but then those orders had been drafted
before Pearl Harbor, which no one expected. He could hardly argue
that Japan and the United States were not now at war. Quezon may
also have asked him, in several frantic telephone calls that morning, to hold his fire, but he was an American general now, not
Quezon's poodle.

Misjudgement turned into tragedy. When the fog cleared and the
Japanese took off, they did so in time to find the B-17s and the

P-40s laid out on the ground in line. Some 110 Japanese aircraft reached Iba airfield and destroyed the 16 P-40s there as they lay in the open. Another 82 Japanese aircraft headed towards Clark base shortly after 12 midday, when the air crews were settling down to lunch. A radio commentator had just broadcast unconfirmed reports that the Japanese were bombing Clark, which raised a hearty laugh among the airmen. Out of the clear blue sky the Japanese appeared, looking, according to the crew of the one B-17 still in the sky, like a thunderstorm. A whole squadron of B-52s was destroyed on the ground, although two others were fortunately in the air off Manila Bay. It was a shattering blow and would render air bases on the north of the island out of commission and virtually without fighter protection.

Brereton soon after had to order most of his remaining aircraft to Australia and Java. The few remaining fighter aircraft fought on, against vastly superior Japanese air power. Deprived of air cover, the Philippines were sitting ducks for Japanese air attack: three days later the huge US naval base at Cavite was blown up. On 16 December it was the turn of the Manila docks. The old defensive plan for the Philippines was in tatters because, after the catastrophe at Pearl Harbor, the navy had decided it could not maintain a supply route to the Philippines: the army would thus eventually run out of supplies. As MacArthur waited for the inevitable land invasion, he surveyed the wreckage of everything he had striven for. His inadequate air defences were destroyed or gone. The islands were blockaded by sea and the navy had all but left. He had worked for more than six years to build up a Philippines defence force, but his militia was still only half-trained and was now demoralized. He was 61 years old and witnessing his worst ever professional setback.

On 22 December a force of 80 Japanese landing craft carrying some 20,000 troops beached at Lingayen Gulf well to the north of Manila. Two days later 7,000 Japanese troops were landed at Lamon Bay. The Japanese were closing in two giant pincers to take Manila. MacArthur, now that the unreal interlude was over, was at his decisive best: he had long realized that to send his inexperienced men to fight in the open on the plain of Luzon would be madness: his army would disintegrate under Japanese air and tank attack. The Japanese, for their part, expected him to dig in and defend Manila, but this was equally hopeless, in MacArthur's view.

MacArthur's armies on north and south Luzon were instead ordered to retreat to the Bataan Peninsula, where they could hold out until the promised reinforcements could be brought up. He ordered Quezon to leave at once, at 2 p.m. on Christmas Eve, for the stronghold of Corregidor, an island two miles off the tip of the Bataan Peninsula. Reaching Corregidor, MacArthur installed himself in Topside, the officers' house on the top of Malinta Hill.

From there he directed by telephone one of the most superbly executed retreats ever staged in history. The chief difficulty was that his armies were divided in two: if one retreated too fast, the advancing Japanese could intercept and cut the other off from reaching Bataan. MacArthur instructed General Jonathan Wainwright, the commander of the northern army, to build a line of defence, wait for the Japanese to mass for an attack, and then retreat to build another line 10 miles back. In this way they could stagger and delay the Japanese advance without losing significant casualties. Some 180 bridges were blown en route. General Masaharu Homma, the Japanese commander, advanced just as MacArthur had expected and was held up by the defensive lines, which allowed the smaller southern army to slip into Bataan ahead of the northern. Even that curmudgeonly old critic of MacArthur, Jack Pershing, called it 'a masterpiece – one of the greatest moves in all military history'.

The two armies – the 28,000-strong northern army and the 15,000-strong southern one – which were once 160 miles apart were united at Calumpit bridge. They spent two days crossing the river, then blew the bridge up and withdrew to the next river crossing at Layao, where they destroyed the bridge on 6 January 1942. By then 80,000 troops had arrived safely in Bataan – 5,000 American soldiers and 65,000 Filipinos. There were, in addition, some 26,000 civilian refugees. Manila was declared an open city.

The Japanese were astonished – they had expected to have to fight for Manila until the last moment. The Japanese general staff in Tokyo noted that 'the Japanese commanders could not adjust to the new situation'. It had been 'a great strategic move' on MacArthur's part. Those on this superb retreat were not to know that, ultimately, many of them might have been better off fighting in the open.

On one count, MacArthur could be badly faulted: prior to the attack, instead of filling Bataan with supplies, he had left most of them outside Manila. It had proved impossible to move them in time. Now the peninsula was greatly overpopulated and food had to be half-rationed.

Three days later the Japanese staged their first air attack on Topside, which lasted nearly four hours. MacArthur coolly watched it in his soft military cap, until forced down on his stomach beside a hedge by an orderly who held his own helmet over the general's head: a piece of shrapnel tore off the back of the orderly's hand and another dented the helmet.

Meanwhile, the real fighting was taking place on the defensive frontline of Bataan as the Japanese chipped away at the bulk of the Philippine and American troops. It was a grim contest, but the defenders held out. The Allied forces were split across the peninsula into a 1st Corps, commanded by Wainwright, and a 2nd Corps, commanded by General George Parker. There was a gap in between the flanks of Bataan's main mountain, which Wainwright considered impenetrable, but 500 Japanese soldiers got through and Sutherland mistakenly ordered Wainwright to pull back, leaving most of his artillery behind. The Japanese landed troops behind the backs of both armies, but Wainwright still managed to launch brilliant attacks that eliminated both beachheads.

Roosevelt conveyed to MacArthur a terrible order to fight to the death and MacArthur rose to the challenge: 'I have not the slightest intention in the world of surrendering or capitulating the Filipino forces of my command. I intend to fight to destruction on Bataan and then do the same on Corregidor.' Privately, he summed the situation up with bitter accuracy: 'never in history was so large and gallant an army written off so callously'. The general prepared to die with his troops. He even considered shooting Jean and

Arthur if they refused to leave the island without him. Both Roosevelt and Eisenhower believed the outcome to be inevitable, although the US chief of staff, General George C. Marshall, disagreed. The possibility of surrendering Bataan never occurred to MacArthur – not least because he knew how the Japanese treated their prisoners. It was better for him to go down gloriously after all the humiliations they had inflicted on the Americans, British and Dutch in Asia. He wrote:

> My heart ached as I saw my men slowly wasting away. Their clothes hung on them like tattered rags. Their bare feet stuck out in silent protest. Their long bedraggled hair framed gaunt bloodless faces. Their hoarse, wild laughter greeted the constant stream of obscene and ribald jokes issuing from their parched, dry throats. They cursed the enemy and in the same breath cursed and reviled the United States; they spat when they jeered at the Navy. But their eyes would light up and they would cheer when they saw my battered, and much reviled in America, 'scrambled egg' cap. They would gather round and pat me on the back and 'Mabuhay Macarsar' me. They would grin – that ghastly skeleton-like grin of the dying – as they would roar in unison, 'We are the battling bastards of Bataan – no papa, no mama, no Uncle Sam'. They asked no quarter and they gave none. They died hard – those savage men – not gently like a stricken dove folding its wings in peaceful passing, but like a wounded wolf at bay, with lips curled back in sneering menace, and always a nerveless hand reaching for that long sharp machete knife which long ago they had substituted for the bayonet. And around their necks, as we buried them, would be a thread of dirty string with its dangling crucifix. They were filthy, and they were lousy, and they stank. And I loved them.

Events took an extraordinary turn. On 23 February 1942, Roosevelt issued the order for MacArthur to travel to Melbourne, Australia, for major reinforcements. MacArthur had a momentary breakdown, threatening to resign his commission and enlist as a private on Bataan, but the following day he said that for the sake of his men he had no alternative but to obey a direct presidential order which was now repeated even more insistently. MacArthur deluded himself that Roosevelt would be true to his pledge to allow him to return and save his men.

On the evening of 11 March, he entrusted the poisoned command of the Philippines to General Wainwright: 'Good-bye, Jonathan. When I get back, if you're still on Bataan, I'll make you a lieutenant general.' The little party then made an extraordinarily dangerous trip through Japanese lines to Cuyon Island. In Melbourne he discovered that Roosevelt had lied once more: there was no army in Australia waiting to return him to Bataan: there were just 32,000 troops altogether, including the Australian army. There was no navy, fewer than 100 working aircraft, and no tanks.

On arrival in Australian territory he had said: 'The President of the United States ordered me to break through the Japanese lines and proceed from Corregidor to Australia for the purpose, as I understand it, of organising the American offensive against Japan, a primary objective of which is the relief of the Philippines. I came through and I shall return.' Those three last words were a stroke of public-relations genius: they instantly became the cornerstone of the MacArthur legend, one of the most famous utterances by a general in history.

For the second surprise on his arrival in Australia – almost as unexpected as the first – was the realization that he had become a hero: not just any hero, but probably the greatest hero of the war so far, a towering figure of resistance. Unlike the British General Arthur Percival who had surrendered Singapore, he had held on grimly, month after month, against irresistible force – the only spoke in the wheel of the relentless Japanese advance. It had been a new Alamo, the stuff of legend, a second Dunkirk, defeat dressed up as victory. The 62-year-old general, so long dogged by failure, had become the symbol of resistance to Japanese aggression in the Far East. In Australia, he was living proof of the US commitment to defend the continent.

In his new position as commander of the Far East, he urged Wainwright to break out of Bataan and join the guerrillas operating in Luzon, but Wainwright's exhausted men could do no such thing.

Running out of food, they surrendered on 19 April. For a further 27 days, the forces in Corregidor held out under intense artillery fire and air attack. On 5 May the Japanese landed in force and, although at first driven back, put five light tanks ashore and threatened to fire right into a tunnel which contained 1,000 injured men. On the next day, Corregidor's defenders surrendered. The first phase of the Pacific War was over: the brave stand of those on Bataan and Corregidor had no more than temporarily halted the otherwise unbroken string of Japanese victories. The Japanese now took their revenge, taking the Bataan prisoners on their terrible 'death march', which caused some 15,000 to perish.

In June 1942, the Battle of Midway, in which the Japanese suffered significant losses in the Pacific, marked the turning point in the naval war; with the US's far superior war production machine, the odds were already lengthening against Japan in the long term. The Americans were to produce 20 carriers against the six produced by the Japanese over the following two years. Midway had been a close run thing, a battle won almost by accident, but it signalled to the Americans that victory was possible in the Pacific and rendered the diversion of precious war resources to the Pacific theatre sensible. And at that stage, the Americans made a number of crucial decisions that were to determine the course of the Pacific War.

The first was to aim for Japan itself as the central strategic objective. There was no intention of merely rolling back the Japanese conquests; the aim was nothing less than to strike at the home islands themselves and extract an unconditional surrender, as Roosevelt made clear at his summit with Churchill in Casablanca early in 1943. The strategy was to neglect the limbs, and strike at the heart. This led to the second key choice: how to get there. In the end a messy compromise was reached between a naval route to the north, led by Admiral Chester Nimitz, the commander-in-chief of the US Pacific fleet, and a separate attack to the south, commanded by MacArthur.

The navy was given charge of the first major American advance in the war, the attack on Guadalcanal, the strongly fortified Japanese outpost off eastern Papua New Guinea, while MacArthur was given charge of the invasion of New Guinea itself and the attack on Japan's command centre in the south at Rabaul. Even as MacArthur began to plan his campaign, American tactics were thrown into confusion by a major Japanese landing at Buna with the objective of crossing the nearly impenetrable mountain jungle of southern New Guinea in order to seize Port Moresby, the capital. Simultaneously, the Japanese responded furiously to the almost unopposed American landing on Guadalcanal: the Japanese regarded this as a major test of their strength and threw everything they could into it.

After establishing their beachhead, the marines had to be supplied down a treacherous channel through which ships came under fire on three sides. On 8 August the Japanese surprised an American flotilla, sinking four cruisers and destroying another. The US hit back on 24 August, sinking a carrier, a cruiser and a destroyer. However, Japanese reinforcements poured in as the fighting spread on the island, and became ever more intense. In November, during the Battle of Guadalcanal, the Japanese were bloodied; a fortnight later, the Japanese failed in a major attempt to intercept the American supply convoys to Guadalcanal. Only in February 1943, after frenzied fighting, was the epic and pyrrhic struggle over: the Japanese force was evacuated.

The tide had turned, painfully and bloodily, in the Allies' favour. There was to be much criticism of the Allies' decision to fight so bitterly for Guadalcanal at such an appalling cost, not least from MacArthur. Yet at that stage in the war, a grim battle of attrition against the Japanese was almost inevitable to drive home the message that they were not invincible, after all. After Guadalcanal, the Imperial Army was never to take the offensive again in the Pacific. It was forced to fight bitterly to hold on to what it had acquired.

The next target was Rabaul, with its large naval base, airfields and supply depots. MacArthur was determined to engage the enemy as infrequently as possible as he moved up the coast of New Guinea, leap-frogging between airstrips and leaving Japanese forces outflanked with their supplies cut off. In fact, the campaign proved much slower and more arduous than expected, requiring a series of landings and difficult amphibious operations. However, one by one his targets were picked off. Woodlark, Kiriwina and Nassau Bay were seized virtually without casualties. MacArthur's forces then marched on Salamanua, a major base which the Japanese evacuated. Thanks to a brilliant encircling move, MacArthur then forced the Japanese to withdraw also from Lae. The Japanese put up stiff resistance at Finschhafen, which fell on 2 October 1943. The bulk of New Guinea was now in allied hands.

Meanwhile, a parallel assault was being mounted by naval forces along the Solomon Island chain to the north. The Russell Islands fell in February, New Georgia in June, followed by Vella Lavella. Japanese counterattacks were unsuccessful. By October 1943, the northern forces were ready to attack Bougainville, the final stepping stone to Rabaul. The American navy was poised to form one part of the pincer movement, MacArthur's forces the other, in Operation Cartwheel, which was intended to surround the Japanese stronghold.

The American air force was now securing victories through a new policy of low-level bombing. In the Battle of the Bismarck Sea, Flying Fortresses sunk four destroyers and a convoy of transport ships. In another aerial engagement in April 1943, Admiral Yamamoto was shot down and killed. MacArthur's advance was then slowed by a probably unnecessary landing on southern New Britain; his Australian forces became bogged down in arduous fighting in the Huon Peninsula.

At the end of 1943, Stalin, Roosevelt and Churchill approved a new strategy in Tehran, which allocated greater resources to the Pacific War. This persuaded Admiral Nimitz to go on the offensive in the northern Pacific, in open competition with MacArthur's forces further south. The general was meanwhile given specific goals: the seizure of Kavieng, New Ireland and Manus, further to encircle Rabaul. Meanwhile, Nimitz wasted no time in making a landing on the Marshall Islands in January 1944 and seizing its western point, Eniwetok, in a bloody battle in February.

The Japanese, horrified at the two-pronged attack, now resolved to try and contain it in one major gamble: to try and lure American naval forces into a trap, where they could make use of their control of airspace and the protection of shore-based guns. The project was called Operation A-go. However, the American naval forces made no move towards the Japanese fleet, preparing to concentrate on island-hopping in the north. On 19–21 June 1944, the Japanese fleet, which had decided to pursue the Americans, met its match. The Battle of the Philippine Sea, which became known colloquially as the Marianas Turkey Shoot, saw the sinking of three Japanese carriers, while two others were severely damaged. Some 330 Japanese planes were lost.

Immediately afterwards, troops seized Saipan after a fierce battle; in July, Guam and Timor also fell after heavy fighting, in which 60,000 Japanese and at least 5,000 Americans were killed. The Japanese fleet was toothless for several months. MacArthur's forces moved forward much faster and more self-confidently to Biak, Noemfoor Island and Sansapor. The Americans now effectively controlled the whole of New Guinea, and were only 500 miles from reaching the Philippines.

The joint chiefs of staff reviewed the situation. In their opinion there was little reason, with the seizure of the Marianas which brought American aircraft within strategic bombing distance of Japan, to get bogged down in a long campaign to liberate the Philippines – it was deemed preferable for MacArthur's land forces to be brought under Nimitz's control, for Formosa to be seized and for an invasion of Japan proper to be prepared. On 26 July 1944, Roosevelt travelled to Pearl Harbor to meet MacArthur, the only senior commander who recommended landing in the Philippines. MacArthur's arguments won the day: in September instructions were issued for American forces to aim for the Philippines. It was to remain MacArthur's conviction to the last that Iwo Jima, Okinawa and a direct invasion of Japan were unnecessary, much less the atomic bombs dropped in order to obviate the need for such an invasion. With its fleet on the defensive and the Philippines in American hands, he declared that Japan could be strangled economically, becoming the biggest of all examples of his wither-on-the-vine philosophy, and forced to sue for peace.

As American forces prepared for the landings in the Philippines, the Japanese rounded up their remaining naval forces for a final attempt to stop the invasion: a large Japanese fleet opposed the US fleet at Leyte Gulf in October 1944. The battle, the largest in world naval history, raged for several days and was a close call for the American fleet, part of which had been mistakenly sent off on a wild goose chase in search of the Japanese carriers, largely as a result of poor coordination between the Nimitz and MacArthur. In the end, however, the Japanese fleet lost four carriers, including their flagship, three battleships, six heavy cruisers, three light cruisers and 10 destroyers. The Japanese fleet was all but destroyed.

The way was open for the landings on the island of Leyte, two-thirds of the way down the Philippine archipelago. The landing proved remarkably successful, but the Japanese followed up with four counteroffensives, throwing so many aircraft into the fighting that American control of the air seemed in danger. For a while it looked as if the offensive was stalled, until American aircraft succeeded in sinking a major Japanese convoy carrying reinforcements to Leyte in November. Even so, the Americans remained bogged down in a massive quagmire of mud for several weeks until MacArthur came up with a bold plan to stage a further landing in December at Ormoc, behind Japanese lines. The landing was successful and panicked the Japanese. The impasse was broken.

The same month, the small outpost of Mindoro was attacked and seized with high casualties. An invasion force of 200,000 men was assembled to move on Luzon, the main Philippine island. The Japanese were now fighting a war of attrition to delay invasion of the home islands. The US fleet supporting MacArthur, under Admiral William Halsey, suffered several setbacks: a typhoon wrecked several ships; an attack on Formosa's airfields was frustrated by the weather; and in January 1945 a series of kamikaze attacks sunk a battleship, two cruisers and a destroyer. But the bulk of the forces landed without opposition.

MacArthur ordered General Walter Krueger to move faster on Manila, where the Americans feared that thousands of prisoners of war were about to be butchered. Two further landings were staged to complete the encirclement of the capital. In a spectacular raid, a contingent of MacArthur's army rushed into central Manila, scattering the Japanese forces, to free some 5,000 prisoners. However, the fight to rid the capital of its 20,000 troops, the recapture of Corregidor and Bataan, and the attempt to get the Japanese out of the central mountains, were to take several, bloody months. The casualty rate was high: some 80,000 Japanese lost their lives on Luzon alone, compared to 7,300 Allied troops. With the southern Philippines liberated, Borneo fell also. MacArthur was dryly to observe that the total killed on Iwo Jima and Okinawa in the navy's northern thrust was greater than that in the whole of his campaign from Papua New Guinea to the Philippines.

In March 1945 preparations began in Japan for the defence of the mainland – Operation Ketsu-go. Japan assumed that the Americans would invade the southern island of Kyushu with 15 divisions in October (in fact, the US's planned Operation Olympic called for 10 divisions to arrive in November). Under Ketsu-go it was intended to muster no fewer than 58 infantry divisions, made up of 2,600,000 soldiers from the regular army, backed up by 3,650,000 reservists and a volunteer militia of 28 million. The prospect of an invasion of Japan, and the likely resistance and casualties, was awesome.

At 9.30 a.m. on 16 June, the joint chiefs of staff arrived at the White House to give President Harry S. Truman the results of a two-day appraisal of the task of invading Japan. General George Marshall outlined the plan for the first attack, with 816,000 troops, on 1 November 1945; this would be followed by an invasion of Honshu around Tokyo with 1,172,000 men on 1 March 1946. The sombre warning given by the chiefs of staff was that a million American lives were likely to be lost in the operation.

A month later, Truman was given an even more dire message by MacArthur. He warned that the Japanese could resort to guerrilla warfare in the event of an invasion and that a campaign might last 10 years. No estimate of the extent of American casualties could be given; nor was any made of the likely number of Japanese dead and wounded, either by MacArthur or by the joint chiefs of staff, but air raids on Japanese cities had already taken some 700,000 lives before August 1945. Military casualties could be reckoned at upwards of a million, with civilian casualties a multiple of that.

In late July, MacArthur had been told of the successful testing of the atom bomb. He was appalled and felt it was 'completely unnecessary from a military point of view'. Nevertheless, he did as he was ordered and went ahead with preparations for a huge American invasion of mainland Japan, involving 1.4 million GIs based in the Philippines and a further 1 million to come. It was said that the Japanese had prepared 5,000 kamikaze aircraft and that securing Kyushu would cause more than 250,000 US casualties. MacArthur told his chief of staff, Sutherland, 'If you can get a way to drag your feet do so, because we are never going to invade Japan.'

———⁓———

'Little Boy', the codename for the atom bomb, was dropped on Hiroshima on 6 August 1945. 'Fat Man' was dropped on Nagasaki three days later. On 30 August 1945, a C-54 aircraft called the *Bataan* took off from Okinawa, bearing the commander of American forces in the Far East, General Douglas MacArthur, and his chief aides across a clear, calm blue sky. If he was nervous, MacArthur tried not to show it. He paced up and down the aircraft, talking about his priorities in the exercise of the awesome powers that in a few hours were to pass to him. He dictated staccato apparently random thoughts: 'First destroy the military power... Then build the structure of representative government... Enfranchise the women... Free the political prisoners... Liberate the farmers... Establish a free labour movement... Encourage a free economy... Abolish police oppression... Develop a free and responsible press... decentralise the political power...' Could he, for the first time in modern history, accomplish that miraculous phenomenon: a successful occupation of a defeated nation? It amounted to a blueprint for the reshaping of a whole oriental society. The plane began the descent to land at Atsugi airbase outside Tokyo.

MacArthur's action appeared to be one of absolute foolhardiness. General Robert Eichelberger, in charge of the advance party at Atsugi, and one of MacArthur's most hard-headed colleagues, repeatedly tried to persuade the commander-in-chief to abandon the venture. The dangers of landing with only minimal protection in the heart of the Kanto Plain, southwest of Tokyo, where 300,000 well-armed Japanese troops were based, and where acts of insubordination and refusal to acknowledge defeat had been commonplace, were only too apparent. Atsugi had been a training base for kamikaze pilots, many of whom had refused to surrender. A mutiny there after the Emperor's announcement of surrender had sputtered on for days. Yet MacArthur ordered his own party to take off their guns before the aircraft landed. He believed the unarmed arrival of the Americans would make it less likely that they would be attacked; moreover, it would rub in the fact that the Japanese had been defeated. MacArthur would come as a conqueror, not as a fighter.

The plane nestled down on the field and MacArthur got out. The showman with dark glasses and corncob pipe, who had proba-bly been as responsible as any for Japan's defeat, descended the air-craft steps and set foot on enemy soil. They found Yokohama like a ghost town, deserted and boarded up. At the city's splendid New Grand Hotel, the staff instantly prostrated themselves before MacArthur. At dinner, he was told that his steak might be poi-soned. He laughed and replied, 'no one can live forever'.

Churchill was later to venture the opinion that 'the outstanding accomplishment' of any commander during the war was General MacArthur's 'landing with such a small force of troops in the face of several million Japanese soldiers who had not yet been disarmed'. MacArthur's unarmed arrival was admired by the Japanese, and threats of an attack against the American immediately dissipated.

The actual Japanese surrender ceremony on 2 September was something of an anticlimax, in spite of MacArthur's attempts to orchestrate a grand finale. In one poignant piece of symbolism, he invited General Jonathan Wainwright, who had surrendered to the Japanese at Corregidor after MacArthur had left the island, and General Arthur Percival, the former British commander at

Singapore, to meet him and then witness the surrender. Nimitz and Halsey were also present for the ceremony, which took place on the massive 45,000-ton battleship, the USS *Missouri*, anchored some 18 miles off Tokyo Bay. The reunion with Wainwright was emotional. MacArthur was shocked by his old comrade's appearance:

> He was haggard and aged. His uniform hung in folds on his fleshless form. He walked with difficulty and with the help of a cane. His eyes were sunken and there were pits in his cheeks. His hair was snow white and his skin looked like old shoe leather. He made a brave effort to smile as I took him in my arms, but when he tried to talk his voice wouldn't come. For three years he had imagined himself in disgrace for having surrendered Corregidor. He believed he would never again be given an active command. This shocked me. 'Why Jim,' I said, 'Your old corps is yours when you want it.'

The Japanese delegation was less impressive than MacArthur might have expected. The Emperor, of course, would not attend. The Prime Minister, Prince Higashikuni Naruhiko, was the Emperor's uncle and had used his royal blood as a pretext for staying away. His deputy, and the real strongman in the government, Prince Fumimaro Konoye, also made his excuses. The short straw was drawn by the foreign minister, Mamoru Shigemitsu, a tough old idealist who had lost his leg in a bomb attack 15 years before and who, appropriately enough, was a vigorous anti-militarist. For the army, General Yoshijiro Umezu, the chief of the army general staff, the figure who had vacillated and then urged Japan to fight on, was ordered to attend. When he had first heard this he had gone pale with anger and threatened to commit *suppuku*, until the Emperor himself prevailed upon him to attend.

MacArthur's broadcast to the American people that day was even oddly moving and thoughtful:

> Today the guns are silent. A great tragedy has ended. A great victory has been won... A new era is upon us. Even the lesson of victory itself brings with it profound concern, both for our future security and the survival of civilization. The destructiveness of the war potential,

through progressive advances in scientific discovery, has in fact now reached a point which revises the traditional concepts of war. Men since the beginning of time have sought peace... Military alliances, balances of power, leagues of nations, all in turn have failed, leaving the only path to be by way of the crucible of war. We have had our last chance. If we do not now devise some greater and more equitable system, Armageddon will be at our door. The problem basically is theological and involves a spiritual recrudescence and improvement of human character that will synchronise with our matchless advances in science, art, literature and all material and cultural developments of the past two thousand years. It must be of the spirit if we are to save the flesh.

MacArthur was now placed in one of the most remarkable positions of any man in world history. He had been given sole charge of a country of 75 million people with a unique tradition of obeisance, deference and hierarchy. He was the first foreign ruler and occupier in 2,000 years of Japanese history. He was perhaps the only example of a true viceroy, appointed to rule over another land, and a huge one at that, in the United States' history of avowed opposition to colonialism. He was Japan's new Shogun, dwarfing the Emperor in power. He had charged himself with no less a task than the transformation of a warlike despotism into a modern, democratic state.

When MacArthur arrived, it seemed that the Americans had intended to rule directly through their own colonial government. This would have been as disastrous as removing the Emperor. For one thing, MacArthur apart, many of those who served under him were woefully inadequate to the task: some, like Sutherland, were highly efficient executives, capable of carrying out orders in brutally efficient fashion, but absolutely blind to the political sensitivities of administering a hostile and dejected people. Others, like Courtney Whitney, were court flatterers, men MacArthur required for fawning adoration but not to run a huge country.

MacArthur issued three peremptory proclamations on 3 September that made English the official language of government, instituted military courts and declared military-issued currency to be legal tender. The foreign minister, Mamoru Shigemitsu, promptly explained this was not the way to do things: the Japanese government, he insisted, would act as MacArthur's administration and carry out whatever he decreed. MacArthur listened, and scrapped the proclamations.

MacArthur's proconsulship of Japan was initially highly successful, and most of the democratic reforms he introduced, as well as the no-war clause in the country's constitution, survive to this day. However, his attempt to reform the oppressive, cartel-based *zaibatsu* economic system failed and provoked mounting opposition to his government. In June 1950, just as his policies seemed to be blocked and the old warrior's career seemed to be coming to an end at the ripe old age of 70, the telephone rang in MacArthur's bedroom:

> It rang with the note of urgency that can sound only in the hush of a darkened room. It was the duty officer at headquarters. 'General,' he said, 'we have just received a dispatch from Seoul, advising that the North Koreans have struck in great strength south across the 38th Parallel at four o'clock this morning'. Thousands of Red Korean troops had poured over the border, overwhelming the South Korean advance posts, and were moving southward with a speed and power that was sweeping aside all opposition.
>
> I had an uncanny feeling of nightmare. It had been nine years before, on a Sunday morning, at the same hour, that a telephone call with the same note of urgency had awakened me in the penthouse atop the Manila Hotel. It was the same fell note of the war cry that was again ringing in my ears. It couldn't be, I told myself. Not again! I must still be asleep and dreaming. Not again! And then came the crisp, cool voice of my fine chief of staff, General Ned Almond, 'Any orders, General?'

—⁓—

By 27 June 1950 the tanks of the 150,000 strong North Korean army were outside Seoul in South Korea. MacArthur desperately reported to Washington 'complete collapse is imminent' and proposed to evacuate American nationals. He was in for a real surprise: Truman had decided to fight. MacArthur, as commander-in-chief of the Far East, was ordered to send US air and naval units to Korea, while a 13-nation force was put together under authority from the United Nations, which Russia was boycotting because of its refusal to oust the Chinese nationalist delegation there.

Now, by accident, as in the Philippines, he had been given a whole new glorious lease of life: he found himself in the frontline of the first real engagement of the Cold War. The challenge was a startling one: the most popular general in America, the hero of the Pacific War, had been turned to again by his nation in its hour of need. He was rejuvenated. Truman, who had been under pressure in the United States for his appeasement of communists, had needed to turn to the very general he hated most. MacArthur happened to be on the spot, but most Americans believed he was the only man capable of rising to the challenge.

This he did, gloriously. Within two days, again displaying his breathtaking courage, he had flown in the unarmed *Bataan* to Suwon airfield, 70 miles south of Seoul. There, he commandeered a black Dodge and several jeeps to tour the front, while under threat of attack, for eight hours so that he could build a first-hand picture of the situation.

The first priority was to land troops from Japan. Truman authorized him to do so within 48 hours. MacArthur rushed three divisions of the US 8th Army to South Korea, instructing their advance guard to delay the North Koreans for the time needed to bring in reinforcements. This worked and in late July 1950 the North Koreans were brought to a stop outside the defensive line 15 miles from the port of Pusan. MacArthur had secured himself a last-minute toe-hold as troops poured in from the 12 allied countries.

MacArthur, though, had no intention of staying on the defensive. On 23 August he convinced senior commanders of his plan: He promised 'I realise this is a 5,000 to 1 gamble. But I am used to taking such odds... We shall land at Inchon... and I shall crush them!' It was, by any standards, an almost lunatic risk. Inchon had no beaches, so the attacking force would have to land on the piers against an entrenched enemy: the tides were 32 feet, one of the highest in the world; withdrawal of the force once landed would be nearly impossible. On the first tide an offshore islet would have to be captured before the main landings could be made on the second. 'We drew up a list of every natural and geographic handicap – and Inchon had 'em all,' said one officer. In response, MacArthur argued that surprise was everything.

On 15 September the landing was made, with MacArthur watching from one of the ships. Two days later he went ashore. He was violently sick as the tension drained away when he appreciated the success of the landing. He exposed himself recklessly to enemy fire. Just over 500 Americans had been killed and 2,500 wounded against enemy losses of 30,000–40,000. By 26 September, Seoul had fallen. American forces broke out of the Pusan beachhead and trapped a further 50,000 North Korean troops between the two pincers, with the remaining 50,000 fleeing northwards. Soon the total captured rose to 130,000. It had been one of the swiftest, boldest and most decisive military triumphs in history – achieved by a 70-year-old general who had not seen active combat for six years. Of all the glories of the MacArthur legend, this was certainly the greatest.

MacArthur was now ordered to destroy the North Korean armed forces. But there were concerns. At a meeting on 15 October with President Truman, MacArthur was asked whether he felt there was any danger of Chinese or Soviet intervention in Korea. MacArthur replied: 'Very little. Had they interfered in the first or second months it would have been decisive. We are no longer fearful of their intervention.' Truman made no comment: he had no information to the contrary, but demanded that if the Chinese were not in the war, they should not be attacked. Both would be proved wrong.

Ten days later MacArthur proposed advancing to a new line 40 miles north of Pyongyang, which was about to fall, and then to 'secure all of North Korea'. However, the Chinese had already infiltrated some 100,000 men into the mountainous territory between the two American armies, and chose this moment to punch at the US's most extended units in the far north. MacArthur was by now deeply concerned: he estimated that there were some 56 Chinese divisions in Manchuria – nearly half a million men, as well as 400,000 reservists.

Meanwhile, 200,000 fresh Chinese troops were infiltrated across the unbombed bridges by 26 November, which saw the worst set-back for American forces since the Second World War. The Chinese, under a brilliant and ruthless commander, General Lin Piao, had concentrated in immense strength, taking advantage of the cover of the winter, and holed up secretly in hamlets and caves along the rugged mountains of the Korean backbone that MacArthur always believed to be uninhabitable and impassable. Some 300,000 hungry, poorly equipped young troops fell upon the American force, outnumbering it 10 to one, from the front, sides and rear, threatening to cut off and surround it. MacArthur, caught by surprise and stunned out of his usual jaunty self-confidence, wired to Washington, 'We face an entirely new war.'

With foolhardy stubbornness – perhaps for the first time betraying the inflexibility of his years – MacArthur continued to order his forces to move forward for four days before bowing to the inevitable and ordering their withdrawal. In a celebrated incident, when the Americans were blocked by a deep gorge, aircraft lowered a whole bridge across it to help them on their way. The 7th Fleet picked up the survivors and carried them down to Pusan. To the south, another allied army was forced back across the 38th Parallel.

A rattled President Truman said at a press conference that nuclear weapons might be used against China and that this was for MacArthur to decide – only to withdraw the threat under British pressure. In fact, the retreat had been superbly handled with a high, but not overwhelming, casualty rate of 25 per cent killed or wounded. Nevertheless, it was a devastating setback, resulting in the near loss of the entire peninsula to the Chinese army.

MacArthur was immediately blamed by much of the world press for failing to predict the attack and, much less fairly, for having 'provoked' it – although it should have been obvious that so massive an offensive (eventually involving nearly 1 million men) had been months in preparation, long before his own limited northward thrust, which had anyway been authorized by the high command.

The extraordinarily accurate Chinese knowledge of troop deployments in Korea had been furnished by two British spies in Washington, Kim Philby and Guy Burgess, and a colleague in London, Donald Maclean. In January 1951, Seoul fell again, this time to the Chinese, and they continued to progress halfway down South Korea.

By this time a fresh American commander, General Matthew Ridgway, had arrived in Korea; he was an energetic, courageous fighter. The following month he boldly launched a counterattack, saying that the Chinese were exhausted, and recaptured Seoul and all territory up to the 38th Parallel: MacArthur, who in the wake of the Chinese offensive had been uncharacteristically defeatist and flustered, was beginning to be regarded by Washington as dispensable in view of Ridgway's successes.

It seems clear that by now MacArthur had decided on provoking the president into dismissing him: he knew that the best possible outcome of the war – restoration of the status quo – would be inglorious and saw no future in commanding the US army there any longer. On 5 April 1951 a story was printed in the London *Daily Telegraph* that MacArthur had told a British visitor that 'United Nations forces were circumscribed by a web of artificial conditions... in a war without a definite objective... It was not the soldier who had encroached upon the realm of the political [but the reverse]. The true object of a commander in war was to destroy the forces opposed to him. But this was not the case in Korea. The situation would be ludicrous if men's lives were not involved.'

On 11 April, Truman summoned the press to the White House and announced MacArthur's dismissal before word of it had reached him, for fear that he would take the opportunity of resigning first. ('The sonofabitch isn't going to resign on me. I want him fired,' declared Truman.) As MacArthur put it later: 'The actual order I received was so drastic as to prevent the usual amenities incident to a transfer of command, and practically placed me under duress. No office boy, no charwoman, no servant of any sort would have been dismissed with such callous disregard for the ordinary decencies.' MacArthur told his wife, 'Jeanie, we're going home at last.'

MacArthur returned to the United States and one of the greatest welcomes for a national hero ever seen. Briefly, he toyed with the idea of becoming president, but was pre-empted by his old chief of staff, Dwight Eisenhower, a much shrewder politician but a bureaucratic general. Thereafter, MacArthur became an occasional adviser to presidents, notably telling President Kennedy not to intervene in Vietnam, before his death, aged 84, in 1964.

—◈—

Douglas MacArthur displayed a thoroughly old-fashioned taste for sharing the risks of the frontline with his men when it had become unfashionable; cool thinking on the battlefield; a huge penchant for seizing military opportunities as they arose as well as a gifted tactical grasp; a devotion to his men; and a desire to keep the numbers of casualties down even among the enemy. He also displayed some skill in selecting officers (although too many were sycophants); superb coordination of command and control in battle; the high intelligence evident in his speeches, his paternalist rule in Japan and his humanist attitude to his profession of war; contempt for disadvantageous odds; and an insufferably charismatic, superior and flamboyant personality. He was almost addicted to insubordination from an early age – towards Pershing, Roosevelt (whom, however, he admired) and then Truman (whom he did not).

Like so many of the mavericks, he became a major political leader and administrator, as proconsul of Japan for six years, following in the footsteps of Clive, Washington, Wellington and Grant. Yet, like all of them except Washington, he was a poor politician on his native soil, failing to understand that military glory, command and proconsular authority abroad cannot readily be transferred to the sphere of democratic politics, with its compromises, half-truths and accommodations with lobbies. In Asia, however, like Caesar, 'he did bestride this narrow world like a colossus'. He was a maverick, one of the very last of the great warriors and a genius in warfare.

Bibliography

Clive

Bence-Jones, Mark, *Clive of India*, London, 1974.

Cambridge, R.O., *Account of the War in India*, Dublin, 1761.

Caraccioli, Charles, *Life of Robert, Lord Clive*, London, 1777.

Chaudhury, N.W., *Clive of India*, London, 1975.

Coke, Mary, Lady, *Journal*, Edinburgh, 1896.

Davies, A. Mervyn, *Clive of Plassey*, London, 1939.

Dodwell, Henry, *Dupleix and Clive*, London, 1920.

——, *Nabobs of Madras*, London, 1926.

Edwardes, Michael, *The Battle of Plassey*, London, 1963.

——, *Clive: The Heaven-Born General*, London, 1977.

Feiling, Keith, *Warren Hastings*, London, 1954.

Forde, Lionel, *Lord Clive's Right-hand Man*, London, 1910.

Forrest, Sir George, *Life of Lord Clive*, 2 vols, London, 1918.

Gleig, G.R., *Life of Clive*, London, 1848.

Gopal, Ram, *How the British Occupied Bengal*, London, 1963.

Gupta, B.K., *Siraj-ud-Daula and the East India Company*, Leiden, 1966.

Harvey, Robert, *Clive: The Life and Death of a British Emperor*, London, 1997.

Hill, S.C., *Bengal in 1756–7*, London, 1905.

Holt, Peter, *In Clive's Footsteps*, London, 1992.

Ives, Edward, *A Voyage from England to India in the Year 1754*, London, 1773.

James, Lawrence, *Raj: The Making and Unmaking of British India*, New York, 1998.

Johnstone, John, *A Letter to the Proprietors of East India Stock*, London, 1776.

Khan, Abdul Majed, *The Transition in Bengal 1756–1775*, Cambridge, 1969.

Langford, Paul, *A Polite and Commercial People*, Oxford, 1992.

Lawrence, Stringer, *Narrative*, Cambridge, 1761.

Macaulay, Thomas Babington, *Essay on Clive*, London, 1840.

Malcolm, Sir John, *Life of Robert, Lord Clive*, 3 vols, London, 1836.

Martineau, Alfred, *Dupleix*, Paris, 1931.

Minney, R.J., *Clive of India*, London, 1931.

Orme, Robert, *History of the Military Transactions of the British Nation in Indostan*, London, 1763–78.

Scrafton, Luke, *Reflections on the Government of Indostan*, London, 1763.

Sinha, N.K., *Economic History of Bengal*, Calcutta, 1956.

Smith, William James (ed.), *The Grenville Papers*, London, 1852–3.

Spear, Percival, *The Nabobs*, London, 1932.

——, *Twilight of the Moguls*, Cambridge, 1951.

——, *India, a Modern History*, Michigan, 1961.

Strachey, Henry, *Narrative of the Mutiny of the Officers*, London, 1773.

Sutherland, Lucy, *The East India Company in Eighteenth-Century Politics*, Oxford, 1952.

Thompson, Virginia, *Dupleix*, New York, 1933.

Thornton, Edward, *History of the British Empire in India*, 6 vols, London, 1841–5.

Vansittart, Henry, *Narrative of the Transactions in Bengal from 1760 to 1764*, London, 1766.

Walpole, Horace, *Letters*, Oxford, 1903–8 and 1918–25.

Watts, William, *Memoirs of the Revolution in Bengal*, London, 1764.

Williams-Wynn, Arthur, *Charles Williams-Wynn*, London, 1932.

Woodruff, Philip, *The Men Who Ruled India*, London, 1953.

Wolfe

Alberts, Robert C., *The Most Extraordinary Adventures of Major Robert Stobo*, Boston, 1965.

'The Assault Landing at Louisburg, 1758', *Canadian Historical Review* 35, 1954.

Eccles, W.J., 'The Battle of Quebec: A Reappraisal', in *Essays on New France*, Toronto, 1987.

Gipson, Lawrence H., *The British Empire Before the American Revolution. Vol. VII: The Great War for the Empire: The Victorious Years, 1758–60*, New York, 1967.

Hibbert, Christopher, *Wolfe at Quebec*, New York, 1959.

Keegan, John, *Fields of Battle: The Wars for North America*, New York, 1996.

Kimball, Gertrude Selwyn (ed.), *Correspondence of William Pitt when Secretary of State with Colonial Governors and Military and Naval Commissioners in America*, New York, 1906.

Knox, Captain John, *An Historical Journal of the Campaigns in North America, for the Years 1757, 1758, 1759 and 1760*, ed. Doughty, Arthur G., 3 vols, Toronto,1914–16.

Moore, Christopher, *Louisbourg Portraits*, Toronto, 1982.

Stacey, C.P., *Quebec, 1759: The Siege and the Battle*, Toronto, 1959.

Stanley, George F.G., *New France: The Last Phase, 1744–1760*, Toronto, 1968.

Steele, Ian K., *Warpaths: Invasions of North America*, New York, 1994.

Willson, Beckles, *The Life and Letters of James Wolfe*, New York, 1909.

Washington

Bowman, Allen, *The Morale of the American Revolutionary Army*, Washington, D.C., 1943.

Callahan, North, *Henry Knox*, New York, 1958.

Coupland, Reginald, *The American Revolution and the British Empire*, New York, 1930.

Curtis, Edward, *The Organisation of the British Army in the American Revolution*, New Haven, Connecticut, 1926.

Dull, Jonathan, *The French Navy and American Independence*, Princeton, New Jersey, 1975.

Egerton, Hugh, *Causes and Character of the American Revolution*, Oxford, 1923.

Ferrie, Richard, *The World Turned Upside Down*, New York, 1988.

Fisher, Sydney, *The Struggle for American Independence*, 2 vols, Philadelphia, 1908.

Freeman, Douglas, *George Washington: A Biography*, 6 vols, New York, 1948–54.

Frey, Sylvia, *The British Soldier in America*, Austin, Texas, 1981.

Freidenwald, Herbert, *The Declaration of Independence*, New York, 1904.

Fuller, J.F.C., *Decisive Battles of the USA 1776–1918*, New York,1942.

Gottschalk, Louis, *Lafayette and the Close of the American Revolution*, Chicago, 1942.

Greene, Nathanael, *Papers*, ed. Conrad, Dennis, 9 vols, Ann Arbor, Michigan, 1971–2001.

Harvey, Robert, *A Few Bloody Noses: The American Revolutionary Wars*, London, 2001.

Headley, W.T., *Washington and his Generals*, 2 vols, New York, 1848.

Hibbert, Christopher, *Redcoats and Rebels: The War for America, 1770–1781*, London, 1990.

Jensen, Merrill, *The Founding of a Nation: A History of the American Revolution 1763–1774*, New York, 1968.

Johnson, Curt, *The Battles of the Revolutionary War*, 2 vols, New York, 1879.

Lafayette, Marquis de, *Mémoires*, Leipzig, 1837.

Lee, Henry, *Memoirs of the War*, New York, 1870.

Madison, James, *Papers*, 3 vols, Washington, D.C., 1840.

Main, Jackson, *The Antifederalists*, Chapel Hill, North Carolina, 1961.

———, *The Social Structure of Revolutionary America*, Princeton, New Jersey, 1966.

Malone, Dumas, *The Story of the Declaration of Independence*, New York, 1954.

May, Robin, *The British Army in North America, 1775–1783*, London, 1998.

Mazyck, Walter, *George Washington and the Negro*, Washington, D.C., 1932.

Merriam, Charles, *A History of American Political Theories*, New York, 1903.

Morris, Richard, *The Peacemakers: The Great Powers and American Independence*, New York, 1965.

Nickerson, Hoffman, *The Turning Point of the Revolution*, New York, 1928.

Quarles, Benjamin, *The Negro in the American Revolution*, Chapel Hill, North Carolina, 1961.

Ramsay, David, *A History of the American Revolution*, 2 vols, London, 1789.

Randall, Willard, *Benedict Arnold: Patriot and Traitor*, New York, 1990.

Robson, Eric, *The American Revolution in its Political and Military Aspects*, London, 1955.

Rochambeau, Marshal Comte de, *Mémoires*, Paris, 1838.

Royster, Charles, *A Revolutionary People at War*, Chapel Hill, North Carolina, 1976.

Schwartz, Barry, *George Washington*, London, 1987.

Simms, William, *Nathanael Greene*, New York, 1858.

Smith, Page, *A New Age Now Begins: A People's History of the American Revolution*, 2 vols, New York, 1976.

Smith, Paul, *Loyalists and Redcoats*, Chapel Hill, North Carolina, 1964.

Syrett, Harold (ed.), *The Papers of Alexander Hamilton*, 26 vols, New York, 1961–79.

Thayer, Theodore, *Nathanael Greene, Strategist of the American Revolution*, New York, 1960.

Treacy, M.F., *Prelude to Yorktown*, Chapel Hill, North Carolina, 1963.

Trevelyan, Sir George, *The American Revolution*, 4 vols, New York, 1899–1907.

Wahike, John, *The Causes of the American Revolution*, Lexington, Massachusetts, 1973.

Walpole, Horace, *Letters*, Oxford, 1903–8 and 1918–25.

Warren, Mercy, *History of the American Revolution*, 3 vols, Boston, Massachusetts, 1805.

Washington, George, *Writings*, 39 vols, Washington, D.C., 1937–44.

Weems, Mason, *A History of the Life and Death, Virtues and Exploits of General George Washington*, Georgetown, D.C., 1800.

Will, Garry, *Cincinnatus: George Washington and the Enlightenment*, New York, 1984.

Wellington

Alcaide, A., *Historia de los dos Sitios que pusieron a Zaragoza en los años de 1808 y 1809*, Madrid, 1830.

Aldington, R., *Wellington*, London, 1946.

Aymes, J., *La Guerra de la Independencia en España 1808–1814*, Madrid, 1975.

Azcarate, P. de, *Wellington y España*, Madrid, 1961.

Becke, Archibald, *Napoleon and Waterloo*, London, 1995.

Brett, Oliver, *Wellington*, London, 1928.

Bryant, Sir Arthur, *Years of Victory 1802–15*, London, 1944.

Cambronero, C., *El Rey Intruso: José Bonaparte*, Madrid, 1909.

Carr, Raymond, *Spain 1808–1975*, Oxford, 1982.

Cassinello, Juan Martín, *El Empecinado*, Madrid, 1995.

Corona, C., *Revolución y Reacción en el Reinado de Carlos IV*, Madrid, 1957.

Crauford, Alexander, *General Crauford and His Light Division*, London, 1891.

Cuenca, J., *La Iglesia Española antes la Revolución Liberal*, Madrid, 1971.

Dallas, Gregor, *1815*, London, 1996.

Davies, D., *Sir John Moore's Peninsular Campaign 1808–9*, The Hague, 1974.

De Lancey, Lady, *A Week at Waterloo in 1815*, London, 1906.

Diz, M., *El Manifesto de 1814*, Pamplona, 1967.

Douglas Reed, *From Valmy to Waterloo: Extracts from the Diary of Captain Charles François*, London, 1906.

Dufour, G., *La Guerra de la Independencia*, Madrid, 1999.

Esdaile, Charles, *The Peninsular War*, London, 2002.

Fletcher, I. (ed.), *The Peninsular War: Aspects of the Struggle for the Iberian Peninsula*, Staplehurst, Kent, 1998.

Flores, F., *El Bandolerismo en Extremadura*, Badajoz, 1992.

Fortescue, Sir John, *History of the British Army*, London, 1930.

Foy, M.S., *History of the War in the Peninsula under Napoleon*, London, 1827.

Glover, Michael, *Wellington's Army in the Peninsula 1808–1814*, New York, 1977.

——, *The Napoleonic Wars: An Illustrated History*, London, 1979.

Glover, Richard, *Peninsular Preparation*, Cambridge, 1988.

Griffiths, Paddy (ed.), *Wellington Commander*, Chichester, 1985.

Hall, C., *British Strategy in the Napoleonic Wars 1803–15*, Manchester, 1992.

Harvey, Robert, *The War of Wars*, London, 2006.

Haythornthwaite, P., *The Armies of Wellington*, London, 1994.

Hibbert, Christopher, *Wellington: A Personal History*, London, 1997.

Holmes, Richard, *Wellington*, London, 2003.

Houlding, J.A., *Fit for Service: The Training of the British Army 1715–1795*, Oxford, 1981.

Howarth, David, *A Near Run Thing*, London, 1968.

Hughes, B.P., *Open Fire: Artillery Tactics from Marlborough to Wellington*, Chichester, 1983.

Iribarren, José, *Espoz y Mina, El Guerrillero*, Madrid, 1965.

Izquierdo, M., *Antecedentes y Comienzos del Reinado de Fernando VII*, Madrid, 1963.

James, Lawrence, *The Iron Duke: A Military Biography of Wellington*, London, 1992.

Linck, Tony, *Napoleon's Generals: The Waterloo Campaign*, Chicago, 1994.

Longford, Elizabeth, *Wellington: The Years of the Sword*, London, 1971.

Lovett, Gabriel H., *Napoleon and the Birth of Modern Spain*, New York, 1965.

Ludovici, A. (ed.), *On the Road with Wellington*, New York, 1925.

Lynch, J., *Bourbon Spain 1700–1808*, Oxford, 1989.

Marte, F., *El Motín de Aranjuez*, Pamplona, 1972.

Maurice, Sir John (ed.), *The Diary of Sir John Moore*, London, 1904.

Maxwell, Sir Herbert, *The Life of Wellington*, London, 1900.

Meyer, J., *The Battle of Busaco: Victory or Defeat*, London, 1989.

——, *The Battle of Vitoria*, London, 1990.

Monton, Juan Carlos, *La Revolución Armada del Dos de Mayo en Madrid*, Madrid, 1893

Muir, Rory, *Britain and the Defeat of Napoleon 1807–1815*, London, 1996.

——, *Salamanca, 1812*, New Haven, Connecticut, 2001.

Muñoz Maldonado, José, *Historia Política y Militar de la Guerra de Independencia*, Madrid, 1833.

Napier, W., *History of the War in the Peninsula*, London, 1840.

Oman, Carola, *Sir John Moore*, London, 1953.

Oman, Sir Charles, *A History of the Peninsular War*, 7 vols, London, 1902–30.

——, *Wellington's Army 1809–1814*, London, 1912.

Paget, J., *Wellington's Peninsular War: Battles and Battlefields*, London, 1990.

Parkinson, Roger, *Moore of Corunna*, London, 1975.

Priego López, Juan, *Guerra de la Independencia 1808–1814*, Madrid, 2000.

Torreno, José María Queipo de Llano, *Historia del Levantamiento, Guerra y Revolución de España*, Madrid, 1853

Read, J., *War in the Peninsula*, London, 1977.

Roberts, Andrew, *Napoleon and Wellington*, London, 2001.

Robertson, Ian, *Wellington at War in the Peninsula 1808–1814*, Barnsley, 2000.

Rocca, Albert de, *In the Peninsula with a French Hussar*, London, 1990.

Rodríguez, Solís, *Los Guerrilleros de 1808*, Madrid, 1887.

Rousseau, I. (ed.), *The Peninsular War Journal of Sir Benjamin d'Urban*, London, 1930.

Rudorff, R., *War to the Death: The Sieges of Saragossa 1808–9*, London, 1974.

Southey, Robert, *History of the Peninsular War*, London, 1832.

Stanhope, Earl of, *Conversations with the Duke of Wellington*, London, 1953.

Suchet, Louis Gabriel, *Memoirs of the War in Spain from 1808 to 1814*, London, 1829.

Teffeteller, G., *The Surpriser: The Life of Sir Rowland Hill*, Brunswick, New Jersey, 1983.

Thompson, Norman, *Wellington*, Manchester, 1990.

Thornton, M.J., *Napoleon After Waterloo*, Stanford, California, 1968.

Urban, Mark, *The Man Who Broke Napoleon's Codes*, London, 2001.

Vaughan, Charles Richard, *Narrative of the Siege of Saragossa*, London, 1809.

Vilar, P., *Hidalgos, Amotinados y Guerrilleros*, Barcelona, 1999.

Weller, Jac, *Wellington at Waterloo*, London, 1992.

Wilcock, Paul, 'An Elegant Sword', *Royal Armouries Journal*, London, 2002.

Nelson

Blanning, T.C.W., *The French Revolutionary Wars, 1787–1802*, London, 1996.

Boselli, Count, *La Prise de Malte*, Rome, 1909.

Brenton, Edward, *Life and Correspondence of John, Earl St Vincent, 1838*, London, 1966.

Bryant, Sir Arthur, *Years of Endurance, 1793–1802*, London, 1942.

Chevalier, E., *Histoire de la Marine Française sous la Première Republique*, Paris, 1886.

Clarke, James and McArthur, John, *Life of Admiral Lord Nelson*, London, 1809.

Clowes, William, *The Royal Navy*, London, 1899.

Coleman, Terry, *Nelson: The Man and the Legend*, London, 2001.

Corbett, Julian, *The Campaign of Trafalgar*, London, 1910.

Davis, Ralph, *The Rise of the English Shipping Industry*, Newton Abbott, 1972.

Fitchett, W., *How England Saved Europe*, London, 1900.

Gardiner, Robert (ed.), *The Campaign of Trafalgar 1803–1805*, London, 1997.

Harbron, J., *Trafalgar and the Spanish Navy*, London, 1988.

Harland, John, *Seamanship in the Age of Sail*, London, 1984.

Harrison, James, *Life of Nelson*, London, 1806.

Hibbert, Christopher, *Corunna*, London, 1961.

——, *Nelson: A Personal History*, London, 1994.

Howard, Frank, *Sailing Ships of War 1400–1860*, London, 1980.

James, William, *The Naval History of Great Britain*, London, 1824.

Jennings, Louis J. (ed.), *The Correspondence and Diaries of the Late Right Honourable John Wilson Croker*, London, 1885.

Kemp, Peter, *The British Sailor, A Social History of the Lower Deck*, London, 1970.

Kennedy, Ludovic, *Nelson's Band of Brothers*, London, 1951.

Lavery, Brian, *The Ship of the Line*, London, 1984.

——, *Nelson's Navy*, London, 1989.

Lloyd, Christopher, *The British Seaman*, London, 1968.

Lyon, David and Gardiner, Robert (ed.), *Nelson against Napoleon: From the Nile to Copenhagen 1798–1801*, London, 1997.

Marshall, John, *Royal Naval Biography*, London, 1835.

Morrison, Edward (ed.), *The Hamilton and Nelson Papers*, London, 1894.

Nelson, Viscount Horatio (with Nicolas, Sir Nicholas), *The Dispatches and Letters of Vice-Admiral Viscount Nelson*, 7 vols, London, 1844–6.

Pettigrew, Thomas, *Memoirs of the Life of Vice-Admiral Lord Nelson*, London, 1849.

Pocock, Tom, *Horatio Nelson*, London, 1988.

——, *The Terror Before Trafalgar: Nelson, Napoleon and the Secret War*, London, 2002.

Pope, Dudley, *The Great Gamble: Nelson at Copenhagen*, London, 1972.

——, *Life in Nelson's Navy*, London, 1997.

Rodger, N.A.M., *The Admiralty*, Lavenham, 1979.

——, *The Wooden World*, London, 1988.

Russel, Jack, *Nelson and the Hamiltons*, London, 1969.

Southey, Robert, *Life of Nelson*, London, 1813.

Tucker, Jedediah, *Memoirs of Earl St Vincent*, London, 1844.

Warner, Oliver, *A Portrait of Lord Nelson*, London, 1958.

——, *The Battle of the Nile*, London, 1960.

Wheeler, H.F.B. and Bradley, A.M., *Napoleon and the Invasion of England*, London, 1908.

White, Colin (ed.), *The Nelson Companion*, London, 1995.

Cochrane

Allen, Joseph, *Life of the Earl of Dundonald*, London, 1861.

Atlay, James B., *The Trial of Lord Cochrane before Lord Ellenborough*, London, 1897.

Bérenger, Charles Random de, *The Noble Stock-jobber*, London, 1816.

Brenton, Edward, *Life and Correspondence of John, Earl of St Vincent*, 2 vols, London, 1838.

Bunster, Enrique, *Lord Cochrane*, Santiago, 1966.

Chatterton, Georgiana, Lady, *Memorials Personal and Historical of Admiral Lord Gambier*, 2 vols, London, 1861.

Cochrane, Thomas, Lord, *Narrative of Services in the Liberation of Chile, Peru and Brazil*, 2 vols, London, 1858.

——, *The Autobiography of a Seaman*, 2 vols, London, 1860.

Cochrane, Thomas, 11th Earl of Dundonald, *The Life of Thomas Cochrane, 10th Earl of Dundonald*, London, 1869.

Cruz, Ernesto de la, *Epistolario de D. Bernardo O'Higgins*, 2 vols, Santiago, 1916.

Ellenborough, Lord, *The Guilt of Lord Cochrane in 1814*, London, 1914.

Finlay, George, *History of the Greek Revolution*, 2 vols, Oxford, 1854.

Gambier, Lord, *Minutes of a Court Martial*, Portsmouth, 1809.

Giffard, Edward, *Deeds of Naval Daring*, London, 1852.

Grimble, Ian, *The Sea Wolf*, London, 1978.

Harvey, Robert, *Cochrane*, London, 2000.

Leon, Henry Cecil, *A Matter of Speculation: The Case of Lord Cochrane*, London, 1965.

Lloyd, Christopher, *Lord Cochrane*, London, 1947.

Mallalieu, J.P.W., *Extraordinary Seaman*, Macmillan, 1958.

Marryat, Florence (ed.), *Life and Letters of Captain Marryat*, 2 vols, London, 1872.

Martel, Alamiro de Avila, *Cochrane y la Independencia del Pacifico*, Santiago, 1976.

McRae, Alexander, *A Disclosure of the Hoax Practised upon the Stock Exchange*, London, 1815.

Pope, Dudley, *Life in Nelson's Navy*, Chatham, 1997

Rodger, N.A.M., *The Wooden World*, London, 1988

Tute, Warren, *Cochrane*, London, 1965.

Thomas, Donald, *Cochrane*, London, 1978.

Zenteno, J.L., *Documentos Justificativos Sobre la Expedición Libertadora del Perú*, Santiago, 1861.

Garibaldi

Garibaldi, Giuseppe, *Memorie*, 6 vols, Bologna, 1932–7.

Guerzoni, Giuseppe, *Garibaldi*, Florence, 1882.

Mario, Jessie White, *Vita di Giuseppe Garibaldi*, Milan, 1882.

——, *Garibaldi e i suoi Tempi*, Milan, 1884.

Mazzonis, Filippo (ed.), *Garibaldi condottiero. Storia, teoria, prassi*, Milan, 1984.

Milani, Mino, *Giuseppe Garibaldi. Biografia critica*, Milan, 1982.

Mola, Aldo A., *Garibaldi vivo*, Milan, 1982.

—— (ed.), *Garibaldi generale della liberta*, Rome, 1984.

Ridley, Jasper, *Garibaldi*, New York, 1974.

Sacerdote, Gustavo, *La vita di Giuseppe Garibaldi secondo i risultati delle piu recenti indagini*, Milan, 1933.

Scirocco, Alfonso, *Garibaldi*, London, 2007.

Grant

Badeau, Adam, *Military History of Ulysses S. Grant*, New York, 1882.

Burne, A.H., *Lee, Grant and Sherman*, Aldershot, 1938.

Cadwallader, Sylvanus, *Three Years with Grant*, New York, 1955.

Catton, Bruce, *U.S. Grant and the American Military Tradition*, Boston, 1954

——, *Grant Moves South*, Boston, 1960.

——, *Grant Takes Command*, Boston, 1969.

Conger, Arthur, *The Rise of U.S. Grant*, New York, 1931.

Fuller, J.F.C., *The Generalship of U.S. Grant*, New York, 1929.

——, *Grant and Lee: A Study in Personality and Generalship*, Bloomington, Indiana, 1957.

Grant, Ulysses S., *Personal Memoirs of U.S. Grant*, 2 vols, New York, 1885–6.

Keegan, John, *The Mask of Command*, London, 1987.

Liddell Hart, B.H., *Great Captains Unveiled*, New York, 1927.

Macartney, C.E.N., *Grant and his Generals*, New York, 1953.

McFeely, William, *Grant*, New York, 1981.

Porter, Horace, *Campaigning with Grant*, New York, 1897.

Sandberg, Carl, *Storm over the Land*, New York, 1939.

Simon, John Y. (ed.), *The Papers of U.S. Grant*, Champaign, Illinois, 1967.

Rommel, Montgomery and Patton

Barnett, Correlli, *The Desert Generals*, London, 1960.

—— (ed.), *Hitler's Generals*, London, 1989.

Bayerlein, Fritz, 'El Alamein', in Richardson, William and Freidin, Seymour (eds), *The Fatal Decisions*, London, 1956.

Baynes, John, *Urquhart of Arnhem*, London, 1993.

Blumenson, Martin, *Rommel's Last Victory*, London, 1968.

Brooks, Stephen (ed.), *Montgomery and the Eighth Army*, London, 1991.

Bullock, Alan, *Hitler and Stalin*, London, 1991.

Carsten, F.L., *The Reichswehr and Politics*, London, 1966.

Carver, Michael, *El Alamein*, London, 1962.

——, *Tobruk*, London, 1962.

——, *Dilemmas of the Desert War*, London, 1986.

Chalfont, Alun, *Montgomery of Alamein*, London, 1976.

Cooper, Matthew, *The German Army 1933–45*, London, 1978.

D'Este, Carlo, *Decision in Normandy*, London, 1983.

Douglas-Home, Charles, *Rommel*, London, 1974.

Eisenhower, David, *Eisenhower at War*, London, 1986.

Fraser, David, *Erwin Rommel*, London, 1993.

Fest, J.C., *Hitler*, London, 1974.

Galante, Pierre (with Silanoff, Eugene), *Operation Valkyrie*, New York, 1981.

Goebbels, Josef (trans. Taylor, Fred), *Diaries 1939–41*, London, 1948.

Hamilton, Nigel, *Monty*, 3 vols, London, 1981–6.

Hildebrandt, K. (trans. Falla, P.S.), *The Third Reich*, London, 1984.

Hoffmann, Peter (trans. Barry, Richard), *The History of the German Resistance*, London, 1977.

Horne, Alistair, *To Lose a Battle*, London, 1969.

Jackson, William, *The North African Campaign 1940–43*, London, 1975.

——, *Overlord, Normandy 1944*, London, 1978.

Keegan, John, *The Mask of Command*, London, 1987.

——, *The Second World War*, London, 1989.

Lamb, Richard, *Montgomery in Europe*, London, 1983.

Lewin, Ronald, *Rommel as Military Commander*, London, 1968.

——, *The Life and Death of the Afrika Korps*, London, 1977.

Liddell Hart, B.H. (ed.), *The Rommel Papers*, London, 1953.

——, *The Second World War*, London, 1970.

Macksey, Kenneth, *Rommel, Battles and Campaigns*, London, 1979.

——, *Guderian*, London, 1975.

von Manstein, Erich, *Lost Victories*, London, 1958.

Montgomery of Alamein, *Memoirs*, London, 1958.

Overy, Richard, *The Road to War*, London, 1990.

Pitt, Barrie, *The Crucible of War*, London, 1980.

Prittie, Terence, *Germans Against Hitler*, London, 1964.

Ruge, Friedrich, 'The Invasion of Normandy' in *Decisive Battles of World War II*, ed. Jacobsen, Hans-Adolf and Rohwer, Jurgen, London, 1965.

——, *Rommel in Normandy*, San Rafael, California, 1979.

Schmidt, H.W., *With Rommel in the Desert*, London, 1951.

Schweppenburg, Geyr von, *The Critical Years*, London, 1952.

Strawson, John, *The Battle for North Africa*, London, 1969.

——, *Alamein*, London, 1981.

Sykes, Christopher, *Troubled Loyalty*, London, 1968.

Taylor, A.J.P., *The Origins of the Second World War*, London, 1961.

Trevor-Roper, H. (ed.), *Hitler's War Directives*, London, 1964.

Westphal, Siegfried, *The Fatal Decisions*, London, 1956.

Wheeler-Bennett, John, *The Nemesis of Power*, London, 1961.

——, *Hindenburg: The Wooden Titan*, London, 1936.

Wilmot, Chester, *The Struggle for Europe*, London, 1952.

Young, Desmond, *Rommel*, London, 1950.

MacArthur

Abaya, Hernando J., *Betrayal in the Philippines*, New York, 1946.

Ambrose, Stephen E., *Duty, Honor, Country: A History of West Point*, Baltimore, 1966.

Appleman, Roy E., *South to the Naktong. North to the Yalu*, Washington, D.C., 1961.

——, *The United States Army in the Korean War*, Washington, D.C., 1961.

Archer, Jules, *Front-Line General: Douglas MacArthur*, New York, 1963.

Barbey, Daniel E., *MacArthur's Amphibious Navy*, Annapolis, Maryland, 1969.

Bateson, Charles, *The War with Japan: A Concise History*, East Lansing, Michigan, 1968.

Belote, James H., and Belote, William M., *Corregidor: The Saga of a Fortress*, New York, 1967.

Brereton, Lewis H., *The Brereton Diaries*, New York, 1946.

Brines, Russell, *MacArthur's Japan*, Philadelphia, 1948.

Cannon, M. Hamlin, *Leyte: The Return to the Philippines*, Washington, D.C., 1954.

Craig, William, *The Fall of Japan*, New York, 1967.

Dexter, D., *The New Guinea Offensives*, Canberra, 1961.

Dower, John, *Embracing Defeat*, New York, 1999.

Eyre, James K., Jr, *The Roosevelt–MacArthur Conflict*, Chambersburg, Pennsylvania, 1950.

Grew, Joseph, *Ten Years in Japan*, New York, 1944.

Gunther, John, *The Riddle of MacArthur: Japan, Korea and the Far East*, New York, 1951.

Harries, Meirion and Susie, *Soldiers of the Sun*, London, 1991.

Harvey, Robert, *American Shogun*, New York, 2006.

——, *The Undefeated*, London, 1995.

Higgins, Trumbull, *Korea and the Fall of MacArthur*, New York, 1960.

Hough, Frank O., and Crown, John A., *The Campaign of New Britain*, Washington, D.C., 1952.

——, *et al.*, *Pearl Harbor to Guadalcanal*, Washington, 1958.

Hunt, Frazier, *The Untold Story of Douglas MacArthur*, New York, 1954.

James, Dorris Clayton, *The Years of MacArthur*, 2 vols, Boston, 1970–5.

Kennan, George F., *Memoirs, 1925–1950*, Boston, 1967.

Kenney, George C., *General Kenney Reports: A Personal History of the Pacific War*, New York, 1949.

——, *The MacArthur I Know*, New York, 1951.

Krueger, Walter, *From Down Under to Nippon*, Washington, 1953.

Lee, Clark and Henschel, Richard, *Douglas MacArthur*, New York, 1952.

Long, Gavin M., *MacArthur as Military Commander*, London, 1969.

MacArthur, Douglas, *Reminiscences*, New York, 1964.

Manchester, William, *American Caesar*, New York, 1978.

Mayer, Sidney L., *MacArthur*, New York, 1971.

——, *MacArthur in Japan*, New York, 1973.

Miller, John, Jr., *Cartwheel: The Reduction of Rabaul*, Washington, D.C., 1959.

Morrison, Samuel Eliot, *New Guinea and the Marianas, March 1944 – August 1944*, Boston, 1953.

——, *The Liberation of the Philippines: Luzon, Mindanao, The Visayas, 1944–1945*, Boston, 1959.

——, *Victory in the Pacific, 1945*, Boston, 1960.

Newton, Clarke, *The Fighting Douglas MacArthur*, New York, 1965.

Nicolay, Helen, *MacArthur of Bataan*, New York, 1942.

Perret, Geoffrey, *Old Soldiers Never Die*, London, 1996.

Reilly, Henry J., *Americans All: The Rainbow at War*, Columbus, 1936.

Reischauer, Edwin O., *The United States and Japan*, Cambridge, Massachusetts, 1950.

Ridgway, Matthew B., *The Korean War*, New York, 1967.

Rovere, Richard H. and Schlesinger, Arthur M., *The General and the President, and the Future of American Foreign Policy*, New York, 1951.

Schaller, Michael, *MacArthur*, New York, 1989.

——, *The American Occupation of Japan*, 1985.

Schoor, Gene, *General Douglas MacArthur: A Political Biography*, New York, 1951.

Sebald, William J. and Brines, Russell, *With MacArthur in Japan*, New York, 1965.

Smith, Robert R., *Triumph in the Philippines*, Washington, D.C., 1963.

Toland, John., *The Rising Sun*, New York, 1970.

Wainwright, Jonathan M. and Considine, Robert (ed.), *General Wainwright's Story: The Account of Four Years of Humiliating Defeat, Surrender and Captivity*, Garden City, New York, 1946.

Waldrop, Frank C. (ed.), *MacArthur on War: His Military Writings*, New York, 1942.

Waters, Walter W., and White, William C., *B.E.F.: The Whole Story of the Bonus Army*, New York, 1933.

Willoughby, Charles A. (ed.), *Reports of General MacArthur*, 2 vols, Washington, D.C., 1966.

Willoughby, Charles A. and Chamberlain, John, *MacArthur, 1941–1951*, New York, 1954.

In addition to the books listed here, I have also consulted various collections housed in libraries: Robert Clive's letters at the National Library of Wales, Aberystwyth; Major John Carnac's letters in the British Library; Robert Orme's papers in the India Office Records, the British Library; the Powis collection in the India Office Records, the British Library; Laurence Sulivan's papers in the Bodleian Library, Oxford and Harry Verelst's papers in the India Office Library, the British Library.

Index

Entries in **bold** indicate battle maps